Modernizing the Central City

Modernizing the Central City:
New Towns Intown , , , and Beyond

Harvey S. Perloff
Tom Berg, Robert Fountain
David Vetter and John Weld

Ballinger Publishing Company ● Cambridge, Mass.
A Subsidiary of J. B. Lippincott Company

International Standard Book Number: 0–88410–414–1

Library of Congress Catalog Card Number: 74–14687

Printed in the United States of America

Library of Congress Cataloging in Publication Data

Main entry under title:

Modernizing the central city.

Includes bibliographies.
1. Urban renewal—United States.   I. Perloff, Harvey S.
HT175.M64   301.36'3'0973   74–14687
ISBN 0–88410–414–1

Contents

v

List of Tables

xi

List of Figures

List of Maps (for Los Angeles)

List of Diagrams

A Special Note

In mid-January, 1975, just as this volume was going to press (at the page-proof stage), the U.S. Department of Housing and Urban Development announced that it will not accept any additional applications for federal assistance to new community projects, covering new towns intown as well as outlying new communities. Thus, the program described in this volume was suspended by the executive branch of the government. As far as the new town intown portion of the program is concerned, given the minimal support provided by the federal government—that is, limited in actual fact to mortgage guarantee assistance—it was unlikely that there would be many applications for assistance under any circumstances. This volume describes, in effect, how *not* to promote an urban development program and what it would take by contrast to give a substantial boost to central city modernization.

Preface

When the federal government launched the new town intown[a] program in 1970, it was the latest in a series of programs aimed at modernizing and revitalizing the central city. Shortly after it was under way, we suggested to the Department of Housing and Urban Development that there would be great value in examining the new program against the lessons of past national experience and initial performance of the new towns intown. Such early monitoring could provide guidelines for program operation so that avoidable errors might be avoided—the kind of errors so common with previous central city programs. Inadequacies in the Federal Title VII legislation also needed diagnosis in order to better realize the full potentiality of the new town intown concept.

It was very much to the credit of HUD staff members that they were willing to support critical evaluation of a program none too firmly established politically, financially, and administratively. We hope our study will contribute to establishing independent evaluation as an integral element of national urban development programs and policies.

Federal housing and urban development programs of the post-New Deal generation have sought—partly explicitly and partly implicitly—to "redevelop" or "renew" the central city and to assist the poorer and less advantaged families in acquiring housing and other basic requirements of city living. Included have been the urban renewal program dating from 1949, the public housing program (initiated in the 1930s) and related programs of housing assistance, and the model cities program dating from 1966. The new town intown program provided for by the Housing and Urban Development Act of 1970—Title VII of which makes federal loan guarantees available for intown land

a. Throughout this study, we use a simplified form of the term rather than the form in the legislation ("new town intown" instead of the earlier "new-town-in-town"), both to avoid three hyphens and to be able to use the term "intown" in a flexible manner—as "intown new town" or "intown program" for example.

acquisition and development, as well as other forms of financial assistance—is the most recent effort with generally similar objectives.

SOME GENERAL LESSONS FROM EXPERIENCE

Our review of federally sponsored central city programs highlighted significant weaknesses in helping central cities come to grips with their major problems. These weaknesses include lack of clarity and consistency of objectives, inadequate scale and scope of activities, and inadequate authority and resources to get difficult tasks accomplished. Most of these weaknesses inhere in the new town intown program as it has been designed and administered to date (mid–1974). Major changes in the program will be needed if it is to contribute importantly to improving life in the central cities.

The lack of clear objectives in federal programs is an obvious problem because "we can't get there if we are not clear where we are going." The most important of the central city programs, urban renewal, particularly suffered in this regard. Its very title—"urban renewal"—suggested the importance of modernizing and reinvigorating the central city. But the initial association of this objective with the physical elimination of slums and blight and the program's later inability to dissociate itself from slum clearance resulted in a strong taint in spite of evident accomplishments in a number of central cities. The urban renewal program also lacked clarity as to whether it was intended to help poorer and less advantaged groups in the central city, or whether it could safely disregard the impact of its activities on such groups.

The lack of clear objectives for the public housing and model cities programs was of a different nature. touching on several inherently complex issues. It was never clear whether these programs were to be (a) merely specialized welfare programs for helping those most in need, (b) improved ways of delivering certain services through a concentrated community focus (low income housing and basic public services), or (c) approaches to changing some elements in the overall structure of the central city in order to create greater opportunities for the poor. Both the public housing and model cities programs, it is evident, were severely limited in scope and impact and did not result in any substantial systemic modernization of our central cities.

Our national history with these three urban programs suggests that in the future any central city program should be concerned initially and fundamentally with articulating a set of basic urban development objectives—if it hopes to be helpful and effective in a significant way.

THE PROBLEM OF MODERNIZING THE CENTRAL CITY

Our detailed review of the older programs, as well as examination of modernization development within central cities, have served to emphasize the logic of the core objectives of the older programs and the need to specify them carefully in future legislation and administrative regulations and guidelines.

Central cities undergo continuous change reflecting technological, economic, and social changes under way nationally and regionally. In some aspects of city life and in some areas, change can be very rapid and profound. But not unexpectedly, some aspects of city life and some geographical areas substantially lag behind perceived needs, or the changes impact the life of urbanites in a seriously negative way. These lags and undesirable changes have adverse effects in different ways: (a) on the *efficiency* with which city business is carried out or city life lived, (b) on *equity*—in that some groups suffer disproportionately, and/or (c) on the *quality of life in general.*

Obsolescence is most readily perceived in the physical elements of the city's fabric as, for example, when a street system inherited from the distant past plays havoc with the efficiency of transportation, or when old buildings become inappropriate for modern industry in terms of their structure and location, or when old public facilities become totally inadequate to service the present population of an area. Land ownership patterns inherited from the past may well be so fractionated as to make private redevelopment too costly and time-consuming to be feasible. Thus, whole sections of a city may be obsolete for modern city life and locked into declining posture because of the inability of existing local institutions, private and public, to modernize and revitalize the city's structure.

This suggests a second key element of urban obsolescence: the inability of local institutions, particularly of local government, to cope with such physical and other attendant forms of obsolescence and decline. City (and county) governments have, of course, changed over the years, but unfortunately their modernization tends to proceed most readily in precisely those traditional functions long assigned to local government—delivery of basic public services (police, fire, health, education, and the like)—and to lag most seriously in the nontraditional areas, particularly development (that is, economic development, physical development, and social development) and developmentally related services.

A tremendously important fact is that American local government has not been modernized adequately in function or structure to undertake responsibility (a) for arresting urban structural obsolescence and (b) actively stimulating development of the central city in directions called for by technological, economic, and social changes currently under way. Only with establishment of the New York Urban Development Corporation (UDC) has any state *or* local government effectively assumed such developmental responsibility *and* evolved at least some of the institutional and programmatic instrumentalities to carry it out. In other places, because no one has direct responsibility for coping with urban obsolescence or for modernization, it is essentially ignored. For example, if local urban renewal agencies has been so encouraged, a new kind of federal-local instrumentality might well exist today for effectively sponsoring central city development. But the federal renewal program was so flawed that no such overall development instrumentality really can be said to exist. Thus, the development and modernization functions have yet to be incorporated into local government.

There is yet a third, and even more complex, element of urban obsolescence—that of "social obsolescence." This is not a term or concept with established meaning, but we need to recognize the importance of the social factor in central city obsolescence. Many aspects are involved. One is the locational mismatch between where poor and minority families can find places to live and places where they can find jobs. Thus, for example, many of these families live cheek-by-jowl with the growing office complexes of the central business district, yet neither our public nor private institutions are organized to adequately prepare workers in these families for high paying jobs in such complexes. Traditional home ownership patterns, traditional patterns of public service delivery, traditional concepts of job holding, and other features of central city life do not seem to meet the needs of life in urban ghettos. There is need for social *innovation*, quite comparable to the need for physical and governmental modernization.

The comparatively recent new town intown program is in even greater danger than the urban renewal program of undercontributing to the modernization of central cities, because of the *self-contained* and *"balanced"* emphasis of such intown new towns.[b] The NTITs quite readily could be just that: relatively self-contained subcommunities that do little to improve the basic efficiency, equity, or quality of life of the central city as a whole. These potential islands could very well induce "displacement effect" similar to that of certain urban renewal projects—that is, merely shift problems of decline to other sections of the city while the project area was being "upgraded." But even if in NTIT projects there was no displacement but merely an "enclave effect"—that is, the creation of small islands of improvement in a sea of decline, the program only would have added to the many such socioeconomic enclaves of the more advantaged that already exist in the average central city, and would hardly justify the expenditure of taxpayers' money.

Thus, one conclusion drawn by the present study is that the modernization objective must be built into future new town intown legislation and, to the extent possible, into current new town intown guidelines and administration. Proposals for federal financial assistance should be able to satisfy the national administrator that the project has potential for helping modernize the central city as a whole and not just to provide new and more convenient housing for the already advantaged.

In this regard, it might be noted that the initial proposal for creating

b. In part, because new towns intown must conform to the same set of guidelines that apply to the development of outlying new communities, despite their inherent differences.

new towns intown (Perloff, 1966) suggested the use of the "new town" label precisely because the effort proposed for the inner cities was to bring about— through coordinated, large scale planning and action—*new and improved patterns of city living and working.* It was in the planned creation of *modernized* patterns of living and working that the intown program should resemble programs for constructing suburban new communities.

The other side of the same coin has been the need to specify objectives for increasing basic services, employment, and housing opportunities available to poorer and less advantaged families in the inner city. This is a need that holds for the new town intown program. Model cities, and to some extent public housing programs, established such objectives, in most cases independent of urban renewal. This weakened both the model cities and renewal efforts or, alternatively, precluded the potential for mutual reinforcement that was otherwise available. Model cities and public housing did little, if anything, about the central city's basic urban fabric or its basic socioeconomic and institutional processes, while urban renewal proceeded with physical redevelopment largely unconcerned for the poorer and less advantaged families. Model cities, public housing, and urban renewal were, however, essentially *central city development efforts* and should have been structurally and administratively integrated from the start and ordered by a clearly articulated set of national and urban-regional objectives.

The fact is that in the United States today, modernization cannot go very far by ignoring the interests of the less advantaged residents of the central city. For one thing, the social dynamite that is stored up makes physical and economic development programs in the older sections of a central city highly risky and extremely costly. For another, such improvement programs, when geared specifically to the interests of the wealthier residents and business groups, are basically inequitable and indecent and have no place in a modern democracy. Politically, they are also not very feasible, as they should not be.

The first line of attack on the problems of the less advantaged families is probably people-oriented, nonplace programs aimed directly at improving their welfare, such as income maintenance programs and the like. However, development, place-oriented programs can also be enormously helpful by increasing economic opportunity and directly improving the quality of life of such families. Past national experience indicates that *only* broadly conceived and "high leverage" modernization and improvement programs are likely to significantly impact the extremely difficult problem of assisting the poor. The key point, then, is that the two objectives—(a) modernizing the central city and (b) assisting the less advantaged—are mutually reinforcing and should be conceived as naturally going together. The new town intown program can achieve importance in central cities—and not end up as essentially a series of elaborate and fancy housing projects—only if it clearly establishes and carries out these twin objectives.

THE STRUCTURE OF THE STUDY

The study as formulated involved five major aspects: (1) examination of the national experience with urban renewal and model cities, specifically in terms of their lessons for the new town intown program; (2) examination in some depth of new towns intown either under way or proposed; (3) interviews with, and a polling of the opinions of, some of the nation's top experts in central city development as to what they think we have learned from urban renewal and model cities and how the new town intown program should best proceed; (4) "close-up" study of the problems and possibilities for undertaking a new town intown effort in a large city; and (5) in-depth study of two subjects of special interest to new towns intown: tax increment financing and a systems approach to housing.

Probing of these five aspects revealed that two basic approaches to central city development have evolved or are evolving: one based on essentially isolated projects or unbalanced programs limited to narrowly defined target areas, the other involving a broad programmatic approach to developing the central city as a whole with individual projects derived from the overall pattern of development. The present volume is, accordingly, organized along the lines of these two approaches. Parts I and II cover the project approach, including the urban renewal and model cities experience as well as the current, first generation new towns intown. Part III discusses the programmatic approach to central city development by reference to the views of the experts, a second generation type new town intown proposal (for Hartford, Connecticut), and the description of a possible NTIT program for a major city (Los Angeles). Part IV presents two special studies while Part V presents a summary and recommendations.

It should be noted that what has been attempted by the study as a whole is essentially an *overview* of the problems and possibilities in central city development. It was designed from the beginning as a first phase effort to be followed by additional study phases. It is concerned more with analyzing what are appropriate *approaches* to modernization than with the details of the present new town intown program. It is assumed that many of the issues will have to be considered in greater detail and specificity to provide definitive program and administrative criteria.

Essentially, then, this study attempts to provide a sturdier knowledge base for central city modernization than we have had in the past. Hopefully, this will make it possible to implement the recently conceived NTIT program with a better understanding of what is involved and to write improved legislation for central city modernization in the future.

Harvey S. Perloff
July 1974

Acknowledgments

This study was carried out as a team effort from beginning to end.

I want first and foremost to acknowledge my debt to my coauthors who were involved in every phase of the study. They helped make working together an intellectual and personal delight.

We have had the continuing assistance—and very great stimulus—of several faculty members of UCLA's School of Architecture and Urban Planning; particularly, John Friedmann, Bernhard Hafner, Leroy Higginbotham, Jurg Lang, Peter Marcuse, George Rand, Helmut Schulitz, and Edward Soja, as well as Frank Mittelbach and David Peterson, and a group of able students (shown in the study staff list). Much of whatever value this study may have is due to the substantial contribution of these colleagues.

We want also to express our gratitude to the many persons at HUD who helped with information and suggestions, and, particularly, to Jack Underhill, HUD project officer, Don Patch, and Ernest Zupancic.

We are also extremely grateful to the excellent SAUP staff who worked on the many different versions of the reports—often giving up free time over holidays to meet deadlines; especially Kitty Bednar, Marsha Brown, Vanessa Dingley, Flyn Harwood, Harriet Higginbotham, Catherine Kroger, Diane Morgan, and Sandra Pritikin. We owe a particular debt of gratitude to Jean King who guided the various reports to completion with skill and dedication. Mimi Perloff took on some of the editorial chores.

H.S.P.
July 1974

UCLA NEW TOWN INTOWN STUDY STAFF

Project Director: Harvey S. Perloff

NATIONAL STUDY STAFF:

Thomas Berg
Robert Fountain
Frank Mittelbach
George Rand
Helmut Schulitz
David Vetter
John Weld

Assisted by: Ross Andrews, Scott Carde, Frank Klett, James McNett, Michael Mekeel, Maggie Mills, Sean O'Laoire, Pamela Palmer, Ivor Prinsloo, Tim Yeomans

LOS ANGELES STUDY STAFF:

Thomas Berg
Robert Fountain
John Friedmann
Bernhard Hafner
Leroy Higginbotham
Jurg Lang
Peter Marcuse
David Peterson
Edward Soja
David Vetter
John Weld

Assisted by: Peter Boland, Eugene Brooks, Michael Durkin, Nicelma King, Francis Polson, Milton Roberts, John Stern

"Shortcut"

FOR A SHORTCUT THROUGH THE VOLUME, READ—

The preface—which discusses central city obsolescence and modernization;

First seven pages of Chapter 1 and summary sections at beginning of the three case studies—which tell what has been happening with new towns intown under way and planned;

First two pages of Chapter 2—which outline differing emphases on various components in NTIT projects;

Tables in Chapter 3—to get a picture of the costs involved in building in the central city;

Chapter 4—which summarizes the strong and weak features of the urban renewal and model cities programs;

Chapter 7—which outlines the rationale behind moving from a project to a programmatic approach in central city development;

First nine pages of Chapter 10—which discuss institutional modernization;

Chapter 11—which discusses various sources of financing central city development;

Chapter 15—which contains the summary and recommendations.

Part I

**New Towns Intown
as Demonstration Projects:
the Title VII Experience**

Chapter One

Case Studies of New Towns Intown

Introduction

National experience to date with the federal new town intown program provides insights into major policy issues for the federal and local governments in advancing central city revitalization. Reviewing this experience reveals some of the major constraints on intown development and suggests strategies for overcoming current stumbling blocks.

Federal financial assistance to encourage development of new towns intown, largely federal mortgage guarantees, is provided for in Title VII of the Urban Growth and Community Development Act, a section of the Housing and Urban Development Act of 1970. Major provisions of the act cover suburban and intown new towns, most often without making a distinction between the two. The inclusion of the new towns intown was an open recognition by Congress of the need to satisfy big city interests if adequate political support was to be engendered for new communities legislation.

The heart of Title VII, the mortgage guarantees, seeks to improve the availability of private mortgage fund capital for new town projects. Federal guarantee of new town obligations makes it possible for developers to use debt instruments similar to corporate bonds which can be offered to a broad capital market. "This method of financing is more favorable to the developer than conventional methods which normally require him to share profits with the lender. Lower interest rates are also possible, and, because a higher loan-to-value ratio is achievable, the amount of equity required of the developer is lower." (Mields, 1973, p. 32). Private developers may be guaranteed an amount covering up to 80 percent of the value of real property before development and 90 percent of the land development costs, while public developers can receive a federal guarantee covering 100 percent of the value of real property and of land development costs. The guarantee also allows the developer to pay interest on his debt only during the first ten years of development, with payment on principal not beginning until the eleventh year.

3

In addition to the loan guarantee, Title VII provides for interest loans, public service grants, and special planning assistance. However, several years after the enactment of the provision, by mid–1974, the Administration had neither requested funds from Congress nor had it expended the relatively small amounts that Congress had appropriated for these purposes. The passage of the Housing and Community Development Act of 1974 reestablished the possibility of employing these aids.

Title VII has stimulated mild interest in the construction of new towns intown by private and public developers and opened up the possibility of supplementary financing sources for intown projects already under way or planned. From the very beginning, there was a substantial amount of ambiguity attached to the Administration's and HUD's handling of the Title VII provisions. Thus, for example, some development entities were interested in obtaining public service and facilities grants, but no federal funds were being made available. Those who felt they would gain little from a federal mortgage guarantee therefore saw no reason for applying under Title VII. An outstanding example was the developer of the Fort Lincoln project in Washington, D. C., who did not apply for assistance even though committed to an expensive new town intown development in the nation's capital.

Because of the complexity and ambiguity of Title VII funding, new towns intown examined in this volume include projects not encompassed by Title VII, as well as those that have received or have applied for Title VII assistance.

To provide an overview for the discussion that follows, two tables have been prepared. Table 1–1 summarizes basic data for various new towns intown under way or planned. Table 1–2 deals with the basic developmental strategies these new towns intown have employed.

Two Models of Central City Development

Analysis of new town intown projects now under way or planned indicates that the federal program stimulated two primary approaches to, or models of, central city development. These differences in approach arise from differences in programmatic and areal scope, impact on central city revitalization, site ownership, and other factors. This differentiation poses significant policy issues concerning central city development for both the cities and federal government because requirements and impacts will vary greatly according to the model followed.

The two models being used are:

Model IA: Development of a single large vacant or abandoned parcel of land outside the central business district (for example, Fort Lincoln, Roosevelt Island, and Pontchartrain).

Model IB: Development of a single large contiguous parcel of underutilized land within the central city, basically similar to the most advanced of the later urban renewal projects (for example, San Antonio, Cedar–Riverside[a] and San Diego).

Model II: Development of a very large mixed use sector of the central city, involving noncontiguous projects (rather than a single project) and joining new town intown approaches with other approaches (for example, Hartford Process, Cleveland, and Chicago).

Case Studies

Problems and potentials of Model I new towns intown as well as issues raised by their development are summarized from a detailed examination of projects under way and planned. The summary is based not only on detailed study of the project applications and prospectuses, but also on extended interviews with developers and local and federal officials.

The main features of three new town intown projects are described in the section following.

ROOSEVELT ISLAND

Summary

The Roosevelt Island[b] new town intown is being developed as a race and income integrated community of 17,000 to 18,000 people on a 140-acre island in New York City's East River. The site is owned by the city, and was underutilized after a number of hospitals and other facilities were abandoned as obsolete. The New York State Urban Development Corporation (UDC) was selected by the city to develop the island. UDC then set up a subsidiary, the Roosevelt Island Development Corporation (RIDC), as the development entity.

The island is two miles long and 800 feet wide at its widest point. The ruins of three major hospitals and their auxiliary buildings occupy a large portion of the site. Two additional hospitals (Goldwater Memorial and Bird S. Coller Hospital) are still functioning and employ about 5,000 people. With the exception of 3,000 patients at the hospitals and 175 residents of a nurses' dormitory, the island was virtually uninhabited when the project was initiated.

Currently, the only access to the island is via the Roosevelt Island Bridge by buses or automobiles. Although buses run from the nearest mainland subway station, commuting to the island is still time-consuming, especially

a. Cedar–Riverside has some characteristics of both Model IA and Model IB. Since the models represent essentially "ideal" types, variations on these models are to be expected. For present purposes, Cedar–Riverside is treated as a Model IB type of development.
b. The island, formerly known as Welfare Island, was recently renamed Roosevelt Island.

Table 1–1.　New Town Intown Projects: Comparative Data

Project Name	Cedar–Riverside *Minneapolis* *Minnesota*	Fort Lincoln *Washington* *D. C.*
Current Status	Under way	Final Planning
Land Area	100 acres	335 acres
Population		
Present	4,000 (1972)	0
(density)*	36/acre	–
Projected	30,000	16,000
(density)*	340/acre	105/acre
Projected Land Use		
Residential %	26%***	45%
Commercial/Industrial %	36%	7%
Circulation %	19%	24%
Open Space, Public Use %	19%	23%
Housing Mix (total units)	12,500	4,625
% Low Income assisted	14%	15%
% Moderate Income assisted	29%	32%
% Unassisted	57%	53%
Projected On-Site Employment	?	7,000
Estimated Cost† Total Project	$40–60 million	$40–60 million
Institutional Framework	private developer & LPA	private developer & LPA
Present Land Use	Low density residential and vacant land	Vacant (Federal surplus land)

　* Gross density: Total population ÷ total project area designated residential
　** Phase I intown component only
　*** % of total urban renewal site
Source: Project applications and related reports

considering that it lies in the heart of the New York metropolitan area. A subway stop at the island is scheduled for completion by 1980. In the meantime, express bus service to the downtown area and adjacent subway stations is planned to increase accessibility of new residents.

　　Some of the newer and more striking features of Roosevelt Island plan include:

　　Exclusion of Automobiles:　On-island transportation will be on foot, bicycle, or electric minibus. Parking garages at the edge will be provided for automobiles, which will not be permitted on the island itself.

　　Land Leasing Arrangements:　The island is being leased from the city by RIDC for a period of 99 years. This eliminates the difficult and time-consuming problem of setting a price for the public land, and then transferring it to the developer. The ground rent paid the city under the terms of the lease depend upon use. Uses producing higher returns (for example, luxury housing)

Table 1–1.   (cont.)

San Antonio New Town San Antonio Texas	Pontchartrain New Orleans Louisiana	Roosevelt Island New York City N. Y.	Hartford Process* Hartford Connecticut
Pending ‡	Final Planning	Under way	Public Discussion Final Planning
558 acres	8,400 acres	140 acres	5,700 acres (approx.)
3,275 (1972)	0	0	70,000
45/acre	–	–	N.A.
20,000	87,000	17–18,000	80,000 (approx.)
130/acre	33/acre	500/acre	N.A.
26%	32%	25%	N.A.
37%	15%	16%	N.A.
22%	20%	15%	N.A.
15%	33%	44%	N.A.
7,058	27,600	5,000	N.A.
42%	30%	30%	20%
20%		25%	20%
38%	70%	45%	60%
15,000	61,000	7,000	100,000+
$80 million	$150–175 million	$250 million	$800 million
private	city public	state develop.	public/private
developer & LPA	develop. corp.	corporation	partnership
Underutilized (residential and commercial	Vacant (largely marsh)	Vacant, abandoned and/or underutilized	Northern half of Hartford, incl. CBD

† These totals are not comparable across projects because of the variations in the amount
of housing and other components.
‡ In suspension (as of mid–1974) awaiting state legislative action.

have higher ground rent than socially desirable uses producing lower returns
(low and moderate income housing).

Means of Financing Infrastructure: RIDC will finance all of the
infrastructure and public facilities except the schools. It will cover these costs by
charging "development fees" and deducting the costs from the rent due to the
city under the terms of the lease. This rent is based on both the ground rent and
a tax equivalent. Cost to RIDC for this infrastructure may approach $40 million.

Housing Cooperatives: Pending a favorable ruling from the IRS,
cooperative housing will be built for higher income families. This will allow these
families to receive substantial tax advantages equivalent to home ownership.

Urban Design: Roosevelt Island will provide a high density urban
environment that makes good use of the island's physical attributes while maintaining its most valuable historical landmarks.

Development of the Roosevelt Island new town intown will be
financed by $250 million tax exempt bonds issued by UDC in 1971. Although

Table 1-2. Prerequisites and Strategies for NTIT Development

	Cedar–Riverside	(Fort Lincoln)*	San Antonio	Roosevelt Island	(Pont-chartrain)*	Hartford Process	(Battery Park)*	(San Diego)*
I. Institutional arrangements to achieve effective public or private entrepreneurship and active support								
A. Private developer and local renewal agency	X	X	X			X		X
B. Public development corporation								
1. State				X		X		
2. City						X	X	
3. Special authority								
II. Achieving competitive capital and operating costs through land acquisition and write down								
A. Creation of usable land								
1. Filling					X			
2. Diking					X			
3. Using air rights								
B. Reuse of underutilized land								
1. Reuse of publicly owned under-utilized land								
a) Sold at "value for use"		X						
b) Leased to public development corporation				X			X	
2. Obsolete use								
a) Waterfront						X	X	
b) Industrial								
c) Other	X		X	X				X
C. Write downs								
1. Title I, urban renewal write down			X					
2. "Tax advantage write down" via various schemes designed to channel tax benefits	X					X		
3. Lease or rental arrangements to lower effective land acquisition costs			X	X				

III. *Financial arrangements to achieve competitive capital and operating costs in central city*

A. Tax increment financing				X		X		
B. Federal or local grants	X	X	X		X	X	X	X
C. Lower cost of debt service								
1. Title VII loan guarantee	X		X		?	X	X	
2. Sale of public bonds		X			?		X	

IV. *Improving the welfare of the less advantaged:* subsidies or programs to raise levels of income and services

A. Housing subsidies								
1. Federal	X	X	X	X	X	X	X	X
2. State			X			X	X	
3. Local			X					
B. Systems to lower building costs	X	X	X		X	X	X	
C. Use of internal subsidies (returns from profitable activities used to provide housing and services for less advantaged)		X	X	X	X	X		
D. Efforts aimed at raising the incomes of the less advantaged								
1. Affirmative action programs for construction jobs and business opportunities	X	X	X	X	X	X	X	X
2. Regional economic development and manpower training		X		X		X	X	X
3. Equity participation	X	X				X		
E. Improved community services for less advantaged inhabitants	X	X	X	X	X	X	X	X

*Not included in case studies

Table 1–3.   Two Models for the Development of New Towns Intown

	Model IA	Model IB	Model II
Land Use before Development	vacant or abandoned	underutilized	vacant or under-utilized or "conservation"
Spatial Configuration	contiguous parcel	contiguous parcel	linked project areas (joining "opportunity" and "need" areas)
Location	outside CBD	edge of or in CBD	large development sector of central city, probably involving CBD
Primary Orientation	project	project	development program
Examples	Roosevelt Island (Pontchartrain)* (Fort Lincoln)*	San Antonio Cedar–Riverside (Battery Park)* (San Diego)*	Hartford Process (Cleveland)* (Chicago)*

*Not covered in case studies

RIDC has applied to HUD for designation as a Title VII new town project, it was motivated by a desire for enhanced preference in the award of HUD public facility grants rather than the need for any federal mortgage guarantees (UDC can float and guarantee its own bonds).

Brief History

In January of 1968, Mayor John V. Lindsay appointed a special committee to make recommendations for the future use of the island. After the report of this committee was published, UDC was selected as developer. In August 1970, with the master plan completed and the 99-year lease signed, the directors of the newly formed RIDC met for the first time.

The decision to lease, rather than buy the land, eliminated the difficult, time-consuming and politically sensitive task of setting a sales price for the land. Herman Kahn of the Hudson Institute reportedly estimated the market value of the island to be $1 billion. Clearly, his estimate was based on the assumption that a developer could put all of the land to its most profitable market use, which would mean little or no low and moderate income housing. The City of New York decided to use the island to demonstrate how a race and income integrated new community could be built in the central city rather than to sell it to the highest for-profit bidder. This meant that some land use decisions on the island be based on social returns generated rather than monetary returns.

One mechanism which allows the developer to meet social objectives is the ground rent formula of the lease. Under this formula the amount paid to the city for the land depends on the use to which the land is put. For example, the ground rent for subsidized housing would be lower than for luxury housing or commercial uses. Another such mechanism allows the developer to deduct its infrastructure costs from the rent and tax equivalency payment due to the city.

Construction had already begun on the first housing when the RIDC decided to apply for assistance under Title VII. RIDC was interested only in the public facilities grants, not in the loan guarantees. What it wanted were the special supplemental grants and priority on other facilities grants. Hence when such grants were not made available, it became apparent that RIDC really received nothing for filing a Title VII application.

Because the island is isolated from the rest of the city and has almost no resident population, RIDC has faced little political opposition. Only when the plans for a tramway[c] were announced were there problems; high income groups on the Manhattan side were opposed to the tramway because of the additional traffic that would be generated.

c. The tramway is planned to serve island residents until the subway station is completed. In addition to political problems, the proposed tramway faces considerable financial constraints, because it might become obsolete overnight when the subway system links up to the island in 1980. There is some discussion that conversion of the tramway to tourist use might make it feasible.

Program Components

1. **Job Development.** Approximately 2,000 jobs would be created in the provision of retail and other types of services for the island's population. The hospitals will continue to employ about 5,000. It is doubtful that these jobs represent a net increase for the region. If the island were not developed, its potential residents would probably locate and generate demand in other areas.

However, it is likely that more jobs will go to minority people than in a typical suburban development. First, more minority persons will live in the NTIT and it will be accessible to large minority group concentrations. Furthermore, UDC will undertake an aggressive affirmative action program to assure that minority groups get a fair share of the opportunities generated. The affirmative action will encompass:

a) employment in construction
b) contracting and subcontracting opportunities
c) firms dealing with UDC
d) business and employment opportunities in the completed NTIT

2. **Service Development.** The main commercial area will be the Town Center which will include offices, restaurants, shops, theaters, a hotel, and other public facilities. Each of the residential "towns" will contain about 30,000 square feet of convenience commercial facilities. Of special interest are the following services:

a) Education. Educational facilities are proposed at the preschool, primary, and secondary levels. The projected number of students is about 3,650 (450 in preschool and 3,200 in school programs). Many of the physical facilities such as the library, gymnasium and classrooms will be used for cultural and recreational purposes. Plans call for the dispersal of these facilities throughout the community.

Responsibility for school planning rests with the Joint Planning Committee for Roosevelt Island, which was created by the Chancellor of the Board of Education. After construction, the Board of Education will either lease or purchase the schools from UDC.

b) Security. No mention is made of plans for enhancing personal security in the application. However, Frank Kristof (RIDC) mentioned that the inaccessibility of the island together with the prohibition of autos might make it a less attractive place for crime. In this sense, the island will be much like a fortress surrounded by a moat. (All it needs is a drawbridge!) Given the high crime rate in most of New York, this image could be quite effective in marketing. A police checkpoint at the entry point could act as a deterrent to crime. Any criminal would have to walk by the checkpoint (cars are prohibited) or swim the East River. If he did commit a crime, how could he know that his victim had not phoned ahead to the police to block his escape? Anyway, Roosevelt Island will provide a way to test the hypothesis that controlling access can reduce crime.

c) Transportation. A subway line connecting the island to both Queens and Manhattan is now under construction; it is scheduled for completion by 1980. Still in the conceptual stage is a tramway system (or possibly a ferry) which would service island residents until the subway link was operational. The short period of heavy use (1974–1980) makes this latter proposal financially problematical.

Internally, a major innovation will be the absence of the private automobile. Visitors and residents will be required to park in parking garages at the edge of the island, with movement within the island accomplished by bicycle, foot, or an electric minibus system. The pedestrian orientation of the project will be stressed.

d) Recreation. RIDC is planning a large program involving maintenance of open space; creation of five parks with connecting bicycle pathways and pedestrian trails and promenades; restoration of seven historic buildings; and construction of other cultural and civic facilities. The recreational opportunities would be open to all New Yorkers.

e) Public Facilities. All necessary facilities and utilities will be provided. One of the more innovative proposals is the disposal system for solid waste. Preliminary studies suggest the feasibility of a vacuumatic refuse system. Connected to disposal chutes in all buildings, garbage and other refuse would be transported to a central facility, where it would be compacted and disposed of.[d] Trash pickups would be eliminated and aesthetic and health conditions enhanced.

3. Housing Development. Current plans envision a resident population of 17,000 to 18,000 occupying 5,000 dwelling units. Housing will be provided for all income groups. RIDC is trying to find a way of providing housing for households in the $10,000–$14,999 group—the group that falls between the Section 236 and Mitchell–Lama programs. UDC is attempting to finance the Mitchell–Lama units at 90 percent of their cost at the going rate for tax free public bonds; tax abatements are also part of the program (see Table 1–4).

Housing in New York is incredibly expensive. UDC-financed limited profit housing (Mitchell–Lama) cooperatives cost about $10,000–$12,000 per room. With 90 percent financing, the carrying charges range from $95 to $110 per room per month. This is the middle income housing.

In conventionally financed housing without tax abatements, carrying costs run to $160 to $180 per room per month. This assumes 87 percent down

d. Either by incineration at a city incinerator or by use as landfill in a designated area.

Table 1–4.   Income Mix for Housing on Roosevelt Island

	Income Level	North Town (finished 1977)		South Town (finished 1979)		Total	
Low Elderly	$2,400–5,472	296	8.7%	204	12.8%	500	10.0%
Low Family	$1,440–7,500	603*	17.7%	397*	24.8%	1,000	20.0%
Moderate (236)	$4,800–14,050	803	23.6%	447	28.0%	1,250	25.0%
Middle (Mitchell–Lama)	$12,000–58,800	700	20.6%	300	18.8%	1,000	20.0%
Conventional	$19,200–80,600	1,000	29.4%	250	15.6%	1,250	25.0%
Total		3,402	100.0%	1,598	100.0%	5,000	100.0%

*35 units added to bring up total to level listed on other tables of the application

Source: New York State Urban Development Corporation, *Welfare Island—A Planned New Town Intown, City of New York, New York, An Application for Determination of General Eligibility Under the Housing and Urban Development Act of 1970, Title VII—Urban Growth and New Community Development, Part B—Development of New Communities,* New York, April 1972, Book I, p. III–10

payments (about \$1,700 to \$1,800 per room). There is some concern that RIDC will not be able to rent such high rent housing on the island. In March 1972, Kristof stated that a full year of negotiations with developers to build 1,250 units of this high rent housing was not successful.

To cope with this problem, Kristof suggested that these units be developed as cooperatives. This would allow a transfer of "income tax benefits from the developers and limited partners to the owner-occupants" (New York UDC, 1972, Exhibit F, p. 4). This would result in substantial savings per room, because in cooperative apartments the interest rate and real estate tax portion of the carrying charge may be deducted from income for computing federal and state income taxes. The carrying charge per room can be up to 37 percent less for the higher income groups than the carrying charges without tax benefits (see Table 1–5).

The projected 5,000 dwelling units will be built on about 35 acres adjacent to approximately 100 acres of open space. While high in comparison to most other cities, 40 to 63 dwelling units per acre on Roosevelt Island is medium density in New York. In Manhattan, the predominant zoning level produces 111 to 247 units per acre.

The experience to date with management of high rise units for lower income families has not been encouraging. For this reason, RIDC is placing a good deal of emphasis on housing management and tenant education.

HUD has defined racial and income integration as important goals of NTIT development and has developed guidelines to this effect. Although RIDC seems to have emphasized integration, HUD has insisted on spelling out exactly what measures it is taking to assure both types of integration.

To develop a racially integrated community of 17,000–18,000 in New York City is to go against very strong demographic trends. As the RIDC application points out:

> During the past decade, segregation patterns tended to intensify with Blacks and Puerto Ricans concentrated in four areas of the City— South Bronx, Central Brooklyn, South Jamaica, and Central Harlem. Over 80 percent of the Blacks within the city lived within one of. . . 26 poverty areas. (New York UDC, 1972, p. VI–1).

During the 1960–1970 decade, the Puerto Rican population jumped by 72 percent and the Black population by 53 percent. Twenty-one percent of the population was Black in 1970, up from 14 percent in 1960. The white population, excluding Puerto Rican whites, dropped by 16 percent during this same decade.

RIDC estimates that 20 to 27 percent of the island's total population would be nonwhite when completed. A vigorous program for attracting minorities has been planned. However, probably the most important factor in determining racial mix is the final rent levels for the project.

Table 1–5.   Benefits of Cooperative Housing: Carrying Cost Per Room at Different Marginal Tax Rates: Two Examples

Annual Income*	Marginal Tax Rate	Example I¹ Carrying Cost of $102/month**		Example II² Carrying Cost of $160/month**	
		Carrying Cost with Tax Benefits	Cost Savings through Tax Benefits	Carrying Cost with Tax Benefits	Cost Savings through Tax Benefits
$22,000	32%	$81.50	$20.50	$127.00	$33.00
$40,000	39%	$75.75	$26.25	$118.00	$42.00
$43,000	48%	$68.25	$33.75	$106.00	$54.00
$54,000	53%	$64.00	$38.00	$99.75	$60.25

* For married taxpayers filing joint returns
** Basic rental without housing cooperative income tax benefits
¹ Down payment: one bedroom units = $4,200; four bedroom units = $8,400
² Down payment: one bedroom units = $6,150; four bedroom units = $12,300

Source: Frank S. Kristof, "Welfare Island—Marketability of Mitchell–Lama and Conventionally-financed Full-taxpaying Housing," in New York State Urban Development Corporation, *Welfare Island—A Planned New Town Intown, An Application for Determination of General Eligibility Under the Housing and Urban Development Act of 1970, Title VII—Urban Growth and New Community Development, Part B—Development of New Communities*, New York, April 1972, Book I, Sec. X, Exhibit F, p. 4

In terms of income integration, as in other NTITs, the objectives must be balanced against the need to assure economic feasibility. RIDC estimates that as of 1974 about 51 percent of the island's households will have incomes of more than $15,000 per year. By 1979, this income group would drop to 42 percent of total households. The Regional Plan Association projects that the $15,000† group would constitute only about 22 percent of the New York region's population (see Table 1–6).

For income groups under $10,000 per year, the projected proportions come closer to those projected for the region in both 1974 and 1979 than other income categories. This is particularly true for the $5,000–$9,999 group.

It is the $10,000–$14,999 income group that is slighted. Although around 28 percent of the region's households are expected to fall into this group by 1980, only about 10 percent of the island's households would be in this category. The reason is that this group falls between the upper income limits for Section 236 housing and below the minimum limits for Mitchell–Lama housing. As mentioned earlier, RIDC is trying to develop housing for this group.

Financial Plan

The NTIT will be financed with $250 million in tax exempt bonds sold by UDC in 1971. While total project costs are not available, projected costs for infrastructure and public facilities total $30.1 million (at 1971 prices). The addition of an 8.0 percent per year allowance for inflation pushes these costs to $38.8 million. Table 1–7 presents a breakdown of the costs by major category. Not included is an additional $16 million of capital cost for new schools which will be paid by the city. Because most of these costs will be incurred early in the

Table 1–6. Projected Income Levels for Households in the New York Region and Roosevelt Island

	New York Region		Roosevelt Island	
	1975	*1980*	*1974*	*1979*
Under $5,000	22.3%	19.1%	16%	11%
$5,000–9,999	36.8	31.7	28	37
$10,000–14,999	25.3	27.5	7	10
$15,000–29,999	13.2	18.2	30	17
$30,000+	2.4	3.5	19	25
Total	100.0%	100.0%	100%	100%

Source: Regional Plan Association, *The Region's Growth,* A Report of the Second Regional Plan, New York, 1967

New York State Urban Development Corporation, *Welfare Island–A Planned New Town Intown, An Application for Determination of General Eligibility Under the Housing and Urban Development Act of 1970, Title VII–Urban Growth and New Community Development, Part B–Development of New Communities,* New York, April 1972, Book I, pp. IV–5, IV–10

Table 1–7.   Cost of Infrastructure and Public Facilities, Roosevelt Island *(Millions of dollars)*

Streets, Sewers, and Other Infrastructure	$16.2
Fire Station	.3
Day Care Centers	3.0
Vacuumatic Refuse Disposal System	3.0
Plazas, Promenades, Town	5.4
Recreation	1.2
Library	1.0
Total Cost at 1971 prices	30.1
Allowance for Inflation (8.0 percent per year)	8.7
	$38.8

Source: New York State Urban Development Corporation, *Welfare Island—A Planned New Town Intown, An Application for Determination of General Eligibility Under the Housing and Urban Development Act of 1970, Title VII—Urban Growth and New Community Development, Part B—Development of New Communities,* New York, April 1972, Book I, p. XI–6, Chart 1

development process when revenues are low, cash flow will be negative during the first eight years of the project's life.

UDC will repay the costs of infrastructure and development by subtracting development costs from rents due the city under terms of the contract. These subtractions, or "development fees," are the charges that UDC makes for its services, and are believed sufficient "to make it a self-sustaining development agency ... UDC's fees provide funds which, when added to reimbursements, will cover the costs, reserves and allowances needed for its operation" (UDC, 3/22/1972).

To be more specific, under the Roosevelt Island lease there are two types of rent: basic and additional. "Basic rent" is the mechanism by which the land value and tax revenues of the new community are applied to payment of the special costs of Roosevelt Island, including infrastructure costs for which the city would otherwise have to budget; and "additional rent" is the mechanism by which the "profits," if any, of development are shared by UDC and the city (UDC, 3/22/1972).

The lease specifies a ground rent and a tax equivalent for each type of development that are used in calculating basic rent. Those uses producing higher returns, such as luxury housing or commercial uses, have higher basic rents than those generating lower returns, such as low and moderate income housing. From this basic rent, UDC can deduct the costs of providing infrastructure and other costs related to the performance of its obligations. The computation of additional rent starts with an estimate of gross income from all sources from which are deducted all costs involved in development. Under current lease agreements, the developer will pay 60 percent of net income to the city (see Table 1–8).

Table 1-8. Lease Arrangements at Roosevelt Island (1969)

A. DEFINITIONS
  1. Basic rent: Ground rent* plus tax equivalent payments* *less* normal allowances** (expenditures for public facilities by the developer) and debt service (for financing of public facilities).
  2. Additional rent: 60 percent of net income of the project
  3. Net income: Gross project income *less* basic rent payments, normal allowances, debt service, and certain specified costs (in addition to normal allowances).

B. COST DATA
  1. Ground rent and tax equivalent payments:
    a) Subsidized Housing.
        Ground rent = $30 per completed unit per year
        Tax equivalent = 10 percent of annual shelter rent
    b) Middle Income Housing.
        Ground rent = $180 per completed unit per year
        Tax equivalent = 10 percent of annual shelter rent
    c) Conventionally Financed Housing.
        Ground rent = $340 per completed unit per year
        Tax equivalent = comparable to units elsewhere in the city
    d) Commercial Space.
        Ground rent = $.60 (sixty cents) per square foot of completed space per year
        Tax equivalent = comparable to commercial space elsewhere in the city
  2. Additional rent: Dependent upon net project income

*Varies with land use of property in question
**Adjusted for any reimbursements repaid by receipts from operation of public facilities. Normal allowances specifically exclude any expenditures or allowances allocable to park development.

Source: City of New York, New York State Urban Development Corporation and Welfare Island Development Corporation, *Lease Agreement Between City of New York (Lessor), New York State Urban Development Corporation (Lessee) and Welfare Island Development Corporation (Subsidiary),* New York, December 23, 1969

This method of financing public facilities and infrastructure is somewhat similar to that of tax increment financing in that the economic returns from development are used to finance the development. The difference is that the development corporation, rather than the city, finances the improvements. In effect, the city is giving UDC the use of the island for a number of years in return for UDC's promise to develop the island according to the approved plan and to provide infrastructure.

The fiscal impact on the city should be positive. Even after deductions, there will be "sufficient net revenue to provide a flow of funds to the city" (RIDC, 8/19/1972). The RIDC application (p. XI-5) states that "the island is estimated to provide monies in excess of one million dollars a year to the city and at the term of the lease, the land and improvements there upon will revert to the city." However, the city must provide services for the island and, until the infrastructure costs are paid, the city will receive very little from the rent to provide such services. No estimates of costs of providing such services to the island have yet been made public.

CEDAR–RIVERSIDE

Summary

The Cedar–Riverside new town intown in Minneapolis was the first intown new community to receive financial assistance under the New Communities Development Act of 1970. Under the terms of the project agreement, the federal government is guaranteeing loans to the developer in the sum of $24 million. The new town intown also receives the FHA housing subsidies.

The Cedar–Riverside project covers an area of 100 acres almost completely contained within the 340 acres of the Cedar–Riverside urban renewal project. The site is roughly triangular in shape, bounded by the Mississippi River and two major highways (I94 and 35w). Cedar–Riverside is strategically located, lying only 12 blocks from downtown Minneapolis and eight miles (a ten-minute drive) from downtown St. Paul (see Figure 1–1).

The new town intown component of the Cedar–Riverside site consists of five distinct neighborhoods totaling about 100 acres. Most of the remainder of the urban renewal site is occupied by five major institutions: the University of Minnesota (West Bank campus), Augsburg College (a private 4-year Lutheran college), St. Mary's Junior College (nursing), St. Mary's Hospital, and Fairview Hospital (see Figure 1–2). Immediately to the west of Cedar–Riverside is the site of the proposed Industry Square urban renewal project.

Cedar–Riverside had a population of about 4,000 in 1970, largely composed of students and retirees but also with a smaller number of professionals and blue collar workers. Median incomes were below the Minneapolis average.

The prevailing land use at Cedar–Riverside was low density residential, largely single family homes and duplexes. There was also a sprinkling of small businesses including small retail stores, artisan/craftsmen shops, and some restaurants and bars. Land uses, before and after project completion, are summarized in Table 1–9.

Current plans project an ultimate on-site resident population of about 30,000 and a daily population of 75,000 (including visitors, workers, and residents). Residents will be accommodated in 12,500 dwelling units clustered in five distinct neighborhoods. These communities will encircle a town center with 1,500,000 square feet of commercial, hotel, office, cultural, and recreational space.

The new town intown will be constructed in ten phases over a period of 15 to 20 years. Phase I began in 1971.

Under the direction of a full time staff backed by an array of special consultants, planning for the Cedar–Riverside project has been both comprehensive and innovative. Outstanding features include:

1. Positive efforts to create a socially and economically integrated community;
2. Deliberate attempts to foster an exciting living environment by subsidizing cultural and social groups via low rents;

Figure 1–1.   Urban Renewal and Public Housing Projects, Minneapolis, Minnesota (1968)

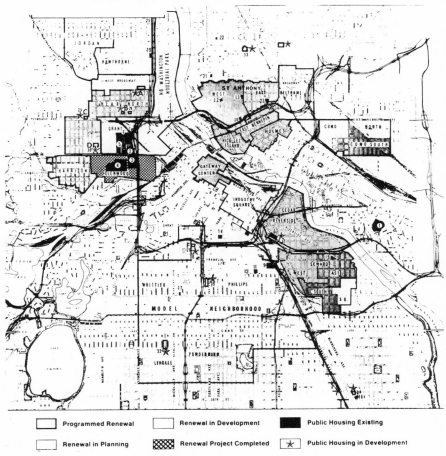

Source: City of Minneapolis, *1967–68 Report,* Minneapolis, 1968, p. 17

3. Planning for a modern pedestrian circulation system at the site;
4. Planning to minimize ill effects of relocation by allowing residents displaced from one area of the site to resettle elsewhere on the site;
5. Close cooperation with area residents, businesses, and other interests;
6. Close working relationships with a wide range of private and public agencies.

Cedar–Riverside will be financed by a combination of federal and private support. Public investment takes the form of federal guarantees for $24 million, coupled with housing subsidies and other federal programs. Private capital is provided by the developer (Cedar–Riverside Associates), joined by a number of limited partners seeking tax shelter.

Figure 1–2.   Cedar–Riverside Renewal Area

Source: Minneapolis Housing and Redevelopment Authority, *Cedar–Riverside Urban Renewal Plan* (R 213), as revised September 12, 1968, Map 2, p. 27

Table 1–9.   Land Use at Cedar–Riverside

	Acres	*Percent*
Before Urban Renewal Plan:		
Residential	110	32.3
Nonresidential	125	36.8
Streets and Alleys	105	30.9
Total	340	100.0
After Urban Renewal Plan:		
Residential	88	25.9
Commercial	11	3.2
Institutional	113	33.2
Parks	56	16.5
Social and Cultural	6	1.8
Circulation	66	19.4
Total	340	100.0

Source: Minneapolis Redevelopment and Housing Authority

Cedar–Riverside Associates, Inc., *Cedar–Riverside New Community, Narrative Description,* Minneapolis, May 9, 1972, p. 2

The project has been troubled by persistent questions raised concerning its unusually high density and by financing difficulties.

History of the Site

What is now Cedar–Riverside originated in the late 1800s as an entry zone for immigrants (largely of Scandinavian and Bohemian decent) to Minneapolis. These original settlers made their living as mill workers and in other occupations associated with the lumber trade. Most of the buildings extant on the site were constructed during this era. Cedar–Riverside reached a peak population of 20,000 in 1912 and began a decline that has continued to the present day. The site's population in 1970 was about 4,000.

As early as 1938 Cedar–Riverside was suggested as a potential candidate for urban renewal. By the 1950s it was apparent to many that the area was in a serious state of decay: the population was shrinking, houses and other structures built at the turn of the century were deteriorating, blue collar workers who provided stability to the site were departing, and the number of transient residents was on the increase. In addition, the University of Minnesota across the river had decided Cedar–Riverside represented an ideal location for expansion of its campus. Other nearby institutions had similar intentions.

Discussions between these institutions, government bodies, and business and citizen groups resulted in the Minneapolis Housing and Redevelopment Authority promulgating its first urban renewal plan for the area in 1960. Due to a lack of agreement among the various interested parties, final approval for this plan was not achieved.

During the 1960s the composition of Cedar–Riverside changed considerably. Many of the blue collar families departed and were replaced by students and other young adults drawn by the proximity to the University of Minnesota. The university had acquired some 80 acres at the site and had begun construction of classrooms and a dormitory. The opening of a new bridge over the Mississippi River (with both vehicular and pedestrian access) made the primary university complex far more accessible and further encouraged student residence. The decline of the area's housing continued.

Planning for Cedar–Riverside's future also continued during the 1960s. The Cedar–Riverside Area Council (a citizen group)—interacting with the Housing and Development Authority, Planning Commission, and other groups—proposed a series of objectives for the area. These became the basis of a 1966 Planning Commission plan and a subsequent urban renewal plan which won final approval in 1968.

Backers of the plan hoped to make Cedar–Riverside into an important new center for Minneapolis. Among the objectives called for in the urban renewal plan was the desire,

> to create in the Cedar–Riverside area an intensively developed major educational, research, and health complex with supporting residential and commercial uses. Coordination of planning and development by the public, institutional, and private developers is intended to create an area of distinguished design which functions effectively. (*Cedar–Riverside Urban Renewal Plan,* section R 213 B. 2, objective c.)

An interesting feature of the 1968 plan was the conditional exclusion from acquisition until 1973 (1979 in some areas) granted to many property owners at the site. This was to allow them time to evolve their own development plans (in keeping with overall development envisioned under the 1968 plan) if they chose. If a development plan for their property was not approved by 1973 (or 1979), the land became subject to condemnation and clearance.[e]

Very few property owners exercised their option. Much of the land was ultimately acquired by Cedar–Riverside Associates, a development corporation which already owned considerable property at the site. This group, which was to build the new town intown, had its beginning in 1962 when the original partners purchased land for a small apartment building. Seeing potential for a larger scale development, the two partners continued to acquire land until they owned a sizable portion of the southwest quadrant of Cedar–Riverside. In 1965 they allied themselves with the B. W. and Leo Harris Company and encouraged them to purchase land in the southwest quadrant as well. The two groups

e. Actually, the *conditionally* excluded property could be condemned prior to 1973 (or 1979) if redevelopment requiring such condemnation was approved by the Minneapolis Housing and Redevelopment Authority.

worked closely together and began comprehensive planning for the future use of the land. Several private consultants were hired to lend their expertise and to allow for a "multidisciplinary approach to the planning process."

The Cedar–Riverside/Harris group supported the 1968 plan for Cedar–Riverside. Their relationship with the Housing and Redevelopment Authority (author of the plan), has evolved into a public-private partnership that has continued until the present day with mutually beneficial results.

> The partnership—as written in the Urban Renewal Plan—was the mechanism, the tool to achievement of [redevelopment of the area]. The partnership was advantageous to the Redevelopment Authority, for it reduced the need to use eminent domain powers . . . ; demanded no funding from the public sector; and . . . allowed the Authority to have direct input into and control over the direction of the project. Private benefits were the knowledge and security that project integrity would not be sacrificed due to "holdout" parcels and the possibility of reducing critical time lags for approvals by increasing intergovernmental cooperation. (Connell, p. 20)

In 1969 the Harris Company sold its share of the project to Henry McKnight, a noted conservationist and Minnesota state senator. He joined the original partners (Keith Heller and Gloria Segal) as the third major partner[f] in a partnership called Cedar–Riverside Associates.

After approval of the Cedar–Riverside Plan in 1968, the developers explored the possibility of using federal land writedowns (under Title I urban renewal provisions) to lower the rents on subsidized housing units. Due to numerous administrative delays and other problems, it was decided this approach offered little potential and that development could be better carried out without federal grants. Cedar–Riverside Associates continued to purchase land at the site; by 1972 they had acquired some 85 acres of their 100-acre goal on a willing seller-willing buyer basis. It was hoped the appreciation in land value brought about by higher density development would be sufficient to repay the initial investment in property.

With enactment of the New Communities Development Act of 1970, the developers recognized the opportunity to create a central city new community on their holdings. With the cooperation of the Office of New Communities Development staff at HUD, they secured a Title VII guarantee for private bonds in 1971 and thus became the first federally supported new town intown.

> It is noteworthy that the new town intown effort was not seen as a negation of the urban renewal project and plan. Instead, the new town route was seen as a complement to urban renewal rather than a

f. Henry McKnight died on December 30, 1972.

disassociation from the renewal goals. The $24 million Title VII commitment received in late June, 1971 will enable long term financing for the development and will assure priority on federal infrastructure grants (Connell p. 20).

Cedar–Riverside will be built in ten 2-year increments until it reaches a projected peak population of 30,000 "with the area serving a resident-visitor-working population of 75,000 daily." The first of these ten development stages is now under construction. At completion the project will contain about 12,500 dwelling units; some 1,500,000 square feet will be devoted to commercial uses. By this time the Cedar–Riverside NTIT will be "the hub of major educational/cultural center for the entire Minneapolis region" (Interview with Cedar–Riverside personnel).

Program Components

1. Housing Development. Construction of housing will be a major focus of the Cedar–Riverside project, with 88 of its approximately 100 acres devoted to this use. The new town intown will incorporate a variety of housing types and sizes, the exact mix dependent on the need and future demand for housing in Minneapolis. As a Cedar–Riverside Associates' publication noted, the

> development plan emphasizes the need for a variety of resident options in type, size, and rental range of housing. This diversity of opportunity for the individual resident is carried out within an architectural framework which does not outwardly distinguish between low, middle, and high income buildings, but is of uniformly high quality in both design and construction. Because an effective housing program cannot be developed in isolation, housing goals, especially relative to density and life style, were considered in conjunction with planning for commercial and community services. (*Cedar–Riverside Associates, 1972 a*, p. 13)

a) Housing Mix. Project planners are striving for a housing mix which will serve a wide range of social and economic groups. The developer has commited himself to provide a significant number of housing units for low and moderate income families and individuals. In the project agreement between HUD and Cedar–Riverside Associates, a housing mix of 43 percent low and moderate income units, 34 percent medium income units, and 23 percent high income units is projected. The sizable proportion of low and moderate income units indicates a desire to create a fully income integrated new community which reflects the income distribution of the metropolitan area.

The first stage of development now under way, Cedar–West, will involve 1,299 units distributed as follows:

Section 23   —   117 units (low income public housing)
Section 236   —   552 units (federally subsidized)
Section 236b   —   408 units (nonsubsidized, market rent)
Section 220   —   222 units (semiluxury units)

Total   1,299 units

(Cedar–Riverside Associates, 1972 a, p. 13)

The Section 23 leased housing originally had been planned as public turn-key (ownership) units, but project planners later decided that leased units would better serve the needs of low and moderate income families. It is interesting to note that the units will not be isolated in their own building, but will be interspersed throughout Phase I development. Experience with this approach will help determine how lower income units should be located in the future.

In addition to income mix, Cedar–Riverside is planned to include a wide variety of age groups, professional and nonprofessional employment categories, and life styles. By project completion, the residential community is expected to have a cosmopolitan atmosphere. Since the residential component is being planned with the realization that the entire Cedar–Riverside project will very likely develop into a major educational/cultural center for the Minneapolis/St. Paul region, events at Cedar–Riverside in the next few years should provide valuable insights into how viable new communities can be created in central city locations.

b) Racial Mix. The Cedar–Riverside experience offers little insight into the question of desirable racial mix for new town intown projects, because unlike most large American cities, Minneapolis' minority population makes up only a small population (seven percent) of the city's total. For the SMSA as a whole the proportion is less than two percent. Most of the minority population are either Blacks or native Americans.

Current HUD new town guidelines do not call for specific racial mixes. Thus, there are no specific plans for specifying a set minimum number of Blacks, native Americans, or other minorities. However, even if HUD should require some racial mix in accord with the city's or the region's profile (as is now the case with income mix), the developer does not anticipate any difficulty in attaining such modest levels (Interview with Cedar–Riverside Associates).

The absence of a large minority population in Minneapolis clearly simplifies Cedar–Riverside Associates planning for the project. They do not have to confront an issue that must be addressed in most new towns intown planned for other areas of the country.

c) Density and High Rise Living. Since Cedar–Riverside Associates assembled its present holdings privately (without recourse to the MHRA's power of eminent domain), its front end investment in property is sizable. To recoup this investment, it is planning for a population of 30,000 by the completion of the project. With some 88 acres allocated to residential use, this works out to a gross project density of approximately 340 persons per acre, which would make Cedar–Riverside one of the most densely populated developments in the entire Midwest. There is great uncertainty at this point as to the ultimate impacts this high rise density would have, both in terms of the living environment for future residents and long term viability of the project financially. As one authority noted,

> We here in the Middle West have never had a Manhattan Island. When you take a 340 acre island, bounded by a river, freeways—and you develop it with densities of maybe 150 units an acre, with families, students, and elderly—we just don't have any experience with that type of dense living (Charles Krusell,[g] Quoted in Connell, p. 28).

Krusell thus raised a key issue: whether the traditional Midwestern orientation toward low density development can adjust to and accommodate the densities for Cedar–Riverside. The developers are confident, however, not only that the high densities will be accepted but can become a selling point for attracting new residents. As Dr. David Cooperman, their consultant for social planning, noted in a working paper, with proper physical design and full consideration of the needs and expectations of the various population groups anticipated at Cedar–Riverside, high density and high rise living might prove to be key assets of the project ("Social Planning for Cedar–Riverside," 1971).

Cooperman did believe, however, that there are two primary prerequisites to a successful high density project. First, every attempt must be made to avoid what he called "movement activity congestion" (that is, traffic and/or pedestrian tie-ups). He felt this could be accomplished through "separation of vehicular and pedestrian traffic, constructing efficient vertical movers (elevators, stairways, ramps), and by using a combination of specific interior dwelling unit designs and management policies which would avoid conflict over territory by groups with competitive demand for the same social space" ("Human Resources Planning, Cedar–Riverside," Appendix I D, p. 5).

More important perhaps is his second prerequisite, the need to avoid "social disorganization" due to high density and high rise living. He believed this can be accomplished by designing structures and open space to reflect the life styles of occupants and to facilitate positive interaction. As Cooperman stated:

> Many of the major gains of Cedar–Riverside as a whole will stem from the vital quality of urban life that results from a combination of population types, graded and optimized use of high densities, and physical planning to avoid congestion and to permit such densities to work well, rather than from any more deliberate attempt to establish

g. Former Director, Greater Minneapolis Metropolitan Housing Authority.

a distinct neighborhood or community of idealized rural models ("Social Planning for Cedar—West," March 11, 1971. p. 14).

Cooperman went on to add a qualifying note, however: "[T]he effect of physical planning (building massing and dwelling unit location, location and planning of pedestrian and vehicular paths, and parking structures) on opportunity structures [sic] has been widely discussed and debated. There is yet much to [be] learned about the subject, especially in relation to high rise, high density developments such as this one" ("Social Planning," pp. 14—15).

Thus, the actual viability of Cedar—Riverside's high density residential development will require the passage of time, since there is insufficient evidence at this date for objective evaluation. It is apparent, though, for the significantly higher densities (by Minnesota standards at least) to prove successful, all of the developers' assumptions and forecasts must be borne out. While many believe that if high densities can be successful anywhere in Minneapolis it will be at Cedar—Riverside (Connell, p. 28), Jack Crimmins'[h] assessment of the situation remains valid:

> We will have to really see how it works out . . . whether high density, combined with FHA subsidy, creates a desirable and livable environment. We really don't know—I don't think anyone in the country knows (Quoted in Connell, p. 28).

d) Relocation. Due to the relatively low density of current residential development, relocation would be less a problem at Cedar—Riverside than at sites with larger populations. In addition, Cedar—Riverside Associates hopes to minimize the impact of relocation by carefully staging development. Since the developer owns most of the housing at the site already, residents displaced in one stage can be relocated in dwellings owned by the developer elsewhere at the site (Cedar—Riverside interview). Experience with relocation to date has been positive:

> Concern for the interim community has been widely evidenced in the types of activities generated by Cedar—Riverside Associates. . . . Relocation for the Stage One Development has been handled by an in-house tenants relocations staff, who have been successful in relocating over one hundred and twenty-five residents in comparable or better housing units at the same rent level (Connell, 1972, p. 21).

2. Job Development. Economic development is a peripheral issue at Cedar—Riverside, because the main thrust of the project is housing (with supportive commercial and cultural facilities). While many jobs will be created

h. Of the Minneapolis Housing and Redevelopment Authority.

during the construction stages, their creation will be a by-product. Most of the permanent jobs at nearby colleges and hospitals would probably have been available without the new town intown, although some jobs may be added to service the growing "youth market" created by the concentration of students (Interview with Del Peterson).

If anything, it would appear that existing economic opportunity actually made the project possible rather than the reverse. The site was selected precisely because of the presence of major educational and health institutions; it was then planned so as to optimize the value of locating near these facilities. The prospect of as many as 60 percent of the working residents finding employment practically within walking distance typifies how the existing job market should enhance marketability of housing units.

There is, of course, wide recognition among public officials in Minneapolis that the new town intown and other components of the urban renewal project should have considerable impact upon the city and region. While specific projections have not been attempted, most believe Cedar–Riverside will become a major institutional and cultural center that will attract people back to Minneapolis. This would certainly aid revitalization of the inner city and to some extent stem the current flight to the suburbs (Interview with Jack Crimmins).

The experience at Cedar–Riverside is thus mixed as regards the present ability of a new town intown of this type (Model IB) to induce economic development. Based on Cedar–Riverside's history, indications are new towns intown modelled after Cedar–Riverside (development of a relatively small section of vacant and/or underutilized land) probably do not lend themselves to an active program of job creation. However they may function as a component of more widely based efforts.

Cedar–Riverside also reemphasizes the close relationship of proximity to employment opportunities and amenity resources with ultimate project success. Without the ready availability of jobs, entertainment, and cultural resources, the project would probably not have come into existence. This reinforces the findings at Fort Lincoln (Washington, D. C.), which indicated that project success will depend on developing a major employment center at or near the site. This also supports the finding of the new town financial model created by the Decision Science Corporation which indicated that accessibility to amenities was the single most important determinant of a new town's financial feasibility.

3. Service Development. A wide array of services has been envisioned for Cedar–Riverside although in many cases these services are contingent upon public financial support. Since no formal mechanism existed to coordinate provision of public and private services, the developer established informal ties and working arrangements with almost every agency and group whose decisions may impact the project. Its full-time activity has led to commitments for many services.

One staff member is quoted as saying:

> We primarily consider outselves facilitators of space and look to many other people to provide services and program. We want to get together with people who have knowledge in specific areas and plan the physical elements in conjunction with program needs. What we're suggesting is that the people best equipped to provide this input are the people who are now providing community services (Robert Kueppers, quoted in Connell, 1972, p. 22).

Cedar–Riverside Associates has stressed the desires and expectations of the resident population. For example, commercial services are designed to fit the needs of residents and visitors. Provision has been made for a "convenience commercial center" in each of the major residential neighborhoods, with space for small stores serving local needs and a local center for cultural and community activities. In addition, there will be one major "elongated commercial centrum" to service the entire resident community plus many expected visitors. This main commercial center will contain:

a) Office space for professional and business services;
b) Specialty shops, retail, and consumer services for local residents, the daytime student population and employment force, and visitors to the hospital and university;
c) Hotel facilities to serve the university and other institutions;
d) Commercial and public recreation facilities for residents and visitors;
e) New service facilities for or related to the University of Minnesota (*Cedar–Riverside Associates, 1972,* p. 19).

Cedar–Riverside is also attempting innovative technological systems wherever feasible. In planning the transportation and circulation system, for example, provision has been made for "climate-controlled" walkways, a coordinated vertical and horizontal circulation system and an integrated parking system. Regarding the parking system,

> under a concept of "joint utilization" now proposed, parking ramps would be located so that, rather than providing solely residential parking or only space for office and University parkers, they would serve both purposes. By utilizing available space for a different parking clientele at different hours during the day, 20 to 40 percent more multiuse space would be made available (*Cedar–Riverside Associates,* 1972, p. 16).

More tentative (dependent on the availability of Department of Transportation and other agencies' funding) are plans for an automated moving ped-sidewalk, a computerized driver information system and a linkup with the proposed Twin Cities' rapid transit system.

The provision of educational, recreational, health, and other services has also been carefully studied.

An important tool is flexible leased space:

> Within this concept, space will be leased by the developers to public entities such as the Minneapolis public schools and to the community. Program direction and initiation will be provided by residents to the public entity while the owner-developer provides space for proposed programs and maintenance. Leased space will permit modification of services in later stages through direct resident participation, and will also allow neighborhood facilities to grow with and adjust to the needs of community. In addition, flexible space will promote multiple use of existing facilities (Cedar–Riverside Associates, 1972, p. 20).

The developer's concern for a wide array of services is one of the outstanding hallmarks of new community development in a central city. Software is viewed as being as important as hardware. A restatement of Cedar–Riverside Associates' own conclusion is appropriate:

> Comprehensive planning for the future "new town-intown" of Cedar–Riverside is an attempt to add to the advantages of living in an urban environment through technological advances which reduce air pollution and traffic congestion as well as provide quality homes and services. Life in a high density urban environment will allow the individual to take advantage of efficiencies which provide more time for leisure, creativity, and social interaction. . . .
>
>   The regeneration of Cedar–Riverside as a thriving urban community promises to show what can be done through the difficult process of multidisciplinary planning and cooperation between the public and private sector. Cedar–Riverside can be considered not only as innovative but potentially, a new model for urban redevelopment (Cedar–Riverside Associates, 1972, pp. 20–21).

Managing and Financing Development. Cedar–Riverside is being developed by Cedar–Riverside Associates, a private development corporation, in conjunction with the Minneapolis Housing and Renewal Authority. The latter can exercise the power of eminent domain on behalf of the project (as yet this has not proven necessary); it also has responsibility for any relocation required, liaison with the city and federal governments, and so forth. Cedar–Riverside Associates has also worked out numerous working relationships with most other local private and public agencies whose activities may affect the project.

The project is being financed by a combination of federally guaranteed bonds and subsidies, and private equity investment. Cedar–Riverside Associates currently has Title VII guarantees for $24 million. The guarantees enabled the developer to assemble relatively large amounts of capital at market rates. The developer also has relied on housing subsidies and may tap other federal programs in the future.

Private capital is supplied by the developer as well as a series of limited partners seeking tax shelter. Considerable revenue for reinvestment is also expected from the project itself, because land values are expected to rise significantly due to site improvements and increased density.

While details of the financial plan remain confidential, indications are that the new town intown would not show an actual "profit" until fairly late in its existence. The project has, in fact, experienced financial difficulties. Because of the confidentiality factor, the causes are not known to us.

SAN ANTONIO

Summary

The proposed San Antonio new town intown (SANT) would cover 557.8 acres in the center city, encompassing most of the northern half of the central business district. The site is bounded on the north and east by freeways (1–37); on its southern and western boundaries it "blends into" the remainder of the central city core (see Figures 1–3 and 1–4).

The resident population at the site was approximately 3,275 in 1972, down from 7,201 in 1960 and 4,719 in 1970. Most residents are housed in substandard housing (71.9 percent of 901 units on site were so classified by the 1970 census).

Based on analysis of census data for the San Antonio central business district and nearby tracts, the area within and surrounding the new town intown can be characterized as a disadvantaged, mixed residential/commercial area, with a declining population, a deteriorating (and aged) housing stock, low median values of owner occupied dwelling units (except in downtown census tracts), low median family incomes, high vacancy rates, unusually high concentrations of the elderly, and a sizable minority population. Minorities in most tracts are Mexican-Americans and other Latin-Americans; two tracts have significant numbers of Blacks as well.

The San Antonio new town intown site contains numerous minor and major commercial enterprise, institutions, and historical sites. (See Figure 1–5)

The new town intown proposal is an innovative attempt to apply the lessons of past central city revitalization efforts. Due to the sizable scale and fortuitous location of the project, it has potential to significantly pact the City of San Antonio and surrounding region.

Figure 1–3. Regional Context: San Antonio New Town

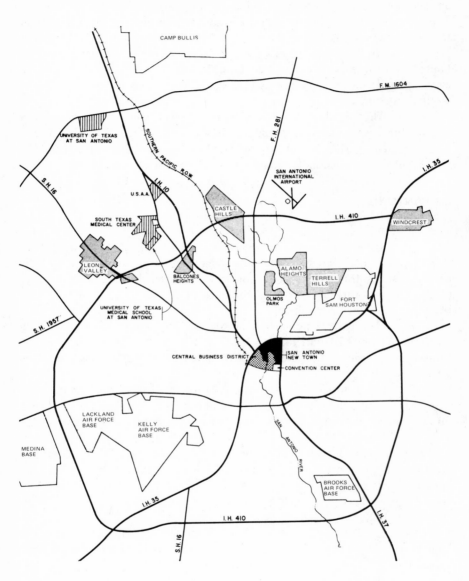

Source: San Antonio New Town, Ltd., *Final Application for San Antonio New Town*, San Antonio, Texas, January 1973, Volume III, Map 1

Figure 1–4.   Land Use Concept: San Antonio New Town

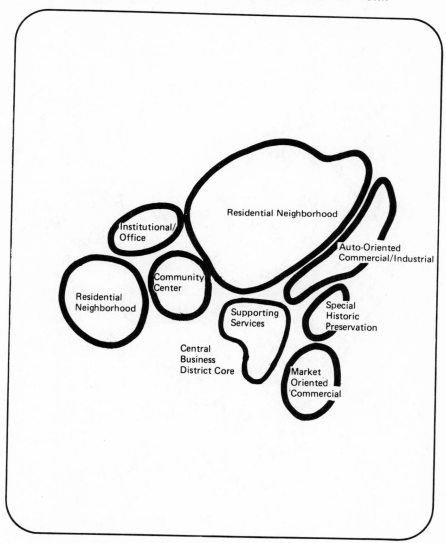

Source: San Antonio New Town, Ltd., *Final Application for San Antonio New Town,* San Antonio, Texas, January 1973, Volume III, Map 4

Figure 1–5.   Institutions and Facilities: San Antonio New Town

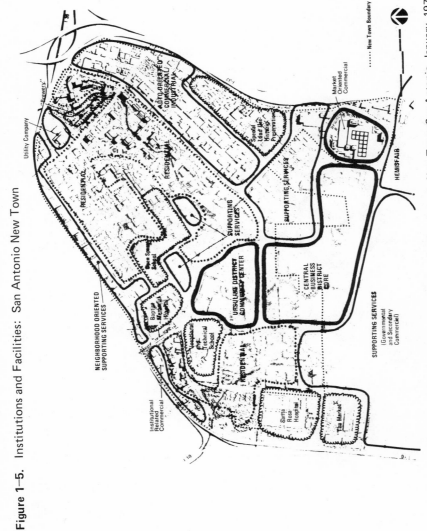

SANT arose with the recognition by many groups in San Antonio of the need for revitalizing the central business district. The City Council, Commissioners of Bexar County School Board, and San Antonio Development Agency (along with other public and private groups) have pledged to support the project (San Antonio New Town, Ltd., *Application,* Exhibit 16, pp. 1).

The principal goals are as follows:

1. To create residential neighborhoods that are attractive and capable of supporting new investment and accommodating approximately 20,000 residents;
2. To strengthen the central business and cultural center of San Antonio and to increase its ability to serve as a major center of employment, business, and community life;
3. To provide a suitable and improved environment for major community facilities including the city auditorium, three high schools, and two major hospitals;
4. To provide for the preservation and improvement of certain key areas or structures of architectural and historical importance;
5. To increase the safety and efficiency of pedestrian and vehicular movement in central San Antonio; and
6. To increase the overall attractiveness and value of the central area to such an extent that it will help generate increased values throughout the central portions of the city (SANT *Application,* pp. III−2 and 3).

As shown in Table 1−10, development plans are purposely flexible and reflect a fluid financial and economic situation. Current plans call for development of only about 46 percent of the project area initially. Depending on future economic conditions, up to another 22 percent of the site would also be developed. The remaining 32 percent will be maintained at present uses.

The SANT project would be built in four stages over a period of twenty years. Ultimately, the resident population should reach a level of 19,415. Present projections envision the construction of 7,058 dwelling units by project completion, of which 43 percent would be assisted units for low and moderate income families.

The revitalization of San Antonio's central business district would be a major thrust of the new town intown:

> The project is well located to serve a multitude of needs implicit in a large scale redevelopment undertaking in the center city area of San Antonio. Its adjacency to the existing Central Business District will allow a continual "cross utilization" of facilities and activities in both areas with mutual benefit. Additionally, the project site is directly in the path of Central Business District growth and development that has been occurring during the past decade. Thus, *the*

Table 1–10.   Land Use Patterns: San Antonio NTIT *(In Acres)*

	Current Land Uses		Proposed Land Uses			Total	
	Acres	%	Redevelop. Area	Potential Redevelop. Area*	Existing**	Acres	%
Residential	72.5	13.0	136.7	–	10.7	147.4	26.4
Commercial/Office	154.8	27.8	36.8	35.5	105.0	177.3	31.8
Special Employment/ Industrial	7.3	1.3	–	22.7	7.3	30.0	5.4
Open Space/River	65.2	11.7	8.8	3.0	25.5	37.3	6.7
Public/Institutional	46.0	8.2	11.9	–	34.1	46.0	8.2
Right-of-Way	212.0	38.0	–	–	119.8	119.8	21.5
Total	557.8	100.0	194.2	61.2	302.4	557.8	100.0

*Development conditional on future financial and economic viability

**Land within the new town intown area not currently earmarked for development activity; *i.e.*, to be maintained at present uses. Thus, for example, the 147.4 acres of residential planned for by the completion of the project would include 10.7 acres of land currently residential that had not been developed, another 61.8 acres of residential land that had been developed, plus 74.9 acres of land now in other uses that had been developed to residential use

Source: San Antonio New Town, Ltd., *Final Application for San Antonio New Town*, San Antonio, January 1973, Vol. I, pp. II–32

project will solidify and greatly enhance the CBD rather than contribute to its further fragmentation (Emphasis added.) (SANT Application, pp. VI–48, VI–49).

Planning for economic development and creation of employment would be flexible, with the goal of exploiting all available resources and opportunities. Current plans project some 10,000 to 15,000 on-site jobs by project completion.

The project would also give high priority to providing an array of resident services so as to create a "responsive New Town social system." (SANT Application, p. V–3). Working closely with public and private agencies, project planners could create action oriented programs shaped to fulfill the needs of the resident population. The social program is thus seen as an integral part of the overall project objective of strengthening and revitalizing San Antonio via the new town intown.

The SANT project would be carried out by a partnership of the San Antonio Development Agency (SADA) and the private developer. SADA sponsored an application to HUD for federal financial support (Title VII and Title I). In addition, it would provide eminent domain powers as needed to effect land acquisition, relocation of displaced residents and businesses, and to act as liaison between the developer and the city government.

The financial plan is tentative. Current plans envision the project requiring in excess of $80 million dollars to be financed by a combination of Title VII guaranteed bonds ($20 million), a Section 102 loan ($32 million), a Title I NDP grant ($15 million), plus private equity capital ($7.3 Million), and other borrowing ($8 million). Payback would be from revenues generated by the project's continuing development.

History of the Development

The new town intown is being developed by San Antonio New Town, Ltd., the same team responsible for the San Antonio Ranch project (a suburban new town development). Most of the team was originally involved with the Flower Mound New Town near Dallas, where they initially demonstrated their expertise. They were sought out subsequently by the owners of the San Antonio Ranch as developer-consultants, which ultimately led to their involvement in downtown San Antonio.

The San Antonio project reflects the concern of public and private sectors for the future viability of the central business district. The decline of population, deterioration of housing, and exodus of firms and retail businesses all contributed to this fear. The new town intown was proposed to reverse these trends and avert a major decline. Given their involvement with the San Antonio Ranch "new town out of town," the ranch's developers were viewed as likely participants in the intown effort.

Actually, the development is only 50 percent owned by the San

Antonio Ranch developers, with the remaining 50 percent equity interest held by city businessmen. Working with the San Antonio urban renewal agency, Central City Development Committee, and other interests, the new town organization was formally established in early 1972.

Since then, most major private and public organizations have endorsed the new town intown project. After considerable analysis and discussion, a pre-application for HUD financial support was prepared and circulated in August, 1972. Upon successful reception, a complete final application was circulated in January, 1973. A draft environmental impact statement and applications for preliminary categorical grants were submitted soon thereafter.

The financial program is key to success of the project. Thus, enabling legislation was introduced in the Texas Legislature in March, 1973 (HB 1471, HB 1472, SB 749, 750, and 751) to allow for tax increment financing and other revisions in state urban renewal laws. Although the House passed the legislation in May, 1973, the state senate adjourned without taking action.

Due to this lack of enabling legislation, the project has been placed on inactive status by HUD until such time as the state senate passes the bills.

Program Components

1. Housing Development. By the time SANT would be completed in the mid–1990s, the area would have a resident population of about 19,500 housed in some 7,000 units (on 150 acres of land). The mix of housing projected for the site is summarized in Table 1–11.

Table 1–11.   Housing Mix: SANT Development Program

	Number	Percent
Projected Population		
In Assisted Units	8,383	43
In Market Rate Units	11,032	57
Total	19,415	100
Projected Dwelling Unit Mix		
Sale Units (Low Density)		
Assisted Units	695	10
Market Rate Units	135	2
Rental Units (Medium Density)		
Assisted Units	1,210	17
Market Rate	640*	9
Rental Units (High Density)	4,378*	62
Market Rate		
Total	7,058	100

*An estimated 1.088 market rate rental units will be priced within the range of low income families and individuals (SANT Application, p. V–33)

Source: San Antonio New Town, Ltd., *Final Application for San Antonio New Town,* San Antonio, January 1973, Volume II, p. VI–72

Four major considerations have been emphasized in planning for the "comprehensive housing program for SANT." First, the needs and expectations of present residents of the site would receive careful consideration. Planners indicate that compensation for acquisition of land or displacement of residents will be reasonable and fair. Second, where feasible, relocation would occur within the project area itself. Displacement outside the project area of residents, businesses, and/or other service facilities within the site would be kept at an absolute minimum.

Project planners are also stressing a wide ranging programmatic approach. Planning will involve coordinating the needs of people with housing commercial, recreational, social, health, transportation, education, and other facilities to be provided. Physical "tie-in" and its impact on the integration of housing, people, services, and facilities is viewed as especially important.

Finally, in accord with HUD guidelines, the ultimate housing and population mix at the site will reflect the mix of the surrounding San Antonio Standard Metropolitan Statistical Area (SMSA) (SANT Application, pp. V–26, V–28).

a) Housing Mix. As noted above, current plans call for a mix of income groups approximating the SMSA. Some 43 percent of the projected ultimate population will have incomes below $5,400 (in 1970 dollar terms), which is approximately the median income level for the SMSA. Some 37 percent of the population is expected to have incomes in excess of $10,500 (see Table 1–12). It is anticipated that most assisted units will be occupied by minority families and individuals (largely Mexican-American).

b) Residential Environment. An important component of the SANT housing plan is creation of an attractive residential environment. San Antonio possesses a wide variety of cultural, historical, and recreational ameni-

Table 1–12. Dwelling Units by Income Range: San Antonio NTIT

Family Income	No. of Units	Percent	SMSA Percent
Market Income (Over $10,500)	2,618	37.1	30
Moderate Income ($7,500 to $10,500)	1,447	20.5	25
Low Income (under $7,500)	2,993*	42.4	45
Total	7,058	100.0	100

*Includes 1,905 assisted units and 1,088 market rate units priced within the range of families and individuals with annual incomes below $7,500 (see SANT Application, p. V–33)

Source: San Antonio New Town, Ltd., *Final Application for San Antonio New Town,* San Antonio, January 1973, Volume II, p. V–25

ties which planners want emphasized in new town intown residential communities. One of the most important is the San Antonio River which adds charm and uniqueness to the downtown. Housing at SANT will have the river (as well as the San Pedro Creek and proposed additional channels) as a primary focus. In addition, project planners want to increase the overall attractiveness of the new town by encouraging multi-use facilities, creating a town center along the lines of a Ghiardelli Square in San Francisco, and improving lighting and police patrols to assure a safe environment.

c) Density. With a projected population of about 19,500 housed on about 150 acres, gross project density works out to about 130 people per acre. The developer has indicated that the lowest density housing (both rental and sales) will be reserved for low and moderate income groups. Density in these subsidized units is planned for 30 to 40 dwelling units per acre for garden apartments and 12 to 18 dwelling units per acre for sales units (SANT Application p. V–33).

Although these relatively low densities for subsidized units complicates financial planning, it reflects the developer's intention to create desirable residential alternatives for all income groups. Noting that the major porportion of those residing in subsidized units will be Mexican-Americans, who "have consistently been shown to avoid high density if at all possible," the developer concludes that relatively low density housing "is the only method by which (they) can provide the kind of housing low and moderate income families want as well as need" (SANT Application, pp. V–32, V–33).

2. Job and Economic Development. A major goal of the new town intown is revitalizing the City of San Antonio. As the developer noted in its Title VII application,

> in terms of the justification for a development of this type (*i.e.,* SANT), there is no area outside of the central city that more demands renovation, upgrading, and improvement. If it is to remain a major center of the area's economic and social structure, then innovative planning, development, and financial commitment must be applied to stablize and ultimately reverse declining population trends, and a diminishing of the area's commercial and office activity importance (SANT Application p. VI–46).

As was shown in Table 1–10, not all of the project area actually would be developed. Operating within 558 acres marked out by the project's boundaries, planners would encourage development of sites with the greatest economic potential. Current plans envision new commercial and office activities taking up 36.8 acres at various locations across the site. If these initial development efforts are successful and other factors are favorable, up to another 35.5 acres of office/commercial and 22.7 acres of "special" employment/industrial may be developed as well. Specific development plans will depend on future economic and political conditions.

a) Job Creation. SANT has the potential to attract an estimated 10,000 to 15,000 jobs. Current (still very tentative) employment projections are summarized in Table 1–13. While it is uncertain that these jobs actually represent a net gain (from a regional perspective), their concentration in downtown San Antonio, rather than in distant suburban developments, should make them more accessible to minority and other less advantaged groups of the central city.

b) Minority Participation. The developer recognizes the importance of full participation and involvement of all segments of San Antonio's economic sector.

In addition, the developer plans to facilitate participation of small minority businesses within SANT by establishing a Minority Enterprise Small Business Investment Corporation (MESBIC) to provide equity funds, long term loans, and management assistance. The developer would commit at least $150,000 of cash equity to generate approximately $2,250,000 in loan potential.

Manpower training programs are also an important element in full participation by less advantaged groups in the employment and entrepreneurial opportunities of SANT. One definite proposal involves pairing the new town manpower programs with a 500-acre vocational technical center at San Antonio Ranch[i]. Many jobs should be made available by the expansion of industry in the project area as well.

Table 1–13. Employment Projections: San Antonio NTIT*

Office	
Finance, Insurance, and Real Estate (FIRE)	3,964
Legal	600
Business Services	1,252
Medical/Dental	718
Miscellaneous	1,091
Total Office Employment	7,625
Luxury Hotel	45
Total Commercial and Retail Employment	2,636
Total Industrial Employment	3,813 to 4,195

*Projected based on fixed ratios of employees to square footage of land estimated to be developed; *e.g.,* FIRE—one employee per 160 sq. feet; Legal—one lawyer and two secretaries per 600 sq. feet, and so forth

Source: San Antonio New Town, Ltd., *Final Application for San Antonio New Town,* San Antonio, January 1973, Volume II, pp. V–18, V–20

i. Also under discussion is the feasibility of pairing the San Antonio MESBIC with that of the intown project. It may be desirable to combine the two into one functional entity. No decision has been made.

c) Marketing. The current image of downtown San Antonio may discourage participation in opportunities created by the new town intown. To correct for this, the developer proposes a marketing effort to sell the project.

> The (marketing) program will be directed at conveying (an image of) a *complete* community with all services, facilities, and amenities situated in the midst of an exciting urban center that is the economic and cultural focus for an entire region. Thus, rather than being marketed as an isolated "island," the project will be marketed as an integral part of the existing and planned activities in the center city . . . .(SANT Application, pp. VI–58).

3. Service Development. Since the site lies completely within the City of San Antonio, public services will be provided by existing governmental agencies. The developer, however, pledges to facilitate provision of public and private services to all socioeconomic groups.

In considering the nature and mix of the social services to be provided or encouraged, planners are devoting equal attention to maintenance and expansion of existing successful services as well as creation of services not presently obtainable. Provision of services is seen as a major determinant of project success. Planners argue that software is as important as hardware in any development that seriously attempts to revitalize the central city.

> As one of the critical life support systems that address human needs, social services are increasingly recognized as the basis for public and private planning and development. The comprehensive social services system proposed for the New Town is based on this need. San Antonio New Town is predicated upon the assumption that neither the physical nor the social environments operate independently of each other. Rather, they augment, complement, and supplement each other to the point that the interrelationship produces a truly viable project which meets human needs (SANT Application, p. V–5).

Programs and activities are planned for a variety of areas. Highlights are as follows:

a) Education. The developer proposes working with the San Antonio Independent School District and a citizens' education committee (composed of parents, students, educators, and manpower representatives) to evolve a "comprehensive, community education system" which includes programs for preschool children, basic education, vocational education, adult education, and continuing college level opportunities (SANT Application, pp. V–55, V–56).

The school district is committed to construct a new high school and a new elementary-middle school complex. It will also assist with preschool and day care programs, which both the developer and district view as extremely important due to an exceptionally large number of less advantaged children. To compensate for their comparative disadvantage, the developer proposes to work with the school district to enlist federal and other support for child development and day care programs. Similar efforts would be made to enlist support for adult and vocational programs on site.

b) Health. Numerous health facilities are immediately adjacent to the project site. However the developer also will consider the feasibility of prepaid health plans, comprehensive health services through contract with appropriate institutions, and other health related services.

To assure community participation, a medical committee would be established to evaluate health needs and make recommendations to appropriate authorities. The health committee would be composed of representatives of all interested parties: consumers, health providers, insurers, and so forth.

c) Recreation and Open Space. Again, the site is accessible to the many recreational, historical, and cultural resources of downtown San Antonio. The San Antonio River Walk, an especially important amenity, gives a distinctive flavor to the project.

Improvement of open space and creation of innovative transportation systems would contribute to the unique residential environment planned for SANT. The developer plans to link residential areas with major activity nodes (recreational, employment, and educational) by pedestrian walk and bikeway systems. The pedestrian and bicycle movement systems would be designed around the San Antonio River and San Pedro Creek.

Major emphasis would be placed on developing recreational facilities whenever feasible. These would include vest pocket parks, increased use of elementary and secondary school playgrounds and facilities, and experimentation with neighborhood recreational opportunities—on rooftops, within private plazas, and above parking structures (SANT Application, p. V−88).

d) Personal Security. In keeping with the image of the new town intown, considerable attention would be directed to creating a sense of personal security in the project. The developer anticipates criminal activities will be kept at a minimum by relying on a carefully planned mix of good building design, innovative lighting and electronic security systems, improved police/community relations, improved police patrolling (including foot beats in lieu of automobile patrols when feasible), and careful mixing of land uses (and the associated activity patterns).

e) Commerical Services. A full range of commercial services would be developed at SANT. In addition to the proposed and existing regionally oriented facilities, four "mini-centers" would be constructed for project residents.

Four 6,000 square foot mini-centers will be developed. . . .Each mini-center will provide convenience services and facilities such as drive-in groceries, cleaners, beauty parlors, quick-food services and so forth (SANT Application, p. VI–78).

Managing and Financing the Project

Management and financing of the new town intown would be accomplished through two entities, San Antonio New Town, Ltd. (SANT), a private development corporation, and the San Antonio Development Agency (SADA), a public agency of the City of San Antonio. A summary of the financial resources to be contributed by each entity is shown below.

SANT is a joint venture comprised of two groups. The first is the San Antonio Ranch, which owns 50 percent equity in the project and provides the operating organization to develop the NTIT. The second group consists mainly of downtown San Antonio businessmen and investors who will contribute the other 50 percent.

The financial plan anticipates a total equity contribution of $7.35 million to occur during the first eight years of the project. After the eighth year, revenues and Title VII escrow disbursements would be adequate to cover development expenditures. Additional private equity and debt capital would be required to finance buildings to be constructed and retained by SANT.

As a municipal entity, SADA provides a means of injecting public funds into the project. SADA is also designated a local public agency for federal urban renewal funds and brings the public power of eminent domain to the project.

SADA is expected to channel $47 million into the project from the following sources: (1) a Section 102 definitive loan of $32 million, and (2) a Title I NDP grant of $15 million. The Section 102 loan is to be repaid from tax revenues generated by NTIT. This is in essence a tax increment financing device, except that a federal loan is used rather than local bonds.

SADA would also assist SANT in the timing of land acquisition expenses. SADA would purchase the land and lease it to SANT as it is needed

Table 1–14. Sources of Financial Resources: San Antonio NTIT

Entity	Source of Funds	Amount (Millions of dollars)
SADA	Title I NDP Funds	$15.0
	Section 102 Definitive Loan	32.0
SANT	Private Equity Capital	7.3
	Title VII Bonds	20.0
	Other Borrowing	8.0
	Total	$82.3

for development. The land outlays of SANT would therefore be timed to the development schedule and avoid the high initial acquisition costs which would otherwise be required. SANT would purchase land from SADA after development has advanced to the point where sufficient revenues are available.

Chapter Two

NTIT Program Implications: Balancing Job, Service, and Housing Development

Experience to date with new town intown development is largely based on the proposals and plans of developers since little NTIT construction has occurred. However, certain conclusions regarding emphasis of program components can be drawn. One fact that stands out clearly is that the mix of program components varies widely from project to project. This is to be expected, because each NTIT is an integral part of its city. Since a NTIT's relationship with the host city's economic base, public and private service systems, and housing markets is much closer than a suburban new community, emphasis placed on economic, service, and housing development must vary according to local context. To take an obvious example, if a NTIT is surrounded by hospitals and educational facilities, as at Cedar–Riverside, it would be inappropriate to require additional medical and educational facilities be provided on site. In other instances, provision of such facilities on site could be a principal aim in NTIT development in order to strengthen the primary job base. Table 2–1 shows the different emphasis placed on jobs, services, and housing in NTIT projects of two primary model types. The emphasis placed on each component varies according to the host city and type of NTIT being developed.

JOB DEVELOPMENT

Current experience with Model I NTITs indicates a growing awareness of the need to use public investment to create functioning *communities* rather than merely supporting housing construction or attaining some other single purpose objective. The HUD New Communities guidelines are quite clear:

> Although a new community need not be completely self-sufficient, it must provide in a single area the housing, social services, public and commercial facilities, and *job opportunities* normally associated

49

Table 2—1.   Component Emphases for Different NTIT Models

	Substantial	*Some*	*Little*
Job Development			
Model IA	Pontchartrain	Fort Lincoln	Roosevelt Island
Model IB	San Antonio	Battery Park	Cedar–Riverside
	San Diego		
Model II	Hartford Process		
	Cleveland		
	Chicago		
Service Development			
Model IA	Fort Lincoln	Pontchartrain	
		Roosevelt Island	
Model IB	San Antonio	Battery Park	
	Cedar–Riverside	San Diego	
Model II	Hartford Process		
	Cleveland		
	Chicago		
Housing Development			
Model IA	Roosevelt Island		
	Fort Lincoln		
	Pontchartrain		
Model IB	Battery Park	San Antonio	San Diego
	Cedar–Riverside		
Model II	Hartford Process		
	Cleveland		
	Chicago		

with a city or town. In determining the degree of internal diversity for a given site, consideration will be given to adequacy of existing or projected services and facilities in the immediate area. However, the community may not consist simply of housing or housing with a minimum of commercial facilities serving only the immediate needs of people for neighborhood shopping. Nor may a new community be predominantly industrial or commercial development, with a minimum supply of new housing (HUD Guidelines, p. 13) (Emphasis added.).

The role of job creation has varied among NTIT projects proposed to date, depending on the situation in and around the site. The widest variation is observed among Model IA developments. This is to be expected because Model IA site location is largely determined by the availability of large parcels of vacant or abandoned land. The presence or absence or economic and/or other potential is fairly coincidental. Economic conditions are most favorable at Pontchartrain, where economic development will be fairly intense, and at Hartford which proposes a NTIT and regional development program, along Model II lines.

New Orleans is in the process of creating a new deepwater port. Since the Pontchartrain NTIT is located immediately adjacent to this facility, many related commercial and manufacturing activities can be carried out efficiently within the NTIT project. Pontchartrain will have a major economic focus in order to fully exploit its developmental potential. Thus, by taking advantage of the current economic trends in New Orleans, the NTIT will be able to generate considerable on-site employment while at the same time facilitating the revitalization of the city's economy and enhancing the financial feasibility of the project.

In addition to its fortunate location, Pontchartrain's enormous size (approximately 8,400 acres) simplifies job creation because so many diverse activities can be carried out within project boundaries. Its range of potential employment generators is far greater than smaller projects where the limited amount of land is determinative. It is interesting to note that Ponchartrain plans to devote about 1,200 acres to economic and institutional development which, excepting Hartford, is practically equal in area to all other NTIT projects combined.

The importance of an employment base to project success is also evident at Fort Lincoln where the General Services Administration will be the primary employer. If the federal government had not committed GSA offices at the site, Fort Lincoln might never have come into existence as a NTIT. At best, it would have developed into little more than a public housing tract. By coordinating the federal decision as to where the facility should be located with project development, project developers greatly increased the likelihood of creating a viable community instead of a stretch of new housing units.

Creation of employment need not always be a primary consideration of NTIT development, however, as is demonstrated by Roosevelt Island. Unlike Pontchartrain and Fort Lincoln, Roosevelt Island is immediately adjacent to a gigantic number of jobs in Manhattan. Creation of additional employment on-site merits relatively low priority since other development needs are greater. A somewhat similar situation exists at Cedar–Riverside where a large number of jobs are available within walking distance of nearby colleges and hospitals.

The programmatic implication is that planning the economic development component of a NTIT must be flexible. Rather than requiring every site be a major employment generator, employment development should be emphasized only where local economic trends are favorable and resident needs require it. In the case of Roosevelt Island and Cedar–Riverside, project size also discourages substantial employment creation, because the sites' economic activities appear too small for sizable impacts on central city needs if the projects are to retain significant housing components. With greater size and favorable location, more potential is opened up for regional scale economic development activities as was noted at Ponchartrain.

An even better example of comprehensive economic development as a means of increasing employment is the Hartford Process. Here, project planners hope to change the central city from a declining manufacturing center to a nodal center for service industries serving local and national markets. They advocate a programmatic approach (Model II) that takes into account the entire city and its needs in planning the development of specific project sites. As at Pontchartrain, the greater scale of programmatic operations allows for considerable flexibility and potential effectiveness than with projects restricted to a small site.

It is significant that, in every case, NTIT developers have shown good judgment in planning their economic development activities with careful consideration of regional economic trends. Rather than attempting to counter negative features of the local economy (as was so often the case in earlier urban renewal and model cities' efforts), the NTITs are meant to take advantage of and augment positive economic features. By investing where marginal returns are likely to be greater (given the constraint of attaining certain social goals), the project planners can achieve more for a given level of public investment.

NTIT developers have recognized the rising importance of service industries in central cities in creation of employment. Fort Lincoln is encouraging government and educational activities, Cedar–Riverside relies heavily on nearby universities and hospitals, and Hartford is clearly oriented toward enhancing service activities. The only project with specific economic plans involving major manufacturing and industrial activity is Pontchartrain which is in many ways unique. Land costs are far lower there than other NTITs while its proximity to a major port makes such economic development logical and desirable. It is a special case that does not invalidate the basic generalization that most NTITs depend on service industries for most of their job creation efforts.

It would appear that most NTIT proposals want to develop employment opportunities for minority groups as well as other workers by federal subsidies provided by HUD or other departments. NTIT developers also hope to create additional economic opportunities for minority groups by stimulating minority businesses. At Pontchartrain, the developer has pledged to set aside a substantial share (starting at 10 percent the first year, and increasing at 5 percent a year until the upper limit of 40 percent is reached) of the dollar volume of construction subcontracts for qualified minority subcontractors. San Antonio's developer would facilitate participation of small businesses by establishing a Minority Enterprise Small Business Investment Company.

NTIT project developers have recognized that enhancing employment and business opportunities is in itself insufficient to effectively aid the disadvantaged in finding jobs. All NTIT proposals acknowledge the need for manpower training by pointing out that many in the resident labor force could not fully exploit new employment opportunities without some training and/or counseling. Child care centers are similarly recognized as as essential prerequisite to single parents and working mothers holding new employment.

Unfortunately, many proposals for child care centers, manpower training programs, and the like have been vague due to problems of financing. Though aware of the need for software programs to support job creation efforts, developers have been constrained by their negative impact on project cash flow—which is critical, given the existing financial limitations of Title VII. This suggests that *in order to carry out a comprehensive program of employment development, additional legislative provision will have to be made for federal financing of necessary but unprofitable social programs.*

Greater involvement of appropriate local, regional, state, and federal agencies and subsidies accordingly is called for. Already most NTIT projects have encouraged local involvement, especially in the area of adult education. Most also seek federal support for manpower training programs. Hartford Process, for example, has been attempting to establish an open line of credit at the Department of Labor for exactly this purpose. Major constraints on the participation of other federal agencies in NTIT activities have limited federal funding while once again manifesting difficulties inherent in coordinating HUD and other federal departments.

Internal subsidies (via tax increment financing, special tax assessments, or other means) offer considerable potential for financing job and related software development. Pontchartrain has some innovative suggestions, recommending establishment of a nonprofit Manpower Planning Service funded in part by a one-time assessment of property owners (and in part by hoped for state and federal subsidies). The Hartford Process also has proposed capturing tax increases engendered by NTIT development for use in financing child care and manpower training.

HUD could encourage such human oriented activities under certain circumstances by reducing the amount of low and moderate income housing required for a given project in return for greater emphasis on software programs.[a] This again argues for greater flexibility in project planning with developers and HUD attempting to aid the less advantaged in the ways most likely to have the maximum benefit given local resources and needs. Such an approach may be practical only in larger NTITs where such tradeoffs could be made without reducing other components to insignificant roles.

Even assuming suitable jobs could be created with the appropriate supportive social services, there may be problems in making jobs equally accessible to all groups. HUD guidelines prohibit discrimination and promote equal

a. The likely situation for such an approach to be desirable would be in an area where housing was not a high priority need or where economic conditions were such that the return on public investment appears greater from employment than housing development.

opportunity for minority groups in on-site employment. The effectiveness of such guidelines, of course, would depend on the vigor with which they are enforced especially after a project existed for several years and HUD was less directly involved.

In general, if new towns intown aim at revitalizing central cities, and particularly the older and more problem-prone areas, then the traditional urban development approach of HUD will have to be joined with an economic development approach (thus far, only haltingly advanced in central cities, excepting only Philadelphia and a few other cities). The NTIT operating agency will probably have to have the authority (and resources) to assist existing industries to stay in the central cities (for example, by providing space for expansion) and to attract appropriate new industries to the central city by tax abatements and other inducements, as well as by making space available. And such an operating agency will need the authority (and resources) to provide the social services appropriately related to an economic development program.

SERVICE DEVELOPMENT

The greater awareness of the importance of software programs in publicly supported development (which was especially evident in some later urban renewal projects), has been carried over into the planning of NTIT projects. This is fortunate, because acceptance that software is as necessary as hardware will do much to increase the effectiveness of public investment in central city revitalization. The HUD New Communities guidelines rightfully note:

(720.10)   *Social*
    (a)   *General.*   A new community must have a social plan and program which, among other things, includes measures to increase the available choices for living and working for full range of people and families of different compositions and incomes . . . and, in cooperation with appropriate local governments, provides a full range of health and social welfare, vocational training, educational, recreational, cultural, commercial, and other services essential to a balanced community. (HUD Guidelines, p. 17).

The exact nature of the "package of services" needed for each NTIT is difficult to determine, because each project's needs (and resources) are likely to be fairly unique. All proposals, of course, provide for the basic commercial, personal service, and public governmental needs of the project residents. In this respect a NTIT is identical with more advanced housing developments. What sets a NTIT apart is concern for the special needs of its residents. In some cases, extra software may not be needed because accessible opportunities already exist elsewhere. This appears to be the case at Roosevelt Island; special services will be primarily resident oriented. At the other extreme is the Hartford Process—a Model II development *program*—which emphasizes improving services and other amenities to make the central city more attractive to private investment. Table 2–2 summarizes the mix of on-site (or immediately adjacent) services proposed for (or already present at) Title VII NTIT projects. As can be seen, all hope to provide a fairly wide range of software and thereby recognize the importance of developing viable communities.

To simplify discussion of this component, two types of services should be identified. First are basic services which cater primarily or entirely to resident needs and are common to all NTIT proposals and most other new community developments. These "base line" services include public and quasi-public amenities such as infrastructure (roads, utilities, sewers, and so forth) and services (schools, police and fire protection, refuse collection, etc.) as well as community oriented private services (shopping, personal services, etc.).

The second type are those physical and programmatic amenities *not* common to all projects but which are included to enhance the community environment and/or to assist specific subgroups (minorities, aged, and so forth). These occur in different mixes in different project proposals depending on economic and human needs of the project and its environs, and the financial resources available. Such extra amenities encompass a myriad of possibilities, including regional shopping centers, manpower programs, development of unique cultural/historical/natural/recreational resources, and child care facilities.

While some of these latter amenities may prove to be profitable investments (since they will increase the value of the site or are self-supporting), most are not. However desirable programs aimed at helping specific groups may be, few can be run profitably without public support. As can clearly be seen in Table 2–2, while all NTIT developers want to provide an array of software programs, in most cases financial support has been very uncertain. If other federal and state agencies do not supply sufficient funding, many will not be provided and much of the social potential hoped for in NTIT development will be lost.

The uncertainty of financial support is the most significant barrier to developing an effective service component in NTITs. While additional software could be encouraged directly by HUD, the fact remains that provision of most human oriented services is not HUD's primary responsibility. Successful financing of the service component of most NTIT developments will require the active support of other federal, state, and local agencies. To date, mechanisms for inducing such cooperation (except on an informal or voluntary basis) do not exist.

HOUSING DEVELOPMENT

Housing has been a major aspect of all new town intown proposals. It is most important in the smaller Model IA NTITs, where the lower cost of vacant and

Table 2-2.   Service Packages for NTIT Projects

	Pont-chartrain	San Antonio	Cedar-Riverside	Fort Lincoln	Hartford Process**	Roosevelt Island
Manpower Programs						
Manpower Training	X*	X*		XXX	XXX*	X
On-the-job Training	X*			XXX*	XXX*	X
Vocational Education	X*	XXX			XXX*	X
Counselling/Job Referral	X*	X*		XXX*	XXX*	
Support for Minority Business	X*	XXX*	XXX	XXX	XXX*	X
Affirmative Action Program	XXX	XXX	XXX	XXX	XXX	XXX
Day Care Facilities	X*	X*	XXX	XXX	XXX*	X
Educational Programs						
Preschool	X*	X*	X*	XXX	XXX	XXX
Primary Education	XXX	XXX	XXX	XXX	XXX	XXX
Secondary Education	XXX	XXX	XXX	XXX	XXX	XXX
Junior College	XXX		XXX	XXX*	XXX	
Four Year College or University			XXX		XXX	
Adult Education	XXX*	XXX*	XXX	XXX	XXX*	XXX
Innovative Public School Programs	XXX*	X*	X	XXX	XXX	X
Special Education Programs (handicapped, bilingual, remedial, and so forth)	X*				XXX*	
Training and Use of Educational Paraprofessionals	X*				XXX*	
Health Programs						
Resident Health Insurance Plan	XXX*	X*		XXX*	XXX*	X
Major Health Facility			XXX		XXX*	XXX
Training and Use of Health Paraprofessionals	X*				XXX*	XXX

Program					
Special Programs (mental health, alcoholism, drug abuse, and so forth)	X*		XXX	XXX*	XXX
Recreational Programs					
Open Space Plan	XXX*	X*	XXX	XXX	XXX
Water Oriented Activity	XXX	XXX	XXX	XXX*	XXX
Cultural Activity	X*	XXX	XXX	XXX*	X
Spectator Sports Facility	X*	XXX	X	X	
Development of Natural/Historical Site Resources	XXX	XXX	XXX	X*	XXX*
Other					
Personal Security	X*	XXX*	X	XXX	XXX*
Innovative Circulation System	X*	X*	X	X	XXX*
Multipurpose Community Center	X*		XXX*	XXX*	XXX**
Social Planning Coordinating Organization	XXX		X	XXX	XXX
Affirmative Action Housing Program	XXX	XXX	XXX	XXX	XXX
Resident Services					
Legal Aid	X		XXX	XXX	XXX
Consumer Education	X*				
Regional Shopping Center	XXX	XXX	XXX	XXX*	XXX
Environmental Conservation	X*	XXX			XXX

Key: X   Mentioned as a possibility
XXX   Discussed in detail

*   Financing uncertain
**   Plans for financing the Hartford Process are not yet completed

Source: Project Applications

abandoned land[b] has made it more economically feasible to construct housing and the relative "lack of space" discourages major economic development. Housing is less predominant at Pontchartrain, because its scale and location. San Antonio NTIT (the only "pure" Model IB), although it would have a sizable housing component, would also emphasize economic development. Located both within and immediately adjacent to San Antonio's central business district, it is in an excellent location to support positive economic trends in the city. In fact, it is likely most Model IB new towns intown will be less focused on housing compared to Model IA, because their boundaries can be shaped according to economic development potential rather than by availability of suitable vacant or abandoned land.

Another important aspect of NTIT housing development has been the mix of people who will reside in the housing. HUD guidelines have noted:

720.10　*Social*
　　(b)　Housing and Population Mix.
　　　(2)　*Housing Mix.*
　　　　　It must have an adequate range of housing and a variety of housing types for both sale and rental for people of all incomes, ages, and family composition, including a substantial amount for people of low and moderate income. . . The Secretary will establish the threshold amount of both low and moderate income housing which is acceptable and determine the sufficiency of housing mix for a given project, taking into account the following factors:

　　　　　(i)　Current regional profile by income, family size, and age and the projected profiles for major development periods in the plan; . . . (HUD Guidelines, p. 18).

All NTIT proposals provide for housing mixes in keeping with current regional profiles, as modified by local supply of and demand for housing and existing patterns of employment opportunities. The social viability of the projected population mixes remains untested, but project developers apparently feel they are workable. In most projects, different income groups would be located in fairly separate parts of the NTIT. At Cedar–Riverside, however, current plans call for interspersal of different groups. One goal is to intersperse low and moderate income units with the market rate and some semiluxury housing.

In developing Model I NTITs, the regional profile concept has assured that less advantaged persons share in the housing opportunity produced by public investment. Some might argue, however, that the less advantaged in some cases might well be provided with less housing so that public investment can be refocused on employment development or service development for these

b.　As compared with built-on land where demolition and relocation costs are involved.

groups. In other words, under certain circumstances the poor might benefit more from additional jobs than new houses. In general, each case must be judged on its own merits, with NTIT developers working closely with the residents (or user groups) to determine that unique combination of programs and facilities that best meets the needs of the less advantaged.

The problem of planning for an appropriate proportion, type, and mix of housing, and of related services and facilities in intown areas is discussed at a later point in the volume.

Chapter Three

The Economics of Model I
New Towns Intown

Two sets of economic constraints are operative for Model I new towns intown. The first bundle of constraints arise from the initial legislative conception and HUD's subsequent administration of Title VII. With (a) a statutory limitation of $50 million in mortgage guarantees (not grants or loans) per new community project regardless of whether suburban or central-city located, and (b) HUD's apparent decision to limit support to only one NTIT project per city, the federal incentives for central city development under NTITs are indeed weak. Moreover, as the preceding chapter demonstrated, the federal government also has not committed itself to effective intergovernmental or financial efforts so as to promote more balanced NTITs—in which economic and service development are balanced against housing development according to the particular needs of the NTIT project and its surrounding locale.

Thus, the lack of a strong federal legislative and administrative commitment to new towns intown does little to help a potential central city developer overcome a second set of economic constraints—the conventional but very powerful forces which discourage private (and public) investments in revitalizing our cities. In general, two conventional economic facts constrain central city developers: (1) building costs in the central city are higher than in suburban areas, and (2) at the present time, the potential returns from intown private investment do not compensate for the higher costs and risk. Since social problems in a central city further enlarge the investment risk (Sternlieb, 1967), too often the result has been a pronounced pattern of center city disinvestment.

New towns intown, that is, development of comprehensive communities capable of revitalizing a central city, should be designed to reverse disinvestment trends by reducing the costs and risk of intown development. The Model I NTITs planned or proposed to date are instructive in this regard because of the basic insights they offer into the cost dynamics of central city development. These insights need to be clearly understood if the Model I NTIT effort,

61

essentially a demonstration program, is to set the stage for more effective and comprehensive federal sponsorship of central city development.

Cost Reduction Strategies

To achieve cost reduction goals, NTIT developers and public agencies have devised several methods of lowering capital and operating costs for the private developer. These methods are aimed at encouraging higher levels of private investment in the central city and reducing the need for direct public financial support. The most important are as follows:

1. Use of Vacant Land. Much of the NTIT activity to date has involved large parcels of vacant land in the central city. Roosevelt Island, Fort Lincoln, and Pontchartrain typify this approach. We refer to this approach as Model IA development. The general applicability of Model IA NTITs to most central cities is uncertain because the availability of such land resources is much in doubt. An unusually hopeful position was taken by Manvel (1968, p. 19) who noted:

> A considerable part of the area of many major cities is still undeveloped. Unimproved land typically makes up about one-third of all private holdings, or more than one-fifth of the total area of cities of 100,000-plus population. Even most cities of over 250,000 have a considerable amount of undeveloped land.[a]

Whether this land is suitable for NTIT development depends on its type. Five types of vacant land need to be considered: (a) remnant parcels, (b) unbuildable parcels (that is, land too steep or in flood plains), (c) corporate reserve, (d) land held for speculation, and (e) institutional reserve. Of these types of land, only the last four could be considered for Model IA NTIT development.

Although remnant parcels would obviously be too small, land that is quite steep or on flood plains might be suitable. For example, the Diamond Heights renewal project in San Francisco involved building on very steep land.

a. Before we can accept this conclusion, however, it must be pointed out that one reason for the alleged high percentage of vacant land shown is the way in which his data was collected. Manvel collected gross totals for 106 cities with a population of 100,000 or more, most of which were central cities for larger SMSAs. The boundaries of these cities sometimes reach out into suburban areas; sometimes they only encompass the downtown or immediately surrounding areas. Obviously, one would expect to find a good deal more vacant ground in the outlying areas than in the older, built-up areas of the city. For example, compare San Francisco and San Diego. The boundaries of San Francisco cover a relatively small and older part of the SMSA. The City of San Diego stretches all the way from San Clemente to the Mexican border. Not surprisingly, 54 percent of the land in San Diego and only 5 percent of the land in San Francisco turn out to be vacant. Use of his data must take into account Manvel's failure to make this distinction.

The manner in which the lots were subdivided made development impossible until public involvement and exercise of eminent domain powers made land assembly possible. Diking part of a flood plain in Hartford also worked, yielding land for what will be the North Meadows industrial park. Land held for speculation or for corporate and institutional reserve could also be used for NTIT development. In communities studied, though, parcels large enough for Model IA NTITs have been fairly rare; in most cases, reserves tend to have drawbacks for major town-size development.

An indication of just how misleading aggregate figures on vacant land can be in assessing the availability of sites for Model IA NTITs can be found in Los Angeles. Manvel's survey of vacant land in Los Angeles identified a total of 29,400 acres of vacant land in the city, of which 100 percent is buildable. However, detailed data from the Los Angeles Planning Department discloses that the majority of this vacant land lies in the suburban San Fernando Valley. An intensive search of the city outside the valley turned up no parcels of more than 40 acres that might be usable for Model IA NTIT development; at best, there were some *underutilized* parcels that might be used for NTIT purposes but only with appropriate public incentives for clearance and development.

2. Creation of New Land by Filling, Diking, or Air Rights. Creation of land by filling and diking can greatly reduce land costs in areas very close to the central city. The Battery Park project is an excellent example. The cost of building the platform and filling for construction was about $40 per square foot while market value of the new land created is approximately $400 per square foot.

Pontchartrain NTIT is another example of filling and diking to reap substantial returns in terms of land value appreciation. A drawback is its limited applicability to major United States cities. Even where feasible, there may in addition be undesirable environmental side effects.

Use of air rights over existing facilities is another way of creating areas for development within the central city. However, cost of building the platforms is prohibitive except where the value of the space created is extremely high. The Sunnyside Yards project in Queens, sponsored by the New York Urban Development Corporation (UDC), has been stalled because of the high costs of building the platform. However, there are some examples of successful use of air rights; a case in point is Prudential Center in Boston which is built over the Massachusetts Turnpike.

3. Re-use of Underutilized Land. Potentially, the most common source of land for new town intown development is land currently utilized for low intensity and/or inappropriate uses. This could be either publicly or privately owned:

a) Development of Publicly Owned Land. President Johnson

proposed that federal lands be used to develop large scale communities for low and moderate income families. Derthick's (1972) penetrating analysis of this unsuccessful program showed that there was very little federal land suitable for NTIT development; political opposition was often insurmountable; and that it was quite difficult to transfer such land from the Federal General Services Administration (GSA) for NTIT development.

The biggest problem is determining the land's price. Fort Lincoln NTIT in Washington, D. C., the only survivor of the surplus lands program, has provided an excellent example of the problems involved. After more than three years of negotiation, the price had still not been set as of mid–1974. The tie-up was due to determination that the land must be appraised at its "highest and best use." However, the appraisers were instructed to assume that there would be no public investment in the area and no renewal plan. Eventually, Washington's Redevelopment Land Agency (RLA) was to buy the land from GSA at its value for "highest and best use." The RLA would, in turn, sell the ground to a private developer at value "for use" or value for development as a NTIT. The price to be paid by the developer could be higher than that paid by RLA with the difference (the "write-up") being used to defray part of the public cost of the project.

The land price paid by the Fort Lincoln developer will depend on the ultimate use of the individual parcels. For example, the price paid by the developer for property to be used for a high rise office or residential tower will be high, because investment returns are also high. For open space, educational, or other public uses, the developer will pay nothing, because he will receive no direct return from these parcels. While value for use is based on capitalized value, in practice it is determined by negotiation. This method allows considerable flexibility in the development plan and encourages socially beneficial but economically unproductive or marginal returns.

Leasing arrangements can eliminate problems of setting a market price and of transferring land from public to private ownership. The amount to be paid for a specific parcel would depend on its use, with the lease payment being much lower for low and moderate income housing or other social amenities than for uses with higher returns. Leasing, rather than selling, public lands to development corporations could be a more expeditious way of transferring land for NTIT development. It would facilitate land transfer, minimize political opposition associated with selling public land to private developers, and eliminate the problem of setting a market price. Roosevelt Island typifies this approach.

b) Underutilized Land in the Central City.   Changes in technology and consumer preferences have rendered some large central city facilities obsolete. This is particularly true of port facilities and railroad yards, many of which have long outlived their usefulness. In some cases, this land is suitable for NTIT development. Part of Battery Park formerly held piers made obsolete by the advent of containerized shipping and the demise of passenger ship travel. NTIT development in port areas often has the added advantage of opening up the waterfront for pedestrian and recreational use.

Prudential Center in Boston was built on the site of an underutilized railroad yard. Combining this reuse with air rights use could be an advantageous land assembly strategy for other cities. However, railroad yard land is not cheap and reuse therefore must be of relatively high intensity to make projects financially feasible without land write-down or other public subsidy.

It has often been suggested that NTITs be constructed in abandoned residential areas. Certainly, the rebirth of areas such as Brownsville in New York City and Woodlawn in Chicago would require large scale efforts. Although many parcels probably could be acquired by the city for back taxes, the basic social maladies that caused abandonment in the first place must be resolved before these areas could be rebuilt without massive subsidies. As long as junkies and other criminal elements dominate these areas, development will be impossible. Social problems cannot be solved by bricks and mortar alone.

4. Channel Development Into the NTIT Via Planning Controls. Under certain circumstances, local governments could use their zoning and planning powers to channel central city development into NTIT areas without direct expenditures of public funds. One example is occurring in New Orleans where the city government has refused to construct additional bridges across the Mississippi River. This effectively precludes major development beyond municipal boundaries until new bridges and highways are authorized by the city.

Other metropolitan areas have also acted to curtail peripheral residential expansion. The best example of a regional approach is in Minneapolis–St. Paul, where the Metropolitan Council (the regional government) uses its A–95 review powers to focus growth and prevent excessive urban sprawl. In both New Orleans and Minneapolis, municipal policies facilitate higher intensity development in already developed areas.

Basic Hardware Costs

Based on analysis of proposals submitted to HUD, NTIT developments involve the following cost items:

Land Acquisition and Development;
Infrastructure;
Relocation;
Building;
Planning and Overhead;
Financing;
Taxes, especially Real Estate Taxes;

Return on Equity Investment;
Builders' and Developers' Profits.

Significant by their absence are the costs of providing services for the unemployed, poor, handicapped, and other less advantaged groups. Provision for such "software" has been a peripheral item in project cash flows because, under HUD's administration of Title VII, these activities basically do not concern a developer (beyond fulfilling commitments to provide specific services which he makes in return for federal mortgage guarantees). Discussion by developers of software costs in project proposals have been almost always qualified with a statement to the effect that implementation is dependent on the financial involvement of some federal, state, or local agency. Although many services proposals have been innovative and socially desirable, their financing generally has not been assured by HUD or the developer.

1. Land Costs.
a) Land Acquisition and Development. Land costs comprise a major cost category for NTIT developers. This section provides some data on levels of central city land prices, variations between metropolitan areas, and costs of acquiring land and preparing it for development.

Table 3–1 shows land acquisition prices in some central city and suburban new towns. The data demonstrate that land prices vary enormously between urban and suburban regions: the price for Battery Park land is 262 times that for Pontchartrain and 394 times that for Columbia and Reston.

Land prices quoted in Table 3–1 are acquisition prices only. The relevant price for analysis for NTITs includes all costs of preparing the land for reuse: these include relocation and demolition costs; landfill and other site preparation; infrastructure costs; and project planning costs. These additional

Table 3–1. New Town Land Cost

	Total Acres	Land Cost	Cost/Square Ft.
1. NTIT[1]			
San Antonio	194.2	$27,067,000	$3.20
Cedar–Riverside	340.0	30,579,000	7.02
Pontchartrain	8,400.0	25,200,000	.06
Battery Park*	91.0	62,403,000	15.76
2. Suburban New Town[2]			
Columbia	14,000	$25,000,000	$ .04
Reston	7,400	13,200,000	.04
Park Forest South	8,200	40,000,000	.11

*Not seeking Title VII support

Source: [1] Project Applications and Prospectus
[2] Mahlon Apgar, "New Business from New Towns?" *The Appraisal Journal,* Volume 41, #1, January 1973, pp. 10–11

costs may be far greater than the acquisition cost, especially where large amounts of relocation or extensive landfill are involved. Table 3–2 shows the relationship between acquisition costs and total cost of prepared sites for selected projects. It should be noted that these prices are not the same as those used by Title VII entities where urban renewal funds or other subsidies have been used or where non-Title VII entities have been borne some costs.

Table 3–2 shows that land acquisition costs are a high percentage of total costs in San Antonio, an occupied central city area, but are a low percentage of total costs in Pontchartrain where land is vacant. (Note that much of the acquisition cost in San Antonio is to be borne by the San Antonio Development Authority, not by the Title VII developer.) Land improvement costs are high in Battery Park and Pontchartrain because of the fill and diking required.

The land prices in the above tables do not necessarily represent the true relationship between prices in those metropolitan areas. A much wider sample is provided by FHA data summarized in Table 3–3. The median price of $1.99 per square foot for land in New York is more than seven times that for land in San Antonio. The data used in deriving Table 3–3 do not allow separation by central city *vs.* suburban locations.

Table 3–2. Costs of Land Acquisition and Development *(Dollars per square foot and Percent of Total)*

Component of Cost	Battery Park (New York)[1]		San Antonio[2]		Pontchartrain[2]	
	Cost (per Sq. Ft.)	Percent	Cost (per Sq. Ft.)	Percent	Cost (per Sq. Ft.)	Percent
Land Acquisition Price	not available		3.20	35.0	.06	10.0
Relocation and Demolition	not available		.80	9.0	–0–	
Other Acquisition Costs	not available		1.52	17.0	–0–	
Total Acquisition Cost	15.76	19.0	5.52	61.0	.06	10.0
Land Improvement and Infrastructure	33.37	40.0	.93	10.0	.22	37.0
Nonconstruction Costs (planning, legal, sales, overhead)	12.14	15.0	2.32	25.0	.10	16.0
Financing Costs	21.82	26.0	.39	4.0	.22	37.0
Total	83.09	100.0	9.16	100.0	.60	100.0

Sources: [1] Battery Park prospectus
[2] Project applications

Note: Costs reported do not necessarily accrue to new town intown developer, and do not reflect any cost subsidies

Table 3-3.　Median Price of Land for Existing Single Family Housing Units ($ per square foot)

	Los Angeles	New York	Washington, D.C.	Minneapolis	San Antonio
1972	1.30	1.99	.86	.64	.27
1971	1.28	1.54	.98	.61	.27
1970	1.18	1.97	.90	.62	.26
1969	1.14	1.65	.78	.58	.28
1968	1.10	1.40	.69	.55	.25
Growth Rate	4.2%	9.1%	5.7%	3.8%	2.0%

Source: United States Federal Housing Administration, *Area Trends—A Supplement to FHA Trends*, Washington, 1968; 1969; 1970; 1971; Second Quarter 1972

Land price increases over time are an important consideration to a developer; the rise may represent a cost increase where acquisition of some project land is deferred, or may represent a revenue increase where land is acquired and held for development at a later time. Some historical trends in land price increases are shown in Tables 3–3 and 3–4; Table 3–4 indicates that land prices for central city areas have risen at a rate of 8.4 percent per year over the period 1952–1966; Table 3–3 gives some indications of the differences between growth rates of price increases between regions, with the fastest rates of increase being found in the more populous areas; unfortunately, data in Table 3–3 are not disaggregated by suburban and central city designations.

Table 3–5 shows the increasing importance of land costs in the price of new single family homes. The site/value ratio has increased from 12 percent in 1950 to 21.4 percent in 1972. Furthermore, the price per square foot of the site has increased from \$.54 to \$1.19 in the period 1966–1972. This indicator (which eliminates effects of changing lot sizes) has increased approximately 120 percent. The market price of the site has increased almost 425 percent since 1950 while the Consumer Price Index has increased roughly 60 percent in the same time period.

b) Infrastructure Costs. Infrastructure costs are another major

Table 3–4. Land Price Indexes for NonMetropolitan, Metropolitan Ring, and Central City Areas, United States, 1952–1966 *(1952 = 100)*

Year	*NonMetropolitan*	*Metropolitan Ring of SMSA*	*Central City*
	(1)	*(2)*	*(3)*
1952	100	100	100
1953	99	135	117
1954	104	143	123
1955	111	180	145
1956	121	200	160
1957	129	230	180
1958	141	250	195
1959	149	270	209
1960	153	290	220
1961	162	310	236
1962	170	325	250
1963	182	345	265
1964	195	360	280
1965	211	370	290
1966	225	390	309
Annual Rate	6.0%	10.2%	8.4%

Source: Grace Milgram, "Estimate of Value of Land in the United States Held by Various Sectors of the Economy, Annually, 1952–1968," in United States Congress, House of Representatives, *House Document No. 92–64, Institutional Investor Study Report of the Securities and Exchange Commission,* 92d Cong., 1st Sess., (Washington. D. C.: Government Printing Office, 1971), Supplementary Vol. I, Pt. 6, Appendix II, p. 329

Table 3–5.   Characteristics of FHA One-Family New Home
Transactions [Sec. 203 (b)] for Selected Years

	Average			
Year	FHA Estimated Property Value	Market Price of Site	Site/Value	Price of Site per Sq. Ft.
1950	$8,594	$1,035	12.0%	N.A.
1952	10,184	1,227	12.0	N.A.
1954	10,847	1,456	13.4	N.A.
1955	12,008	1,626	13.5	N.A.
1956	13,334	1,887	14.2	N.A.
1958	14,326	2,223	15.5	N.A.
1959	14,605	2,372	16.2	N.A.
1960	14,855	2,477	16.7	N.A.
1961	15,125	2,599	17.2	N.A.
1962	15,460	2,725	17.6	N.A.
1963	16,189	2,978	18.4	N.A.
1964	16,522	3,130	18.9	N.A.
1965	17,176	3,442	20.0	N.A.
1966	17,984	3,627	20.2	$ .54
1967	18,964	3,777	19.9	.59
1968	19,974	4,154	20.8	.65
1969	21,030	4,300	20.4	.68
1970	23,559	4,952	21.0	.84
1971	24,330	5,150	21.2	1.02
1972	25,324	5,420	21.4	1.19

Source: United States Federal Housing Administration, *FHA Trends of Home Mortgage Characteristics,* Washington, D.C., 1950–1972

subcategory of land costs to a developer. Infrastructure costs include such items as water, gas, and electricity connections; street and sidewalk construction; and other site and project related costs. Table 3–6 itemizes the range of some infrastructure costs for selected suburban developments; the table shows a range of $.41 to $.73 per square foot, with more dense uses having less cost per square foot. Similar estimates have been obtained from other sources.[b] The data in Table 3–6 may not be relevant for central city developments, however.

In addition to those infrastructure costs included in Table 3–6, the developer may also be required to bear some or all of the cost for providing schools, parks and open space, and community services. There is no way to estimate how much of these costs will accrue to NTIT developers; the agreements which are worked out between local government and a NTIT developer on these community-wide infrastructure items may have a large impact on project land costs.

c) Relocation Costs. The Uniform Relocation Act of 1970 places a

b. For example, the Los Angeles County Assessors Manual, AH–531.20, pages e–h, shows infrastructure costs for single family residences ranges from $.45 and $.58 per square foot.

Table 3-6. Analysis of In–Tract Site Development Costs

February, 1973

Development Cost Items	S. F. Development Youngstown, Ohio	S. F. Development E. Chicago Heights, Ill.	Multifamily Shenango Valley, Pa.	Multifamily Brooklyn Illinois
Number of Lots (units)	248	132	84	50
Average Lot Size	7200 sq. ft.	5500 sq. ft.	7882 sq. ft.	8712 sq. ft.
Grading and Clearing	$175	$157	$390	$373
Utility Trench Excavation	250	300	27	180
Sanitary Sewer	250	95	90	160
Storm Drainage	782	395	400	480
Water	535	365	225	480
Gas	585	365	210	373
Electric Power	676	500	240	373
Paving–Parking, Walks and Patios	780	805	2505	676
Landscaping	450	1025	500	600
				355
Total Lot Improvement Cost	$4483	$4007	$4587	$3570
Cost per Square Foot of Lot	$ .62	$ .73	$ .58	$ .41

Source: Madison–Madison–International, *Adequacy and Cost Analysis of New Community Infrastructures*, (Washington, D. C.; Madison–Madison–International Publishing Company, 1973)

substantial burden on projects which would displace a considerable number of households, individuals, or businesses. The *HUD Statistical Yearbook 1971* shows that the average moving expense per family in 1969 was $85 and the average location adjustment payment was $378. Payments to individuals in 1969 was $57 for moving and $409 for relocation adjustment payments (primarily for the elderly). Although complete statistics have not been compiled showing the effects of the 1970 Uniform Relocation Act (Congressional Research Service, p. 59), interviews with HUD relocation officials produced the following estimates of relocation costs:

National Averages (estimated)

Homeowner Displacement	$8,000 per family unit
Tenant Displacement	$2,500–3,000 per family unit
Moving Expenses	$400 per family unit
Business (varies by type)	$5,000 per business

For a recent renewal project in San Diego, California, the relocation cost averages were estimated by local officials as follows:

Homeowner Displacement	$10,500 per family unit
Tenant Displacement	$3,500 per family unit
Moving Expenses	$400 per family unit
Business Displacement	$6,500 per business

In addition to these relocation expenditures, the displacing agency is responsible for the costs of administering the relocation program. The developer must either establish a relocation program or use local government facilities if available. Either way, the developer must pay the cost of the program. In San Diego the administration costs were approximately $132,000 per year, representing about 50 percent of total relocation expenses.

      The lack of substantial data on relocation costs under the Uniform Relocation Act is due in part to the fact that few projects with significant relocation have been undertaken since the Act became effective. Despite the lack of data, several authors have speculated on the ultimate impact of the legislation on future publicly funded renewal projects. While there has been some disagreement on the basic equity of the Act,[c] most observers agree the financial feasibility of projects involving substantial relocation has been greatly complicated. This is especially true because after July 1, 1972 local authorities must bear relocation costs on the same basis as other project costs (although prior to 1970 the federal government assumed 100 percent of these costs). Given the severe

c. Gorland (1972, pp. 137–138) argued the Act is overly generous; others have felt it goes a long way towards correcting inequities of the past. (Hubbard, 1972; Miller, 1972)

revenue problems facing most local jurisdictions, this provision may needlessly hinder central city modernization programs. There has been considerable feeling that the federal government should resume full responsibility for relocation costs (Gorland, 1972, p. 138; Hubbard, 1972a, p. 213; Miller, 1972, p. 214).

On a more positive note, it would appear the 1970 Act may reduce community opposition to renewal by eliminating one major source of complaint. This has proven to be the case in at lease one current program (Portland, Oregon: Sieber, 1972, pp. 455–456).

2. Building Costs.

a) Basic Building Costs. Building costs are the second major category of housing cost; they, too have a major impact on the feasibility of NTIT projects. Because of the higher density in central cities, building costs assume a greater importance than in suburban development projects.

Basic building costs for a variety of types of structures are given in Table 3–7. The basic costs include normal builders' profit and overhead but must be adjusted for three effects: (1) building height, as described in footnotes 1 and 2 of Table 3–7; (2) geographical area, as shown in Table 3–8; and (3) total building size, as shown in Table 3–9.

The major effect of building height is the height limitation on various types of structures. For example, to proceed from three-story, wood frame apartments to four-story concrete apartments raises average cost from $13.68 to $15.11 per square foot. An even more pronounced jump in average cost occurs when the six-story height limit on concrete is exceeded; seven-story reinforced structures would cost at least $19.04 per square foot.

b) Regional Variations. Building costs also vary widely with geographical area. The local multipliers are given in Table 3–8. These multipliers are multiplied by the basic costs in Table 3–7 to give local building costs. There is a wide variation in local building costs; average cost in New York is 32 percent higher than San Antonio. (It should be noted that while building costs vary widely, the variation is much less than the variation in land cost, as discussed earlier.)

c) Unit Size. Another influence on building cost is unit size. Table 3–9 shows building costs for multiple residences of wood frame construction; as total floor area per unit increases, average cost per square foot decreases. This occurs because the costs of the relatively expensive parts of the unit (kitchens, bathrooms, electrical and plumbing hardware) rise less than proportionately with increases in total area.

3. Nonconstruction Costs.
Several types of costs incurred by NTIT developers are described as nonconstruction costs. These include:

Planning and Engineering
Legal;

Table 3–7. Basic Building Costs

			Average Square Foot Base Costs ($)			
Frame Type	*Single Family Home*[1]	*Low Rise Apartments*[1]	*High Rise Apartments*[2]	*Commercial*[1]	*Office*[1]	*Industrial*[1]
Fireproofed Structural Steel		20.28	24.59	20.61	26.46	15.08
Reinforced Concrete		19.04	23.94	18.49	24.56	13.51
Concrete or Masonry	16.46	15.11		14.51	18.30	9.83
Wood or Open Steel	15.14	13.68		12.35	14.90	8.27

Sources: [1] Marshall and Stevens, *Residential Cost Handbook*, (Los Angeles: Marshall and Swift Publishing Company, 1971), pp. B–77 through B–81. Add to basic figure .8 percent base cost for every floor above three; e.g. for fourth floor of concrete office, square foot base cost increases to $18.45, fifth floor $18.60, and so forth
[2] Marshall and Swift Publication Company, *Marshall Valuation Service, Rapid Method of Computing Approximate Building Values*, (Los Angeles: Marshall and Swift Publication Company, August 1972), p. 11. Add to base cost .7 percent for every floor above three
Maximum height for wood frame construction is three floors; for concrete, six floors; for reinforced concrete, sixteen floors

Table 3-8. Local Building Cost Multipliers

City	Frame Type			
	Wood	Concrete	Reinforced Concrete	Fireproof Steel
Los Angeles	1.19	1.19	1.20	1.21
Washington D.C.	1.19	1.19	1.19	1.21
New Orleans	1.10	1.10	1.11	1.11
Boston	1.23	1.23	1.23	1.24
Minneapolis	1.22	1.22	1.23	1.24
New York (Manhattan)	1.38	1.38	1.39	1.41
San Antonio	1.05	1.05	1.05	1.07

Source: Marshall and Stevens, *Residential Cost Handbook*, (Los Angeles: Marshall and Swift Publishing Company, 1971). Local multipliers apply to basic building costs in Table 3–7

Table 3-9. Effect of Unit Size on Building Cost[1]

Sq. Ft. Per Unit	Cost Per Sq. Ft.
800	$14.77
1000	14.09
1200	13.43
1400	12.91
1600	12.52
1800	12.20
2000	11.91

[1] This example, for wood frame multiple dwellings, is included for illustrative purposes only

Source: Marshall and Stevens, *Residential Cost Handbook*, (Los Angeles: Marshall and Swift Publishing Company, 1971), p. B–84

Sales and Promotion;
Management and Overhead;
Financing.

Nonconstruction costs for the projects reviewed were between 14 and 52 percent of total costs accruing to the Title VII entity. The wide range is due to the fact that non-Title VII entities assumed some nonconstruction costs for some projects.

Planning and engineering costs for the projects reviewed ranged between $2.6 million and $4 million. A substantial part of planning and engineering costs occurs in the first two years of the project and are associated with Title VII application procedures.

Projected legal costs ranged between $600,000 and $1,450,000. Like planning costs, legal costs were high during the application stage (about $100,000 per year) and fell to much lower levels ($25,000 to $50,000) in subsequent years.

Projected management and overhead costs ranged from $8 to $12 million. Management costs consist of two major components: costs incurred during the application stage (typically about $250,000), and costs related to continuing activities which vary according to types of activities which the Title VII entity engages in. Minimal costs would accrue to the Title VII developer who engages in land development only; costs would be higher for those who engage in continuing construction, rental, and other activities.

Promotion and sales costs consist of costs of advertising, marketing, and sales or rental commissions. Advertising and marketing costs also occur in the early project years and were typically set at about $200,000 during the first two years. Sales costs and commissions become significant when project land is sold or leased; one estimate is that sales costs of about seven percent of sale value can be expected.

Financing costs include all costs of raising the capital required for land acquisition, improvement, and resale or development. For projects reviewed, financing costs ranged from 8.6 to 16.5 percent of total project costs. A list of financing costs incurred by Title VII developers is shown below.

a) Project application charge: $10,000;
b) Commitment charge: 0.5 percent of guarantee amount up to $30 million, 0.1 percent above $30 million;
c) Guarantee fee: 3 percent of guarantee (can be waived for public developers);
d) Annual fee: 0.5 percent of outstanding guarantee amount for first seven years, 1 percent thereafter (can be waived for public developers);
e) Interest on Title VII bonds: currently about 7 percent per year;
f) Bond underwriting costs: 1 to 3 percent of principal amount;
g) Interest on non-Title VII debt.

Title VII application costs consist of planning, legal, and management efforts required to meet HUD requirements. For several projects investigated in this study, total application costs ranged between about $700,000 to more than $1,100,000. The major cost item was attributed to planning costs. There is no way to determine how much of these costs would be incurred for non-HUD-sponsored projects; however, interviews with principals in NTIT projects indicate that a substantial amount of application costs are incurred in activities specific to HUD requirements.

4. Profit. Profits for private NTIT developers have to be viewed in respect to two considerations: (a) the range of activities in which the Title VII entity engages and (b) the timing of costs and revenues.

The range of activities may include at the simplest level, acquisition, improvement, and resale of land. Other Title VII entities may retain land ownership and acquire revenues through lease income. A higher level of involvement would include building activities and rental or lease of buildings. The appropriate level of profits, and the means of acquiring the profit has varied widely according to the type of NTIT activity.

The construction activities and long term ownership and management of buildings have been usually performed by entities other than the Title VII entity. In many cases, these other entities are owned by the same individuals as the Title VII entity, and in some cases partnerships or other legal devices link the Title VII entity to these other entities. As a result, the profits (and losses) from Title VII activities can be shifted to the other entities. This makes it very difficult to identify appropriate levels of profit for the Title VII entity.

The second consideration is the timing of costs and revenues. Costs are incurred, typically, long before revenues are received; hence a method of discounting revenues and costs must be used to give a true picture of profitability.

Wilburn and Gladstone have identified two measures of profitability (and the expected range of values associated with each): Return on Investment and Return on Equity. Return on Investment (ROI) is an approximate measure of the economic feasibility of the project in the broadest sense, without regard to financing or distribution of returns between equity contributors and debt holders. ROI is defined as net profit divided by total cost where all costs and revenues are discounted to the present. Wilburn and Gladstrone suggested that ROI between 15 and 25 percent (before income tax) is appropriate for new town projects given the level of risk involved. Hence the profit to be shared by equity holders (in the form of profit) and debt holders (in the form of interest) can be expected to fall in the 15 to 25 percent range.

Return on Equity (ROE) is a measure of the profitability to the project's owners, the equity contributors. ROE is defined as total profits minus financing costs divided by contributed equity. While ROI measures economic profits provided by the project regardless of financing, ROE measures profits which accrue to equity holders and fully reflects the leverage obtained by borrowing. Wilburn and Gladstone indicated that ROE must be higher than 15 to 20 percent for long term projects such as new towns.

The discounting required to relate distant profits (realized toward the end of a 20-year NTIT project) with present investment (required at the beginning of the project) requires that high dollar amounts of profit be realized if profits occur late in the project. To obtain a 20-percent rate of return, $38 of profit in the 20th year would be required for each dollar of investment made in the initial year of the project. This example demonstrates the critical nature of timing investment outlays and project revenues on profitability.

Socioeconomic Viability of Alternative Densities

The higher densities planned for new towns intown reflect the need to reduce land cost per dwelling unit by increasing the number of dwelling units per acre. A brief review of proposed Model I NTITs reveals a wide latitude in the acceptable densities. Table 3–10 shows that proposed densities range from 10 to 178 units per acre.

In determining residential density, a NTIT developer is directly concerned with the type of residential units to be constructed. To increase density the developer may need to change building types from single family homes to low or high rise apartments. The National Association of Homebuilders has published data representative of densities for different types of structures, shown in Table 3–11.

A more comprehensive study of density was carried out by Hanke in 1966. He prepared a diagrammatic representation showing the various relationships among density, open space requirements, and other spatial variables according to building type, which he called the Land Use Intensity (LUI) Scale. His chart is reproduced as Figure 3–1. Although the chart may not necessarily represent optimum spatial ratios for NTITs, it is valuable in relating type of structure to density.

As published by the Federal Housing Administration, Hanke's LUI

Table 3–10. Proposed NTIT Densities

NTIT	City	Residential Acres	Dwelling Units	Gross Density
Battery Park	New York	79	14,100	178.0
Welfare Island	New York	34.9	5,000	141.4
Fort Lincoln	Washington D.C.	155	4,625	30.0
Cedar–Riverside	Minneapolis	88	12,500	142.0
Pontchartrain	New Orleans	2,700	27,600	10.2
San Antonio	San Antonio	136.7	7,058	51.6

Source: Project Applications and Prospectuses

Table 3–11. Density and Number of Persons Per Acre

Type of Unit	Average Density Per Acre	Average No. Persons Per Unit	Average No. Persons Per Acre
High Rise	67.73	3.3	273.5
Medium Rise	45.00	3.3	148.5
Garden	19.55	3.4	66.5
Townhouse	13.62	3.5	47.7
Single Family	2.50	3.6	9.0

Source: National Association of Homebuilders, *Profile of a Builder and His Industry*, Washington, D.C., 1970

Figure 3–1. Land Use Intensity Standards

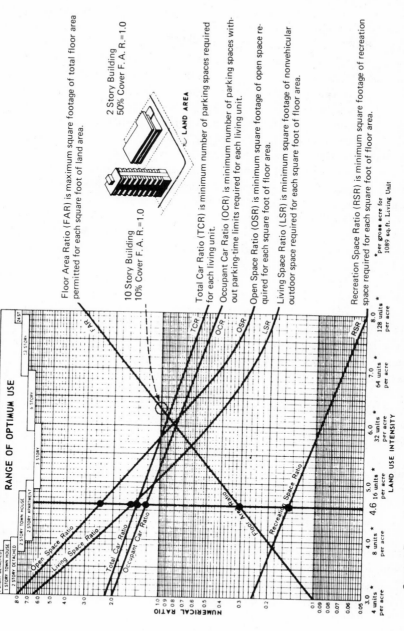

Floor Area Ratio (FAR) is maximum square footage of total floor area permitted for each square foot of land area.

2 Story Building
50% Cover F. A. R.=1.0

10 Story Building
10% Cover F. A. R.=1.0

Total Car Ratio (TCR) is minimum number of parking spaces required for each living unit.

Occupant Car Ratio (OCR) is minimum number of parking spaces without parking-time limits required for each living unit.

Open Space Ratio (OSR) is minimum square footage of open space required for each square foot of floor area.

Living Space Ratio (LSR) is minimum square footage of nonvehicular outdoor space required for each square foot of floor area.

Recreation Space Ratio (RSR) is minimum square footage of recreation space required for each square foot of floor area.

* per gross acre for
1089 sq.ft. Living Unit

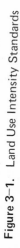

Source: Byron R. Hanke, *Land Use Intensity Standards, The LUI Scale and Zoning*, Federal Housing Administration, 1966, p. 8

Scale indicates the maximum amount of floor space and minimum area for recreation, open space, living space, and parking facilities required for FHA-insured planned unit developments and multifamily housing. Once FHA has determined an appropriate LUI number (based on location, community environment, project staging and timing, site features, and the housing market), the ratio of required land uses can be readily determined. An example by Hanke for a project rated 4.6 on the LUI Scale appears in Figure 3–1 (Hanke, p. 7–a).

It is possible to derive the relationships between land costs per dwelling unit, building costs per dwelling unit, and density. Figure 3–2 shows the relationship between building costs and density; the figure shows that building cost per square foot decreases as density increases in the range of 1 to 30 units per acre, up to the maximum density for wood frame (two- or three-story maximum) apartments. Building costs rise steadily throughout the rest of the density range, reflecting the progressively higher costs of concrete, reinforced concrete, and steel frame construction. The total range of costs begins at $15.14 per square foot for single family residences, has a minimum at $13.68 for wood frame apartments, and rises to $31.47 for 40 story steel buildings. The figure assumes a constant dwelling unit size so that a two-dimensional presentation can be made.

The combined effects of increasing density on building costs, which vary as shown in Figure 3–2, and land costs per dwelling unit, which are a declining proportion to density, can be illustrated in the following example. As shown in Table 3–12, for example, we have relied upon the basic building costs from Table 3–7, and assumed land cost to be $5 per square foot. Figure 3–3 demonstrates graphically the relationship between costs and density for the data summarized in Table 3–12. As can be seen, minimum cost ($22,038 per dwelling unit) occurs at a density of 32 units per acre using a concrete four-story apartment. Obviously, this indicates that minimum cost configurations do not necessarily result at highest density, because of the steep rises in building costs at higher and higher densities.

It should be noted, however, that merely minimizing cost is not a sufficient goal for development activities. A more reasonable and realistic goal is to maximize total revenues minus costs. When the demand side of the equation is considered, the effect of consumers' preferences regarding density becomes an additional density related variable.

Expert opinion on density remains divided. Indeed, the question of alternative densities and their impact on human life is quite controversial. Lewis Mumford, leading critic of present-day cities, has recommended the development of linked urban settlements of manageable size as an alternative to high density living (Mumford, 1961). Others share his views (for example, Gutking, 1962). Some authors believe density to be a contributing factor in increased social disorganization and related problems.

On the other hand, some researchers have argued that density *per se*

Figure 3–2.   Effect of Increasing Density on Building Costs

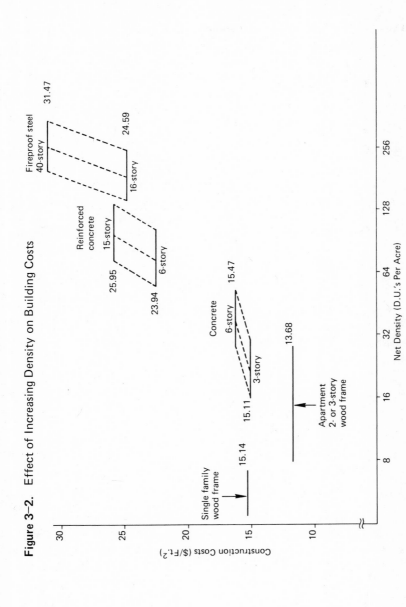

Sources: Density Data: Bryon R. Hanke, *Land Use Intensity Standards, the LUI Scale and Zoning*, Federal Housing Administration, United States Department of Housing and Urban Development, Washington, D.C., 1966, Fig. 5, p. 8
Building Costs: [2] Marshall and Stevens, *Residential Cost Handbook*, (Los Angeles: Marshall and Swift Publishing Company, 1971). No regional cost multiplier has been used; costs will increase to as high as 1.39 times those shown according to geographical area

Table 3–12.   Hypothetical Example of Effect of Increasing Density on Cost of Dwelling Unit

Density Dwelling Unit Per Acre	Building Type	Cost Per Square Foot[1]	Total Building Cost Per Dwelling Unit[2]	Land Cost Per Square Foot[3]	Total Land Cost Per Dwelling Unit	Total Cost Per Dwelling Unit
8	Single Family Wood Frame	$15.14	$15,140	$5.00	$27,225	$42,365
16	Apartment 3-Story Wood Frame	13.68	13,680	5.00	13,600	27,280
32	Concrete 4-Story	15.23	15,230	5.00	6,806	22,038
64	Reinforced Concrete 7-Story	24.71	24,710	5.00	3,403	28,113
128	Reinforced Concrete 13-Story	25.85	25,850	5.00	1,702	27,552
256	Steel 20-Story	27.00	27,900	5.00	850	28,750

[1] Assumes basic costs from Table 3–7
[2] Assumes 1,000 square feet per dwelling unit
[3] Arbitrary assumption

Figure 3-3. Land and Building Costs and Density: A Hypothetical Example

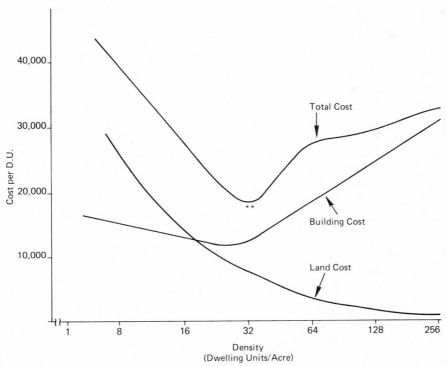

*Based on data summarized in Table 3-12.
**Minimum cost per unit occurs where density = 32 units acre;
   average cost per unit = $22,038.

is not the problem, that it is how the development is designed that is the crucial factor. High density of itself is not necessarily undesirable (Jensen, 1966; Alexander, 1967; Rainwater, 1970; Whyte, 1970).

Cedar–Riverside is particularly interesting, because it will have one of the densest developments in the Midwest—142 units per acre. The developer's consultant, Dr. David Cooperman of the University of Minnesota, concluded that such densities are feasible assuming good design; that is, avoidance of "movement activity congestion," reliance on well thought out physical planning, recognition of the importance of open space, and so forth. ("Social Planning for Cedar–West," March 11, 1971). Some local officials, however, have withheld judgment to see whether the NTIT succeeds or fails in the Minneapolis housing market (Connell, 1972, p. 28).

Densities at other new town projects will be at lower levels. For example, densities at the San Antonio new town intown would be kept fairly low, at least for low income families, in recognition of traditional values and preferences of the prospective residents (*San Antonio New Town Application,* Vol. II, pp. V–32, V–33). Pontchartrain would also be at a relatively low density and in keeping with local attitudes.

A study by the Urban Land Institute fairly well expresses current attitudes on density and development. In a study of townhouses and condominiums, they put forth the following points:

1. Customer satisfaction decreases as density increases;
2. Price is inversely related to density. The lower the price the higher the density;
3. Density alone is not a guarantee of either good or bad quality. It depends on how the density is used ("Townhouses and Condominiums," *Urban Land News and Trends in Land Development,* March, 1973.).

The Urban Land Institute report thus presented the view that the actual density is not as important as the feeling of density that the occupants have. The major factors concerning the illusion of density are:

1. Families per acre: as density increases dissatisfaction increases;
2. Density in the immediate neighborhood: views of nearby open space create a feeling of lower density;
3. Dissatisfaction increases geometrically with the size of the project;
4. Project layout has a direct effect on creating the feeling of density;
5. Noise has a strong effect on the feeling of density.

A consumer's preferences with regard to density and the price (cost) of housing units interact through the demand function to establish the revenue curve facing the developer as he increases density. Under some circumstances it is possible that the density which results in minimum cost is higher than that which a consumer finds desirable.

Accordingly, optimum density for new towns intown is determined by three factors: land cost, building costs, and consumer preferences. While the effects of density of land and building costs are known, the effect on consumer preferences cannot be systematically measured or predicted at present, and are, in any event, intimately related to local attitudes and perceptions of what is and is not acceptable.

Need for Housing Subsidies

The most important housing issue is whether housing mixes can incorporate *any* low and moderate income families without public subsidies. It appears abundantly clear that unsubsidized construction of low and moderate income housing is not economically feasible under current conditions. In almost every conceivable situation, the maximum rents even a "well off" moderate income family can afford (based on FHA guidelines) are too low to adequately compensate an unsubsidized builder. With low income families the situation is even less competitive and, thus, far more serious.

If the Federal NTIT program is to construct dwelling units for low and moderate income groups, housing subsidies must continue to be an important part of the NTIT financial package.

Before the economic infeasibility of constructing housing units for low and moderate income families can be demonstrated, a methodology for estimating financial feasibility is introduced and discussed. A basic method used by land developers to show feasibility of land use is "land value residual pro forma analysis." This method relates projected revenues to projected costs (such as construction, financing, equity returns, and so forth) but omits the cost of land. The discounted value of the costs (excluding land cost) is subtracted from the discounted value of the revenues; the remaining amount is assumed to be the value of the land under the proposed use. If this land value residual equals or exceeds the actual cost of the land, then the activity is feasible. An example of a land value residual analysis is shown in Table 3–13; the example is for rental residential property.

Based on this methodology, the feasibility of providing low-moderate income housing can be estimated (if building costs, land costs, and rental limits for low-moderate income families are known). A variety of *hypothetical* types of projects were tested using data for three metropolitan areas, and the results are reported in Table 3–14.

Before proceeding, several conclusions from the previous sections on costs of construction, land cost, and density should be pointed out:

a) Building costs per unit area decrease as the type of structure proceeds from single family to low rise apartments, but rise sharply with high rise structures. For any given type of structure, costs per unit area decrease as dwelling unit size increases and also decrease as project size increases;

b) Infrastructure costs per dwelling unit, which are normally capitalized into land costs, go down as project density increases;

c) Market rent decreases as density increases, holding all other factors constant. The amount by which market rents decline as a function of density cannot be estimated systematically at the present time.

Several types of structure and densities were tested for each metropolitan area to show the trade-off between construction cost and land cost as density increases. The large increments in construction costs for taller structures more than offset the related decrease in land costs at some point in each metropolitan area except New York; the extremely high land costs there make high rise construction the only feasible type. In New Orleans and San Antonio,

Table 3–13.   Example of Land Value Residual Pro Forma Analysis

Improvement Costs

1.	Basic Construction Costs $12 per sq. ft. x 1,000 sq. ft.	$12,000
2.	Nonconstruction Costs (15% of Basic Costs) Fees, permits, utility hookups, building profit, real estate taxes and finance costs during construction	1,800
3.	Landscaping, site work, and so forth (2% of Basic Costs)	240
4.	Total Improvement Cost	14,040

Net Income and Cash Flow

5.	Scheduled Rent (Annual @ $200/mo)		2,400
6.	Less: Vacancy and collection allowance (5%)		120
7.	Operating expenses	(25%)	600
8.	Real Estate taxes	(10%)	240
9.	Annual Net Income		1,440
10.	Less: Mortgage payment (line 14)		975
11.	Net Cash Flow		465

Financing Costs

12.	Economic Value Annual Net Income (line 9) Capitalized at 9.5%	15,158
13.	Mortgage Amount 75% of Economic Value	11,368
14.	Mortgage Payment Mortgage Amount, repaid in 35 years with 8.0% interest, constant = 8.58%	975

Calculation of Land Residual Value

15.	Return to Equity: net cash flow (line 11) capitalized at 15%	3,100
16.	Mortgage (line 13)	11,368
17.	Total Supportable Costs	14,468
18.	Less: Improvement Cost (line 4)	14,040
19.	Residual Value of Land per D.U.	428
20.	Residual Value per acre at 10 Dwelling Units per acre	4,280

Table 3–14. Required Rents for Selected Metropolitan Areas and Densities

Metropolitan Area	Density and Type of Structure[1]	Building Costs		Land Costs		Required Annual Rent[6]	Maximum Rent for Low-Moderate Income Families[7]
		Per Square Foot[2]	Per Dwelling Unit[3]	Per Square Foot[4]	Per Dwelling Unit[5]		
New York	Steel High Rise Apartments 40 Floors 178 D.U.'s Per Acre	43.03	43,030	83.09	20,334	9,879	1,945
	Reinforced Concrete Medium Rise Apartments 12 Floors 100 D.U.'s Per Acre	35.37	35,370	83.09	36,194	11,570	
	Concrete Low Rise Apartments 6 Floors 50 D.U.'s Per Acre	21.50	21,500	83.09	72,388	14,637	
New Orleans	Reinforced Concrete Medium Rise 12 Floors 100 D.U.'s Per Acre	26.55	26,550	.61	265	4,181	

Table 3–14. (cont.)

Metropolitan Area	Density and Type of Structure[1]	Building Costs		Land Costs		Required Annual Rent[6]	Maximum Rent for Low-Moderate Income Families[7]
		Per Square Foot[2]	Per Dwelling Unit[3]	Per Square Foot[4]	Per Dwelling Unit[5]		
	Concrete Low Rise Apartments 6 Floors 50 D.U.'s Per Acre	17.10	17,100	.61	531	2,750	1,181
	Wood Frame Low Rise Apartments 3 Floors 16 D.U.'s Per Acre	16.70	16,700	.61	1,660	2,862	
	Condominium or Garden Apartments 8 D.U.'s Per Acre	15.11	15,110	.61	3,321	2,873	
San Antonio	Steel High Rise Apartments 40 Floors 178 D.U.'s Per Acre	32.66	32,660	9.16	2,242	5,441	

Reinforced Concrete 12 Floors 100 D.U.'s Per Acre	26.80	26,800	9.16	4,182	4,830	1,384
Concrete 6 Floors 50 D.U.'s Per Acre	15.47	15,470	9.16	8,364	3,720	
Wood Frame 3 Floors 16 D.U.'s Per Acre	14.36	14,360	9.16	26,136	6,313	

[1] Densities are maximum for that type of structure as indicated by Hanke (see Figure 3–2)

[2] Basic construction costs (from Table 3–7) multiplied by geographical index (Table 3–8) and building height multiplier

[3] *Assumes* 1,000 square feet per dwelling unit

[4] Computed from data in column 5 ("Land cost per dwelling unit") using in column 2 ("Density and type of structure")

[5] Total costs of land acquisition, infrastructure, and nonconstruction costs from selected project applications

[6] Computed using formula in Table 3–13, *assuming* .75 loan to value ratio, 35 years eight percent mortgage (8.6 percent mortgage factor), 15 percent equity capitalization rate, 9.5 percent income capitalization rate

[7] See Table 3–19

minimum cost per dwelling unit would be achieved using medium rise (six-story) concrete construction and moderate densities.

The assumptions used in the calculations were chosen to bias the analysis toward feasibility if at all possible. Minimum cost buildings, high land use densities, low expense to revenue ratio, minimum market interest rate, and maximum mortgage terms were used. Despite the deliberate bias, it appears that no building configuration and density can achieve housing for low-moderate income families in any of the metropolitan areas tested without some type of subsidy. This is true even in New Orleans where land costs have been minimal and low rise, low cost construction cost estimates were used.

Housing Finance Strategies

Given the financial impossibility of constructing housing for low and moderate income families without subsidy, several means of reimbursing a developer for unprofitable housing have been employed or are available. Obviously, public subsidies can reduce the costs of low-moderate income units. A brief summary of the principal cost categories of housing construction appears on Table 3–15.

If revenues generated from housing sales or rentals do not cover total costs, obviously some kind of subsidy will be required or low-moderate income units will not be built. A subsidy can be supplied to reduce costs or to increase revenues. Various strategies of providing subsidies are discussed below.

1. **Land Subsidies.** Various subsidies can reduce land costs for low-moderate income housing. A direct write-down using Title I urban renewal funds was used most often in the past. Although write-downs have been popular because land represents a major cost item, the economic efficiency of land write-downs has been challenged. Further, the higher density of land uses in NTITs has made land write-downs less attractive; Table 3–15 shows that land costs may represent only 13 percent of total costs in high density projects.

Table 3–15.   Principal Housing Cost Categories *(Percent of Total Price)*

Cost Category	Single Family Homes		Elevator Apartments	
Lot		22.5%		13.0%
Construction		52.5		60.0
(Materials)	(36.7)		(38)	
(Labor)	(15.8)		(22)	
Sales		5.0		–
Finance		8.0		12.0
Profit and Overhead		12.0		15.0
		100.0%		100.0%

Source: President's Committee on Urban Housing, *A Decent Home: Report of the President's Committee on Urban Housing,* (Kaiser Report) (Washington: President's Committee on Urban Housing, 1968), p. 119

Another method for extensively reducing land costs would be leasing land, owned by local or state governments, at less than market rates. Examples include Battery Park and Roosevelt Island where market rate lease prices would have precluded developing low and moderate income housing. San Antonio proposed a variation on the concept; land would be leased from the LPA until occupancy is complete and revenues are sufficient to allow eventual purchase from the LPA.

The public lease method for reducing land costs is not limited to HUD-sponsored projects. An increasing number of private suburban developments have been relying on ground rental or lease schemes, especially for townhouse or condominium types of units. This allows a property owner to retain tax benefits of land ownership, recover holding costs through land rentals, and still have access to possible capital gains at the termination of the lease period.

2. **Building Costs.** Building costs comprise the other major cost category of producing housing. Table 3–15 shows that building costs make up to 60 percent of housing costs in central cities.

Tables 3–16 and 3–17 show that although building costs vary widely with type of structure, there is less variation between geographical areas than is found for land costs.

In Table 3–16, it can be seen that in proceeding from single family residences toward low rise wood frame apartments, building costs per unit area fall substantially. In addition, average size of dwelling units also decreases in proceeding from single family units to apartments.

Costs per dwelling unit climb sharply when high rise construction is contemplated. Table 3–16 indicates that construction costs per square foot for high rise are substantially above that for single family units. As a result, con-

Table 3–16. Construction Costs for Selected Types of Structures

Type of Structure	Construction Cost Per Square Foot
Single Family	$15.14
Apartments	
Low Rise	
Wood	13.68[1]
Concrete	15.11[1]
High Rise	
Reinforced concrete	
(up to 15 floors)	23.94[2]
Steel	24.59[2]

[1] Add .8 percent times base cost for every floor above three
[2] Add .7 percent times base cost for every floor above three
Source: Table 3–7

Table 3–17. Geographical Variations in Construction Costs
(Mean value for all four frame types)

Area	Local Cost Multiplier[1]
Boston	123.25
Los Angeles	119.75
Minneapolis	122.75
New Orleans	110.50
New York	139.00
San Antonio	105.50
Washington, D.C.	119.50

[1] Multiply by basic costs from Table 3–7
Source: Table 3–8

Table 3–18. Rise in Construction Costs Indexes *(1966–1972)*

Year	Construction Materials		Construction Wages	
	Index of Wholesale Prices	*Annual Growth Rate (%)*	*Index of Union Weekly Wage for Selected Trades*	*Annual Growth Rate (%)*
1966	98.8		146.26	
1967	100.0	1.2	154.95	5.3
1968	105.6	5.6	164.93	6.6
1969	111.9	6.3	181.54	8.8
1970	112.5	0.6	195.98	13.4
1971	119.5	7.0	212.24	15.0
1972	126.6	7.1	224.22	9.2
1973	140.1		237.38	
1967–72 Average*		5.3		9.7

*Estimates
Source: Domestic and International Business Administration, U.S. Department of Commerce, *Construction Review,* Washington, D.C., Vol. 19, No. 7, July 1973, pp. 51, 63

struction costs at high densities (assuming high rise is implied) can rise fast enough to more than offset the savings in land costs.

Construction costs have risen rapidly in recent years, as shown in Table 3–18. Construction costs are related to costs of construction materials, labor wage rates and productivity, and innovations in construction techniques. Barriers to innovation have been a major factor in the rapid rise of construction costs. Despite federal programs such as Operation Breakthrough, construction costs have continued to rise rapidly and at rates higher than for other industries.

No indirect federal subsidy techniques for construction costs have been attempted. Possibilities include federal subsidies of construction materials, innovative programs such as design of modular and factory produced housing, increase of the number of skilled employees in building trades, and research for developing better materials, techniques, and designs.

The possibilities for innovations in construction techniques appear to be very good for NTITs. The large scale and, in some cases single ownership, of NTIT projects should be conducive to factory scale mass production of components and units. The effectiveness of mass production in improving productivity and decreasing costs have been noted. The large gains which could accrue to NTIT developers by innovative techniques make it likely that a small subsidy, such as research and development grants or research subsidies, could stimulate major efforts by developers.

3. Finance Costs. Finance costs are another major category of occupancy costs. Several techniques have been used to reduce these costs relative to low and moderate income housing.

One indirect subsidy of interest rates is the Title VII loan guarantee. The risk reduction achieved by a Title VII guarantee may possibly reduce the interest rate on a development loan as much as 2 percent. For a $50 million loan over a 20-year payback period, this could mean a saving up to $15 million in interest costs depending on amortization schedule and other variables.

Direct interest rate subsidies to owners of low and moderate income housing, as through the Sections 235 or 236 programs, have effectively increased the ability of low and moderate income families to afford decent housing. An example of the effect of alternative levels of financial support on interest rates and housing costs appears in Table 3–19. As can be seen, an interest rate decrease of 2 percent (from 9 percent down to 7 percent) would lower the monthly rental by about $16 and mortgage payments by $27 per month.

Table 3–19. **Selected Examples of Effect of Interest Rates on Housing Costs**

Interest Rate (Percent)	Required Rental for Rental Units[1]	Monthly Mortgage Payment Sale Units[2]
9.0%	$201	$168
8.25[3]	194	158
7.0[4]	185	141
5.0	170	117
3.0	156	95

[1] Assumes unit with economic value of $15,000, 75 percent mortgage, 35-year term, net income 60 percent of scheduled gross income at market interest rate, expenses and return to equity do not vary with interest rate

[2] Assume $20,000 mortgage, 25-year term

[3] Approximate market interest rate on conventional mortgages in effect in May, 1972, including charges and discounts

[4] Approximate interest rate on recent Title VII loans

Table 3-19 indicates that interest rate subsidies affect the mortgage component of sale units more sharply than rent levels. This is somewhat misleading, however, because mortgage payments cover only part of the occupancy costs of owner occupied housing.

One alternative to Sections 235 and 236 programs would be to use Title VII funds to finance sales and construction of low and moderate income units. This would reduce financing costs by about 2 percent—assuming the current difference between conventional mortgage rates and rates of Title VII guaranteed debts is due to the federal mortgage guarantee. The positive effects of a 2 percent decrease in interest costs have been pointed out previously. The only cost to HUD would be the increased risk of broader Title VII guarantees, secured partially by buildings instead of improved land. Of course, greater ease of financing the construction activity at the site might tend to increase the odds of project success and thus offset the risk of a broader guarantee.

Three examples can illustrate the importance of this provision. (1) The Mitchell–Lama program in New York uses state bonds to raise funds which are in turn used to finance middle income housing. Interest rates are thereby reduced from market mortgage rates to the state bond rate. (2) The Veterans Home and Farm Program in California does essentially the same for veterans. (3) UDC finances most of its projects using similar procedures.

The use of funds raised through Title VII guarantees could similarly reduce interest rates on mortgages, especially in new towns developed by private entities. One important aspect of financing housing construction through Title VII is that shortages in mortgage funds from conventional sources, which may occur during tight money periods, could be eliminated. Further, financing through Title VII would allow the new town developer to finance residential construction early in the development process before confidence of the conventional institutional sources of mortgage funds is won or in areas of a city where conventional lenders are hesitant to enter.

Table 3-20 estimates the increase in guaranteed loan amounts which would be required if HUD guaranteed 100 percent of the cost of low and moderate income housing at three selected NTIT projects. As can be seen, Title VII loans would have to be increased substantially to include financing of low to moderate cost units. To correct for this, the term of the Title VII agreement might have to be extended beyond the present 20 to 35 years. Possibly, HUD could guarantee only a portion of the cost on the ground that a significant part of the initial cost would be covered by the rents of the less advantaged. HUD then would only subsidize the difference between what the actual rents could support and what it actually cost to provide the housing.

4. Real Estate Taxes. Real estate taxes on land and buildings are a large part of total occupancy costs. Some data on real estate taxes are shown in Table 3-21. Netzer has estimated that property taxes as a percent of occupancy

Table 3–20. Additional Financing Required for Low-Moderate
Housing

NTIT Project	Existing or Proposed Title VII Land Development Loan (Millions)	Estimated Cost of Low-Moderate Housing[1] (Millions)
Cedar–Riverside	24	83.1
Pontchartrain	50	124.0
San Antonio	7	66.6

[1] Estimate based on $15,000 cost per low-moderate income housing unit. Number of low-moderate units used are: San Antonio, 4,440; Pontchartrain, 8,300; Cedar–Riverside, 5,539
Sources: Project Applications and Prospectuses

Table 3–21. Real Estate Taxes as Percent of Value

Type of Unit	Annual Real Estate Taxes (Percent of Value)
Single Family	1.4%
Apartments (5–50 units)	2.0
Apartments (over 50 units)	2.7

Source: Netzer, Dick, *Economics of the Property Tax,* (Washington, D. C.: The Brookings Institute, 1966), p. 79

costs may be as high as 25 percent in large central city areas. Data for recent projects show that real estate taxes comprise 21 percent of rentals in Battery Park (Preliminary Prospectus, p. 37), 16 percent in Pontchartrain (Gladstone Associates, 1972, p. 111), and 11 percent in major suburban new town projects (Wilburn, 1972, p. 111). This part of the cost can be reduced through tax abatement agreements with the local government. An example is provided by the Fenway urban renewal project in Boston. The scheme provides for some increase in tax revenue to local government over and above municipal costs, but results in a tax rate lower than surrounding communities. Tax increment financing is another type of subsidy used to reduce project financing costs. Yet another variation occurs when a local government commits real estate tax revenues for provision of infrastructure items, cultural or recreational facilities, or otherwise to reduce costs of the project developer or increase marketability—hence revenues—of the project.

5. Internal Subsidies. In the absence of direct subsidies for low and moderate income housing, it may be possible in some projects to subsidize these units at the expense of high income, commercial, and industrial land users. In economic terms, the developer would be acting as a price discriminator. This

implies that the market for high income residential, commercial, and industrial land is imperfect. If there were perfect competition, the developer would be unable to raise the price of high income and nonresidential land above competitive prices.

In more real terms, the internal subsidy means that the commercial and high income residential user would be provided with fewer amenities, lower quality, or less space than would otherwise be the case. The question of how much the developer can reduce the level of amenities and still reach the target market would be determined chiefly by the level of competition.

The internal subsidy method may greatly increase the risk of a NTIT project if competition exists for commercial and high income residential property. A competing commercial or high income residential development which did not have to subsidize low-moderate income housing could provide more amenities for its customers; such a competitor could capture some of the most profitable activities away from the NTIT, leaving only the less profitable activities. A NTIT facing such competition would have its financial position seriously endangered. This suggests that to ensure the success of NTIT efforts, external subsidies are preferable.

6. Rent Supplements. In addition to the various means of lowering the costs of providing new housing to the less advantaged another means of reimbursing the developer would be to enhance potential residents' ability to pay rents appropriate to the builder's investment. Possibly some sort of rent supplement could be incorporated into plans for public support of low and moderate income housing construction in NTIT developments.

Although the rent supplement program was under heavy political fire from its enactment in 1965, there is a renewed interest in direct allowances to tenants and homeowners. One advantage of this housing allowance approach is that it gives the recipient greater freedom of choice and movement than he would have under the capital subsidy approach whereby the subsidy is tied to a specific unit. On the other hand, some predict that a rapid switch to the allowances would result in inflationary increases in demand. It is obvious that any set of housing programs for lower income families must be aimed at increasing the amounts that these families can spend on housing as well as the supply of lower cost housing. Just how rent supplement programs can best be incorporated into an NTIT development is uncertain, although the idea appears to offer considerable potential. The concept of rent supplements is now being evaluated through a series of experiments in a number of communities; these evaluations can be expected to provide useful insights into how rent supplement programs might ultimately be incorporated into new town intown development efforts.

Summary

Our review of experience with new towns intown to date (mid–1974) suggests the following conclusions:

1. The federal new town intown program has stimulated few actual projects; in fact, by mid–1974, only one project under way (Cedar–Riverside) could be said to be a direct product of the federal program. Against the background of common knowledge that central city development is difficult and costly, the incentives and subsidies held out by the federal government are clearly not seen as adequate to induce a large volume of private and/or public investment in such development.

2. The new towns intown which have been proposed under the federal program have been of two distinct types, requiring different approaches and different forms and types of financing, although in the administration of the federal program all proposals have been treated as essentially the same. One involves single *projects* on contiguous tracts of land (what we have labeled Model I projects); the other involves long-term *programs* of central city development, encompassing a series of projects, which may cover anything from open land to highly built-up areas that need developmental attention, (or what we have called a Model II approach to new towns intown).

3. The new town intown program has promoted interest in the various components of development, including jobs, services and facilities, and transportation as well as housing, not just housing alone. This has marked a significant forward move in the realm of central city development. However, the full impact of federal pressure for a rounded concern for all the important aspects of development has not been felt, since federal support for services and facilities specifically geared to central city development has not been forthcoming (even though provided in Title VII).

4. The federal program has induced new town intown plans to incorporate in each project a "reasonable" proportion of low and moderate income housing, but again the full impact of this pressure has not been felt because, in the last few years, federal funds to subsidize such housing has not been available, and it has been established that, under current conditions, low and moderate income housing cannot be built in the central city without "outside" subsidy.

5. The problem of making central city development competitive with development in suburban areas remains. The slow pace of new town intown construction under the federal program has served, in fact, to highlight this problem more sharply than ever. A variety of means through which such development costs might be reduced have been detailed; ultimately, most of them involve some form or other of governmental subsidy.

Part I

Bibliography

Abbott, Sidney. "New Hope for New Towns," *Design and Environment,* Vol. 3, No. 1 (Spring 1972), pp. 28–37.

Alexander, Christopher. "The City as a Mechanism for Sustaining Human Contact," in William R. Ewald Jr., *Environment for Man* (Bloomington: Indiana University Press, 1967), pp. 60–109.

American City Corporation. *The Greater Hartford Process.* Report prepared for the Greater Hartford Corporation and Greater Hartford Process, Inc. (Hartford: April 1972).

Anders, Michael. "Fort Lincoln Clears Hurdle, To Sell Stock," *The Evening Star Daily News* (Washington D. C.: July 26, 1972).

Apgar, Mahlon IV. *Managing Community Development: The Systems Approach in Columbia, Maryland* (New York: McKinsey & Company, 1971).

Apgar, Mahlon IV. "New Business from New Towns," *The Appraisal Journal,* Vol. 41, No. 1 (January 1973), pp. 7–35.

"Automobile-Free New Town," *HUD Challenge,* Vol. IV. No. 3 (March 1973), pp. 26–27.

Bailey, James & Simpson Lawson. *Fort Lincoln New Town, Washington D. C.,* Joint Development Strategies Study No. CPM–1586–72, Case Study P–2 for the Department of Housing and Urban Development (Washington D. C. : March 1973).

Barton-Aschman Associates, Inc. *Fort Lincoln New Town Project Management System, Overview: Summary and Recommendations,* Prepared for the District of Columbia Redevelopment Land Agency (Chicago: June 1973).

Battery Park City Authority. *Preliminary Official Statement,* Prospectus (April 20, 1972).

Browne, Richard P. & Associates. *Cleveland New Town Intown, A Conceptualization at the Mid-Point – Phase One* (Cleveland: September 1972).

Bryan, Jack. "Twin Cities of Minneapolis, St. Paul Have New Set of Twins," *Journal of Housing,* Vol. 29, No. 3 (March 1972), pp. 119–131.

Building Systems International, Inc. and Westinghouse Corporation. *Fort Lincoln New Town—Report of the BSI/Westinghouse Joint Venture* (Washington, D. C.: January 1972).

Cameron, Gordon C. *Regional Economic Development: The Federal Role* (Washington, D. C.: Resources for the Future, 1970).

Cedar–Riverside Associates, Inc. *Cedar–Riverside New Community, Narrative Descriptions* (Minneapolis, May 9, 1972 a).

Cedar–Riverside Associates, Inc. *Human Resources Planning, Cedar–Riverside* (Minneapolis, July 1972 b).

Centex Corporation, *A Management Program for the Planning of Pontchartrain New Town Intown, New Orleans, Louisiana,* Working Paper (Dallas 1971).

City of Minneapolis. *1967–1968 Report* Minneapolis 1968).

City of New York, New York State Urban Development Corporation, and Welfare Island Development Corporation. *Lease Agreement Between City of New York (Lessor) and New York State Urban Development Corporation (Lessee) and Welfare Island Development Corporation (Subsidiary)* (New York, December 23, 1969).

Clawson, Marion. *Suburban Land Conversion in the United States: An Economic and Governmental Process* (Baltimore: The John Hopkins Press 1971).

Connell, Kathleen M. *Regional New Towns and Intergovernmental Relations* (Detroit: Metropolitan Fund Inc., February 1972).

Cooperman, David. "Social Mix and Social Planning," Mimeo. prepared for Cedar–Riverside Associates, Inc. (Minneapolis, December 1969).

Cooperman, David. "Report on Density, Neighborhood, and Social Planning, Cedar West." Mimeo. prepared for Cedar–Riverside Associates, Inc. (Minneapolis, March 1, 1971).

Cooperman, David. "Social Planning for Cedar West," Mimeo. prepared for Cedar–Riverside Associates, Inc. (Minneapolis, March 11, 1971).

Cooperman, David. "Social Activity Analysis for Development and Use of Cedar–Riverside Open Space." Mimeo. prepared for Cedar–Riverside Associates, Inc. (Minneapolis, August 26, 1971).

Criminal and Social Justice Coordinating Committee for the Greater Hartford Process, Inc. "Corrections," *Greater Hartford Process, Inc.* Hartford, February 1972), pp. 123–26.

Criminal and Social Justice Coordinating Committee for the Greater Hartford Process, Inc. "Policing," *Greater Hartford Process, Inc.* (Hartford, February 1972), pp. 120–22.

Decision Sciences Corporation. *New Communities Annotated Bibliography,* NTIS Report No. PB–206–880 (Springfield, Virginia: National Technical Information Service, U. S. Department of Commerce, November 1971).

Decision Sciences Corporation. *New Communities—Systems for Planning and Evaluation,* Prepared for the Department of HUD, NTIS Report No. PB–206–882 (Springfield, Virginia: National Technical Information Service, U. S. Department of Commerce, November 1971).

Decision Sciences Corporation. *A Review of the State of the Art in Community Analysis, Simulation, and Modeling,* NTIS document No. PB–206–883 (Springfield, Virginia: National Technical Information Service, U. S. Department of Commerce, November 1971).

Decision Sciences Corporation. *Advanced NUCOMS System, General Design Report,* Prepared for the U. S. Department of Housing and Urban Development, Contract No. H–1877 (Jenkintown, Pennsylvania: Decision Sciences Corporation, November 30, 1972).

Decision Sciences Corporation. *Advanced NUCOMS System, Developer Financial Model,* Prepared for the U. S. Department of Housing and Urban Development, Contract No. H–1877 (Jenkintown, Pennsylvania: Decision Sciences Corporation, January 18, 1973).

Derthick, Martha. "Defeat at Fort Lincoln" *Public Interest* (Summer 1970), pp. 3–29.

Derthick, Martha. *New Towns Intown: Why a Federal Program Failed* (Washington, D. C.: The Urban Institute 1972).

District of Columbia Redevelopment Land Agency. "Administrative History of the District of Columbia Redevelopment Land Agency—The Southwest Projects," Mimeo. (Washington, D. C. 1961).

District of Columbia Redevelopment Land Agency. *Annual Report, 1970* (Washington, D. C. 1970).

District of Columbia Redevelopment Land Agency and National Capital Planning Commission. *Urban Renewal Plan for the Fort Lincoln Urban Renewal Area* (Washington, D. C., July 26, 1972).

District of Columbia Redevelopment Land Agency. "Checklist of Major Security Guidelines," Mimeo. (Washington, D. C., 1973).

Douglas, Paul H. *Building the American City.* National Commission on Urban Problems (Washington, D. C.: U. S. Government Printing Office 1968).

Downs, Anthony. *Urban Problems and Prospects* (Chicago: Markham, 1970).

Duncan, Otis Dudley and Beverly Duncan. *The Negro Population of Chicago, A Study of Residential Succession* (Chicago: University of Chicago Press, 1957).

Edson, Charles F. "The Housing and Urban Development Act of 1970," *The Urban Lawyer,* Vol. III, No. 1 (Winter 1971), pp. 142–148.

Educational Planning Associates and General Learning Corporation. *A Community Education System for Welfare Island,* Draft prepared for the New York State Urban Development Corporation (New York, July 6, 1970).

Fort Lincoln Advisory Panel. *Fort Lincoln New Town: Report and Recommendations on Program Objectives* (Washington, D. C.: Washington, Center for Metropolitan Studies, June 1968).

General Electric Company—Tempo. *Developing a Methodology for the Evaluation of Proposed New Communities,* Prepared for the U. S. Department of Housing and Urban Development, NTIS No. PB–207–719 (Springfield, Virginia: National Technical Information Service, U. S. Department of Commerce, October 1971).

Gladstone Associates. *Pontchartrain New Town Implementation Plan, Financial Plan, Fiscal Impact Analysis,* Confidential, Prepared for Pontchartrain Land Development Corporation (Washington, D. C., July 1972).

Gladstone Associates and Wallace, McCarg, Roberts & Todd. *Social Plan, Pontchartrain New Town New Orleans, Louisiana,* Prepared for Pontchartrain Land Development Corporation (Washington, D. C., July 1972).

Gorland, Emanuel. "Relocation Inequities and Problems Emergent as a Result of the 1970 Uniform Relocation Act," *Journal of Housing,* Vol. 29, No. 3 (March 31, 1972), pp. 137–138.

Greater Hartford Process, Inc. *A Learning System for 1980* (Hartford, March 1972 a).

Greater Hartford Process, Inc. *The New Hartford (Phase I): A Community Development Model* (Hartford, March 1972 b).

Greater Hartford Process, Inc. "Work in Progress," Newsletter (Hartford, 1972 c).

Greater Hartford Process, Inc. "Work in Progress: A Progress Report 1972–1973," Newsletter (Hartford, August 1973).

Gruen, Juna J. and Claude Gruen. *Low and Moderate Income Housing in the Suburbs: An Analysis for the Dayton, Ohio Region* (New York: Praeger, 1972).

Gruzen & Partners and the Lefrak Organization, Inc. *A Feasibility Study for the Multiple Use of Air–Rights Over the Sunnyside Yards,* Prepared for the New York State Urban Development Corporation (New York, 1972).

Gutking, E. A. *The Twilight of Cities* (New York: The Free Press of Glencoe, 1962).

Handman, Arthur L. and Robert Bogen. *"A New Mobility for the Capitol Region: Analysis, Plan and Program for Comprehensive Transportation Facilities and Services,"* Greater Hartford Process, Inc. (Hartford, February 1972).

Hanke, Byron R. *Land–Use Intensity Standards, The Lui Scale and Zoning* (U. S. Federal Housing Administration, Washington, D. C., 1966).

Hanson, Royce. *Managing Services for New Communities* (Washington, D. C.: Washington Center for Metropolitan Studies, 1970).

Harman, O'Donnell & Henninger Associates, Inc. *New Town Potential in Northeastern Kansas City, Missouri,* Prepared for Curry Investment Company (Denver, May 1971).

"Hartford has a Process for Tackling Urban Problems with Regional Action," *House & Home,* Vol. 43, No. 5 (May 1973) pp. 12,16.

Heller, Keith R. "Statement of Keith R. Heller, President, Cedar–Riverside Associates, Inc. Before the Subcommittee on Housing of the Committee on Banking and Currency, U. S., House, May 30, 1970," Mimeo. Cedar–Riverside Associates (Minneapolis, May 1973).

Hoffman, Morton & Co. *Response to the Questions Submitted by District of Columbia Redevelopment Land Agency Covering the January, 1972, BSI/Westinghouse Joint Venture General Development Proposal for*

Fort Lincoln New Town, Washington D. C., Prepared for the District of Columbia Redevelopment Land Agency (Baltimore, February 19, 1972).

Hubbard, Robert. "Letters to the Editor," *Journal of Housing,* Vol. 29, No. 5 (May 31, 1972 a), pp. 213–214.

"HUD–Guaranteed New Communities," *HUD Challenge,* Vol. III, No. 8 (August 1972 b), pp. 17–23.

Jensen, Rolf. *High Density Living* (New York: Praeger Publishers, 1966).

Johnson, Philip and John Burgee. *The Island Nobody Knows* (New York: New York Urban Development Corporation, October 1969).

Johnson, Philip and John Burgee. *The Plan for Welfare Island, Technical Report, October 7, 1969* (New York: New York State Urban Development Corporation, October 7, 1969).

Kaitz, Edwin M. and Herbert Harvey Hyman. *Urban Planning for Social Welfare: A Model Cities Approach* (Washington D. C.: Praeger Publishers, 1970).

Karmin, Monroe W. "Greater Hartford: Businessmen, Politicians Seek to Renew a City and Help Suburbs, Too," *The Wall Street Journal,* Vol. CLXXX, No. 17 (Wednesday, July 26, 1972), pp. 1, 12.

Keiser, A. Kay. "A New System of Health Care for 1980, A Proposal," *Greater Hartford Process, Inc.* Mimeo. (Hartford, November 1972) 78 pages.

Keyes, Langley C. *The Rehabilitation Planning Game* (Cambridge: The M. I. T. Press, 1969).

Landrieu, Moon. "The Address of Moon Landrieu of the City of New Orleans Before the Housing Subcommittee of the House on Banking and Currency Committee in Washington, D. C., May 31, 1973," Mimeo. (Office of the Mayor: New Orleans, May 1973).

Lansing, John B., and W. W. Clifton, J. N. Morgan. *New Homes for Poor People: A Study of Chains of Moves* (Ann Arbor: Institute of Social Research, 1969).

Lawson, Simpson F. *Workshop on Urban Open Space* (Washington D. C.: U. S. Department of Housing and Urban Development, 1969).

Levitan, Sar. *Federal Aid to Depressed Areas, An Evaluation of the Area Redevelopment Administration* (Baltimore: John Hopkins Press, 1964).

Lilley, William III. "GPR Report/Parties, Agencies Scrambling to Shape Future of New Communities Program," *National Journal,* Vol. II, No. 14 (April 4, 1970) pp. 726–735.

Linton, Mields & Coston, Inc. *Final Report Government Plan, Analysis of Federal Program Assistance Applicable to the Development of the Pontchartrain New–Town–In–Town,* Prepared for the Pontchartrain Land Corporation (Washington D. C., July 1972).

Logue, Edward J. *Recommended Program Objectives, Fort Lincoln New Town,* Submitted to the District of Columbia Redevelopment Land Agency, Contract DC–RLA–1042 (Washington D. C., July 15, 1968).

Logue, Edward J. *Fort Lincoln New Town Final Planning Report,* Submitted to District of Columbia Redevelopment Land Agency, Contract DC–RLA–1042 (Washington D. C., April 1969).

Logue, Edward J. "Goals, Guidelines, Concerns of the New York State Urban Development Corporation, January 1971," Pamphlet, Adapted from "President's Statement," *The New York State Urban Development Corporation Annual Report,* 1970 (New York, 1970).

Long, Norton E. "The Local Community as an Ecology of Games," *American Journal of Sociology,* Vol. 63 (November 1958), pp. 251–261.

Los Angeles County Assessor's Office. *Los Angeles County Assessor's Manual AH–531.20* (Los Angeles, 1973).

Madison–Madison–International. *Adequacy and Cost Analysis of New Community Infrastructures* (Washington D. C.: Madison–Madison–International Publishing Company, 1973).

Manvel, Allen D. "Land Use in 106 Large Cities," in National Commission on Urban Problems. *Three Land Research Studies,* Research Report No. 12 (Washington D. C.: Government Printing Office, 1968) pp. 19–59.

Marshal and Stevens. *Residential Cost Handbook* (Los Angeles: Marshal and Swift Publishing Company, 1971).

Marshal and Swift Publishing Company. *Marshal Valuation Service* (Los Angeles: Marshal and Swift Publishing Company, August 1972).

Matthews, Trevvett. "Old Wine In New Bottles: A Formula for Success in Regional Renewal Efforts," *The Mortgage Banker,* Vol. 32 (September 1972) pp. 20–30.

Meer, Bernard, and Edward Freedman. "The Impact of Negro Neighbors on White Owners," *Social Forces* (September 1966) pp. 11–19.

Metropolitan Fund, Inc. *Regional New Towns, Alternatives in Urban Growth* (Detroit: Metropolitan Fund, May 1970).

Metropolitan Fund, Inc. *Regional New–Town Design: A Paired Community For Southeast Michigan* (Detroit: Metropolitan Fund February 1971).

Meyer, Douglas K. "Spatiotemporal Trends of Racial Residential Change," *Land Economics* (February 1972), pp. 62–65.

Meyer, Eugene L. "White House Backs New Town Project At Fort Lincoln Site," *Washington Post* (May 20, 1972), p. B–2.

Meyer, Eugene L. "Fort Lincoln 'New Town' Fund Cleared," *Washington Post* (November 19, 1972), p. D–1.

Mields, Hugh Jr. "The Federal New Communities Program: Prospects for the Future," in Perloff, Harvey S., and Neil C. Sandburg (eds.) *New Towns: Why–and for Whom:* (New York: Praeger Publishers, 1973 a), pp. 81–92.

Mields, Hugh Jr. *Federally Assisted New Communities: A New Dimension in Urban Development* (Washington D. C.: The Urban Land Institute, 1973 b).

Milgram, Grace. "Estimate of Value of Land in the United States Held by Various Sectors of the Economy Annually, 1952–1968," in U. S., Congress, House of Representatives, *Institutional Investor Study Report of the Securities and Exchange Commission,* House Document No. 92–64, 92d Cong., 1st Sess. (Washington D. C.: Government Printing Office 1971), Supplementary Vol. 1, Pt. 6, Appendix II.

Miller, Lawrence. "Letters to the Editor," *Journal of Housing,* Vol. 29, No. 5 (May 31, 1972), pp. 214–215.

Minneapolis Housing and Redevelopment Authority. *Urban Renewal and Housing in Minneapolis* (Minneapolis, 1966).

Minneapolis Housing and Redevelopment Authority. *Cedar–Riverside Urban Renewal Plan* (R 213) as revised September 12, 1968 (Minneapolis, 1968).

Minneapolis Housing and Redevelopment Authority. *Annual Report* (Minneapolis, 1970).

Minneapolis Housing and Redevelopment Authority. "MHRA," Pamphlet (Minneapolis, April 1972).

Moore, John L. "Urban Report/Congress Gathers Wide Support for Reshaping Administration's Community Development Bill," *National Journal,* Vol. 5, No. 22 (June 2, 1973), pp. 797–808.

Mumford, Lewis. *The City in History: Its Origins, Its Transformations, and Its Prospects,* Vol. II (New York: Harcourt, Brace & World, 1961), p. 286.

Naftalin, Arthur. "Minneapolis: A Case Study in a Unified Attack on Urban Problems," *Journal of Housing,* Vol. 26, No. 11 (November 1969), pp. 615–618.

National Association of Homebuilders. *Profile of a Builder and His Industry* (Washington D. C., 1970).

National Commission on Urban Problems. *Building the American City: Report of the National Commission on Urban Problems to the Congress and to the President of the United States,* 91st Cong., 1st Sess., Housing Document No. 90–34 (Washington: Government Printing Office, 1968).

National Kinney Corporation and United Housing Foundation. *Liberty Harbor, A Plan for a New Community on Jersey City's Waterfront* (Jersey City, March 1973).

Netzer, Dick. *The Economics of the Property Tax* (Washington, D.C.: The Brookings Institution, 1969).

New York State Urban Development Corporation and the New York State Office of Planning Coordination. *New Communities for New York* (New York, December 1970).

New York State Urban Development Corporation. *Welfare Island—A Planned New Town In Town, An Application for Determination of General Eligibility Under the Housing and Urban Development Act of 1970—Urban Growth and New Community Development, Part B—Development of New Communities* (New York, April 1972).

Newman, Oscar. *Crime Prevention Through Urban Design—Defensible Space* (New York: Macmillan, 1972).

Peachey, Paul. *New Town, Old Habits: Citizen Participation at Fort Lincoln,* Community Governance Paper No. 1, Washington Center for Metropolitan Studies (Washington, D. C., 1970).

Perloff, Harvey S. "New Towns Intown," *Journal of the American Institute of Planners,* Vol. XXXII, No. 3 (May 1966), pp. 152–162.

Perloff, Harvey S., David M. Vetter, and Thomas Berg. *Lessons From Urban Renewal (for NTITs), A Review of the Literature,* Unpublished (School of Architecture and Urban Planning, University of California at Los Angeles, November 1972).

Perloff, Harvey S. "New Towns Intown In a National New Communities Program," in Perloff, Harvey S., and Neil C. Sandburg (eds.) *New Towns: Why—And For Whom?* (New York: Praeger Publishers, 1973), pp. 159–178.

Perloff, Harvey S., and Neil C. Sandburg (eds.). *New Towns: Why—And For Whom?* Praeger Special Studies Program (New York: Praeger Publishers, 1973).

Pontchartrain Land Corporation. *Application for Pontchartrain New Town In Town, Presented to the Office of New Community Development, Department of Housing and Urban Development,* Vols. I, II (Dallas, Texas, July 1972).

Pontchartrain Land Corporation, with Wallace McHarg Roberts and Todd (Physical, Ecological and Social Planning), Tippetts, Abbett, McCarthy, Stratton (Engineering and Transportation Planning) and Gladstone Associates (Economic and Social Planning) *Pontchartrain New—Town–Intown, New Orleans, Louisiana, A Project for the Pontchartrain Land Corporation (New Orleans, New Orleans East, Inc., 1972).*

President's Committee on Urban Housing. *A Decent Home: Report of the President's Committee on Urban Housing* (Washington, D. C.: Government Printing Office, 1968).

Rainwater, Lee. *Behind Ghetto Walls* (Chicago: Aldine Publishing Company, 1970).

Raspberry, William. "Ft. Lincoln's Best Hope," *Washington Post* (May 12, 1972), p. A–27.

Real Estate Research Corporation. *Economic and Financial Feasibility Models for New Community Development,* Prepared for the Department of HUD (NTIS No. PB–206–925) (Virginia: National Technical Information Service, U. S. Department of Commerce, August 1971).

Regional Plan Association. *The Region's Growth, A Report of the Second Regional Plan,* Vol. II (New York: May 1967), p. 287.

Research Analysis Corporation. *New Community Development,* Prepared for the Department of HUD (Contract No. H1309) (McLean, Virginia: Research Analysis Corporation, December 1971), Vol. I (Primary Investigations); Vol. II (The New Community Development Model).

Rose, Harold M. "The Development of an Urban Sub–System: The Case of the Negro Ghetto," *Annals, Association of American Geographers* (March 1970), pp. 1–17.

San Antonio New Town, Ltd. *Final Application for San Antonio New Town,* Vols. I, II, and III (San Antonio, Texas, January 1973).

Scharfenberg, Kirk. "Blacks Win Share in Ft. Lincoln Profits," *Washington Post* (July 26, 1972), pp. C–1, C–7.

Sieber, Philip E. "Uniform Relocation Act Can Be A Force For Citizen Support of Community Development," *Journal of Housing,* Vol. 29, No. 9 (October 24, 1972), pp. 455–456.

Slidell, John B. *A User's Guide to the GE–UNC New Towns Financial Feasibility Model–Long Program* (University of North Carolina at Chapel Hill: Center for Urban and Regional Studies, May 1972).

Smith, Fred. *Man and His Urban Environment, A Manual of Specific Considerations for the Seventies and Beyond,* Man and His Environment Project (New York, 1972).

Stanback, Thomas M., and Richard V. Knight. *The Metropolitan Economy* (New York: Columbia University Press. 1970).

Taeuber, Karl E. and Alma F. Taeuber. *Negroes in Cities* (Chicago: Aldine Publishing Company, 1970).

Texas Instruments, Incorporated. *Final Report on a Study of Broadband Cable Communications in Pontchartrain New Town Intown,* Report No. 8–72–37, Prepared for the Centex Corporation, Dallas, Texas (July 8, 1972).

"Townhouses and Condominiums," *Urban Land; News and Trends in Land Development,* Vol. 32, No. 3 (March 1973), pp. 3–12.

Twentieth Century Fund. *CDCs: New Hope for the Inner City, Report of the Twentieth Century Fund Task Force on Community Development Corporations* (New York: The Twentieth Century Fund, 1971), with background paper by Geoffrey, Faux.

U. S., Bureau of the Census. *Census of Housing: 1970, Final Report HC–1* (Washington, D. C.: Government Printing Office, 1972).

U. S., Bureau of the Census. *Census of Population: 1970, General Social and Economic Characteristics* (Washington, D. C.: Government Printing Office, various dates).

U. S., Congress, House, Committee of the Whole House on the State of the Union. *Report: The Housing and Urban Development Act of 1970,* Report No. 91–1556, 91st Cong., 2d Sess. (Washington, D. C.: Government Printing Office, 1970).

U. S., Congress, House, Committee of the Whole House on the State of the Union. *Report: The Housing and Urban Development Act of 1972,* Report No. 92–1429, 92d Cong., 2d Sess. (Washington, D. C.: Government Printing Office, September 21, 1972).

U. S., Congress, House, Committee on Banking and Currency. *Basic Laws and Authorities on Housing and Urban Developments* (Revised through January 31, 1971), 92d Cong., 1st Sess. (Washington, D. C.: Government Printing Office, 1971).

U. S., Congress, House. *Message From the President of the United States: Community Development,* Document No. 93–57, 93rd Cong., 1st Sess. (Washington, D. C.: Government Printing Office, March 8, 1973).

U. S., Congress, House. *Message From the President of the United States: Fifth Annual Report on Housing Goals,* Document No. 93–141, 93rd Cong., 1st Sess. (Washington, D. C.: Government Printing Office, August 14, 1973).

U. S., Congress, House, Special Subcommittee on Economic Development Programs of the Committee on Public Works. *Hearings: Evaluation of Economic Development Programs, Pt. I,* October 1, 7, 1969, 91st Cong., 1st Sess. (Washington, D. C.: Government Printing Office, 1969).

U. S., Congress, House, Subcommittee on Housing of the Committee on Banking and Currency. *Hearings: Housing and Urban Development Legislation–1970,* 91st Cong., 2d Sess. (Washington, D. C.: Government Printing Office, 1970), Pt. I (June 2, 3, 4, and 5, 1970), Pt. II (June 8, 9, 10, and 11, 1970; and Appendix).

U. S., Congress, House, Subcommittee on Housing of the Committee on Banking and Currency. *Hearings: Housing and Urban Development Legislation–1971,* 92d Cong., 1st Sess. (Washington, D. C.: Government Printing Office, 1971), Pt. I (August 3, 5 and September 8, 1971), Pt. II (September 9, 10, 13, and 14, 1971), Part III (September 15, 16, and 17, 1971; and Appendix).

U. S., Congress, House, Subcommittee on Housing of the Committee on Banking and Currency. *Hearings: Oversight Hearings on HUD New Communities Program,* 93rd Cong., 1st Sess. (Washington, D. C.: Government Printing Office, 1973).

U. S., Congress, House, Subcommittee on HUD–Space–Science–Veterans of the Committee on Appropriations. *Hearings: HUD–Space–Science–Veterans Appropriations for 1973,* 92d Sess. (Washington, D. C.: Government Printing Office, 1973).

U. S., Congress, Senate, Committee on Banking and Currency. *Report: Housing and Urban Development Act of 1970,* Report No. 91–1216, 91st Cong., 2d Sess. (Washington, D. C.: Government Printing Office, 1970).

U. S., Department of Housing and Urban Development. "Surplus Land for Community Development: Action Program Guidelines," Mimeo. (Washington, D. C., December 1968).

U. S., Department of Housing and Urban Development. "Development Standards for Surplus Land for Community Development Program (SLCD)" Mimeo. (Washington D. C., March 1969).

U. S., Department of Housing and Urban Development. "Surplus Land for Community Development Program (SLCD): Summary Program Description" (Washington D. C., March 1969).

U. S., Department of Housing and Urban Development. *New Communities,* Publication No. M/IP 109 (Washington, D. C., June 1969).

U. S., Department of Housing and Urban Development. *Draft Regulations: Urban Growth and New Community Development Act of 1970* (Washington D. C., 1971).

U. S., Department of Housing and Urban Development. *HUD Statistical Yearbook, 1970* (Washington D. C., 1970).

U. S.., Department of Housing and Urban Development. *Urban Renewal Directory* (Washington D. C., December 31, 1971).

U. S., Department of Housing and Urban Development. *Commemorative Parks from Abandoned Public Cemeteries: A Legal Report* (Washington D. C.: Government Printing Office, 1972).

U. S., Department of Housing and Urban Development. *Financing New Communities Government and Private Experience in Europe and the United States*, Office of International Affairs (Washington D. C., 1972).

U. S., Department of Housing and Urban Development, Community Development Corporation. *Regulations for Assistance for New Communities* "HUD Guidelines," 24 CRF Pt. 720 (Washington D. C., 1972).

U. S., Department of Housing and Urban Development. *The Changing Demand for Local Capacity—An Analysis of Functional Programming and Policy Planning,* Community Evaluation Series No. 12 (Washington D. C.: Government Printing Office, 1973).

U. S., Department of Housing and Urban Development. *Local Government Approaches to Capacity Building,* Community Evaluation Series No. 15 (Washington D. C.: Government Printing Office, 1973).

U. S., Domestic and International Business Administration. *Construction Review,* Washington D. C., Vol. 19, No. 7 (July 1973).

U. S., Economic Development Administration. *Jobs for America,* Annual Report (Fiscal 1970).

U. S., Federal Housing Administration. *Regular Limits for Section 235 and 236 Housing* (Based on 135 percent of Public Housing Admission Limits) FHA 4400.30 (Washington D. C., October 1969).

U. S., Federal Housing Administration. *Area Trends—A Supplement to FHA Trends* (Washington D. C., 1968; 1969; 1970; 1971; Second Quarter 1972).

U. S., Federal Housing Administration. *FHA Trends of Home Mortgage Characteristics* (Washington D. C., 1950 to date).

U. S., Federal Reserve System, Board of Governors. "Data for New Conventional First Mortgages" (Washington D. C., December 1972).

U. S., Office of Revenue Sharing, Department of the Treasury. *4th Entitlement Period Allocations, With Adjustments for Entitlement Periods 1, 2, and 3* (Washington D. C.: Government Printing Office, July 1973).

Weiss, Shirley F. *et al.* (eds.). *New Community Development: Planning Process, Implementation, and Emerging Social Concerns* (Chapel Hill: Center for Urban and Regional Studies, University of North Carolina, October 1971).

Welfare Island Planning and Development Committee. *Report of the Welfare Island Planning and Development Committee, Submitted to John V. Lindsay, Mayor, City of New York, February 1970* (New York, February 1969).

Whyte, William H. *The Last Landscape* (New York: Doubleday and Company, 1970).

Wilburn, Michael D., and Robert M. Gladstone. *Optimizing Development Profits in Large Scale Real Estate Projects,* Technical Bulletin No. 67 (Washington D. C.: The Urban Land Institute, 1972).

Part II

Lessons from Urban Renewal and Model Cities

Chapter Four

The Problem of Objectives

Introduction
The new town intown program, included in Title VII of the Housing and Urban Development Act of 1970, was a direct outgrowth of the national experience with two other major federal programs designed to help central cities—the urban renewal program initiated in 1949 and the model cities program started in 1966. The new town intown provisions of the Act do not reveal what was intended to be the exact relationship between the prior developmental programs and the proposed new one, any more than do the congressional hearings. What emerges is that new towns intown could conceivably draw upon the other programs in an unspecified manner. Actually, as we have seen, the early new towns intown have relied on urban renewal provisions and funds, or have proposed such reliance. In addition, some of the proposed service packages in the NTIT projects have characteristics similar to existing model cities programs. However, neither the act itself nor the implementation of the new town intown program has provided guidelines for how the three are to be interrelated in proposed NTIT projects. The phasing out of the federal urban renewal and model cities in their present forms has added uncertainty and ambiguity to an already ambiguous situation.

Aside from the practical features of which legal provisions and funds are or are not available for central city development—something that clearly should be specified if the new town intown program is to evolve strongly—there are important lessons to be learned from the nation's experience with the two prior programs of evident significance to the new town intown program or any future program looking to central city development. The chapters that follow seek to draw these lessons. Because urban renewal has provided a much longer and more substantial experience than have the model cities, major attention is focused on the former. The purpose of the present study is not to provide a full and balanced description of the urban renewal experience, but, rather, to draw out those lessons that seem to be of direct relevance for the new town intown program as we have come to understand it and its future potential. The treatment, thus, is highly selective, looking only to the broader implications for central city development, and is, inevitably, unbalanced.

Because there have been a sizable number of in-depth studies of our urban renewal experience, and also of the model cities experience, we have relied largely on the literature, rather than launch yet another examination of this much studied subject. Below we present our findings based on this review. The specific lessons that can be applied to the administration of the existing new town intown program, or to the evolution of a future program, are attached to some of the sections.

Evaluating Changing Objectives

1. **Urban Renewal.** Urban renewal (born as "urban redevelopment") was the initial national effort to assist the central city and to improve the working and living conditions of central city residents. It evolved an organizational and funding partnership between Washington and the localities. It authorized the public assembly of privately held real estate in the central city if in accordance with a locally devised renewal plan. The program permitted sale of the cleared land (plus site improvements and supporting facilities) at an economically feasible price to private redevelopers, with the federal government meeting two-thirds to three-quarters of the difference between the cost and the market value for reuse. As of March 1973, the federal renewal administration had authorized contracts for 2,118 local renewal projects, with an estimated total gross cost of slightly over $9 billion (HUD, Housing and Urban Development Trends, December, 1973, Table E 16–17, pp. 44–45).

Over the 25 years of its existence, the renewal program evolved through a number of stages, including new legislative and administrative guidelines, with the program both broadening and deepening its scope and activities. By the time the renewal program was being phased out by the Nixon Administration, the emphasis in a number of major cities had changed from a limited redevelopment project-by-project approach to a broad citywide program for neighborhood-by-neighborhood improvement. These changes, which took place in different cities at different times and at different scales, make evaluation unusually complex. (One of these programs, that of Boston, is described in a later chapter.)

In addition, evaluative schema used by analysts of the urban renewal program changed considerably as techniques evolved and as more was learned about the dynamics of the urban system. The following review of these analyses and evaluations aims at providing insights into the "social learning" that took place in the program. Every analyst was faced with the problem of discerning the objectives of the renewal program. These objectives, as well as their interpretation, varied considerably as the program evolved. According to Page (1965), five major objectives could be discerned:

1. Increasing national income: economic efficiency;
2. Improving the competitive position of the central city intraurban redistribution of income (geographical place prosperity);
3. Mitigating poverty: interpersonal redistribution of income (people prosperity);
4. Eliminating blight and slums;
5. Beautifying the nation's cities. (pp. 2–3)

Earlier and later analysts agreed with some or all of the above listing but placed widely varying emphasis on the different objectives.

It is obvious that there are potential conflicts among the objectives listed by Page. For instance, the objective of economic efficiency could, and often did, conflict with both the intraurban and interpersonal redistributions of income objectives. Furthermore, the objective of intraurban redistribution of income (geographical place prosperity) often conflicted with, or at least did not necessarily contribute to, more equitable interpersonal distribution of income (people prosperity). Analysts normally had to assume away or ignore these conflicts to permit evaluation within a cost-benefit framework. Table 4–1 provides a schematic view of how economic analyses of the renewal program evolved.

The liberal use of limiting assumptions made it possible for an economist to use many of his most sophisticated mathematical tools in analyzing and then evaluating public policies and programs. A good example of this limited approach was the "pure theory of urban renewal." Its creator, Otto Davis (1960), proposed that the city's Local Public Agency (LPA) should act as "a rational entrepreneur" in deciding what urban renewal projects to undertake. As a rational entrepreneur, it should undertake only those projects "for which expected revenues exceed the costs of acquisitions, improvements, and interest charges" (p. 223). The LPA would, therefore, act in much the same way as a private entrepreneur by maximizing its "profits" in the form of tax revenues (Schaaf 1969a). As might have been expected, this proposal generated quite a bit of controversy (Shussheim 1960; Lichfield 1963). Bellush and Hauskencht (1966) presented a broader view of the entrepreneurial role of the LPA.

Nonetheless, early renewal efforts often reflected this very narrow conception of the entrepreneurial role of the LPA. Obviously, an unconstrained LPA trying to maximize tax revenues would seek to get rid of the poor and encourage the return of affluent families, and to change land from residential to commercial and industrial uses. James C. Mao (1966) argued that the renewal effort should seek "a superior pattern of resource allocation" as well as to remove blight and improve the fiscal position of the city. But on closer examina-

Table 4–1. Evolution of Evaluative Schema for Renewal

	Davis (1960)	Hartman (1964)	Mao (1965)	Page (1965)	Rothenberg (1967)	Friedly (1968)
Objectives Considered in Schema						
1. Increasing National Income (Economic Efficiency)	XX		XXX	XXX	XXX	XX
2. Intraurban Redistribution of Income (Place Prosperity)	XXX		XXX	XX	XX	XXX
3. Interpersonal Redistribution of Income (People Prosperity)		XXX	XX	XX	XX	XXX
4. Eliminating Blight			X	X	XX	XX
5. Beautifying Cities				X	X	X
Analytical Framework						
1. Market Economics (Maximize Prosperity of Entrepreneur)	XXX					
2. Welfare Economics (Maximize Welfare)			XXX	XXX	XXX	XX
3. Social Indicators (Array Costs and Benefits for Decision Maker)		XXX				XXX

XXX = Primary emphasis
XX = Secondary emphasis
X = Mentioned as important, but not really integrated into schema

tion, it became obvious that for Mao a superior resource allocation and improved fiscal position of the city were almost synonymous:

> If there is to be an improvement in resource allocation . . . it will result from one or more of the three transformations of land use: (1) transformation in income class—land is transferred from low income to high income users, (2) transportation in density—land transferred from low to high density uses . . . (3) transformation in activity—land transferred from residential to industrial or commercial use, or vice versa (p. 96).

Clearly, both Mao and his predecessor Davis ignored equity problems of interpersonal wealth distribution in their analyses. In their concern to increase city revenues, both would advocate displacing the poor who contribute little in terms of tax revenue and require costly services. Forrester's (1968) *Urban Dynamics* model led to essentially the same strategy. (For critical analysis of this work, see Garn and Wilson (1970).) It was hardly a startling conclusion that cities would be richer if they could discourage poor people from in-migrating or could encourage an outward exodus of those already there.

The work of Davis and Mao accordingly reflected the early orientation of the renewal program. During this phase LPAs in general sought to maximize the prosperity of the central city, and a whole literature on cost-revenue studies emerged (Mace 1961, 1964). Soon after the program began, many observers began to argue that by increasing place prosperity the program was decreasing the prosperity of those relocated by renewal projects (for example, Winnick 1966). The simple fact was that the people and businesses who were forced to relocate were also forced to absorb substantial costs.

Besides being uprooted from homes and neighborhoods, with all of the out-of-pocket dollar and psychic costs involved, many of those relocated ended up paying higher rents (Marris 1963; Fried 1963; and Hartman 1964). In addition, their new housing frequently was little better than the housing they were forced to leave. Clearly, the poor were not being helped by tearing down their housing, destroying their neighborhoods, and forcing them to pay higher rents. Since the poor were inadequately compensated for their losses and costs, they were forced to absorb a large part of the cost of renewal. Downs (1970b) provided the most extensive listing and analysis of nonconstruction costs of the renewal program to date.

More recent cost-benefit analyses (Page 1965; Rothenberg 1967; Friedly 1968) at least acknowledged the importance of dealing with both efficiency and equity problems of the urban renewal process. In earlier studies, only efficiency received consideration. The notion of socioeconomic welfare, however, involves considerably more than the amount of monetary value created per unit of expenditure (efficiency). The distribution of the created value and how the desired distribution is implemented must also be considered (equity).

Economists are normally more comfortable with the technical questions of efficiency since questions of income redistribution are not answerable by quantifiable analyses alone. But this does not mean that questions of income distribution are off limits. As Franklin Fisher (1956) put it: "The refusal to make a value judgment . . . is in itself a value judgment, not only in the sense that one is saying that one ought to abstain from making value judgments, but also in the sense that the results obtained are those that would result from glorifying the present distribution" (p. 381).

While cost-benefit analyses of renewal did not ignore redistribution, they did not dwell on it either. For example, Page (1965) argued that renewal should improve the welfare of slum occupants and suggested that "renewal be analyzed in terms of its impact on the rental position of slum occupants" (p. 5). However, in his calculations the increase in rent of slum dwellers was treated as just another cost of renewal: "A survey of eight families showed that without renewal their average monthly rent was $60 a month, whereas with renewal their average monthly rent was $88. Multiplying average change in monthly rent by twelve months and by a present value factor . . . the reallocation of income by the relocatees to rent was $64,000" (p. 9). These were social costs for which they were not compensated.

Page then compared the cost of increased rent for the slum dwellers with the other costs and benefits accruing to the city but without allowing for the marginal utility of dollars for different income groups. Eighteen dollars a month more in rent for a rich family might not mean much, but for a poor family it will normally mean sacrifices in more essential expenditures. These sacrifices could lead to significantly reduced welfare for the family. Since Page admitted the prime beneficiaries of the projects were often middle class families, under his cost-benefit system a project could result in reduced welfare of the poor and still be judged worthwhile. What matters is that the present value of the other benefits generated by the project exceed the present value of the other costs.

There is still another problem common to these cost-benefit analyses. All required discounting the stream of costs and benefits to present value at a *social* rate of discount. Unfortunately, no one has ever developed a generally acceptable way to calculate the social discount rate. As Marglin (1963) has shown, the prevailing interest rate established by atomistic markets is *not* a suitable surrogate measure for the social rate of discount. Needless to say, the discount rate used is often the deciding factor of positive net benefit streams and project "feasibility," especially for projects with long lives. For example, a project judged desirable under one social discount rate might be judged undesirable under another rate. The decision maker is always left with the difficult and ultimately unresolvable question of which of several discount rates is more appropriate for measuring anticipated net benefits-costs of the urban renewal project.

Rothenberg's *Economic Evaluation of Urban Renewal* (1967) was by far the most comprehensive and thoughtful of the cost-benefit analyses. However, even this study rested on welfare economics and was subject to most of the criticisms leveled against this approach (Arrow 1951; Little 1957). Rothenberg's approach to the problem of aggregating individual welfare was to compromise between enumeration of the project impacts on individual persons and/or specific groups on one side and on the city as a whole on the other. But the approach of enumerating project impacts for individual persons or special groups was not operationalized. Hence considerations of citywide "efficiency" still received much more attention than personal equity consideration. Messner (1967) applied Rothenberg's method to the renewal program in Indianapolis.

The cost-benefit work of Friedly *et al.* (1968) marked a significant departure from the utilitarian dream of a "value calculus" by moving instead toward a social indicators approach. The authors suggested a set of indicators: "These indicators, by reflecting changes in community welfare that result from renewal activities, can be used to detect and, in some cases, measure the movement toward the various goals of the renewal program" (p. 2). In this broader indicators approach, cost-benefit analysis becomes a way of arraying relevant information for the decision maker. This indicators approach is more flexible and workable than the cost-benefit framework employed in earlier studies. The analyst need not worry about the often impossible task of translating and quantifying multidimensional outputs of the program into dollar terms.

This step back from the cost-benefit framework stemmed from the author's realization that "the comparability, the trade-offs, the rules of choice between such a variety of effects in the program do not objectively exist. The ability to make choices in these situations depends critically on the set of values, tastes, and priorities of the agent who is to choose, or on whose behalf the choice is to be made" (p. 23).

The renewal program was an excellent example of how innovative programs can evolve over time. The original program was modified by a series of amendments and supplemented by new programs including rent supplements, housing subsidies, tenant and homebuyer counseling, and relocation assistance. These kinds of shifts characterize most innovative legislation.

The main thrust of urban renewal proved to be elimination of blight and slums. Other associated objectives included improving housing, increasing the local tax base, revitalizing the downtown, and strengthening such urban institutions as hospitals and universities. Emphasis was upon developing geographic place rather than people prosperity. While slum and blight removal was consistently the prime objective, emphasis on other objectives varied widely over the years in response to criticism, political pressure, and changes in perceived needs of community groups.

In 1967 HUD Secretary Robert Weaver, responding to mounting criticism, identified three major goals for urban renewal: (a) conservation and expansion of housing for low and moderate income families, (b) development of new job opportunities, and (c) physical renewal of areas with critical and urgent needs. In the years following, there was some movement away from what many regarded as undue emphasis on housing *per se* and toward a more comprehensive approach to urban problems. The Neighborhood Development Program, for example, signaled recognition of a more flexible, programmatic approach to urban renewal. As one evaluator noted, although plagued with funding problems and bureaucratic delays, "NDP afforded a faster and more flexible method of carrying out renewal on a broad front than has been possible under the segmented project approach of the past 20 years" (Bryan 1971).

2. **Model Cities.** From its inception, model cities was intended to overcome some of the shortcomings of urban renewal; notably, the lack of coordination between government agencies and too much central control, insufficient funding and the emphasis on hardware at the expense of needed services and human welfare programs. As spelled out in the original Demonstration Cities legislation, major objectives were as follows:

a) Concentrate available resources—in planning tools, in housing construction, in job training, in health facilities, in recreation, in welfare programs, in education—to improve the conditions of life in urban areas;
b) Join together all available talents and skills in a coordinated effort;
c) Mobilize local leadership and private initiative so that local citizens will determine the shape of their new city—freed from the constraints that have handicapped their past efforts and inflated their costs (United States Congress, House *Message from the President,* 1966).

Model cities called for a two-phase effort, one year for initial planning and program formulation and five years for implementation. Some 80 percent of planning costs were funded by federal grants. The implementation phase was to be funded by existing federal grants-in-aid supplemented by special grants (which could cover up to 80 percent of the nonfederal contributions required for traditional aid programs). As of March 1973, 147 cities had received model cities "supplementary" (nonplanning) grants totaling $2 1/4 billion (HUD, Housing and Urban Development Trends, December, 1973 Table E-10, p. 46).

Several major evaluative studies of model cities have been attempted. The Booz, Allen study for HUD concentrated on the program's influence upon dispersal and concentration of model neighborhood residents. It observed that the program had had relatively little effect on upward mobility—in part because of insufficient funding (annual per capita expenditures averaged less than $83, with over 60 percent of all funds spent to obtain goods and services beyond project boundaries), and in part because dispersion had never been an explicit goal of the program. They concluded that model cities, while somewhat successful in providing certain physical improvements, failed to enhance services, employment opportunities, or incomes sufficiently to facilitate dispersal of residents to more desirable areas of the cities studied (Booz, Allen, 1970; Congressional Research Service, 1973, pp. 68–84).

A report by the General Accounting Office (1972) explored model cities' success in coordinating the activities of federal agencies engaged in central city programs. The GAO concluded: (a) model cities had achieved relatively little in this area; (b) the problems involved in effecting meaningful interagency cooperation were severe; and (c) true coordination may have been impossible without major legislative and administrative changes (GAO 1972).

The role of community participation in model cities has also been studied. A HUD evaluation examined many aspects of the process and concluded that community involvement "had been most evident in the setting of priorities and selection of projects and least evident in the development of project proposals and administration of the program itself" (HUD, *Citizen Participation in the Model Cities Program,* 1972, p. 26). While the role of citizen participants varied from city to city (depending on local political environment, governmental structure, degree of community organization, and so forth) and had been admittedly imperfect, nonetheless many observers felt citizen participation was one of the more successful aspects of the program (Holland 1971, p. 9; James 1971, pp. 843–45; Washnis 1971, pp. 77–80; HUD, *Citizen Participation,* 1972).

One of the most significant outcomes of model cities was its positive impact on local government institutions. Several evaluators noted that the capacity of many central city governments to deal with their urban problems had been enhanced through model cities involvement (Horton 1971, pp. 19–21; James 1971, pp. 845–855; Jordon 1971, pp. 7–8). The program also trained a substantial number of minority persons, who might otherwise not have had the opportunity, in the arts of government and program development.

Model cities attempted to rectify the hardware bias of urban renewal by a more comprehensive approach that allowed for supportive social programs. Although handicapped by restriction to the least viable sectors of the city, insufficient funding, lack of interagency cooperation and coordination, and other handicaps, model cities demonstrated the importance of an effective balance between hardware and software in central city revitalization programs. This is a key lesson for new town intown developers.

On a more negative note, model cities concentrated resources in a single target area, the Model Neighborhood. This represented a step away from a programmatic approach to a city's problems (the direction in which urban renewal had been evolving). In addition, although the Model Cities program was fairly successful in combining substantial urban renewal and social program funds in the Model Neighborhoods, its very success meant both model cities and urban renewal moved toward concentrating resources in the economically least viable parts of a city. Since even these funds were never really sufficient to provide a "critical mass" for inner city development, the impact of these expenditures was limited. This suggests the NTIT program might benefit by combining the best elements of both model cities and urban renewal, utilizing the NDP programmatic approach to attain the broad social objectives stressed by model cities.

Chapter Five

Urban Renewal as a Tool of Overall Central City Development

The lack of clear objectives in a federal program is obviously damaging because it is "impossible to get there if we are not clear as to where we are going." The most important of the central city programs, urban renewal, has particularly suffered in this regard. Its very title—"urban renewal"—suggests the sensed importance of modernizing and reinvigorating the central city. But the initial association of this objective with the physical elimination of slum and blight and the program's later inability to disassociate itself from slum clearance, has strongly tainted it in spite of its evident accomplishments and great importance in reinvigorating a number of central cities (one of which will be described later). The urban renewal program has also suffered from a lack of clarity as to whether (a) it was intended to help poorer and less advantaged groups in the central city or (b) it could safely disregard the impact of its activities on such groups.

Since the purpose of this review is to derive lessons for the new towns intown program, which clearly must make a major contribution to the modernization and revitalization of the central city if it is to have a meaningful impact, the sections that follow examine the urban renewal program from the standpoint of its contribution to the basic socioeconomic development of the central city. To do this, it is necessary first to note the major changes that have been taking place in central city economies and the implications of these for future city development.

Dealing with Changing Central City Economics

Despite many pronouncements about the decline of the central city, relatively little hard research has been done on the subject. One reason is a serious shortage of systematically collected and published data. Most data are presented only for the Standard Metropolitan Statistical Area. A notable excep-

123

tion is some of Ganz' more recent work. He and his associates (1972) "manufactured" from existing sources sufficient data for a hard look at the changing role of the central city. This work provided valuable insights into the role of the central city in the late 1960s and was the best work on the topic since Hoover and Vernon's excellent study, *Anatomy of A Metropolis* (1962).

Essential in Ganz's (1972) analysis is the distinction between two roles of cities: the production role and the residence role. Cities are both (1) "producers of goods and services" and "creators of jobs and generators of income," as well as (2) "places of resident population" (p. 2). While there has always been a good deal of information about the resident population of cities, there is a great information gap about the cities' role as generators of goods, services, jobs, and income. Ganz argued that this information gap has concealed a very important phenomenon: *the role of the central city as a producer of jobs and incomes has been expanding significantly even as the population of cities declined.* Long (1972) and Sternlieb (1972) take the opposite position.

While certain forces have caused wholesaling and manufacturing firms to move toward the suburbs, gains in the service industries have often more than made up for these losses. As in the national economy, employment in the service industries is growing at a much higher rate than in manufacturing industries (Fuchs 1965). Although there are a number of factors which make the suburbs more attractive for certain manufacturing, wholesaling, and retailing operations, agglomeration economies make the central city an increasingly attractive place for some types of service industries.

Four factors are normally cited (Hoover and Vernon 1962; Meyer *et al.* 1965; Kain 1967; Stanback and Knight 1970) to explain the increasing dispersal of some manufacturing, wholesaling, and retailing firms:

a) Recent technological changes have lowered the relative importance of transportation costs in production. Containerization, miniaturization, and transport technology have reduced the relative proportion of transport costs to total production costs. Automation has made it less important to locate plants close to labor markets, and labor has often moved to the suburbs with the industry;

b) Furthermore, technological innovations in communications and information handling have made it possible to separate the various functions of a firm. For example, the management function can be, and often is, separated from a production plant;

c) Modern manufacturing, wholesaling, and retailing plants are generally land intensive which makes the vacant land at the edges of cities more attractive;

d) Billions of dollars in public investment have produced a highway system which has substantially reduced the cost per mile of transporting goods and people and encouraged decentralization.

Opposed to these dispersed forces are agglomeration economies which make central city concentration more attractive for other industries. These include: economies of scale for the individual firm; localization economies for firms wanting to locate near other firms; and general urbanization economies that accrue to all firms located in a city (Lampard 1968, p. 85). Agglomeration economies are particularly important for some service industries. The large, centralized operations of many insurance, financial, and real estate firms indicate economies of scale. (Armstrong and Pushkarev 1972.) In addition, many firms— for example, legal firms—tend to concentrate around banks and other downtown businesses using their services.

Last, but certainly not least, the concentration of activities in the central city leads to an increasing division of labor (Stigler 1951; Artle 1971). This division of labor allows for job specialization and leads to increased productivity and capacity for innovation (Yavitz and Stanback 1967; Friedmann 1969; Artle 1971).

Recent studies give some idea of the "types" of SMSAs that can be expected to grow rapidly. Stanback and Knight (1970) classified metropolitan labor markets (MLMs) according to the distribution of the labor force among industry groups. The six classifications are: nodal, manufacturing, medical/educational, resort, government, and mixed.

One of the most dynamic is the nodal metropolitan labor market. A nodal MLM specializes in exporting services to hinterland, regional, national, and international markets. MLMs ranking in the top quartile in terms of percentage of total labor force employed in the following six service industries were classified as nodal:

Transportation;
Communication;
Finance, insurance, and real estate (FIRE);
Business and repair services;
Retail;
Wholesale.

San Francisco, Boston, New York, New Orleans, Miami, Houston, Denver, Los Angeles, and Seattle are among the more illustrious examples of nodal labor markets.

Metropolitan areas specializing in provision of labor-intensive services have grown more rapidly than those specializing in manufactured goods. Table 5–1 shows that nodal, medical/educational, resort, and government MLMs grew more rapidly in the 1960–70 period than those MLMs specializing in manufacturing. This reflects the very rapid growth of employment in service industries relative to manufacturing industries—what Ganz (1972a, 1972b) called the "services revolution."

Table 5–1. Growth Characteristics of Metropolitan Labor Markets 1950–1960 *(Medians of percentage increases in employment, regional growth indexes, and job decrease/job increase)*

	Net Employment Increase, 1950–1960		Ratio of Job Decreases to Job Increases (Urban-type employment only)[b]
	Percentage Increase	Regional Growth Index[a]	
Nodal	23.5%	1.73	.11
Small	18.2	1.81	.14
Medium	26.1	1.76	.07
Large	12.3	1.02	.24
Manufacturing	13.0	1.36	.20
Small	13.0	1.49	.18
Medium	15.3	1.27	.20
Large	10.6	1.09	.34
Medical/educational	31.8	2.60	.08
Resort	76.6	4.24	.04
Government	41.6	2.14	.04
Small	42.2	2.36	.06
Medium	44.8	1.40	.04
Large	27.1	2.08	.02
Mixed	13.3	.84	.18
Small	11.7	.69	.27
Medium	21.2	1.16	.09
Large	15.8	1.38	.20
368 MLMs	21.3	Not computed	Not computed

a. Regional growth indexes are computed for each city by computing the ratio of the city's percentage net employment increase to that of the region in which it is located

b. Job decreases are total decreases in employment in those nonagricultural industrial classifications which showed declines from 1950 to 1960. Job increases are total increases in employment in nonagricultural industrial classifications which showed increases

Source: Stanback, Thomas M., Jr. and Richard V. Knight, *The Metropolitan Economy*, (New York: Columbia University Press, 1970), p. 151

In this connection, it is interesting to note the regional development strategy of the Hartford Process. It would structurally shift Hartford's economic base from that of a rapidly declining manufacturing center to a nodal center. This strategy would build on Hartford's already strong insurance industry to develop other labor intensive service industries which export to markets near and far.

The "services revolution" has important implications for the central city. As Stanback and Knight (1970, p. 232) pointed out,

> The importance of services should provide a good indication of the CBD. In a Nodal city the CBD may be expected to dominate; in a manufacturing city it will be of much less importance.

It is likely that these relationships hold important implications for growth. The city with a large, well-developed CBD is more likely to be amenity-rich as well as rich in business services. Theaters, museums, good restaurants, night clubs, and public libraries tend to be found where the business and professional services flourish. Thus the larger and better developed is the CBD, the more services and amenities are found there and the more attractive the city becomes to the relatively fast-growing footloose manufacturing and service industries.

Ganz (1972a) showed the tremendous increase in the importance of office based, high level services in some SMSAs. This increase was reflected in building booms in several CBDs during the last decade. With the exception of Washington, D. C. (obviously a government MLM), 9 (of the 21) SMSAs listed on Table 5–2 showing the greatest increases in square feet of private and public office space in their downtown areas during the 1960–70 period were classified as nodal in 1960. Detroit and Pittsburgh, both of which were classified as manufacturing MLMs in 1970, also showed a good bit of office construction. This reflected the shift in these MLMs toward the service sector.

Note that the growth of office space was rapid in both SMSAs with (a) relatively high concentrations of office employment in the downtown such as Houston (68 percent downtown) and (b) in SMSAs with more dispersed office employment such as Los Angeles (14 percent downtown). Clearly not all service firms find it to their advantage to locate in a CBD. Clustering of service firms to take advantage of agglomeration economies can also be found in suburban areas. Such clusters may be in regional shopping centers, around airports such as O'Hare or Los Angeles International Airport, in outlying office parks (Knight and Ito, 1972) or along corridors such as Wilshire Boulevard in Los Angeles.

However, certain types of labor-intensive industries, especially finance, insurance, and real estate firms, seem to find the CBD particularly attractive. Those professional and business services of the FIRE group tend to locate close to the firms they serve. Corporate headquarters also have a tendency to cluster in the CBD. This is true even in Los Angeles which has experienced a downtown building boom in recent years.

Impact of Urban Renewal on Central City Development

A development program could conceivably stimulate a central city to generate jobs, income, and services by

a) Eliminating or compensating for "neighborhood effects:"
b) Assisting in land assembly;
c) Preserving and enhancing major urban institutions;
d) Investing in public facilities which complement the central city's expanding role for producing goods, services, jobs, and income.

Table 5–2.   Total Office Employment in Selected SMSAs and Estimated Intraregional Distribution

Office employment, 1960* (In thousands)

	SMSA	Central City	Suburban Ring	Down-town	% Office Employment in Downtown	Estimated Gross Private and Public Office Space in Downtown (millions of sq. ft.)		Increase 1960–70
						1960	1970	
*New York SMSA	1,334	1,113	221	840	63%	179	247	68
*Los Angeles SMSA	703	376	327	100	14	16	33	17
*Chicago SMSA	688	488	200	275	40	47	63	16
*Philadelphia SMSA	397	240	157	120	30	26	34	8
Detroit SMSA	316	183	133	80	25	16	23	7
*San Francisco SMSA	306	175	131	100	33	16	26	10
*Boston SMSA	297	142	155	120	40	24	34	10
Pittsburgh SMSA	188	79	108	70	37	15	22	7
St. Louis SMSA	188	110	78	35	19	4	8	4
Washington SMSA	288	199	89	180	63	36	54	18
Cleveland SMSA	183	126	57	50	27	8	11	3
*Newark SMSA	178	85	93	50	28	12	14	2
*Minn.-St. Paul SMSA	168	124	44	65	39	10	12	2
*Houston SMSA	118	100	18	80	68	13	22	9
Milwaukee SMSA	120	90	30	60	50	12	14	2
*Paterson SMSA	97	24	72	5	5	1	1	0
*Dallas SMSA	124	93	31	80	65	16	22	6
Cincinnati-SMSA	106	71	35	45	42	10	12	2
*Kansas City SMSA	113	76	37	30	27	6	9	3
*Atlanta SMSA	111	77	34	45	41	8	17	9
Wilmington SMSA	34	17	17	10	29	2	3	1
Total SMSAs	6,055	3,990	2,065	2,440	40%	477	631	

Table 5-2 (cont.) Notes and Sources

*Office employment located at office, factory, store, institution, and other sites. Does not include sales workers in offices except for downtown estimates

Notes: Detailed figures may not add to totals because of rounding. The data on downtown office employment are estimates rounded to the nearest five thousand and apply to major central business districts only

Sources: Employment estimates constructed by Regional Plan Association from data in U.S. Census, *Census of Population: 1960 Detailed Characteristics*, and *Journey to Work*. Floor space estimates from a survey of respective city planning agencies and, when not locally available, constructed by Regional Plan Association. Armstrong & Pushkarev, 1972, p. 49

The urban renewal program has assisted central cities to adapt to their changing roles by making at least some contribution to each of these developmental aspects.

1. Eliminating or Compensating for "Neighborhood Effects." Davis and Whinston (1961) argued that neighborhood effects and other market imperfections cause private property owners and investors to make suboptimal investment decisions in urban land markets. The return on urban real estate investment depends largely on the neighborhood in which the investment is made.

For example, if an investor in a declining neighborhood decides to renovate his building and add off-street parking, other property owners would benefit from his improvements and reduced street congestion. The benefits would spill over to all in the neighborhood. However, the neighborhood could also detract from the value of the rehabilitated building, reducing the impact of his investment. One way to eliminate such a problem would be by encouraging all property owners in the neighborhood to invest simultaneously. This could produce a higher return than otherwise had each property owner acted separately.

Just how important external diseconomies are in causing decay has been much debated. Unfortunately, there has been little hard research to establish even rough estimates of the magnitude of negative externalities (Mills 1972). Because of so little information, arguments have tended to be based on ideological grounds. Those who support urban renewal have stressed the importance of positive externalities and of government intervention to produce an efficient allocation of resources. Those against government intervention have argued that externalities are not all that important—that free markets can be relied upon for an efficient allocation of resources.

Local public agencies (LPAs) frequently acted as a kind of public entrepreneur to coordinate individualistic investment decisions, and, by so doing, tended to internalize externalities (Davis and Whinston 1961). They accomplished this by bargaining, by inducing property owners to make joint development investments, and by using powers of eminent domain to assemble large tracts of land for urban renewal. In this role of public entrepreneur, they marshalled economic and political resources to attain *what they believed* was in the best interests of the community.

Sometimes local public agencies were instrumental in setting up development corporations able to pool resources and assure that sufficient financial resources were available at attractive rates. Lowe (1967) provided a detailed description of such a development corporation in Philadelphia.

2. Assisting in Land Assembly. Redevelopment normally requires that large tracts be assembled. One problem is that "The supply curve for . . . land . . . is quite discontinuous" (Winnick 1961, p. 294). As each land parcel in a project area is essential, any one property owner can hold out for a monopoly price. The large number of small parcels in most central cities increases the probability of holdouts. Thus, firms that would like to either expand or locate in the central city can be thwarted by the high costs and risks of land assembly. The renewal program allowed land to be assembled at its "fair market value" via the power of eminent domain. Properties could, therefore, be acquired at prices comparable to the rest of the city. Exercise of eminent domain could break the monopoly power of the individual landholders, and lead to a more efficient allocation of resources. (Schaaf 1960, 1964).

Surveys in Boston and New York have shown that lack of space for expansion is a major factor in inducing firms to leave the central city. A study by the Boston Economic Development and Industrial Commission found that "two-fifths of the manufacturing firms were considering moving from Boston due to lack of space for expansion" (Ganz 1972, p. IV-19). Schulz *et al.* (1972) found that lack of space was also a major factor in the flight of manufacturing firms from New York.

Land assembly problems can also inhibit development of new office complexes and commercial facilities in the central city. Studies have shown (Foley 1959; Knight and Ito 1972) that difficulties in land assembly and lack of certain amenities in the central cities are primary factors causing service firms to relocate. Typically, relocation in the suburbs has caused problems in obtaining adequate secretarial, manual, and janitorial staffs. Further, some firms could no longer enjoy easy access to specialized services and activities of the central city. In other words, they could no longer take advantage of central city agglomeration economies. A public development program to facilitate land assembly might have enabled these firms to locate on more efficient sites in the central city. An added attraction would have been maintenance or improvement of job accessibility for disadvantaged populations.

3. Preserving and Enhancing Major Urban Institutions. The renewal program often assisted the expansion of universities, hospitals, and other major institutions. Rothenberg (1967) argued that "if there are substantial economies of scale—as indeed there are—in university and hospital operation, adjacent expansion can save a great deal over nonadjacent expansion by making it unnecessary to duplicate overhead facilities like libraries and laboratories." (pp. 73-77)

These institutions are vital to growth and development of an urban economy because they usually represent the institutionalization of the entrepreneurial functions of invention and innovation. As Thompson (1968) observed, the real economic base of the larger metropolitan region is "the creativity of its universities and research parks, the sophistication of its engineering firms . . . the flexibility of its transportation system . . . and all other dimensions of infrastructure that facilitate the quick and orderly transfer from old dying bases to new growing ones" (p. 52).

In many cases, cultural, aesthetic, recreational, social, and institutional development was aided by urban renewal. Subsidies encouraged better design and inclusion of parks, playgrounds, stadia, museums, concert halls, promenades, and other neighborhood facilities in project areas. Strengthening of services and facilities has been cited by renewal supporters as one of the most significant end products of the renewal programs.

4. Investing in Public Facilities which Complement the Central City's Expanding Role in Producing Goods, Services, Jobs, and Income. Ganz (1972) has pointed to a very interesting paradox: as the productivity of the central cities' economies has grown, their fiscal resources have declined. Thus, rows of shiny new office buildings have sprouted up in an environment of decaying public services.

One reason for Ganz's paradox is that cities do not generally tax the expanding income that they have been generating. "The revenue base, attuned mainly to the declining population role and the tax on property value (principally residential), has not grown commensurately with the cities' economic base" (Ganz, pp. I–8 to I–9). Furthermore, increases in the economic base have occurred primarily in the labor intensive service sector. "Office building based service activity has a high ratio of value, which, in addition, frequently benefits from tax abatements in large cities" (Ganz, p. I–9).

Due to this revenue gap, some cities have cut back public services and reduced capital expenditures so as to overcome budget deficits (National League of Cities 1971). This trend is clearly counterproductive and underscores the need for additional revenues to cope with intown problems.

In a sense, the renewal program redressed some inequities of the property tax system. It provided cities with capital funds to meet the demands of the "services revolution." It allowed cities to modernize obsolete infrastructure. There is, however, a question as to how much economic growth was induced by tax abatements. In most cases, abatements were probably aimed at reducing tax rates to levels similar to suburban areas which also often offered tax abatements to attract economic development.

Ghetto Development Versus Ghetto Dispersal (and a Side Glance at Model Cities)

Several authors have argued that low income, unemployment, and slum living problems cannot be solved within the bounds of the ghetto (Kain 1967, 1968, 1969; Vietorisz and Harrison 1970; Downs 1970). Kain (1967) argued that job opportunities are increasingly concentrated in the outlying parts of a metropolitan area not accessible to ghetto workers. The argument was that racial segregation in housing makes jobs inaccessible to minority groups (Kain 1969; Pascal 1967; Meyer *et al.* 1965). Lack of adequate public transportation or access to a car aggravates the problem.

However, firms in suburban areas may not hire minority workers even if they could get to the jobs. One finding of a demonstration project in Watts was that merely providing transportation for the jobless did not, in itself, cure unemployment. This project underlined something at times forgotten—"that adequate transportation is a necessary but not sufficient condition for people to have access to job opportunities. If jobs are not available, for whatever reason, no amount of transportation will create them" (H. Davis 1970, p. 20). A similar demonstration project in Boston drew essentially the same conclusion (Greenwald and Syron 1969).

In the same vein, it is not sufficient merely to develop job opportunities close to the jobless. Pressman and Wildavsky (1972) have shown that capital subsidy programs often led firms to substitute capital for labor and did not lead to new jobs. Pressman and Wildavsky, along with Kain (1968) and Perloff (1971), argued for a labor subsidy for employers hiring and training those certified as hardcore unemployed. A note of caution must be issued here. If there is not full employment, a labor subsidy can result in shifting unemployment from one group to another. Employers would lay off unsubsidized workers to hire subsidized ones.

All of the strategies above differ sharply from ghetto development schemes, such as model cities, in which public funds were invested in the least viable part of the urban economy. Such efforts have not been very successful (Olken 1971).

Some have argued that strategies of ghetto dispersal and ghetto development are not contradictory. The Twentieth Century Fund's report on community development corporations (1972) argued that ghetto "development and dispersal are . . . complementary. Development assures that as barriers fall, those in the inner city will be able to respond to the pull of outside society, with its greater opportunities and, for most, more attractive living conditions" (p. 9). Job opportunities should be developed in industries outside of the ghetto, but at the same time public investment in human and physical capital should also assure that ghetto residents can take advantage of outside opportunities as they become available (Perloff 1969, p. 67).

Poverty Groups and Poverty Neighborhoods

The urban renewal program started as an effort to clear the slums. Somehow such clearance was to be helpful to the poor living there, although the manner in which this was to happen was never specified. Actually because of the economics of renewal, the pressure was to turn the former slum areas to economically more "productive" uses and to let the former residents fend for themselves or, later in the life of the program move to relocation housing.

Neighborhoods inhabited by low income transient groups or experiencing high turnover of low income residents were often prime targets for renewal. Their welfare was considered secondary to physical renewal. What was ignored was that these areas often served as ports of entry for recent immigrants and provided opportunities for assimilation into urban society (Seeley 1959; Frieden 1964; Shannon and Shannon 1964).

Oftentimes the older, less attractive neighborhoods of America's central cities have served the vital function of springboard for upwardly mobile migrants. Newcomers having gained their first foothold in such neighborhoods, could begin to climb "upward and outward." Unfortunately, renewal projects tended to eliminate these points of entry in the misguided attempt to create stable neighborhoods (Frieden 1964). In effect, these projects tried to create islands of stability in a dynamic field. Frieden suggests that this may have seriously damaged the capacity of cities to assimilate newcomers.

> The assimilation of newcomers is still an urgent problem of the city, and decent low cost housing is a key requirement. . . . In time, urban minority groups . . . will surely vacate the old neighborhoods in their search for better housing. But the present level of migration to cities, the slow pace of minority movement from central cities to suburbs, and the high birth rates of incoming groups suggest that few cities will be ready for wholesale clearance within the next decade or two (pp. 4–5).

In more recent years, because of the increasing resistance to slum clearance and relocation of poor families, urban renewal in several cities sought out underutilized land for projects and provided low and moderate income housing on project sites. The history of urban renewal since the inauguration of the Neighborhood Development Program (in 1968), a new approach for financing project activities on an annual basis, suggests that had the renewal program continued, it would have evolved in the direction suggested by the underlying principles associated with the new town intown program. A case in point is the Hunters Point Redevelopment Project in San Francisco.

> The Hunters Point area will contain 1,902 new housing units, park and recreational facilities, elementary schools, churches, and neighborhood shops. By constructing new housing on presently vacant land, the project will be phased so that residents can relocate in new housing before the old temporary housing (wartime housing built by the federal government during the early years of World War II) is removed . . . the emphasis of the Hunters Point housing program is for families of low to moderate income (San Francisco Redevelopment Agency, 1972, p. 39).

Renewal projects of this type were beginning to look directly to the welfare of the poorer residents of the city, even if on a very limited scale.

The model cities program, which was started two years before the Neighborhood Development Program of urban renewal, was, of course, aimed

directly at helping residents in poverty neighborhoods. Here, as already suggested, the limited "target area" approach, by restricting development efforts to the
least economically viable areas of the city, had built-in disadvantages.

This does not necessarily mean that it was not successful in combat-
ing poverty. There may have been a kind of "Catch 22" built into the program.
For if the program was the least bit successful in increasing personal income in a
target area, the residents would have been able to demand better services, housing, and neighborhood environment. In time-honored American fashion, they
could have chosen to move to better neighborhoods. Thus, the paradoxical
situation could be produced where the more successful a program is in actually
reducing poverty, the faster the target area would decline as those left behind
tended to be the "ne'er-do-well," unemployed, elderly poor, social misfits and
the like. In short, the target area could become a "behavioral sink," like certain
public housing projects, simply because the more successful residents became
upwardly and outwardly mobile.

All this suggests that, to ensure a positive impact, a central city
development program must encompass a substantial portion of the central city
rather than a highly limited "target area," and must move parallel to strong
people oriented programs that seek to cope with the problems of the most
disadvantaged residents.

Racial Mix

There was always a good bit of rhetoric about achieving racial integration in renewal areas, but nobody yet knows how to foster such integration.
Generally, all a developer in a renewal area had to do was to guarantee that he
would not discriminate in renting or selling. Even this came as a relatively recent
advance in HUD requirements.

There have been some attempts to analyze (a) the methods and
motivations in racial discrimination (Becker 1957; McEntire 1960), (b) the
impact of changes in racial composition on property values (Laurenti 1960;
Downs 1960), and (c) the growth of ghettos (Duncan and Duncan 1957;
Taeuber and Taeuber 1956; Morrill 1965; Meer and Freedman 1966; Rose 1970;
and D. Meyer 1972). Boyce and Turoff (1972) assembled a complete bibliography of research on minority groups and housing. One of the most insightful
treatments was the Anthony Downs's (1970a) "Alternative Futures for the
Ghetto." He began by dividing the future into three kinds of alternatives:

1. Degree-of-Concentration Alternatives. (Will the nonwhite population become
   more concentrated in the central cities?)
2. Degree-of-Segregation Alternatives. (Will the neighborhoods within the Standard Metropolitan Statistical Area be integrated?)
3. Degree-of-Enrichment Alternatives. (How much will be invested in upgrading
   the human resources in the area?) (p. 40).

In its early days, the renewal program in many areas tried to bring the white middle class back into the central city. Having had little success while generating a storm of criticism, this goal was dropped. With several notable exceptions, the program in its later form probably did little to change the major trend toward increased concentration of nonwhite populations in central cities (Congressional Research Service 1973, pp. 11–13, 92–102). The forces influencing racial composition and integration of neighborhoods are normally beyond the control of the neighborhoods themselves. The white population seeks to dominate the environment (Downs 1972). When they feel their dominance threatened by increased nonwhite or other minority population, normally they will leave. Increasing minority populations in the central cities guaranteed that many neighborhoods would eventually reach the tipping point and go all minority. The renewal program had little to do with upgrading human resources; hence it did not cause minority incomes to rise. Without higher incomes, it is impossible for minorities to demand housing in better neighborhoods. Without higher incomes, their city governments have a difficult time responding to their needs, much less in so improving services so that they could attract whites back to the central city.

On the other hand, a number of authors have recently begun to challenge the whole concept of racial balance. Gans (1972) challenged the idea that creating a community in which the racial mix "duplicates the prevailing demographic mix in the metropolitan area, the region or even the nation" (p. 21) is a viable goal for planning. Different communities serve different functions. One argument frequently advanced in behalf of balanced communities is that persons of lower status will somehow benefit by living closer to those of higher status. Gans (1972) pointed out that "there is no reliable evidence that poor people are actually benefitted by contact with their so-called betters" (p. 22).

Gans' distinction between microintegration (neighborhood integration) and macrointegration (community integration) helped in clarifying the notion of "balance." Macrointegration is more feasible at the current time, he argued, and it has the advantage of still allowing minority groups access to better jobs and services. Both Gans (1972) and Downs (1972) would agree that macrointegration might be the best interim strategy for development.

Friedmann (1972) argued that the best strategy would be to encourage formation of "affinity environments." The word "ghetto" implies a residential choice forced by racial, ethnic, or class prejudice. But it is often the case that many groups freely decide to live in the same neighborhoods. As Friedmann (1972) observed, "There are areas for swingers and areas for families with school-age children; there are Bohemian sections. . . . There are districts studded with Catholic churches and others where gospel churches and synagogues predominate" (p. 8). These areas where groups sharing different life styles, occupations, age, ethnic culture, family status, religion, or income levels voluntarily choose to live are not ghettos, but affinity environments. Although these affinity environments might be quite diverse on many levels, they can be demo-graphically homogeneous—they can be comprised primarily of one ethnic, racial, or income group.

The problem is to insure freedom of residential choice so that neighborhoods are actually affinity environments rather than ghettos—which is, of course, no easy task.

In fact, we still know little about how to attain the objective of increasing residential choice of all groups. A report to HUD by the National Academy of Sciences and National Academy of Engineering suggests that we face up to this situation and consciously attempt to learn more (1972, pp. 56–57):

> Carefully planned experiments on a number of different scales and patterns from neighborhood to new town should be undertaken to determine the conditions under which residential mixing of families or individuals of different racial and economic categories may be most feasible.

Such experimentation is definitely needed to enable better planning of NTITs over time.

Housing Development

One reason why so much low cost housing was destroyed through the urban renewal program was the initial view of slums as social and physical pathologies—cancers calling for drastic surgery (Shorr 1963). In the zeal to eradicate these "cancerous growths," a rather obvious fact was forgotten that many of the areas called slums served as low cost housing for families who could scarcely afford to spend more of their meager incomes on housing. Neighborhoods can decline because a large number of poor families demand low cost housing.

Emphasis on slum demolition in the early program's stages led to the oft-repeated charge that the renewal program materially reduced the supply of low cost housing at the cost of billions of federal dollars. Grigsby (1965) argued that "Housing conditions are not improved by demolishing *occupied* substandard housing, if, in the process, the total supply of accommodations which the displaced families can afford is reduced. To as great an extent as possible, demolition should be the consequence of abandonment, not the cause of it" (p. 285).

More rehabilitation in residential areas was long touted as a way of renewing neighborhoods without reducing the supply of low cost housing (Nash 1959); McFarland and Vivrett 1966; Keyes 1969; Schaaf 1969b). The problem was that rehabilitation costs large sums of money. Also, rehabilitated housing rents for more than unrehabilitated housing. Hence, poor people could not afford to live in rehabilitated units without subsidies. Large numbers of low income families in fact were displaced from renewal projects stressing rehabilitation (National Commission on Urban Problems 1968). The Federally Assisted Code Enforcement program (FACE) was established to provide for rehabilitation on a neighborhood basis.

Gradually it began to dawn on the Congress that the crux of the housing problem is that poor people could not afford decent housing. Therefore, either the incomes of the poor must be raised or rent supplements provided if the poor are to be decently housed. This led to a wide range of subsidy programs beginning with the below market interest rate programs (Section 221−d [3]), then subsidies for home ownership (Section 235), for rental housing (Section 236), and for rehabilitation (Sections 312 and 115). The 235 program became increasingly controversial with a series of damaging administrative scandals. (U. S. Commission on Civil Rights 1971, U. S. Committee on Banking and Currency 1970). The need for more tenant and homebuyer counseling also became increasingly apparent (Eudey 1970, Marcuse 1971).

Every aspect of experience with central city development—urban renewal, model cities, and the various housing efforts, as well as the limited experience with new towns intown—point to the conclusion that little can be done to improve the housing of low income groups without substantial federal housing subsidies.

Services Development

The importance of linkages between job and service development cannot be overemphasized. More and better jobs increase effective demand for both public and private services. Better personal services render a workforce more productive, as do manpower and educational programs. Better services can increase the comparative economic advantage of a central city. The provision of these services creates jobs, many of which can be filled by disadvantaged workers. Provision of better services is a means not only of improving the quality of urban life but also of providing jobs. As mentioned previously, employment in central city service industries is growing more rapidly than in other sectors (Fuchs 1965). Harrison (1969, 1971, 1972) and Sheppard (1969) have presented a strong case that public service employment will provide an important source of jobs for the disadvantaged worker. Harrison's argument (1969, p. 1) "is based not only on income requirements of the poor themselves, but also and more fundamentally on the growing needs of *all* residents of urban areas for expanded public services." Others have stressed the importance of the service sector in economic growth and development (Greenfield 1966, Artle 1971, Ganz 1972).

The renewal program emphasized investment in public facilities and other physical capital rather than human capital. There is increasing evidence that investment in human capital can often bring higher returns than equivalent investments in plant and equipment (Schultz 1961, Becker 1962, Mincer 1962).

This seems particularly true of investment in training for public service jobs. For example, Harrison (1969) estimated

> the present value of the *direct* social benefits from a public service job development program to be between $29,600 and $36,300 per worker employed, and the costs of training him to be $3,000–$7,000. . . . Considering only the direct impact of a public jobs program on GNP over the next five years, a dollar invested now in a new worker . . . may return anywhere from $.23 to as much as $12.10 in extra GNP (p. 18).

Model cities programs concentrated on a multitude of services for the disadvantaged, but lack of resources and knowledge, together with poor administration, greatly hampered the program in most cities. For example, evaluation of the New Careers Program revealed many such weaknesses (AVCO 1968, Harrison 1969). Model Cities' success with employment development was also limited (HUD 1972, p. 23; Congressional Research Service 1973, p. 29).

All of this emphasizes the strong linkage between economic development and development of public and private services. None of the central city development programs to date have been in a position to stimulate a mutually beneficial relationship between jobs and services. The inherent difficulties and complexities are such that it would take a sustained program, one that could plan for years in advance, and with authority and resources to relate service needs to jobs with adequate refinement. Clearly, a let's-improve-everything-at-once approach, which characterized Model Cities in most communities, could not hope to exploit the potentialities of the jobs-service relationship.

INSTITUTIONAL AND POLITICAL COMPONENTS OF INTOWN DEVELOPMENT

The renewal and model cities programs were a testing ground for theories of planning and social change. New institutions, legal precedents and administrative techniques evolved over time in this testing process.

Urban Development as a "Political Game"

Some writers have suggested that a fruitful way to look at the renewal process was as a "game" (Long 1958; Keyes 1969). The renewal game was normally played by four principal players: the local public agency, local government, community organizations, and HUD, but there were always local variations. Sometimes different groups entered the game. At other times the main participants sat out the game on the sidelines or sent in substitute players. As in any game, the output depended on the skill of the players, the amount of control they could exert, and luck. Information played an important part. Some players had much more information than others and used it to dominate their opponents. Collaboration among players was of the essence. Players able to form the strongest coalition usually won. It was nearly impossible to predict the outcome of such games—as difficult as a game of chess. But there was a vast source of information on past games from which one could derive clues. There were also rules written into the laws and bureaucratic regulations.

1. **The Local Public Agency.** The LPA normally was one of the more powerful players of the urban renewal game. Its role could be that of public entrepreneur, carefully marshalling political and economic resources to attain its objectives (David 1960; Bellush and Hauskneckt 1966; Kovaks 1972). Generally, the LPA had a great deal of latitude in defining its objectives, but more recently these powers were curbed somewhat by HUD.

In some cases, the LPA dominated the renewal game. Some powerful LPAs had been associated with the names of certain individuals: Moses of New York (Jacobs 1968), Danzig of Newark (Kaplan 1963), and Logue of New Haven (Dahl 1961) and Boston (McQuade 1966). However, in most cases, the LPA had to rely heavily upon other participants in the game. The typical ally was the mayor or other powerful local officials.

The power of the LPA stemmed largely from its access to funds from the federal government and its control over information. Only the LPA knew where the next project would be or the real plans for an area. Large staffs of highly trained professionals gave the LPA a sizable capacity to generate and analyze information. Often others in the game had to accept the LPA's information simply because they lacked the resources to get their own data base. Public hearings could be carefully staged to make it difficult for others to argue against the LPA's proposals (Lowe 1967). This is not to say that the LPA could not be beaten. Some community groups have humbled a LPA. Normally, the middle and upper middle classes were heavily represented in these successful community groups (Kovaks 1972). This was no accident, for these groups not only had more political power but were also more proficient in getting and using information.

2. **The City Government.** The city government was generally represented in the renewal game by the mayor although this depended largely on the structure of the local government. This structure determined who had power and who would benefit from renewal. A strong mayor such as Mayor Lee of New Haven (Dahl 1961) could use renewal as a tool for gaining political support. Other mayors let the LPA play for them and provided support from the sidelines.

The city council (or legislative body) normally could veto a renewal project and would do so if sufficient political pressure were exerted. Nonetheless, there were strong incentives for the city government to work with the LPA. One such incentive was the LPA's access to federal funds. The LPA could pursue a policy of maximizing the prosperity of the city—a strategy with certain appeal to many councilmen.

The city government could play an important role in mobilizing political support for a project. Some city agencies also supported the LPA when it was beneficial for them to do so. Planning departments frequently played a peripheral role in renewal because they had little expertise in the kind of action oriented planning done by the LPA and often saw their role strictly in terms of long-range planning.

The city government, in addition, had access to a good deal of important information and the staff for handling this information. Also, since the key people in city government were always either elected or appointed by elected officials, it was generally more responsive to community pressures than the LPA (Kovak 1972).

3. Community Groups. Although community participation was required by HUD, the role of community groups varied enormously from project to project. In early projects, these groups were often used as sounding boards for the LPA and as a tool for informing the community about the LPA's decisions (Dahl 1961; Kaplan 1963; and Wilson 1966). But as the nature of the renewal program became more evident, the position of residents and groups in renewal areas began to grow. After all, it was often these people who involuntarily bore a major part of the program's cost.

The power of community groups to stop or even alter the plans of the LPA varied greatly. In general, the poorer and less educated the population, the less likely it would be able to influence the LPA. As Kovak observed, "If the protest or dissent over a renewal project can be rooted in certain social classes (middle, upper middle), then a greater change for organization will tend to occur, and a different renewal outcome (project defeat) will result" (p. 359). The poor and powerless generally were no match for the LPA. There were many reasons for this. Banfield and Wilson (1964) argued that higher income groups were more likely to participate in the renewal process because they shared a "community-regarding" or "public-regarding ethos." These higher income people supposedly attached "a high value to communitywide and neighborhood-wide goals, even in some cases when these goals . . . entail sacrifice in personal, material satisfactions" (Wilson 1965, p. 412). Gans (1972) took a similar position. Keyes (1969), however, found no evidence of a strong linkage between class and community participation in the South End of Boston.

Even if there was no relationship between class and community participation potential, there certainly was a strong link between class and effectiveness in blocking projects. For instance, the Hyde Park–Kenwood community was heavily populated by professionals from the University of Chicago (Rossi and Dentler 1961; Perloff 1965). This gave them considerably more potential for struggling with the renewal agency since this group had an unusual capacity for organizing and utilizing information. Community leadership was also important. None other than Jane Jacobs became the nemesis of Robert Moses in New York.

Institutions sometimes provided the basis for renewal planning. The University of Chicago exercised an important role in renewal of the surrounding Hyde Park-Kenwood area. And other universities also participated in the renewal process (Kovak 1972).

4. The Federal Government. In the first years of the renewal program, the Urban Renewal Administration allocated funds on a first-come first-served basis. As Rothenberg (1968) put it, "they acted as though resources were not scarce. Eventually, it became clear that some planning would have to be done to insure that resources were allocated efficiently."

Thus, it was written into the Housing Act of 1954 that every community had to have a workable program in order to qualify for federal assistance. Although this led to a surge in plan production, it was doubtful that these master plans had any real impact on the way local resources were allocated (Altchuler 1965). The federal agency did not enter into the renewal game by requiring these plans. Once the plan was done, the community was normally free to do what it wanted, and the plans could always be changed.

The Community Renewal Plans (CRPs) were another step in the direction of comprehensive planning but in a different way. Each community was supposed to develop a comprehensive plan for dealing with problems of urban blight. Unfortunately, there was often no provision for incorporating the CRP into the political process which actually made the decisions.

For example, in San Francisco the Planning Department paid Arthur D. Little (1966) $1 million to do the CRP. Despite its technical sophistication and academic acclaim, it was never used in the decision making process (SPUR,[a] 1972). Whether this has been the case in other cities is not clear. What is clear is that the CRP represented another prerequisite for funding but did not really give the federal government any direct influence over how the city spends its funds.

In response to the wave of criticism in the middle 1960s, HUD finally began to allocate renewal funds on the basis of three criteria: (1) creation of jobs, (2) increase in the supply of low and moderate income housing, and (3) help in the case of disasters. Just how much this influenced resource allocation in subsequent years is uncertain, but regional offices did go through a complex evaluation procedure in allocating funds. Projects with the highest scores were funded first. It is difficult at present to determine how effective this evaluation was in selecting projects meeting the above criteria. In the early 1970s, a new tack in selection criteria appeared. While not adopted in their entirety, the objectives spelled out by the President's Task Force on Urban Renewal were suggestive of the perspective of the current administration. The

a. San Francisco Planning and Urban Renewal Association

Task Force recommended the following as the primary objectives of the urban renewal program:

a) To enhance the efficiency of land use;
b) To improve the fiscal and economic condition of the community by increasing the tax base or through savings in municipal services, or a net increase in personal or business income;
c) To decrease the threat of Balkanization and polarization of American society . . . and to help in exorcising the spectre of economic and ethnic apartheid (President's Task Force on Urban Renewal, 1970, p. 4).

In terms of project selection, the Task Force agreed with the administration's emphasis on greater local decision making and local determination of priorities. They, and the administration, downplayed the importance of low and moderate income housing that had characterized the selection criteria of the mid−1960s.

Role of Community Participation
Community participation in the urban renewal program was, as Kaplan put it in 1963, "more honored in the breach than in the actual performance" (p. 24). As with other aspects of urban renewal, however, the role of community participation evolved over the life of the program and appeared to be developing into a more significant force.

Community participation in urban renewal was approached in two general ways in the literature, either through theoretical discussions or empirical studies.

James Q. Wilson's article for the *Journal of the American Institute of Planners* (1963) was one of the better known theoretical pieces. He argued that the level of community participation in renewal decision making was directly related to the extent to which the local residents possessed an "enlarged view of the community and a sense of obligation towards it." Such high "community-regarding" or "public-regarding" persons generally possessed

> high income, high education, high sense of personal efficacy, a long time perspective, a general familiarity with and confidence in city-wide institutions, and a cosmopolitan orientation toward life (pp. 412−413).

Unfortunately, since most urban renewal areas were not populated by such "public-regarding" individuals, Wilson felt prospects for meaningful community participation were poor. Given the typical renewal area residents "low sense of personal efficacy," "limited time perspective," "difficulty in abstracting from concrete experience," Wilson believed the most that could be expected from the community was acquiescence. When there was community participation, its role would most likely be negative—acting in response to "threats rather than acting to create opportunity."

Other authors shared Wilson's low estimation of most urban renewal communities to participate meaningfully in the renewal process. Kornhauser (1959) warned that "unorganized mass participation can lead to extremism" since low income people have fewer attachments to their community and hence less incentive "to support the rules by which community affairs are generally governed" (pp. 50–51).

Sigel (1968) supported Kornhauser's negative position, suggesting "that it is naïve and even cruel to expect the inarticulate masses to devise urban renewal schemes" (p. 51). Sigel generally felt only persons with "discernable skills" should serve on citizen planning committees. While low income folk might have some role for implementation of renewal plans, it was "least appropriate" that they be involved in translating general goals "into technical and detailed blueprints" (p. 52).

Other authors shared this general approach to participation of low income citizens in the urban renewal process. Crain and Rosenthal (1967) undertook an empirical study which appeared to support the hypothesis that

> the greater the socioeconomic status of the population of a community, the greater the level of community participation in day-to-day community decision making (p. 970).

They felt "community participation in the planning process means more opposition, more issues to be negotiated with more people, and more chance of failure," implying that

> if public officials are going to do the right thing, the people should leave them alone while they do [it] (p. 984).

Opposed to this school of thought, with its pessimism about citizen participation, were those authors taking an advocate position and supporting participation in the urban renewal process even if it involved major changes in the present political/economic structure.

Jean and Edgar Cahn (1968) attacked the validity of Wilson's appraisal of low income people's ability to participate. They attributed the poor's "low sense of personal efficacy" not to basic individual psychological shortcomings but to their "manipulation" by the system. Their apparent passivity was due to the society that stereotyped and dealt with them as such. Given greater recognition and opportunity to participate, the poor were quite capable of involving themselves in the decision making process.

Marris and Rein (1967) shared this view, arguing that urban renewal could not take the poor's desires into account unless they were involved in the decision making process. They saw community participation in urban renewal serving the dual purpose of

> involving and accommodating target area residents to the demands of urban society, while at the same time holding out the possibility of pressuring institutions to better adapt to the needs of their constituencies (quoted in Spiegel, 1968, p. 6).

Milton Kotler (1967) took the most extreme view of the advocate authors. Arguing that effective community participation could not occur under present institutional arrangements, he advocated major changes involving the return of authority and decision making to the poor. He pictured urban renewal and development in the inner city as being carried out by the community itself.

The empirical evidence was mixed, but it appears citizen participation became more important as the renewal program evolved and matured. The earliest studies were generally the most negative.

One of the most comprehensive studies was prepared in 1959 by Gerda Lewis, who reviewed progress in every city (91 in all) that had approved workable programs as of July 31, 1956. She concluded that

> the findings . . . indicate that citizen participation in urban renewal . . . [has] not yet developed to a stage where by any stretch of the imagination could it be said to represent a revitalization of the democratic process (p. 83).

Specific studies of selected cities produced similar findings. Floyd Hunter (Atlanta, 1953), Martin Meyerson (Chicago, 1955), Peter Rossi (Chicago, 1961), Herbert Gans (Boston's West End, 1962), and Harold Kaplan (Newark's North Ward, 1962) all generally agreed with Kaplan's findings in Newark that citizen participation had been relatively "insignificant."

In each of these studies, citizen participation was found to take a negative role, aiming at delaying or preventing urban renewal plans prepared without their consultation. In some cases where communities were involved in the urban renewal process, their record was little better. Dahl (1964) found that community participation in New Haven functioned largely as a rubber stamp. Not one of the local renewal authority proposals was ever modified by the Citizen Advisory Board. Goldblatt (1966) found a similar apathy among low income people in Washington, D. C.'s urban renewal areas.

Opposed to these studies were a set of empirical findings indicating the poor could effectively participate given the proper conditions. Loring (Washington Park, 1957), Edmund Burke (Kansas City, 1966), and the Columbia Law Review (Philadelphia, 1966) all described cases where the poor were able to become involved and contribute to the renewal process in their communities.

The more recent Hunters Point urban renewal project (which is also a model cities neighborhood) in San Francisco demonstrated how community participants effectively involved themselves in urban renewal. A private renewal coalition study described it as a "remarkable resident-Agency cooperative effort." (SPUR Report, 1972, Appendix 6). Working closely with several "advocacy planning" groups, the community at Hunters Point successfully shaped its own future (SPUR 1972; Marshall Kaplan 1969).

Certain factors appear to have been related to successful community participation by the poor in the urban renewal process. It seems certain that areas with stable populations were likely to be the most effective. As Kaplan (1969) noted in Newark, even though all efforts ultimately failed to prevent implementation of Newark's plan, it was the communities with "stable populations and many single family homes" which mounted the most effective opposition. Territories with transient populations witnessed little or no community attempts to impact the urban renewal plan.

The level of local community organization was also key to meaningful community participation. Based on their experience with the Hyde Park–Kenwood section of Chicago, Rossi and Dentler (1961) concluded that

> it seems likely that successful urban renewal in large cities—successful in the sense of being widely accepted both within and without the neighborhoods under urban renewal—will come primarily either in neighborhoods that have an indigenous successful organization or in neighborhoods in which some outside agency manages to create one (p. 292).

Social learning was also involved in the rise in importance of community participation in urban renewal. Rossi and Dentler (1961) found that community organizations in Chicago learned from earlier failures and thus were able to function more effectively. Experience in San Francisco supported this conclusion, because there was a clear rise in the importance of community participation from its almost complete absence in Western Addition I to its vital role in Hunters Point (SPUR Report 1972).

The nature of the urban renewal project being undertaken also affected the level of community participation likely to occur. As Hyman (1967) noted in a recent dissertation:

> there appears to be an inverse relationship between the degree of citizen participation and the degree of LPA's control over the planning process in relation to the treatment method used in a project area. Land clearance appears related to minimal citizen participation and maximum LPA control. Conservation, at the other extreme, involves maximum citizen participation and minimal LPA control. Rehabilitation appears to be the middle case in which there is a more

or less equal but insecure partnership between the citizen organizations and the LPA (pp. 18–19).

With conservation and rehabilitation, community participation was not only desirable, it was a necessary prerequisite. Hyman (1967) further noted:

> a strong working relationship with citizens is required in order to successfully persuade the local home owners to spend their own money to upgrade their homes, while at the same time prevent the neighborhood influences from coalescing into a unified vocal opposition (p. 13).

The increasing importance of community participation in urban renewal also may have been attributable to changes in the traditional viewpoints of many urban renewal planners and decision makers. Urban renewal planners tended to engage in what Hyman called design planning:

> In this model of planning, plans were imposed on citizens who had little or no part in their creation. They were shown the plans mainly for their endorsement and education (pp. 19–20).

In recent years, though, there was a movement away from "pure" design planning as more planners became concerned with the impacts of their plans on the lives of those directly affected by the renewal process. Realizing the need to involve those who would feel the consequences of the planning effort, the urban renewal planning process, at least in some areas, began to incorporate elements of what Hyman (1967) called "consensus planning," Friedmann (1971) "transactive planning," and Marshall Kaplan (1969) "advocacy planning." In essence, rather than handing down completed plans to an expectant community, the planner would attempt to work with and through the community in shaping the plan. This, of course, presupposed substantial community involvement.

Increased citizen participation of model neighborhood residents was one of the central aims of the model cities program. Yet, despite the rhetoric, there were many difficulties in bringing these residents into the development process. A report by the Congressional Research Service (U. S. Subcommittee on Housing and Urban Affairs 1973, p. 79) summed up a HUD evaluation of citizen participation in model cities (1972) as follows:

> If the fifteen cities study of citizen participation can conclude, as it does, that "citizen participation in the Model Cities Program has generally achieved results that are consistent with its goals," this conclusion is diluted to some extent with respect to some of the important ancillary findings also part of the study. Among these are the fact that only about one percent of MNA residents have ever

directly contributed to the program, that citizen groups have often been given the main task of agreeing to or disagreeing with plans drawn up by nonresidents, and that concrete resident benefits (jobs) from the program have been limited.

The lesson for the NTIT program is fairly clear. Over the years, the federal government has become more aware of the need for meaningful participation for reasons of pragmatism as well as basic equity considerations. The *Columbia Law Review's* conclusion (1966, p. 603) regarding community participation appears equally valid for the NTIT program:

> The success of the program will be determined by the degree of local activity, responsibility, and cooperation which it generates.

The problem is how to develop institutions which can translate the objective of true community participation into reality. This tough problem calls for innovative experimentation as well as further study.

Chapter Six

Renewal in Boston: Approaching an Urban Development Program

Introduction

Boston has one of the largest and most diverse renewal programs in the country. Twenty projects cover 3,000 acres of the city; about $1.2 billion in private and $278 million in public funds have been invested in project areas. (See Tables 6–1 and 6–2 and Figure 6–1). Of the 116,000 people in these project areas before renewal, 36,000 (31 percent) were relocated. The projects range from the first, brutal clearance operations such as the infamous West End project to large scale, residential rehabilitation projects. The Boston Redevelopment Authority (BRA) points with justifiable pride at the architectural excellence of such projects as Government Center and restoration of the waterfront area.

The Boston experience with urban renewal is a valuable source of information, not only because of its size and programmatic emphasis, but also because so much has been written about the program and its impacts. In addition to a high concentration of 'urbane intellectuals' (and dissertation-hungry Ph.D. candidates) in Boston and Cambridge who have extensively reviewed the program, BRA's own staff has produced some of the best internal evaluation reports in the country.[a]

Renewal in Boston, as in most of the country, got off to a slow start. As Charles Abrams (1965) pointed out:

> Up to 1954, urban renewal lay in the dumps. Some 211 localities were interested, but only 50 had reached the land acquisition stage. . . . The passage of five years with almost nothing to show for all the fanfare was hardly progress (P. 86, quoted from Keyes 1969, p. 3).

a. We would like to thank Alexander Ganz, Director of Research for the Boston Redevelopment Authority, for his very generous help with this section. Many of the insights presented here are from the excellent reports prepared by him, Thomas O'Brien, and the research staff. We are, of course, solely responsible for what appears here.

149

Table 6-1.   Summary of BRA Activities*

Total Acres in Renewal Areas: 3070

Public Cost	
Total federal capital grants	$180,000,000
Total local contributions	98,000,000
Total Public Cost	$278,000,000
Total Public and Private Investment	
Total residential	$361,000,000
Total commercial	421,000,000
Total rehabilitation	59,000,000
Total institutional	333,000,000
Total Investment	$1,174,000,000
Tax Revenue Increment in Renewal Areas	
Total annual municipal revenue after renewal	$18,000,000
Total annual municipal revenue before renewal	8,000,000
Increase in Total Annual Revenue	$10,000,000**
Total Population in Project Areas	
Before renewal	116,000
After renewal	116,000
Change	00
Total Population Relocated	
Population relocated	36,000
Percent of total population relocated	31%
Impact on Housing Stock in Renewal Areas	
Total residential units after renewal	58,000
Total residential units before renewal	54,300
Net Gain in Stock	3,700

*This summary was done in 1969 and, therefore, does not include the following projects approved after this date: Campus High School, Boylston–Essex, or Brunswick–King. It also does not include Prudential Center which was not financed with federal renewal grants

**Figure does not take into account interim period between clearance and purchase and construction when little or no tax revenues were generated

Source: Boston Redevelopment Authority, "BRA Approved, City Council Approved, and URA Approved/Pending Urban Renewal Projects," (mimeo) Boston, 1969, p. 1

The first two projects were examples of the complete clearance "bulldozer" approach. The New York Streets project received final federal approval to clear 22 acres of land for industrial and commercial uses. This project involved demolition of 947 housing units with *no* new residential construction (See Table 6–2 for more details).

Figure 6-1. Urban Renewal Projects, Boston, Massachusetts

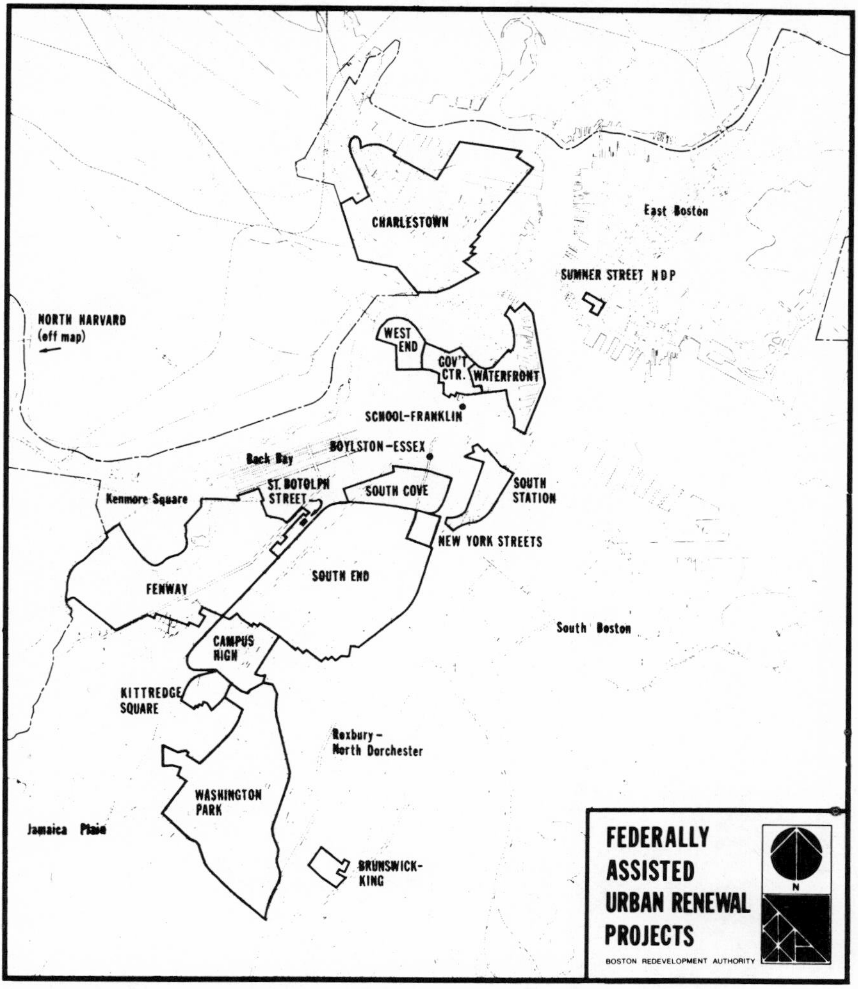

Source: Boston Redevelopment Authority

The controversial West End project was not approved until 1958. This project demolished 3,671 housing units in a closely knit, Italian–American community. Gans (1962) and Fried (1963) described the high social costs imposed on those forced to relocate from the project area. Later events highlighted the injustice. BRA sold the land for construction of 2,286 high rise luxury housing units. As Keyes (1969, p. 27) put it, the West End became a "classic symbol of the way urban renewal should not be handled."

The political furor raised by West End along with legislative changes

Table 6–2.   Statistics for BRA Projects With Over 20 Acres

Project	New York Streets	West End	Washington Park	Water-front	Govern-ment Center	Charles-town	South End	South Cove	Fenway	South Station	Campus High
Date of Federal Approval	1955	1958	1963	1964	1965	1965	1965	1966	1967	1971	1972
Acreage	22	47	502	104	61	520	606	97	507	82	130
Population before Project	2,000	11,000	26,300	217	1,711	20,638	33,735	4,140	15,501	**	**
Population in 1970	0	2,058	20,081	4,967	0	15,353	22,680	2,389	17,691	0	1,749
Housing											
Units Demolished***	947	3,671	2,518	0	584	675	2,496	676	810	**	483
Units Constructed***	0	2,286	1,922	1,948	0	823	3,769	1,113	2,475	0	542
Units Rehabilitated***	0	0	4,562	0	0	1,662	2,611	205	1,250	0	197
Relocation											
No. of Families	**	3,076	1,669	0	264	286	1,730	133	460	**	**
No. of Individuals		900	662	0	170	179	1,820	402	357	**	**
Total Persons Relocated	2,000	11,000	7,304	–	1,711	1,863	7,520	987	1,967	**	**
% of Project Area Pop.	100%	100%	27.9%	0%	100%	9.0%	22.3%	23.8%	12.7%	**	**
Uses after Renewal											
Residential		X	X	X		X	X	X	X	X	X
Commercial	X	X		X	X			X	X		X
Recreational				X				X	X		X
Institutional		X			X	X	X	X	X		X
Industrial										X	
Public Cost (millions)											
Federal											
Capital Grant	$3.2	$11.7	$29.0	$29.9	$35.2	$25.9	$32.8	$19.2	$8.6	$9.0	$18.6
Relocation	0	.3	2.4	2.5	3.1	2.8	4.3	3.7	5.7	1.5	3.5
Local Share	1.6	5.9	37.7	14.0	19.7	11.4	16.4	12.7	14.7*	4.5	6.7
Total	$4.8	$17.9	$69.1	$46.4	$58.0	$40.1	$53.5	$35.6	$29.0	$15.0	$28.8

Table 6–2. (cont.)

Project	New York Streets	West End	Washington Park	Water-front	Govern-ment Center	Charles-town	South End	South Cove	Fenway	South Station	Campus High
Private Investment	$17.0	$75.0	$25.0	$126.3	$100.0	$12.2	$141.0	$100.0	$400.0	**	**
Tax Increment (millions)											
Municipal Tax Before	.2	.6	.7	1.0	1.7	.9	2.4	1.6	.7	**	**
Municipal Tax After	.3	1.3	.4	2.7	2.5	.8	3.3	1.9	2.3	**	**
Total Tax Increment	.1	.7	-.3	1.7	.8	-.1	.9	.3	1.6	**	**

*Includes $12.7 million in Section 112 institutional credits. This section of the National Housing Act allowed a LPA to count institutional investment as part of the local share

**Not available

***Includes both actual and scheduled

Source: Boston Redevelopment Authority, 1973

in the Federal Housing Act of 1954 transformed the program "from one aimed at bulldozing residential slums to one concerned with conserving and rehabilitating the existing stock of housing within the broad framework of the Workable Program" (Keyes 1969, p. 3).

The Logue–Collins Era. John Collins won the mayoral race in an upset victory in 1959. After taking office, he hired Edward Logue, then head of New Haven's aggressive renewal program, as a consultant to develop a renewal plan for Boston. Logue came up with "The 90 Million Dollar Development Program for Boston." Collins subsequently hired Logue and gave him sweeping powers to implement the plan.

Logue's plan had two main thrusts: residential renewal and downtown revitalization. Both thrusts involved large areas of the city. Residential rehabilitation projects begun during Logue's reign covered over 1,700 acres. The Government Center, Waterfront, and Prudential Center projects cover almost 200 acres in the downtown area.

The White–Kinney Era. Logue ran for mayor in 1966 but was defeated by Kevin White. White seemed to be stressing a much broader approach to development. Rather than concentrating investments in project areas, he sought to stimulate public and private capital investment in the city. The current director, Robert T. Kinney, stresses working with the inhabitants of each community. Part of this is based on political philosophy, but part is undoubtedly political pragmatism. After Logue, communities were not about to put up with "top-down" planning.

Program Components

1. Economic Development.

> Production of goods and services in the City of Boston measured in real terms, in dollars of constant value at 1970 prices, rose by $4 billion from 1947 to 1970—a growth of 72 percent. More than two-thirds of this growth, some $2.8 billion, occurred in the decade of the 1960s. As of mid-year 1970, the City of Boston was an economy with a $9.6 billion annual level of production of goods and services, by 516,000 workers. Boston's output per worker (productivity) is higher than in the metropolitan area, and in the United States economy as a whole. (Ganz 1972, p. III–3)

During this 1947–70 period, Boston changed from a declining port and manufacturing area to a booming service center for international, national, regional, and hinterland markets. It, therefore, conforms quite closely to what Stanback and Knight (1970) call a nodal region and displays many of the dynamic characteristics displayed by other nodal regions in the country. This structural shift is reflected in the composition of employment (see bottom of Figure 6–2). In 1947, the top four employers were manufacturing (21.7 percent of the workforce), retail trade (17.9 percent), transportation (14.1 percent), and services (13.8 percent). By 1970, employment in government (15.3 percent) and

Figure 6–2. Structural Transformation of the City of Boston Economy

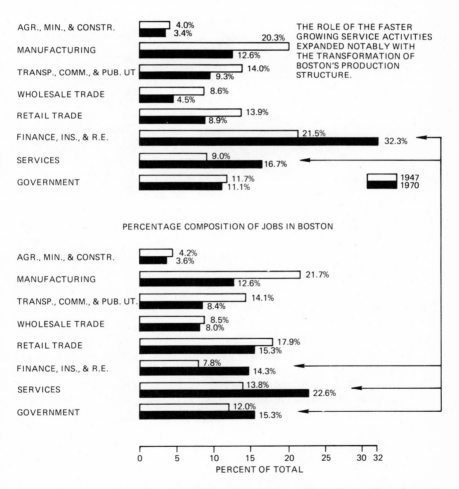

PERCENTAGE COMPOSITION OF THE PRODUCTION OF GOODS & SERVICES IN BOSTON

AGR., MIN., & CONSTR. — 4.0% / 3.4%
MANUFACTURING — 20.3% / 12.6%
TRANSP., COMM., & PUB. UT — 14.0% / 9.3%
WHOLESALE TRADE — 8.6% / 4.5%
RETAIL TRADE — 13.9% / 8.9%
FINANCE, INS., & R.E. — 21.5% / 32.3%
SERVICES — 9.0% / 16.7%
GOVERNMENT — 11.7% / 11.1%

THE ROLE OF THE FASTER GROWING SERVICE ACTIVITIES EXPANDED NOTABLY WITH THE TRANSFORMATION OF BOSTON'S PRODUCTION STRUCTURE.

1947
1970

PERCENTAGE COMPOSITION OF JOBS IN BOSTON

AGR., MIN., & CONSTR. — 4.2% / 3.6%
MANUFACTURING — 21.7% / 12.6%
TRANSP., COMM., & PUB. UT. — 14.1% / 8.4%
WHOLESALE TRADE — 8.5% / 8.0%
RETAIL TRADE — 17.9% / 15.3%
FINANCE, INS., & R.E. — 7.8% / 14.3%
SERVICES — 13.8% / 22.6%
GOVERNMENT — 12.0% / 15.3%

0   5   10   15   20   25   30 32
PERCENT OF TOTAL

Source: Alexander Ganz, *Our Large Cities: New Light on Their Recent Transformation: Elements of a Development Strategy, A Prototype Program for Boston,* M. I. T. Laboratory for Environmental Studies, Supported by Office of Economic Development, Department of Commerce, February 1972

finance, insurance, and real estate (14.3 percent) had displaced manufacturing and transportation from the top four (Ganz 1972).

The top part of Figure 6–2 shows how finance and service activities produce an increasing portion of Boston's total output of goods and services. In 1970, finance, insurance, and real estate industries accounted for 32.3 percent and services for 16.7 percent of total production. Together FIRE and service industries account for nearly half of Boston's total production in 1970; in 1947, they accounted for less than a third of total production. The fact that FIRE industries produce 32.3 percent of total production with only 14.3 percent of the total work force attests to their high productivity per worker.

Figure 6–3 presents a clear view of just how important finance has become in terms of Boston's export role and the rest of the metropolitan area. In dollar terms, finance and services (public, personal, and business) are the primary export industries of Boston. All other industry groups show net exports, but not nearly so high.

BRA assisted these structural changes by coordinating public and private investment decisions, assisting in land assembly, providing public facilities and infrastructure, and enhancing amenities of the downtown. Land write-downs provided a considerable incentive for development investments. Other factors such as improved amenities and economies of agglomeration in the office based service sector also served to attract firms to the area.

To a certain extent, federal funds for land write-down and public facilities redressed inequities of the existing property tax system. For although the economy of Boston is booming, most activity is in the labor intensive service sector. Since the only tax the city can levy is on land (and improvements), Boston must rely upon property taxes in order to provide for the needs of its growing service sector, of disadvantaged residents, and related needs. In addition, property tax abatements for businesses have caused residential taxes to rise, thereby discouraging construction and rehabilitation while encouraging out-migration. These abatements are geared to suburban tax levels in order to encourage relocation or retention of major businesses within the city.

The regional economy of Boston is increasingly concentrating manufacturing employment in suburban areas, and service and financial employment in the central city. This leads to an increase in total commuting as less skilled workers living in Boston often commute out to manufacturing jobs, and more skilled managers and professionals commute from the suburbs to central city offices.

Urban renewal funds in Boston have been invested almost exclusively in physical capital (hardware). Concomitant investment in human beings is necessary to assure that less skilled, as well as the more skilled, workers participate in jobs being created. A community development approach combining investments in both human and physical capital would assure a more equitable distribution of program benefits.

Figure 6–3. Export Role of the City of Boston Economy and that of the Metropolitan Area Suburban Ring

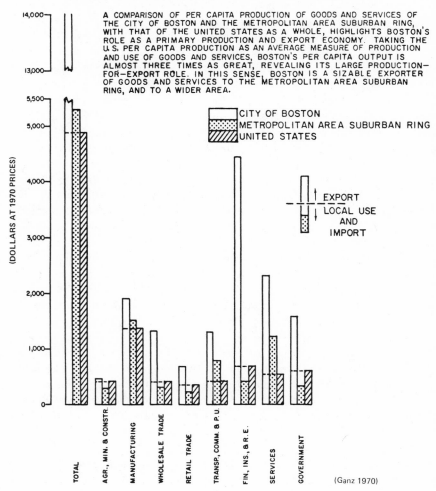

PER CAPITA PRODUCTION OF GOODS AND SERVICES, 1969

A COMPARISON OF PER CAPITA PRODUCTION OF GOODS AND SERVICES OF THE CITY OF BOSTON AND THE METROPOLITAN AREA SUBURBAN RING, WITH THAT OF THE UNITED STATES AS A WHOLE, HIGHLIGHTS BOSTON'S ROLE AS A PRIMARY PRODUCTION AND EXPORT ECONOMY. TAKING THE U.S. PER CAPITA PRODUCTION AS AN AVERAGE MEASURE OF PRODUCTION AND USE OF GOODS AND SERVICES, BOSTON'S PER CAPITA OUTPUT IS ALMOST THREE TIMES AS GREAT, REVEALING ITS LARGE PRODUCTION–FOR–EXPORT ROLE. IN THIS SENSE, BOSTON IS A SIZABLE EXPORTER OF GOODS AND SERVICES TO THE METROPOLITAN AREA SUBURBAN RING, AND TO A WIDER AREA.

(Ganz 1970)

Source: Boston Redevelopment Authority, Research Dept.

2. Development of Services, Housing, and Neighborhoods. In a recent study for the Brookings Institute, Aaron (1972) argued that housing programs in the inner city which aim only at providing housing and housing related amenities are doomed to failure. His argument was that the whole package of residential services such as schools, parks, commercial facilities, transportation, and security, should be emphasized. These services are what make for decent and attractive living environments. Without these services, housing units in the central city tend to become uninhabitable and abandoned.

BRA long recognized the importance of improving residential services for large areas of the city. In rehabilitation projects such as Washington Park, Charlestown, South End, and Fenway (see Table 6–3), extensive investments in physical infrastructure were made in each. Because the city could apply many of these investments as noncash contributions toward the local share of net project cost, there was a strong incentive to locate public facilities within renewal areas.

Undoubtedly investment in housing related physical improvements can be helpful. However, these investments often should be supplemented with investments in the people who provide and use the services. Building new police stations or equipping existing stations with expensive information systems ultimately may be less effective in reducing crime than more effective police training and community programs. Provision of residential services requires investment in both hardware and software. As the local renewal agency, BRA did not have jurisdiction over software programs, but through its community planning efforts, the agencies with such control were often induced to improve their services.

Another question is: services for whom? Those forced out of a project area by the higher rents of new or rehabilitated housing probably did not benefit. In fact, those relocated often bore a disporportionate share of the cost. The West End is probably the most unfortunate example of transfer of costs to the poor for construction of luxury housing (See Table 6–3).

Scale

It is important to distinguish between the size of a project and the area of actual impact. For example, each project in downtown Boston was relatively small individually, but together they covered most of the CBD and impacted the entire region. Creation of job opportunities downtown undoubtedly influenced housing markets in the Back Bay and other parts of the city.

Looking at individual projects as part of a general renewal program gives quite a different picture than looking at each separately. In all but the early clearance projects, BRA has tended to look at each project within at least a city-wide context. This development strategy has allowed BRA to build up the city resources. Examples include:

The clustering of projects in the central city allows office based service firms to take advantage of agglomeration economies;

Rehabilitation projects aim at upgrading areas with strong image and organization;

Table 6–3. Housing Units Completed, Under Way, and Proposed in Planning Districts With Renewal Projects: 1960–1972

Planning District	Conventionally Financed	Regular FHA	Low Income**	Moderate Income***	Total
1. East Boston (Summer Street NDP)*	76	0	359	1,400	1,835
2. Charlestown (Charlestown)*	8	0	96	599	703
3. Central (Waterfront, Government Center, West End)*	2,348	3,582	150	1,358	7,438
4. Back Bay (St. Botolph St)*	1,452	0	0	0	1,452
5. South End (South End)*	222	0	102	2,146	2,470
6. Fenway–Kenmore (Fenway)*	252	268	134	655	1,309
7. Washington Park (Model Cities, Campus High, Washington Park, Kittredge Squire)*	32	38	454	2,218	2,742
Total	4,390	3,888	1,295	8,376	17,949

*Renewal projects in the planning district in parenthesis
**Only developments directly administered by the Boston Housing Authority and Turnkey housing
***Units subsidized under state or Federal programs including Sections 221 (d) 3, 236, and 235

Source: Boston Redevelopment Authority, Research Department, *New Housing in Boston: 1960–1972.* Unpublished working paper, Boston, August 1972

The waterfront project opened up abandoned port facilities for commercial, recreational, and residential uses.

Programmatic Approach: An Example

Boston's urban renewal projects are suggestive of the possibilities inherent in a programmatic approach to central city development. For purposes of discussion, we will focus on the Fenway project and review it from a new town intown programmatic perspective.

The Fenway project, taken in conjunction with the nearby privately developed Prudential Center, demonstrates how a town scale effort (538 acres, population around 20,000) can create a viable, income and racially integrated community. It is also of interest financially, since property tax increments resulting from development could have financed the total public cost.

Prudential Center was developed on the site of an underutilized railroad yard and an antiquated civic auditorium (see Figure 6—4 and Table 6—4). The 31-acre area now houses a 52-story office tower, a 5,800-seat auditorium, a large department store, and three high rise, luxury apartment buildings. Approximately 7,500 people are currently employed in the center. No federal renewal funds were involved, but the developer will receive a tax abatement for 40 years.

Table 6—4. Prudential Center

Size: 31 acres	
Location: In Back Bay area adjacent to the Fenway renewal project	
Use before development: Underutilized railway yard and antiquated convention hall	
Construction: 52-story office tower	
5,800-seat auditorium	
29-story hotel	
Large department store	
Three 26-story, luxury apartment buildings	
Total Employment: 7,500	
Percent of employees living outside of Boston: 62%	
Population relocated: None	
Net impact on housing stock:	
781 luxury housing units	
No housing cleared	
Public Cost:	
Approximate total tax without abatement	$4 million
Approximate total tax with abatement	3 million
Total tax reduction per year	$1 million
Private Investment (estimate)	$150 million
Tax Increment:	
Estimated municipal tax before renewal	$ 721,000
Estimated municipal tax after renewal	3,000,000
Total tax increment per year	$2,279,000

Source: Boston Redevelopment Authority, Research Staff, "The Prudential Center, Part One: Its Direct Impact on Boston," BRA Research Report, Boston, September 1969

Figure 6–4.   Urban Renewal Projects in Boston and the Fenway–Kenmore Planning District

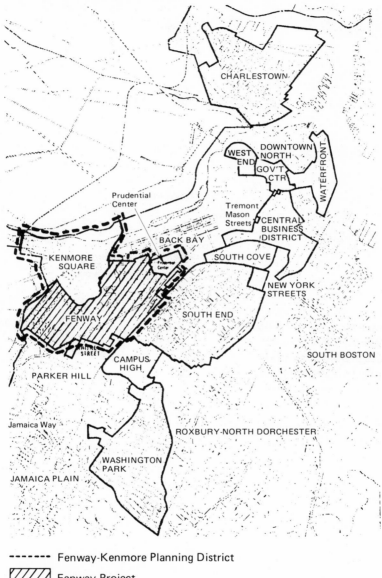

- - - - - - -   Fenway-Kenmore Planning District

/////   Fenway Project

Source: Boston Redevelopment Authority

Even with this abatement, the estimated annual tax increment is about $2.3 million.

Immediately adjacent to the center lies the 507-acre Fenway project (see Table 6–5). The primary aims of this project have been:

Table 6–5.   Fenway Urban Renewal Project

Size: 507 acres
Population in the renewal area (1970): 17,691

Population in the Fenway–Kenmore Planning District:

1950	1960	% Change 1950–60	1970	% Change 1960–70
36,649	32,963	−10.1	32,965	0.0

Income mix in the Fenway–Kenmore Planning District compared with that of the City of Boston, 1960 and 1970: (Dollars of constant value at 1970 prices)

	(Residents) *Boston*		*(Residents)* *Fenway–Kenmore*		*(Employees)* *Prudential Center*
	1960	*1970*	*1960*	*1970*	*1970*
$ 0–6,999	47.8%	34.5%	59.9%	48.0%	54.0%
$ 7,000–14,999	42.7	47.7	33.6	40.6	35.0
$15,000–24,999	7.5	14.8	4.6	8.5	11.0
$25,000+	2.0	3.3	2.1	2.9	
	100.0	100.3	100.0	100.0	100.0

Racial Mix in the Fenway–Kenmore Planning District and Boston

	Boston		*Fenway–Kenmore*		*Fenway Project*
	1960	*1970*	*1960*	*1970*	
Percent nonwhite	9.8	18.1	9.1	9.1	(not available)

Population relocated from renewal area:
Families	460	(Total population 1,967)
Individuals	357	

Net impact on housing stock:
Units cleared	810	
Units constructed	2,475	(all low and moderate income units)
Net gain	1,665	
Units rehabilitated:	1,250	

Public Cost: *(millions)*
Federal capital grant	$ 8.6	
Relocation and rehabilitation grants	5.7	
Local share	2.0	(Also $12.7 million in Section 112
	$16.3	noncash institutional credits)

Tax Increment for Development Parcels:
Estimated municipal tax before renewal	$ 661,000
Estimated municipal tax after renewal	2,300,000
Total increment per year	$1,639,000

Source: Boston Redevelopment Authority

Construction of low and moderate income housing;
Rehabilitation of deteriorated units;
Provision of land for institutional uses;
Improvement of commercial and recreational facilities.

In 1970, 17,691 people lived in the project area. Total public outlay from federal and local sources will be about $16.3 million; an additional $12.7 million will be spent by public and private educational and medical institutions in the area. The tax increment on development parcels is about $1.7 million per year.

The Fenway project and Prudential Center provide one example of how development of underutilized land can be linked to rehabilitating surrounding neighborhoods to bring about town scale modernization of the central city. Judging by the Fenway/Prudential Center experience, the cycle of decline in central city neighborhoods can be reversed by public investment and intervention to stimulate confidence by private investors. Public investment (in this instance emphasizing health and educational institutions) can also serve to strengthen the employment base of an area.

The Fenway experience likewise indicates that income and racial integration may be more feasible in rehabilitated rather than rebuilt, residential areas. Low interest loans, assurance that property taxes would not be increased, and the threat of condemnation were the key incentives for rehabilitation.

There are financial lessons to be learned as well. The total public cost of Fenway was $16.3 million. Municipal investment amounted to $2 million supplemented by $12.7 million in institutional funds which are counted toward the local share (under Section 112). Significantly, these investments generated approximately $400 million in private investment. There are several reasons for this sizable return on public investment:

> The area had not declined very far when public action was initiated;
> Investor confidence was high because of construction of Prudential Center and expansion of other institutions in the area;
> Because the area was declared a renewal area, all homeowners were constrained to upgrade their property. Neighborhood quality would rise, thus adequate returns on rehabilitation investment.

The high levels of public investment result in a tax increment of $1.7 million per year, an amount sufficient to pay back the public cost in a few years.

In terms of employment, Prudential Center is an excellent example of the benefits and difficulties of employment development. One clear intown development lesson is that it may be very difficult to create employment which neatly matches the needs of city residents. It may be more efficient to enhance accessibility to jobs at other locations or provide job training rather than to create jobs for the existing work force.

On the positive side, a successful development program can certainly create employment. At Prudential Center some 7,500 jobs opened up, of which 4,100 (55 percent) are in new firms, new branches of chains, or firms relocating from outside of Boston. These jobs represent a net increase in employment for the city. The remaining 5,400 jobs are in firms which shifted from previous locations in Boston.

On the other hand, the jobs created in Prudential Center generally do not match the skills of workers living in Boston or Fenway. Sixty-two percent of those employed at the Center live in the suburbs. One reason is the high proportion of skilled workers employed at the Center. As Table 6–6 shows, 34 percent of the workers are in professional, technical, or managerial occupations as opposed to 22 percent for Boston's resident labor force. While 44 percent of Boston's resident labor force is employed as craftsmen, foremen, operatives, laborers, or service workers, only 11 percent of Center workers is so employed. Ganz and O'Brien (1972) concluded that:

> The types of firms which have been attracted to these high rise office and commercial buildings do not provide jobs which match the occupational skills of a significant share of Boston's resident labor force. This circumstance highlights the urgent need to adapt manpower training policy and programs to provide the occupational skills required by the nature of jobs emerging in Boston. Such new policies and programs must be complemented by a major effort to

Table 6–6. 1970 Employment (by Occupation) of Boston's Resident Labor Force, Fenway–Kenmore Planning District, and Prudential Center

	Boston's Resident Labor Force		Fenway–Kenmore Planning District		Prudential Center	
	Number	*Percent*	*Number*	*Percent*	*Number*	*Percent*
Total	266,505	100.0%	16,003	100.0%	7,310	100.0%
Professional and Technical	44,894	16.8	5,000	31.2	1,525	21.0
Managerial	15,035	5.6			977	13.0
Clerical and Secretarial	71,655	26.9	5,110	31.9	3,094	42.0
Sales	15,073	5.7	767	4.8	641	9.0
Craftsmen and Foremen	27,157	10.2	715	4.5	118	2.0
Operatives	36,695	13.8	985	6.2	67	1.0
Laborers and Service	53,714	20.2	3,311	20.7	573	8.0
Other	2,282	.8	115	.7	315	4.0

Sources: Tomkins, Mary, "Data Tables," from the 1970 Census of Population and Housing, First Count Summary Tape, (Mimeo) (Boston Redevelopment Authority, December 1972); Ganz, Alexander, and Thomas O'Brien, *The City Sandbox, Reservation or Dynamo,* Unpublished manuscript, Boston, 1972

hold on to those manufacturing jobs now fleeing Boston, which do provide opportunity for lesser skilled workers.

Unfortunately, stopping the movement of manufacturing and wholesaling jobs to land intensive operations in the suburbs appears difficult and expensive. Whether such a strategy is desirable requires consideration of regional impacts as well as the financial investment required. Also, if it is difficult to bring manufacturing and wholesaling firms (and jobs) back from the suburbs, housing workers closer to suburban jobs may be equally difficult due to insular social and political forces. As is well known, suburban communities have developed very effective measures to block in-migration of lower income and minority workers.

A comprehensive new town intown (as typified by the Fenway/Prudential Center complex) could help provide a solution. Continued growth of office based, service industries in the central city could generate additional tax revenues, particularly through tax increments. These revenues could finance less remunerative public investments needed to develop and revitalize older central city neighborhoods, as well as intensive manpower training programs. Tax increment revenues could be combined with general and special revenue sharing funds for greater financial impact. Such a development strategy would go with, rather than against, economic trends concentrating service employment in the central city. Accordingly, it should boost the efficiency of such industries, increase their prospects for further growth, and in turn generate additional tax revenues for central city development.

Moreover, many local residents could be employed in these central city service industries. Most of the service jobs at the center are clerical and secretarial—a category represented in considerable numbers in the area around the Center (see Table 6—6). There are, however, few jobs for lower skill workers. This problem could be attacked on the supply side via manpower and educational programs, and by increasing accessibility to employment elsewhere in the region.

With this interim strategy, out-commuting by central city workers would still be required. However, rather than expending large sums to bring relatively few jobs back into Boston, public investment could be used to better advantage: (a) in increasing accessibility to existing job opportunities throughout the city; (b) improving neighborhoods intown for those unwilling or unable to move to the suburbs; and (c) funding training programs so that more city workers can fit into existing service jobs. Such an approach is in many ways less than ideal, but it seems to be workable and would probably generate a higher return on the limited public funds available.

Part II

Bibliography

Aaron, Henry J. *Shelter and Subsidies: Who Benefits from Federal Housing Policies* (Washington: The Brookings Institution, 1972).

Abrams, Charles. *The City is the Frontier* (New York: Harper and Row, 1965).

Abrahamson, Julia. *A Neighborhood Finds Itself* (New York: Harper, 1959).

Adde, Leo. *Nine Cities: The Anatomy of Downtown Renewal* (Washington: The Urban Land Institute, 1969).

Aiken, M., and R. Alford. "Community Structure and Innovation: The Case of Urban Renewal," *American Sociological Review,* Vol. 35 (August 1970), pp. 843–64.

Alonso, William. "A Theory of the Urban Land Market," *Papers and Proceedings of The Regional Science Association,* Vol. 6 1960, pp. 149–158. Also in Bourne (1971), pp. 154–169.

Alonso, William. "The Historic and the Structural Theories of Urban Form: Their Implications for Urban Renewal," *Land Economics,* Vol. XL, No. 2 1964, pp. 227–231. Also in Bourne (1971), pp. 437–441.

Altshulter, Alan A. *The City Planning Process* (Ithaca: Cornell University Press, 1965).

American Institute of Planners. "Planning the City's Center," Special issue of the *Journal of the American Institute of Planners.* Vol. XXVII (February 1961).

Anderson, Martin. *The Federal Bulldozer: A Critical Analysis of Urban Renewal, 1949–1962* (Cambridge: M.I.T. Press, 1964).

Anderson, Martin. "Fiasco of Urban Renewal," *Harvard Business Review,* (January–February 1965), pp. 6–17, 20, 160, 161.

Armstrong, R. B. and Boris Pushkarev (eds.), *The Office Industry: Patterns of Growth and Location* (Cambridge: M.I.T. Press, 1972).

Arrow, Kenneth J. *Social Choice and Individual Values* (New York: John Wiley and Sons, 1951).

Artle, Roland. "Urbanization and Economic Growth in Venezuela," *Papers of The Regional Science Association,* Vol. 27, 1971.

Asbury, Charles A. "Yesterday's Failure," *Washington Post* (October 15, 1972), p. B 4.

AVCO Economic Systems Corporation. *Pilot Evaluation of Selected New Careers Projects,* U. S. Department of Labor, Office of Manpower Policy, Economic Opportunity Act (August 1968).

Banfield, Edward C. *The Unheavenly City: The Nature and Future of Our Urban Crisis.* (Boston: Little, Brown and Company, 1970).

Banfield, Edward C. and James Q. Wilson. *City Politics* (New York: Random House, 1966).

Beckham, Robert. "In or Out? Changes are on the Way as 'Model Cities' Face Community Development," *Journal of Housing,* Vol. 29, No. 10 (November 1972), pp. 494–497.

Becker, Gary. *The Economics of Discrimination* (Chicago: University of Chicago Press, 1957).

Becker, Gary. "Investment in Human Capital: A Theoretical Analysis," *Journal of Political Economy* (October 1962: Supplement), pp. 9–49.

Becker, Gary. *Human Capital: A Theoretical and Empirical Analysis with Special Reference to Education* (New York: Columbia University Press, 1964).

Bellush, J. and M. Hausknecht. "Entrepreneurs and Urban Renewal: The New Men of Power," *Journal of American Institute of Planners,* Vol. 32 (September 1966), pp. 289–297. Reprinted in the following collection, pp. 209–224.

Bellush, J. and M. Hausknecht (eds.). *Urban Renewal: People, Politics, and Planning* (New York: Doubleday, 1967).

Berry, Brian J. L., S. J. Parsons, and R. H. Platt. *The Impact of Urban Renewal on Small Business: The Hyde Park–Kenwood Case* (Chicago: Center for Urban Studies, The University of Chicago, 1968).

Bogart, Raymond George. *The Effects of Urban Displacement on Retail Businesses in Cincinnati.* Unpublished Dissertation, University of Cincinnati, 1958. Abstract on Page 3266 of Vol. 2901A of Dissertation Abstracts. University Microfilms Order No. 69–6330.

Booz, Allen. Public Administration Services. *Study of the Concentration and Dispersion Impact of the Model Cities Program.* Prepared for the U. S. Department of Housing and Urban Development, Mimeo. Washington, D. C. (June 1971).

Boston Redevelopment Authority. *New Housing in Boston: 1960–1972.* Unpublished Working Paper, Boston (August 1972).

Boston Redevelopment Authority. "Fact Sheets," *Public Information Office,* Boston (December 1972).

Boston Redevelopment Authority. *Boston's Social and Economic Development: Meeting the Needs of the City and Its People.* Unpublished Working Paper, Boston (1973).

Boston Redevelopment Authority. *Rebirth of Boston as a Place to Live, Reversal of Two Decades of Population Decline.* Boston (February 7, 1973).

Bourne, Larry S. *Private Redevelopment of the Central City* (Chicago: Department of Geography, University of Chicago, Research Paper No. 112, 1967).

Bourne, Larry S. (ed.). *Internal Structure of the City: Readings on Space and Environment* (New York: Oxford University Press, 1971).

Boyce, Byrl N. and Sidney Turoff. *Minority Groups and Housing: A Bibliography 1950–1972,* Center for Real Estate and Urban Economics, University of Connecticut, Storrs, Connecticut (1972).

Breagy, James C. "Boston, Leader in Use of Categorical Aids for Urban Renewal, is Searching for Organizational Structure to Maintain the Pace Under Community Development," *Journal of Housing,* Vol. 30, No. 7 (July 31, 1973), pp. 327–332.

Brown, W. A., Jr. and Charles B. Gilbert. *Planning Municipal Investment: A Case Study of Philadelphia,* (Philadelphia: University of Pennsylvania Press, 1961).

Brownfield, Lyman. "The Disposition Problem in Urban Renewal," *Law and Contemporary Problems,* Vol. 25 (Autumn 1960), pp. 732–76.

Bryan, Jack. "Breakthrough Begins, Housing Enters the Industrial Age," *Journal of Housing,* Vol. 27, No. 3 (March 31, 1970), pp. 127–139.

Bryan, Jack "NDP in Review: Does it Move Renewal Faster, Farther?" *Journal of Housing,* Vol. 28, No. 2 (February 26, 1971), pp. 65–74.

Burke, Edmund M. "Citizen Participation in Renewal," *Journal of Housing,* Vol. 23, (January 1966), pp. 18–25.

Business Week (eds.) "Breakthrough's Progress is Slow," *Business Week* (November 14, 1970), pp. 86–87.

Cahn, Edgar S. and Jean C. Cahn. *Citizen Participation.* Mimeographed Draft, (1968).

Cahn, Edgar and Barry A. Passett (eds.). *Citizen Participation: Effecting Community Change* (New York: Praeger Publishers, 1971).

Case, Frederick E. *Black Capitalism: Problems in Development: A Case of Los Angeles* (New York: Praeger Publishers, 1972).

Case, Frederick E. *Inner-City Housing and Private Enterprise: Based on Studies in Nine Cities* (New York: Praeger Publishers, 1972).

Clark, T. "Community Structure, Decision Making, Budget Expenditures, and Urban Renewal in 51 American Communities," in F. Wirt (ed.), *Future Directions in Community Power Research: A Colloquium* (Berkeley: Institute of Governmental Studies, 1971), pp. 43–94.

Coleman, J. *Community Conflict* (Glencoe Illinois Free Press, 1957).

Coleman, James S. *et al. Equality of Educational Opportunity,* U. S. Department of Health, Education and Welfare (Washington, D. C.: Government Printing Office, 1966).

Columbia Law Research Staff. "Citizen Participation in Urban Renewal," *Columbia Law Review,* Vol. 66 (March 1966), pp. 485–607.

Committee for Central City Planning, Inc. "Detoxification and Rehabilitation Program," *Central City Los Angeles 1972/1990: Preliminary General Development Plan* (Los Angeles: April 1972), pp. 101–102.

Congressional Research Service, Library of Congress, *The Central City Problem and Urban Renewal Policy,* Study prepared for the Subcommittee on Housing and Urban Affairs, Committee on Banking, Housing, and Urban Affairs, United States Senate, (Washington, D. C.: Government Printing Office, 1973).

Crain, R. and E. Katz, D. Rosenthal. *The Politics of Community Conflict* (New York: Bobbs–Merrill, 1969).

Crain, R. and D. Rosenthal. "Community Status and a Dimension of Local Decision Making," *American Sociological Review,* Vol. 32, No. 6 (December 1967), pp. 970–984.

Creswell, Richard W., *et al.* "Nashville Model Cities: A Case Study," *Vanderbilt Law Review,* Vol. 25, No. 4 (May 1972), pp. 729–844.

Dahl, R. *Who Governs?* (New Haven: Yale University Press, 1961).

Davidoff, Paul, Linda Davidoff, and Neil N. Gold. "Suburban Action Advocate Planning for an Open Society,"*Journal of the American Institute of Planners,* Vol. XXXVI, No. 1 (January 1970), pp. 12–21.

Davies, Clarence J. *Neighborhood Groups and Urban Renewal* (New York: Columbia University Press, 1966).

Davis, Harmer E. *Transportation–Employment Project, South and East Los Angeles Interim Final Report,* Project No. CAL–MTD9, State of California Business and Transportation Agency (January 1970).

Davis, Otto A. "A Pure Theory of Urban Renewal," *Land Economics,* Vol. 36 (May 1960), pp. 220–226.

Davis, Otto A. "Urban Renewal: A Reply to Two Critics," *Land Economics,* Vol. 39 (February 1963), pp. 99–108.

Davis, Otto A. and Andrew B. Whinston. "The Economics of Urban Renewal," *Law and Contemporary Problems,* Vol. 26, No. 1 (Winter 1961), pp. 105–117. Also in Wilson (1966) pp. 50–67.

Derthick, Martha. *New Towns In–Town: Why a Federal Program Failed* (Washington: The Urban Institute, 1972).

Dorfman, Robert (ed.). *Measuring Benefits of Government Investments* (Washington: The Brookings Institution, 1965).

Downs, Anthony. "An Economic Analysis of Property Values and Race," *Land Economics* (May 1960), pp. 181–188.

Downs, Anthony. "Comments" (on Rothenberg's paper, "Urban Renewal Programs") in Dorfman (1965), pp. 342–351.

Downs, Anthony. "Alternative Futures for the Ghetto," *Urban Problems and Prospects* (Chicago: Markham, 1970a), pp. 27–74.

Downs, Anthony. "Uncompensated Nonconstruction Costs Which Urban Highways and Urban Renewal Impose Upon Residential Households," in Julius Margolis (ed.) *The Analysis of Public Output* (New York: Columbia University Press, 1970), pp. 69–113.

Dugger, G. S. "The Relation of Local Government Structure to Urban Renewal," *Law and Contemporary Problems,* Vol. 26 (Winter 1961), pp. 49–69.

Duncan, Otis Dudley and Beverly Duncan. *The Negro Population of Chicago: A Study of Residential Succession* (Chicago: University of Chicago Press, 1957).

Dunn, Edgar S. *Economic and Social Development: A Process of Social Learning* (Baltimore: Johns Hopkins Press, 1971).

Dyckman, John W. "National Planning for Urban Renewal: The Paper Moon in the Cardboard Sky," *Journal of American Institute of Planners* (February 1960) pp. 49–59.

Dyckman, John W. and Reginald R. Isaacs. *Capital Requirements for Urban Development and Renewal* (New York: McGraw–Hill, 1961).

Eudey, Elizabeth. *A Move to Home Ownership* (San Francisco: San Francisco Development Fund, 1970). Available from National Technical Information Service, No. PB196720.

Fisher, Franklin M. "Income Distribution, Value Judgments, and Welfare," *Quarterly Journal of Economics,* Vol. 70 (August 1956).

Foard, Ashley A. and Hilbert Fefferman. "Federal Urban Renewal Legislation," *Law and Contemporary Problems,* Vol. 25 (Autumn 1960).

Foley, Donald L. *The Suburbanization of Administration Offices in the San Francisco Bay Area* (Berkeley: University of California, Bureau of Business and Economic Research, Real Estate Research Program Research Report No. 10, 1957).

Forrester, Jay W. *Urban Dynamics* (Cambridge: M.I.T. Press, 1968).

Fraser, Stephen A. *Citizen Participation in Decision Making by Federal Agencies: Selective Service System, Bureau of Land Management, Office of Economic Opportunity, Department of Housing and Urban Development.* Unpublished Dissertation. Johns Hopkins University. Abstract on page 2597 in Vol. 300–A of Dissertation Abstracts, 1965. University Microfilms Order No. 69–21, 090.

Fried, Marc. "Grieving for a Lost Home," in Leonard J. Duhl (ed.) *The Urban Condition* (New York: Basic Books, 1963), pp. 151–171.

Fried, Marc. "Transitional Functions of Working Class Communities Implications for Forced Relocation," in M. Kantor (ed.) *Mobility and Mental Health* (Chicago: Charles C. Thomas, 1965).

Frieden, Bernard J. *The Future of Old Neighborhoods: Rebuilding for a Changing Population* (Cambridge: M.I.T. Press, 1964).

Friedly, P. H. *et al. Benefit–Cost Applications in Urban Renewal: Summary of The Feasibility Study.* Prepared for HUD by Resource Management Corporation (Washington, D. C.: Government Printing Office, 1968), 35 pp.

Friedmann, John. "A General Theory of Polarized Development," in Niles Hansen (ed.) *Growth Centers in Regional Economic Development* (New York: The Free Press of Glencoe, 1972).

Friedmann, John. "The Future of the Urban Habitat," in Donald McAllister (ed.) *A New Focus for Land Use Planning,* Research Applied to National Needs, National Science Foundation, Washington, D. C. (Government Printing Office, 1973), pp. 57–82.

Friedmann, John. *Retracking America: A Theory of Transactive Planning* (Garden City: Doubleday and Anchor Books, 1973).

Fuchs, Victor R. "The Growing Importance of the Service Industries," *Journal of Business,* Vol. VII, No. 4 (October 1965), pp. 344–373.

Gans, Herbert J. "The Human Implications of Current Redevelopment and Relocation Planning," *Journal of the American Institute of Planners,* Vol. XXV (February 1959), pp. 15–25.

Gans, Herbert J. *The Urban Villagers* (New York: The Free Press of Glencoe, 1962).

Gans, Herbert J. "The Failure of Urban Renewal," *Commentary,* Vol. 39 (April 1964), pp. 29–37. Also in Bellush and Hausknecht (1967), pp. 465–484.

Gans, Herbert J. *People and Plans: Essays on Urban Problems and Solutions* (New York: Basic Books, 1968).

Gans, Herbert J. "The Possibilities of Class and Racial Integration in American New Towns." Paper prepared for the *Symposium on Human Factors in New Town Development* (Los Angeles: University of California, School of Architecture and Urban Planning, June 1972).

Ganz, Alexander. *Our Large Cities; New Light on Their Recent Transformation; Elements of a Development Strategy; A Prototype Program for Boston.* (Cambridge: M.I.T. Laboratory for Environmental Studies, supported by Office of Economic Research of the Economic Development Administration, U. S. Department of Commerce, February 1972).

Ganz, Alexander and Tina Freeman. *Population and Income of the City of Boston, Recent Evolution and Future Perspective* (Boston: Boston Redevelopment Authority, June 1972).

Ganz, Alexander and Peter Menconeri. *The Expanding City of Boston Economy* (Boston: Boston Redevelopment Authority, June 1970).

Ganz, Alexander and Thomas O'Brien. *The City: Sandbox, Reservation, or Dynamo.* Unpublished Paper, Boston 1972.

Garn, Harvey A. and Robert H. Wilson. *A Critical Look at Urban Dynamics: The Forrester Model and Public Policy* (Washington, D. C.: The Urban Institute, 1970).

Glazer, N. "The Renewal of Cities," *Scientific American,* Vol. 213 (September 1965), pp. 195–204.

Gold, Robert. "Urban Violence and Contemporary Defensive Cities," Journal of *the American Institute of Planners,* Vol. XXXVI, No. 3 (May 1970), pp. 146–59.

Goldblatt, Harold. *Citizen Participation in Urban Renewal* Health and Welfare Council of the National Capital Area. (Washington, D. C., January 1966).

Goldstein, Jon H. *The Effectiveness of Manpower Training Programs: A Review of Research on the Impact on the Poor.* Staff study prepared for the use of the Subcommittee on Fiscal Policy of the Joint Economic Committee, Congress of the United States (Washington, D. C.: Government Printing Office, November 20, 1972).

Goldston, Eli, Allan O. Hunter and Guido A. Rothrauff, Jr. "Urban Redevelopment—The Viewpoint of Counsel for a Private Redeveloper," *Law and Contemporary Problems,* Vol. 26 (Winter 1961), pp. 118–177.

Gorland, Emanuel. *Urban Renewal Administration: Practices, Procedures, Record Keeping* (Detroit: Wayne State University Press, 1971).

Gorland, Emanuel. "Relocation Inequities and Problems Emergent as a Result of the 1970 Uniform Relocation Act," *Journal of Housing,* Vol. 29, No. 3 (March 31, 1972), pp. 137–138.

Greenfield, Harry I. *Manpower and the Growth of Producer Services* (New York: Columbia University Press, 1966).

Greenwald, Carl S. and Richard Syron. "Increasing Job Opportunities in Boston's Urban Core," *New England Economic Review* (Federal Reserve Bank of Boston, January 1969), pp. 30–40.

Greer, Scott. *The Emerging City: Myth and Reality* (New York: The Free Press of Glencoe, 1962).

Greer, Scott. *Urban Renewal and American Cities; the Dilemma of Democratic Intervention* (New York: Bobbs–Merrill, 1965).

Greer, Scott and D. Minar. "The Political Side of Urban Development and Redevelopment," *Annals* (March 1964), pp. 63–73. Reprinted in Bellush and Hausknecht (1967), pp. 157–171.

Grigsby William G. *Housing Markets and Public Policy* (Philadelphia: University of Pennsylvania Press, 1963).

Groberg, Robert P. "Urban Renewal Realistically Reappraised," *Law and Contemporary Problems,* Vol. 30 (Winter 1965), pp. 212–229.

Gutking, E. A. *The Twilight of Cities* (New York: The Free Press of Glencoe, 1962).

Haggart, John C. *Authority in Municipal Organizations for the Integration of Urban Renewal Plans.* Unpublished Dissertation. University of California, Los Angeles. Abstract on page 3129 in Vol. 2408 of Dissertation Abstracts, University Microfilms Order No. 64–2241.

Harrison, Bennett. "Public Service Jobs for Ghetto Residents," *Good Government* (Fall 1969), pp. 1–20.

Harrison, Bennett. *Public Employment and Urban Poverty* (Washington, D. C.: Urban Institute, 1971).

Harrison, Bennett. "Employment, Unemployment and Structure of the Urban Labor Market, *Wharton Quarterly* (Spring 1972a), pp. 4–7, 26–30.

Harrison, Bennett. "Education and Unemployment in the Urban Ghetto," *American Economic Review,* Vol. 72, No. 5 (December 1972b), pp. 796–812.

Harrison, Bennett, H. L. Sheppard and W. J. Spring. "Public Jobs, Public Needs: Government as the Employer of First Resort," *The New Republic* (November 4, 1972), pp. 18–21.

Harrison, Bennett. "Participation in Ghetto Residents in the Model Cities Program," forthcoming in the *Journal of the American Institute of Planners.*

Hartman, Chester. "The Limitations of Public Housing . . . Relocation Choices in a Working–Class Community," *Journal of the American Institute of Planners,* Vol. XXXIX, No. 4 (November 1963), pp. 283–96.

Hartman, Chester. "The Housing of Relocated Families," *Journal of the American Institute of Planners* (November 1964), pp. 266–286.

Hartman, Chester. *Yerba Buena* (San Francisco: Glide Publications, 1974).

Hawley, A. "Community Power and Urban Renewal Success," *American Journal of Sociology,* Vol. 68 (June 1963), pp. 422–431.

Hawley, A. and F. Wirts (eds.). *The Search for Community Power* (Englewood Cliffs: Prentice–Hall, 1968).

Herbert, Ray. "Model Cities: Millions Spent but Little to Show for It," *Los Angeles Times* (April 9, 1972).

Hines, Mary Alice. *Retailing Opportunities in Federal Urban Renewal Projects.* Unpublished Dissertation. Ohio State University, 1967. Abstract on page 3301 in Vol. 2809A of Dissertation Abstracts. University Microfilms Order No. 68–3002.

Hoover, Edgar M. and Raymond Vernon. *Anatomy of Metropolis: The Changing Distribution of People and Jobs Within the New York Metropolitan Region* (Garden City, N. Y.: Anchor Books, 1962).

Horton, Gerald T. "Strengthening Local Government," *Model Cities Service Center Bulletin*, Vol. II, No. 9 (June 1971), pp. 17–21.

Hubbard, Robert. "Letters to the Editor," *Journal of Housing* Vol. 29, No. 5 (May 31, 1972), pp. 213–214.

Hunter, Floyd. *Community Power Structure,* (Chapel Hill: University of North Carolina Press, 1953).

Hyman, Herbert H. *Organizational Response to Urban Renewal.* Unpublished Dissertation, Brandeis University, 1967. Abstract on page 2803 of Vol. 2807 of Dissertation Abstracts. University Microfilms Order No. 67–16, 557.

Jacobs, J. *The Life and Death of Great American Cities* (New York: Random House, 1968).

James, Judson Lehman. "Evaluation Report on the Model Cities Program," in U. S., Congress, House, Committee on Banking and Currency. *Papers Submitted to Subcommittee on Housing: Panels on Housing Production, Housing Demand, and Developing A Suitable Living Environment,* 92d Cong., 1st Sess. (Washington, D. C.: Government Printing Office, 1971) Pt. 2, pp. 839–856.

Jencks, Christopher, *Inequality, A Reassessment of the Effect of Family and Schooling in America* (New York: Basic Books, 1972a).

Jencks, Christopher, and Mary Jo Bane. "Schools and Equality," *Washington Post* Outlook Section (September 17, 1972b), pp. B 1, B 5.

Jensen, Rolf. *High Density Living* (New York: Praeger Publishers, 1966).

Jordan, Fred. "Model Cities in Perspective," *Model Cities Service Center Bulletin* (NLC/USCM), Vol. 2, No. 9 (June 1971), pp. 4–8.

Kain, John F. "The Journey-to-work as a Determinant of Residential Location," *Papers and Proceedings of the Regional Science Association* Vol. 9 (1962), pp. 137–139.

Kain, John F. "The Distribution and Movement of Jobs and Industry," *The Metropolitan Enigma,* James Q. Wilson (ed.) (Washington, D. C.: Chamber of Commerce of the United States, 1967), pp. 1–34.

Kain, John F. and Joseph J. Persky. *The Ghetto, the Metropolis and the Nation,* Discussion Paper No. 30, Program on Regional and Urban Economics, M.I.T.–Harvard Joint Center for Urban Studies (March 1968).

Kain, John F. "Coping with Ghetto Unemployment," *Journal of the American Institute of Planners,* Vol. XXXV, No. 2 (March 1969), pp. 80–83.

Kaitz, Edward M. and Herbert Harvey Hyman. *Urban Planning for Social Welfare: A Model Cities Approach* (New York: Praeger Publishers 1970).

Kaplan, Harold. *Urban Renewal Politics, Slum Clearance in Newark* (New York: Columbia University Press, 1963).

Kaplan, Marshall. "Advocacy and the Urban Poor," *Journal of the American Institute of Planners,* Vol. 35, No. 2 (May 1969), pp. 96–101.

Kaplan, Marshall, Gans and Kahn. *The Model Cities Program: The Planning Process in Atlanta, Seattle and Dayton* (New York: Praeger Publishers 1970).

Keller, S. *Urban Neighborhoods—A Sociological Perspective* (New York: Random House, 1968).

Keyes, L. C. *The Rehabilitation Planning Game* (Cambridge: The M.I.T. Press, 1969).

Kilbridge, M. D., R. P. O'Block, and P. V. Peplitz. "Part II: Economic Models for Housing Analysis," *Urban Analysis* (Boston: Division of Research, Graduate School of Business, Harvard University, 1970).

Knight, David B. and Tatsuo Ito. "Office Parks: The Oak Brook Example," *Land Economics,* Vol. XLVIII (February 1972), pp. 65–69.

Kornhauser, William. *Politics of Mass Society,* (Glencoe, Illinois: The Free Press of Glencoe, 1959).

Kotler, Milton. "Two Essays on the Neighborhood Corporation," in *Urban America Goals and Problems.* Materials prepared for the Subcommittee on Urban Affairs of the Joint Economic Committee, Congress of the United States (Washington, D. C.: Government Printing Office, (August 1967).

Kovak, Richard M. "Urban Renewal Controversies," *Public Administration Review* (July/August 1972), pp. 359–372.

Lampard, Eric E. "The Evolving System of Cities in the United States: Urbanization and Economic Development," in Perloff and Wingo, pp. 81–139.

Lansing, John B., W. W. Clifton and J. N. Morgan. *New Homes for Poor People: A Study of Chains of Moves* (Ann Arbor: Institute of Social Research, 1969).

Laurenti, Luigi. *Property Values and Race* (Berkeley: University of California Press, 1960).

Leach, Richard H. "The Federal Urban Renewal Program: A Ten-Year Critique," *Law and Contemporary Problems,* Vol. 25 (Autumn 1960), pp. 777–92.

Legates, Richard T. *Can the Federal Welfare Bureaucracies Control Their Programs: The Case of HUD and Urban Renewal,* Working Paper No. 172 (Berkeley: Institute of Urban and Regional Development, May 1972).

Lewis, Gerda. "Citizen Participation in Renewal Surveyed," *Journal of Housing,* Vol. 16, No. 31 (March 1959) pp. 80–87.

Lichfield, Nathaniel. "Benefit-Cost Analysis in City Planning," *Journal of the American Institute of Planners,* Vol. 26 (November 1960), pp. 273–279.

Lichfield, Nathaniel. "Relocation: The Impact on Housing Welfare," *Journal of the American Institute of Planners,* Vol. 27 (August 1961), pp. 199–203.

Lichfield, Nathaniel. *Cost Benefit Analysis in Urban Redevelopment,* Real Estate Research Program, Institute of Business and Economic Research, University of California, Berkeley (1962).

Lichfield, Nathaniel. "A Pure Theory of Urban Renewal: A Further Comment," *Land Economics,* Vol. XXXIX, No. 1 (February 1963), pp. 99–103.

Lichfield, Nathaniel. "Spatial Externalities in Urban Public Expenditures, A Case Study," in Julius Margolis (ed.), *The Public Economy of Urban Communities* (Baltimore: Johns Hopkins Press, 1965), pp. 207–50.

Lilley, William III. "The Model Cities Program Faces Uncertain Future Despite Romney Overhaul," *National Journal,* Vol. II (August 11, 1970), pp. 1467–1468.

Lindbloom C. and M. Farrah. *The Citizen's Guide to Urban Renewal,* West Trenton, N. J.: Chandler Davis (1968).

Linton, Mields and Coston, Inc. "A Study of the Problems of Abandoned Housing and Recommendations for Action by the Federal Government and Localities," in U. S., Congress, House, *Hearings Before the Subcommittee on Appropriations,* 92d Cong., 2d Sess. (April 1972), pp. 41–52.

Lipset, S., M. and R. Bendix (eds). *Class, Status and Power* (Glencoe, Illinois: The Free Press of Glencoe, 1953).

Lipset, S. M. *Political Man* (New York: Doubleday, 1960).

Little, Arthur D., Inc. *The San Francisco Renewal Plan.* San Francisco (October 1965).

    Technical Paper No. 1 Simulation Model for Renewal Programming (October 1964).

    Technical Paper No. 2 Models for Condition Aging of Residential Structures (November 1964).

    Technical Paper No. 3 Amenity Attributes of Residential Locations (May 1965).

    Technical Paper No. 4 Estimated Cost of New Construction and Rehabilitation of Existing Residential Structures (June 1965).

    Technical Paper No. 5 Some Studies on the San Francisco Economic Environment (September 1965).

    Technical Paper No. 6 Renewal Attitudes Survey (October 1965).

    Technical Paper No. 8 Simulation Model for Renewal Programming, Phase II.

Little, Arthur D., Inc. *Community Renewal Programming: A San Francisco Case Study* (New York: Praeger Publishers, 1966).

Little, I. M. D. *A Critique of Welfare Economics* (New York: Oxford University Press, 1957).

Logue, Edward J. "Comment on the Housing of Relocated Families," and Chester W. Hartman, "Rejoinder by the Author." *Journal of the American Institute of Planners.* Vol. XXIX, No. 4 (November 1965), pp. 338–344.

Long, Norton E. "The Local Community as an Ecology of Games," *American Journal of Sociology,* Vol. 63 (November 1958), pp. 251–261.

Long, Norton E. "Local Government and Renewal Policies," in Wilson (1966) pp. 432–434.

Long, Norton E. "The City as Reservation," *Public Interest* (Fall 1972), pp. 23–38.

Loring, William C. Jr., Frank L. Sweetzer, and Charles F. Ernst. *Community Organization for Community Participation in Urban Renewal* (Boston: Massachusetts Department of Commerce, 1957).

Lowe, Jeanne R. *Cities in a Race with Time: Progress and Poverty in America's Renewing Cities* (New York: Random House, 1967).

Luedtke, Gerald. *Crime and the Physical City. A Pilot Study Prepared for the National Institute of Law Enforcement and Criminal Justice* (Springfield, Va.: National Technical Information Service, June 1970, PB 196 784.

Mace, Ruth L. *Municipal Cost-Revenue Research in the United States* (Chapel Hill: Institute of Government, University of North Carolina, 1961).

Mace, Ruth L. *Costing Urban Development and Redevelopment* (Chapel Hill: Institute of Government, University of North Carolina, 1964).

Mao, James C. T. *Efficiency in Public Urban Renewal Expenditures Through Capital Budgeting.* Research Report 27. Center for Real Estate and Urban Economies. Institute of Urban and Regional Development: University of California, Berkeley (1965).

Mao, James C. T. "Efficiency in Public Urban Renewal Expenditures Through Benefit-Cost Analysis," *Journal of the American Institute of Planners,* Vol. 32 (March 1966), pp. 95–107.

Marcuse, Peter. *Home Ownership for the Poor: Economic Implications for the Owner/Occupant.* Working Paper 112–126. (Washington: Urban Institute, 1971).

Marglin, Stephen A. "Objectives of Water-Resource Development: A General Statement," Chap. 2, Pt. 1, in *Design of Water Resource Systems* (Cambridge: Harvard University Press, 1962).

Marglin, Stephen A. "The Social Rate of Discount and the Optimal Rate of Investment," *Quarterly Journal of Economics* (February 1963), pp. 95–111.

Marris, Peter. "The Social Implications of Urban Redevelopment," *Journal of the American Institute of Planners,* Vol. XXVIII (August 1962), pp. 180–186.

Marris, Peter and Royce Rein. *Dilemma of Social Reform* (London: Atherton, 1967).

Mayor's Committee for Economic and Cultural Development. *A Partnership for Action: The Mid-Chicago Economic Development Project* (Chicago, May 1970). A Technical Assistance Project funded by the Economic Development Administration of the U. S. Department of Commerce. Available from the Technical Information Service or The Mayor's Committee, Civic Center, Room 302, Chicago, Illinois 60602.

McDonough, Edward F. *A Cost-Benefit Analysis of a Hartford, Connecticut Urban Renewal Project.* Unpublished Dissertation. University of Massachusetts (1968). Abstract on page 1026 of Vol. 2904A of Dissertation Abstracts. University Microfilms Order No. 68–14, 586.

McEntire, Davis. *Residence and Race* (Berkeley: University of California Press, 1960).

McFarland, Carter and Walter Vivrett. *Residential Rehabilitation* (Minneapolis: School of Architecture, University of Minnesota, 1966).

McGee, Henry W. Jr. "Urban Renewal in the Crucible of Judical Review," *Virginia Law Review,* Vol. 56 (June 1970), pp. 826–894.

McQuade, Walter. "Urban Renewal in Boston," in Wilson (1966), pp. 259–277.

Meer, Bernard and Edward Freedman. "The Impact of Negro Neighbors on White Owners," *Social Forces* (September 1966), pp. 11–19.

Mermin, Alvin A. *Relocating Families: The New Haven Experience 1956 to 1966* (Washington: NAHRO, 1970).

Messner Stephen D. *A Cost-Benefit Analysis of Urban Redevelopment: A Case Study of the Indianapolis Program* (Bloomington: Bureau of Business Research, Indiana University, Report No. 43, 1967).

Meyer, Douglas K. "Spatiotemporal Trends of Racial Residential Change," *Land Economics,* Vol. XLVIII (February 1972), pp. 62–65.

Meyer, J. R., and J. F. Kain, M. Wohl. *The Urban Transportation Problem* (Cambridge, Mass: Harvard University Press, 1965), pp. 9–54.

Meyerson, M. and E. Banfield. *Politics, Planning and the Public Interest* (Glencoe, Illinois: The Free Press of Glencoe, 1955).

Mikens, Alvin. *Manpower Perspectives for Urban Redevelopment* (Manpower Training Series), Center for the Study of Unemployed Youth, New York University (1967).

Miller, Lawrence. "Letters to the Editor," *Journal of Housing,* Vol. 29, No. 5 (May 31, 1972), pp. 214–215.

Mills, Edwin S. *Urban Economics* (Glenview, Illinois: Scott, Foresman and Co., 1972).

Millspaugh, Martin. "Problems and Opportunities of Relocation," *Law and Contemporary Problems,* Vol. XXVI, No. 1 (Winter 1961), pp. 6–36.

Millspaugh, Martin. *The Human Side of Urban Renewal* (Ives Washburn, 1960).

Millspaugh, Martin (ed.). *Baltimore's Charles Center: A Case Study of Downtown Renewal.* Technical Bulletin 51 (Washington, D. C.: Urban Land Institute, 1964).

Mincer, Jacob. "On-the-Job Training: Costs, Returns, and Some Implications," *Journal of Political Economy* (October 1962: Supplement), pp. 50–79.

Mitchell, Robert B. (ed.). *Urban Renewal: Goals and Standards. Annals of the American Academy of Political and Social Science* (March 1964).

Morrill, Richard. "The Negro Ghetto: Problems and Alternatives," *Geographical Review* (July 1965), pp. 339–361.

Mumford, Lewis. *The City in History: Its Origins, Its Transformations, and Its Prospects* (New York: Harcourt, Brace & World, 1961).

Muth, Richard F. "Urban Residential Land and Housing Markets," in Perloff and Wingo (1968), pp. 286–333.

NAHRO Program Policy Research. "Uniform Relocation Assistance and Real Property Acquisition Policies Act of 1970: A Title-by-Title Summary," *Journal of Housing,* Vol. 28, No. 2 (February 1971), pp. 82–85.

Nash, William W. *Residential Rehabilitation: Private Profits and Public Purposes* (New York: Action Series, 1959).

National Academy of Sciences. *Segregation in Residential Areas: Papers on Racial and Socioeconomic Factors in Choice of Housing.* Amos H. Hawley and Vincent P. Rock (eds.) (Washington: National Academy of Sciences, 1973).

National Academy of Sciences and National Academy of Engineering. *Freedom of Choice in Housing: Opportunities and Constraints.* Report prepared for the Advisory Committee to the Department of Housing and Urban Development by the Social Science Panel (Washington: National Academy of Sciences and National Academy of Engineering, 1972).

National Commission on Urban Problems, *Building the American City.* Report to the National Commission on Urban Problems to the Congress and to the President of the United States, 91st Cong., 1st Sess., House Document No. 91–34, (Washington: Government Printing Office, 1968).

National League of Cities, "The Fiscal Plight of American Cities." U. S., Congress, House, Committee on Ways and Means, *General Revenue Sharing. Hearings,* 92d Cong., 1st Sess., Pt. 2 (Washington: Government Printing Office, 1971).

Newman, Oscar. *Crime Prevention Through Urban Design—Defensible Space* (New York: MacMillan, 1973).

Nourse, Hugh O. "The Economics of Urban Renewal," *Land Economics,* Vol. 42 (February 1966), pp. 65–74.

O'Block, R. P. and P. H. Keuhn. *An Economic Analysis of the Housing and Urban Development Act of 1968* (Boston: Division of Research, Graduate School of Business, Harvard University, 1970).

O'Brien, Thomas. *The Prudential Center, Part One: Its Direct Impact on Boston* (Boston: Boston Redevelopment Authority, September 1969).

O'Brien, Thomas. *The Prudential Center, Part Two: Its Effect on the Surrounding Area* (Boston: Boston Redevelopment Authority, December 1969).

O'Brien, Thomas, *Government Center* (Boston: Boston Redevelopment Authority, February 1970).

O'Brien, Thomas. *The Prudential Towers and Charles River Park Apartments: The Effect of High Rise on Boston's Population* (Boston: Boston Redevelopment Authority, July 1970).

O'Brien, Thomas and Alexander Ganz. *A Demographic Revolution: The Impact of Office Building and Residential Tower Development in Boston* (Boston: Boston Redevelopment Authority, December 1972).

Olken, Charles E. "Economic Development in the Model Cities Program," *Law and Contemporary Problems,* Vol. XXXVI, No. 2 (Spring 1971), pp. 205–226.

Olympus Research Corporation. *The Total Impact of Manpower Programs: A Four-City Case Study,* Department of Labor, Contract No. PB 202 929 (Washington, D. C. 1971). Two volumes.

"Operation Breakthrough, Current Progress Report; Site Plans," *Architectural Forum,* Vol. 134, No. 4 (May 1971), pp. 58–61.

Page, David A. *Urban Renewal.* Paper presented to Bureau of the Budget Staff. (August 10, 1965), dittoed, 50 pp.

Pascal, A. H. *The Economics of Housing Segregation* (Santa Monica: The Rand Corporation, Memorandum RM–5510–RC, 1967).

Patman, Wright. *The Housing and Urban Development Act of 1972: Report Together with Supplemental Additional and Individual Views* (to accompany H. R. 16704), House Report No. 92–1429, 92d Cong., 2d Sess., (September 21, 1972).

Pearl, Augusta. "First Operation Breakthrough Project Completed," *Journal of Housing* (May 1972), pp. 166–169.

Perloff, Harvey S. *Urban Renewal in a Chicago Neighborhood, An Appraisal of the Hyde Park–Kenwood Renewal Program* (Chicago: Hyde Park Herald, Inc., August 1965).

Perloff, Harvey S. "New Directions in Social Planning," *Journal of the American Institute of Planners,* Vol. XXXI, No. 4 (November 1965), pp. 297–304.

Perloff, Harvey S. and Lowdon Wingo, Jr. (eds.). *Issues in Urban Economics* (Baltimore: Johns Hopkins Press, 1968).

Perloff, Harvey S. "What Economic Future for the Inner City Ghetto?" *Science and Technology and the Cities,* A compilation of papers for the tenth meeting of the Committee on Science and Technology, U. S., House, 1969, pp. 89 ff.

Perloff, Harvey S. "National Urban Policy: Stage I: Building the Foundation" in *Spatial, Regional and Population Economics: Essays in Honor of Edgar M. Hoover.* Mark Perlman, Charles J. Leven, and Benjamin Chinitz (eds.). (New York: Gordon & Breach, 1972), pp. 313–31.

Perloff, Harvey S. "New-Towns-Intown in a National New Communities Program," in H. S. Perloff and N. C. Sandberg (eds.). *New Towns: Why and For Whom?* (New York: Praeger Publishers, 1973a).

Perloff, Harvey S. "Life Styles and The Future Planning Game," *Planning: The ASPO Magazine* (June 1973b), pp. 2–5.

Perloff, Harvey S. "Alternatives for Future Urban Land Policy," with Marion Clawson, *Modernizing Urban Land Policy,* Marion Clawson (ed.). (Baltimore: Johns Hopkins Press, 1973c), pp. 221–39.

Polsby, N. *Community Power and Political Theory* (New Haven: Yale University Press, 1963).

Popenoe, David. *Costs and Benefits in Urban Renewal Decision: A Study of the Theory of Rational Planning in the Public Sector.* Unpublished Dissertation. University of Pennsylvania (1963). Abstract on page 1683 of Vol. 2404 of Dissertation Abstracts. University Microfilms Order No. 63–7077.

President's Committee on Urban Housing. *A Decent Home: Report of the President's Committee on Urban Housing* (Kaiser Report) (Washington: President's Committee on Urban Housing, 1968).

President's Task Force on Model Cities. *Model Cities: A Step Toward the New Federalism* (Washington, D. C., 1970).

President's Task Force on Urban Renewal. *Urban Renewal: One Tool Among Many* (Washington, D. C., 1970).

Pressman, Jeffrey and Aaron Wildavsky. *Implementation: How Great Expectations in Washington are Dashed in Oakland; or Why it's Amazing that Federal Programs Work at All, This Being a Saga of Economic Development Administration as Told by Two Sympathetic Observers Who Seek to Build Morals on a Foundation of Ruined Hopes.* (Berkeley: University of California Press, 1973)

Rapkin, Chester and William G. Grigsby. *Residential Renewal in the Urban Core* (Philadelphia: University of Pennsylvania Press, 1959).

Ratcliff, R. *Private Investment in Urban Redevelopment.* University of California, Berkeley, Real Estate Research Program (1961).

Rawson, Mary. *Property Taxation and Urban Development.* Research Monograph 4, Urban Land Institute (1961).

Real Estate Research Corporation. *Possible Program for Counteracting Housing Abandonment.* Prepared for the Office of Research and Technology, Department of Housing and Urban Development, Chicago (June 1971).

Rose, Harold M. "The Development of an Urban Subsystem: The Case of the Negro Ghetto," *Annals, Association of American Geographers* (March 1970), pp. 1–17.

Rossi, Peter H. and Robert A. Dentler. *The Politics of Urban Renewal: The Chicago Findings* (Glencoe, Illinois: The Free Press of Glencoe, 1961).

Rossi, P. H. and R. A. Dentler. "Power and Community Structure," *Midwest Journal of Political Science,* Vol. IV (November 1960), pp. 394–401.

Rothenberg, Jerome. *Economic Evaluation of Urban Renewal: Conceptual Foundation of Benefit-Cost Analysis* (The Brookings Institution: Washington, D. C., 1967).

Rustin, Bayard. "Equal Opportunity and the Liberal Will," *Washington Post,* 'Outlook' Section (October 5, 1972), pp. B 1, B 4.

Sayre, W. and H. Kaufman. *Governing New York City* (New York: Russell Sage Foundation, 1960).

Schaaf, A. H. *Economic Aspects of Urban Renewal: Theory, Policy and Area Analysis,* Research Report 14, Real Estate Research Program, Institute of Business and Economic Research, University of California, Berkeley (1960).

Schaaf, A. H. "Public Policies in Urban Renewal," *Land Economics,* "An Economic Analysis of Justification and Effects," Vol. XL, No. 1 (February 1964), pp. 67–78.

Schaaf, A. H. "Effects of Property Taxation on Slums and Renewal: A Study of Land Improvement Assessment Ratios," *Land Economics,* Vol. XLV, No. 1 (February 1969a).

Schaaf, A. H. "Economic Feasibility Analysis for Urban Renewal Housing Rehabilitation." *Journal of the American Institute of Planners,* Vol. XXXV, No. 6 (November 1969b), pp. 399–404.

School of Law, Duke University. "Community Economic Development," Pts. I, II, *Law and Contemporary Problems,* Vol. XXXVI, Nos. 1, 2 (Winter and Spring 1971).

Schorr, Alvin. *Slums and Social Insecurity,* Research Report No. 1, U. S. Department of Health, Education, and Welfare (Washington: Government Printing Office, 1963).

Schrank, Robert and Susan Stein. "Industry in the Black Community: IBM in Bedford–Stuyvesant," *Journal of the American Institute of Planners,* Vol. XXXV, No. 5 (November 1969), pp. 248–351.

Schultz, Harvey W., and G. G. Schwartz, Z. Fribourg. "Planning for Jobs: New York City Attempts to Retain and Create Blue Collar Jobs," *Planners Notebook,* Vol. II, No. 1 (February 1972).

Schultz, T. W. "Investment in Human Capital," *American Economic Review,* Vol. 51 (March 1961), pp. 1–17.

Schussheim, Morton. "Determining Priorities in Urban Renewal," *Papers and Proceedings of the Regional Science Association,* Vol. 6 (1960), pp. 195–205.

Schussheim, Morton. "A Pure Theory of Urban Renewal: A Comment," *Land Economics,* Vol. XLV, No. 4 (November 1969), pp. 395–396.

Seeley, John. "The Slum: Its Nature, Use and Users," *Journal of the American Institute of Planners,* Vol. XXV (1959), pp. 7–14. Also in Bellush and Hausknecht (1967).

Shandler, Irving W. "Alcoholics of Special Community Concern," *Comprehensive Community Services for Alcoholics: The Williamsburg Papers,* National Institute for Mental Health, Chevy Chase, Maryland (1970), pp. 15–34.

Shannon, Lyle W. and Magdaline Shannon. "The Assimilation of Migrants to Cities: Anthropological and Sociological Contributions," in Leo F. Schnore (ed.), *Social Science and the City: A Survey of Urban Research* (New York: Praeger Publishers, 1964) pp. 49–75.

Sheehan, Joseph C. *Community Participation in Urban Renewal Planning.* Unpublished Dissertation, University of Maryland (1969). Abstract on page 5548 in Vol. 3012A of Dissertation Abstracts. University Microfilms Order No. 70–11, 640.

Sheppard, Harold L. *The Nature of the Job Problem and the Role of New Public Service Employment* (Kalamazoo, Michigan: Upjohn Institute, January 1969).

Sieber, Philip E. "Uniform Relocation Act Can Be a Force for Citizen Support of Community Development," *Journal of Housing,* Vol. 29, No. 9 (October 24, 1972), pp. 455–456.

Sigel, Roberta S. "Citizens' Committees—Advice versus Consent," *Transaction*, Vol. 4 (May 1967), pp. 47–52.

Silverman, Jane and Constance Whitaker, "Regional Government: To More and More People It's the Way to Define Urban America and Help Solve its Problems," *Journal of Housing*, Vol. 30 No. 1 (January 1973), pp. 23–36.

Simpson, Lawson. "The Pitiful History of the Pilot Neighborhood Center Program," *City*, Vol. 6, No. 2 (March–April 1972).

Slayton, William L. "Rehabilitation Potential Probed for Urban Renewal, Public Housing," *Journal of Housing*, Vol. 22 (December 1965).

Spiegel, Hans B. C. (ed.). *Citizen Participation in Urban Development: Volume I, Concepts and Issues*, Selected Readings Series 7 (Washington, D. C.: Center for Community Affairs, NTL Institute for Applied Behavioral Science, 1968).

Stanback, Thomas M., Jr. and Richard V. Knight. *The Metropolitan Economy* (New York: Columbia University Press, 1970).

Sternlieb, George. "Abandonment and Rehabilitation: What is to be Done?" in *Papers Submitted to Subcommittee on Housing Panels, Part 1*, Committee on Banking and Currency, House, 92d Cong., 1st Sess. (June 1971a) (Washington, D. C.: Government Printing Office, No. 55–294), pp. 315–372.

Sternlieb, George. "The City as a Sandbox" *Public Interest* (Fall 1971b) pp. 14–21.

Stigler, George J. "The Division of Labor is Limited by the Extent of the Market," *Journal of Political Economy*, Vol. LIX (June 1951), pp. 185–195.

Stokes, Charles J., and Philip Mintz, Hans von Gelder. "Economic Criteria for Urban Redevelopment," *American Journal of Economics and Sociology*, Vol. XXIV (July 1965), pp. 249–55.

Strange, John J. (ed.). Special Issue: "Citizens' Action in Model Cities and CAP Programs: Case Studies and Evaluation," *Public Administration Review*, Vol. XXXII (September 1972), pp. 377–470.

Stuart, Darwyn G. *Strategy Analysis in Urban Planning: Evaluating Model Cities Alternatives*. Unpublished Dissertation. Northwestern University (1969). Abstract on page 4582 of Vol. 3010A of Dissertation Abstracts. University Microfilms Order No. 70–6540.

Tabb, William K. *The Political Economy of the Black Ghetto* (New York: W. W. Norton & Company, 1970).

Tabb, William K. "A Cost Benefit Analysis of Location Subsidies for Ghetto Neighborhoods," *Land Economics*, Vol. XLVIII (February 1972), pp. 45–52.

Taeuber, Karl E. and Alma F. Taeuber. *Negroes in Cities* (Chicago: Aldine Publishing Company, 1965).

Terrell, Henry S. *The Fiscal Impact of Negroes on the Central Cities*. Unpublished Dissertation. Stanford University (1969). Abstract on page 1732 of Vol. 3005A of Dissertation Abstracts. University Microfilms Order No. 69–8291.

Thompson, Wilbur. "Internal and External Factors in the Development of Urban Economies," in Perloff and Wingo (1968), pp. 43–62.

Tompkins, Mary. "Data Tables" Compiled from the 1970 Census of Population and Housing, First count summary tapes (Boston: Boston Redevelopment Authority, December 1972).

Tompkins, Mary and Barbara Dumke, Margaret O'Brien, Alexander Ganz. *Boston's Population: Reversal of Two Decades of Population Decline: Rebirth of the City as a Place to Live: Emergence of New Age Structure and Neighborhood Patterns* (Boston: Boston Redevelopment Authority, July 1973).

Twentieth Century Fund. *CDCs: New Hope for the Inner City, Report of the Twentieth Century Task Force on Community Development Corporations* (New York: The Twentieth Century Fund, 1971a), with background paper by Geoffrey Faux.

Twentieth Century Fund. *Report of the Twentieth Century Task Force on Employment Problems of Black Youth* (New York: Praeger Publishers, 1971b).

United States Commission on Civil Rights. *Home Ownership for Lower Income Families: A Report on the Racial and Ethnic Impact of Section 235* (Washington, D. C.: Government Printing Office, 1971), Stock No. 0500–0061.

U. S., Congress, House, Committee on Banking and Currency. *Investigation and Hearings of Abuses in Federal Low- and Moderate-Income Housing Programs: Staff Recommendations,* Report No. 52 018, 91st Cong., 2d Sess. (Washington, D. C.: Government Printing Office, 1970).

U. S., Congress, House. *Message from the President of the United States: Recommendations for City Demonstration Programs.* (January 26, 1966), 89th Cong., 2d Sess. (Washington, D. C.: Government Printing Office 1970).

U. S., Congress, House, Select Subcommittee on Real Property Acquisition of the Committee on Public Works. *Study of the Compensation and Assistance for Persons Affected by Real Property Acquisition in Federal and Federally Assisted Programs,* Committee Printing No. 31, 88th Cong., 2d Sess. (Washington, D. C.: Government Printing Office, 1965).

U. S., Congress, Senate Subcommittee on Housing and Urban Affairs of the Committee on Banking and Currency. *Progress of the Model Cities Program, Hearings,* 91st Cong., 1st Sess. (June 6, 1969). (Washington, D. C.: Government Printing Office, 1969).

U. S., Department of Housing and Urban Development. *The Demonstration Cities Program,* Library of Congress, Legislative Reference Service (October 5, 1966).

U. S., Department of Housing and Urban Development. *Improving the Quality of Urban Life: A Program Guide to Model Neighborhoods in Demonstration Cities* (Washington, D. C.: Government Printing Office 1967).

U. S., Department of Housing and Urban Development. *The Model Cities Program: A Comparative Analysis of the Planning Process in Eleven Cities* (Washington, D. C.: Government Printing Office, 1970a).

U. S., Department of Housing and Urban Development. *Operation: Breakthrough* (Washington, D. C.: Government Printing Office 1970b).

U. S., Department of Housing and Urban Development. *Citizen Participation in the Model Cities Program.* Community Development Evaluation Series No. 2 (Washington, D. C.: Government Printing Office 1972a).

U. S., Department of Housing and Urban Development. *The Federal Grant Process—An Analysis of the Use of Supplemental and Categorical Funds in the Model Cities Program* Community Development Evaluation Series No. 10 (Washington, D. C.: Government Printing Office, August 1972b).

U. S., Department of Housing and Urban Development. *Planned Variations: First Year Survey,* Community Development Evaluation Series No. 7 (Washington, D. C.: Government Printing Office, October 1972c).

U. S., General Accounting Office. *Improvements Needed in Federal Agency Coordination and Participation in the Model Cities Program.* Report No. B–171500 (Washington, D. C.: U. S. General Accounting Office, January 14, 1972).

"Urban Renewal: In Review, In Prospect," *Journal of Housing,* Vol. 27, No. 9 (October 1970), pp. 468–469.

Vernon, Raymond. *The Changing Function of the Central City* (New York: Committee for Economic Development, 1959).

Vietorisz, Thomas and Bennett Harrison. *The Economic Development of Harlem* (New York: Praeger Publishers 1970).

Villecco, Marguerite. "Technology: Operation Breakthrough," *Architectural Forum,* Vol. CXXXIV, No. 4, pp. 58–62.

Vincent, Phillip E. *Public Expenditure Benefit Spillovers and the Central City Exploitation Thesis.* Unpublished dissertation. Stanford University, (1969). Abstract on page 3753 in Vol. 2911A of Dissertation Abstracts. University Microfilms Order No. 69–8291.

Washnis, George J. "An Overview of the Program's Progress," *Model Cities Service Center Bulletin* (NLC/USCM), Vol. 2, No. 9 (June 1971), pp. 77–80.

White, Kevin H. *Boston's Development Prospects, Commitment to the City's Future* (Boston: Boston Redevelopment Authority, January 1973).

White, Kevin H. *Boston's Outstanding Prospects: Commitment to the City's Growth* (Boston: Boston Redevelopment Authority, 1972).

Wilson, James Q. "Planning and Politics: Citizen Participation in Urban Renewal," *Journal of the American Institute of Planners,* Vol. XXXIX, No. 4 (November 1963), pp. 242–249. Also in Wilson (1966), pp. 407–421.

Wilson, James Q. "Urban Renewal Does Not Always Renew," *Harvard Today* (January 1965).

Wilson, James Q. (ed.). *Urban Renewal: The Record and the Controversy* (Cambridge: M.I.T. Press, 1966).

Wilson, James Q. (ed.). *Metropolitan Enigma* (Washington, D. C.: Chamber of Commerce of the U. S., 1967).

Wingo, Lowdon, Jr. "Urban Renewal: Objectives, Analyses, and Information Systems," in Werner Z. Hirsch (ed.) *Regional Accounts for Policy Decisions* (Baltimore: Johns Hopkins Press, 1969), pp. 1–29.

Winnick, Louis. "Economic Questions in Urban Redevelopment," *American Economic Review,* Vol. 51 (May 1961), pp. 290–8.

Winnick, Louis. "Place Prosperity vs. People Prosperity: Welfare Considerations in the Geographic Redistribution of Economic Activity," *Essays in Urban Land Economics* (Los Angeles: Real Estate Research Program University of California, 1966), pp. 273–283.

Yavitz, Boris and Thomas M. Stanback, Jr. *Electronic Data Processing in New York City: Lessons for Metropolitan Economics* (New York: Columbia University Press, 1967).

Zimmer, Basil G. *Rebuilding Cities* (Chicago: Quandrangle Books, 1964). Partially reprinted in Wilson (1966), pp. 380–403.

Part III

Programmatic Approach to Central City Development

Chapter Seven

The Programmatic Approach to Central City Development: Introduction

The preceding review in Parts I and II of the national experience with Title VII new towns intown, urban renewal, and model cities leads to one salient conclusion:

> Federally sponsored urban programs—especially those serving development functions such as redevelopment and the public provision of housing, jobs, and services in limited project situations—have not substantially reversed pronounced patterns of disinvestment in most, if not all, American central cities.

Similarly, any additional extension of the NTIT, urban renewal, or model cities type programs—regardless of whether funded directly through federal (or state) categorical grants-in-aid or indirectly through some form of revenue sharing—would merely constitute "more of the same."

While carrying over this established approach into the mid–1970s may be attractive politically and administratively, to do so would overlook the limitations of isolated projects on one side and attractive programmatic opportunities on the other. The governments of the United States are at a national watershed for instituting a second generation urban development approach. On the one hand, there has been an extended suspension of former national policy programs and project activity, while on the other, the first generation lessons with urban renewal, model cities, NTITs, and related programs have become apparent.

In clear contradistinction to the "more of the same" approach is the possibility of second generation urban development that would selectively incorporate and synthesize the best features of NTITs, urban renewal, and model cities into one comprehensive urban development program. Part III subsequently outlines the structure of such a second generation program, drawing on expert opinion, forward-looking proposals generated in Hartford, Connecticut (as well as in Chicago and Cleveland), and a very extensive study of developmental problems and potentialities in a major city—Los Angeles.

1. National Expert Opinion. As part of the UCLA research project, a number of experts who are recognized authorities in the problems, processes, and opportunities of central city development were surveyed. Their opinion was sampled through a two-step Delphi survey method which sought answers to *the* fundamental urban policy question of the 1970s—where should we as a nation go from here in terms of modernizing and revitalizing our central cities?

Their replies, reported in the next chapter, demonstrated a marked willingness to innovate in order to make the urban development process more efficient and more equitable. This was particularly evident in their receptivity toward urban development corporations and new finance methods, as well as in insisting upon a development strategy that would be both comprehensive and balanced. Such a strategy, it should be noted, would substantially deemphasize housing development, an apparently sharp break away from the conventional wisdom. In their view, housing should be one of numerous components of comprehensive central city development, and its relative importance should be determined locally, according to local needs and priorities, rather than being predetermined and handed down from Washington.

2. The Hartford Process. The most advanced, and thus prototype, NTIT development program in the United States is emerging as the Hartford Process. The Process, now underway for the Hartford, Connecticut central city and region, would selectively incorporate and synthesize NTITs, urban renewal, model cities, and related development programs. But it tends to go considerably farther in proposing an urban-regional development process guided by three objectives.

a) Promoting place prosperity. This would be accomplished by an economic, physical, and housing development strategy aimed at: reversing a declining central business district by retaining industry and introducing service (labor intensive) firms; developing a large, vacant site located nearby for industry; and renewing housing and infrastructure in a decaying, older residential section comprised of Blacks and less advantaged groups.

b) Promoting people prosperity. Economic and social strategies here would concentrate upon economic and job development to raise incomes of less advantaged workers. The income strategy would be supplemented by a "life support" system focusing on neighborhood service centers, education programs, health care and facilities, and the like.

c) Promoting comprehensive urban-regional development. The instrument for realizing the dual objectives of place and people prosperity would be a single comprehensive program of four components: economic and job development (model cities, urban renewal); service development (model cities), physical development (urban renewal), and housing development (subsidized housing, urban renewal). The program is under the centralized direction and management of a single developmental entity, a regional development corporation. Finance provisions are similarly innovative in stressing coordination and concentration of public investments in project areas according to a development program, and targeting investments so as to directly generate tax increments and indirectly raise worker purchasing power (income) to amortize capital improvement bonds.

3. Los Angeles Proposed NTIT.

An outgrowth of the UCLA research was to test its general application in a major city, one personally familiar to the researchers, so as to better discern the functional dynamics of a second generation development program. A possible Los Angeles new town intown policy and program is summarized in Chapters 10–12.

Like the Hartford Process, a Los Angeles NTIT would incorporate conceptually the three program objectives of promoting place prosperity, people prosperity, and comprehensive integrated development. Economically, it views the downtown as centrally located within a robust regional economy so that central city development and modernization would need to move with, rather than oppose, regional investment forces—unless massive urban development subsidies are presumed. Although Los Angeles's downtown is considerably less powerful economically and politically than traditional CBDs in eastern cities, it has an inherently strong development potential nurtured by its central location, a very large urban renewal project, the trend toward service industries, including major headquarters, and a potential mass transit system.

Accordingly, the downtown and certain other relatively "strong" areas would comprise a development sector ("resource and opportunity areas") to be functionally linked with high need ("primary impact") project areas. These linkages could avoid several first generation mistakes including: displacing the poor from their houses, jobs, and neighborhoods to make room for urban renewal; attempting job and economic development in the inner city under a "worst first" approach; and attempting to modernize the central city with thinly dispersed public investments and fragmented programs. Another advantage is that the scale of Los Angeles, which could absorb the Hartford region five times over, creates considerable intrajurisdictional flexibility for a city sponsored development corporation.

Limitations of Model I New Towns Intown

A feature of a second generation urban development program, in addition to selectively superseding prior efforts, would be the explicit statement and definition of development goals. Without such explicit goals, it is exceedingly difficult to: (a) analyze and evaluate the program while in process and to make on-line adjustments, and (b) determine the fidelity by which such goals were being interpreted and applied by HUD and related agencies. While the former observation is self-evident, the latter requires illustration.

The process of policy evolution, as Parts I and II demonstrated, was without enabling state legislation; and the Roosevelt Island project became bureaucratically entrapped, seeking not-to-be-had Title VII supplementary facilities grants (not the mortgage guarantee). Moreover, numerous other applications were bottled up in preapplication or application review processes. And as finally applied by HUD, all NTITs planned or proposed (except Hartford, Cleveland, and Chicago) are of the Model IA or IB type.

From an extensive review of preliminary and final NTIT applications for Title VII assistance and from the three case studies described in Part I, it seems evident that Model I new towns intown in most instances do not properly constitute the basis for comprehensive urban development sponsored either at national or local levels.

A Model IA project essentially entails development of a single large vacant or underutilized site normally located at some distance from the central city business district. Roosevelt Island and Fort Lincoln are examples. Accordingly, Model IA development is a direct function of relatively cheap land, already assembled, and under single prior ownership. Since such resources are extraordinarily rare in most American cities, a Model IA new town intown is a special case, cannot be replicated nationally, and thus should not be emphasized by HUD in distributing Title VII mortgage guarantees. Standing alone, a Model IA cannot be the basis for a local development program, except in unusual cases (especially in smaller cities).

Moreover, the development outputs of a Model IA project are inherently ambiguous and uncertain, because, as discussed above, the twin development goals of central city modernization and assisting the less advantaged (which progressively undergirded all federal urban programs) are not expressly incorporated in the HUD Guidelines. The outputs of Roosevelt Island and Fort Lincoln, in terms of comprehensive development and improvements in the lot of the less advantaged, are likely to be negligible, if not indiscernible, for the New York and Washington, D. C. metropolitan areas. (The Pontchartrain project for all practical purposes is a suburban new community which, due to the happenstance of jurisdictional boundaries, is located within the jurisdiction of the City of New Orleans.) Although a Model IA project would have meager development leverage, that does not minimize its potential as one type of new town intown *project* within an integrated, general development program.

The structural limitations of a Model IB NTIT are less evident, because such limitations are related to federal administration and project and metropolitan scale rather than availability of cheap, contiguous landholdings. A Model IB project involves redevelopment of a single, large site of underutilized land located within the central city. The structure of the San Antonio and Cedar–Riverside projects illustrates the potential of integrating urban renewal with new towns intown.

However, this kind of programmatic integration is (a) a hope rather than a requirement of federal policy, and (b), even if achieved, final outputs of

moving toward a national development policy characterized by two primary goals:

1. To stimulate modernization and revitalization of the decaying central city; and,
2. To stimulate the accessibility of less advantaged persons to standard housing, education, job, health, social services, and economic opportunities.

Logically, it can be said that the uncertain performance of the first generation programs might be attributable either to the fact that: (a) these two primary goals were inherently dysfunctional, or (b) the programs expressing these two goals were inadequately conceived, interpreted, applied, and/or financed. While the former has never been given a meaningful national test, there is ample evidence of the latter failure in program design and execution. And inadequate program conception, interpretation, administration, and/or finance would necessarily preclude a fair test validating the twin goals of modernizing the central city while upgrading opportunities for the less advantaged.

The Title VII new town intown program illustrates the case in point. Here, the twin development goals are functionally implied in the 1970 Housing and Urban Development Act, but are inadequately conceived, interpreted, funded, and applied. In the legislation the Congress declared national policy should:

> . . . refine the role of the federal government in *revitalizing existing communities and encouraging planned, large-scale urban* and new community *development* . . .

> . . . *treat comprehensively* the problems of *poverty and employment* (including erosion of tax bases, and the need for better community *services and job opportunities*) which are associated with *disorderly urbanization*. . . (Emphasis added.).

As interpreted by HUD, however, this declaration of legislative policy, while obviously developmental in thrust, loses something in translation into the federal guidelines for Title VII NTITs. Rather than refine the legislative policy, the Guidelines merely hint at them in oblique fashion: a Title VII new town intown " . . . must contribute to the social and economic welfare of the entire area which it will importantly affect" (HUD Office of New Communities Guidelines 720.6 (a) (3)).

As funded and otherwise encouraged by HUD, only one NTIT (Cedar–Riverside) has received (as of mid–1974) any federal financial assistance under Title VII. The Fort Lincoln project became ensnarled in GSA land appraisal methods and various financing issues; the San Antonio project was disabled

these projects cannot be assumed to constitute a comprehensive urban development program. The former observations require some additional elaboration.

Because the federal new town intown program emerged legislatively *after* urban renewal, model cities, and subsidized housing, it necessarily made some assumptions distinguishing it from its predecessors. The Congressional Record indicates that new towns intown, although spawned in political compromise, could serve three purposes:

1. To enlarge generally the scope and content of existing central city development programs;
2. To overcome recognized problems with the urban renewal, model cities, and housing programs;
3. To be supplemented by urban renewal in providing funding and land assembly powers for urban development flowing under Title I.

Thus, a federal NTIT program under Title VII, if integrated with urban renewal, model cities, and housing programs, logically could have been the foundation for a second generation approach—provided the twin development goals underlying all federal urban programs were openly acknowledged and made to be controlling factors.

In addition, some of that potential can be glimpsed at the Cedar–Riverside and San Antonio projects, as the case studies indicate. However, the development potential of Model IB projects is also clearly a direct function of project and metropolitan scale. Thus, while SANT could have profound effects upon assisting less advantaged populations in downtown San Antonio as well as modernizing the central business district, it would have negligible impacts upon a large city (similarly, for Cedar–Riverside). As a result of HUD's administration of NTITs and urban renewal, particularly in distributing financial and program incentives, Model IB new towns intown are structurally constrained to small to medium size American cities. It is doubtful that Congress intended that Title VII be so interpreted and applied as to inherently exclude significant application in large cities. But like a Model IA project, Model IB NTITs could be primary components in comprehensive urban development programs.

Features of a Second Generation Programmatic Approach to Urban Development

A second generation national urban development program should be organized differently than the present new town intown effort to encourage citywide (and possibly even regionwide) programs of the type evolved in Hartford (and of the kind suggested for Los Angeles in a later chapter). Such a program could be expected to encompass these features: (1) provide for a local selected balance among key development components, including economic development (jobs), housing, physical development, and services; (2) provide for the incorporation of individual projects (of the Model IA and IB variety) into what we have called Model II development programs; and (3) establish an adequate and *long-term* commitment to urban development in American cities, with effective stimulus to required institutional and financial support.

These features will be developed in the chapters that follow as we outline the views of the experts, review the proposals in the prototype Model II (Hartford), and establish what is needed in a major effort to modernize a large American city (Los Angeles).

Chapter Eight

Lessons from the Experts

Introductory Summary

In order to tap existing reservoirs of knowledge concerning intown development, a policy "Delphi" was conducted as part of the new town intown study. Believing the personal experiences of those intimately involved with central city revitalization could provide valuable insights, the Delphi technique was employed to give each participant a vehicle for expressing his views and making inputs to the overall evaluative effort.

The Delphi approach was selected because it is a means of systematically contacting a significant number of knowledgeable persons in a short period of time. Moreover, since the Delphi technique is a cumulative process in which individual inputs are (anonymously) fed back to all participants, each "expert" contacted has the opportunity to reevaluate the positions he has taken in the first round in the light of this feedback. The Delphi can thus be used to evaluate and stimulate a consensus and spread of opinion among the "expert" population being sampled.

The Delphi was designed to complement other sources of information on new towns intown with a more structured instrument whose output was suitable for statistical interpretation.

The Delphi was carried out in two distinct rounds, with each round consisting of the completion and mail return of a written questionnaire. The first questionnaire was aimed at gaining a general impression of the range of opinion about major issues; the second was far more specific, with the participants asked to evaluate a series of policy statements derived from the results of the first round. The sample population contacted via the Delphi involved 67 individuals, with a response rate of about 55 percent for each round.

Detailed discussions of all aspects of the Delphi are contained in the following sections. Very briefly, however, several policy conclusions which stood out, due to the unanimity of support among those contacted during the Delphi exercise, can be mentioned.

In terms of the *objectives of future central city revitalization programs,* most respondents agreed there was need for a *"multifocus"* program approach to central city revitalization. Narrowly defined efforts were felt by many to be dysfunctional. More specifically, a substantial majority indicated that the traditional emphasis on housing in and of itself may have been misplaced; most agreed it should not be the first priority objective of the new town intown program (due to the need for more broadly defined objectives).

A consensus of opinion also appeared regarding several important issues related to *institutional arrangements for new town intown efforts* and central city revitalization in general. There was wide agreement that effective central city programs require a wide array of legal and financial powers, most notably the power of eminent domain, the ability to write down cost of land, and the ability to subsidize costs in other areas. A majority (though not all) of the respondents indicated a *public development corporation* of some sort offered considerable potential to actually administer and carry out effective programs of central city revitalization. In addition to innovations at the local level, the need for revision of the decision making process involved in obtaining federal financial support was also universally acknowledged.

In terms of *financing* new town intown programs, there was also general agreement on several issues. It was almost unanimously asserted that a successful national program of central city revitalization cannot be carried out without sizable direct federal subsidies. It was further agreed that federal Title VII loan guarantees (unsupported by other public funding) are insufficient to finance a meaningful new town intown program, due to the scale of the costs involved. In a related area, many respondents expressed an interest in the potential of a development bank of some type to supply additional financial support for public central city development efforts.

Summary of Responses to Round I

Of the 67 Round I Delphi questionnaires distributed to persons knowledgeable of central city development, 41 had been returned by the final deadline.[a] Of these, 37 were in usable form (3 were filled out incorrectly; 1 was returned blank with a note indicating dissatisfaction with the form and content of the questionnaire).

Sufficient returns were received from persons belonging to three of the subgroups to warrant tabulation of their responses as well. The rate of returns for each subgroup was as follows:

---

a. A list of the participants is contained in Attachment B.

Subgroup	No. Distributed	No. Returned
Academicians and Researchers	22	14
Local Government Officials	15	9
State Government Officials ·	5	2
National Government Officials	8	1
Private Developers, Builders, Consultants	17	8
"Other" categories or not classifiable	–	3
Total Sample	67	37[b]

The results of the Round I Delphi are summarized in Tables 8–1 thru 8–4. Each chart reports group attitudes, for the total sample and three of the subgroups within the sample, for a given issue (objectives, funding, etc.)[c] Summaries of typical comments appear in Attachment A.

Very briefly, the results of Round I of the UCLA–NTIT Delphi were as follows:

TABLE 8–1. FUTURE PRIORITIES FOR CENTRAL CITY DEVELOPMENT PROGRAMS

As can be seen in Table 8–1, the sample believed *upgrading urban services* to be the highest priority objective of public central city development programs, followed by the need to *arrest physical decay* as the second priority and to *create employment* opportunity the third priority objective. Each of the subgroups contained within the total sample identified these objectives as being of primary importance, although with differing orderings of priority. Local government officials gave *arresting physical decay* as their highest priority objective while academics felt *creation of employment opportunity for the disadvantaged* should be the highest priority objective.

Comments associated with this issue indicate many felt no one objective should be singled out, arguing the complexity of central city problems requires solutions which involve a broadly based attack on many fronts.

TABLE 8–2. FUTURE PRIORITIES FOR FUNDING CENTRAL CITY DEVELOPMENT PROGRAMS

In regard to sources of funds for public central city development programs, the responses of the various subgroups were quite similar, both to each others'

b. An additional four returns were not in usable form.
c. Group priorities were determined by arbitrarily assigning a value of 5 points to each 1st priority choice, 4 points to each 2nd priority choice, 3 points to each 3rd priority choice, 2 points to each 4th priority choice, and 1 point to each 5th priority choice. The policy alternative with the highest overall total point count was rated as the 1st priority choice for the group, the second highest as the 2nd priority choice, and so forth. See Attachment I–A for additional details.

responses as well as the responses of the sample as a whole. The total sample singled out *direct federal subsidies* as the most important financing tool, with federal insuring of loans second, direct *state subsidies* third, and *property tax incentives* fourth in importance. Only developers answered differently, assigning *property tax incentives* the first priority in their estimation. The only other notable difference of opinion among the subgroups was the academic subgroup's emphasis on *special revenue sharing* as a high priority source of funds for central city development programs.

Again, comments stressed the need for a flexible system of financing, utilizing a variety of sources in a mix appropriate to each local situation.

TABLE 8–3. PRIORITIES OF ALTERNATIVE INSTITUTIONAL ARRANGEMENTS FOR CENTRAL CITY DEVELOPMENT PROGRAMS

With the exception of local government officials, each subgroup's responses agreed with the total sample's opinion that a *locally based public development corporation* was the most effective of the possible institutional arrangements for public inner city development programs, with *a combination of private development corporation working with a local government agency* the second most effective. Local government officials indicated they believe the *local public renewal authority* is the most effective institutional arrangement.

Comments indicated "optimal" institutional arrangements ultimately depend on the needs and resources of the local situation, arguing a mechanism effective in one situation may prove unworkable under other conditions in another locale.

TABLE 8–4. PRIORITIES OF LEGAL AND FINANCIAL POWERS FOR CENTRAL CITY DEVELOPMENT PROGRAMS

Opinions regarding the relative importance of legal and financial powers were generally uniform for the total sample and the subgroups. All groups identified *the power of eminent domain* as the single most important power. All groups except academics identified *the ability to write down the cost of land* as the second in importance. Academics, however, assigned their second priority to *the ability to subsidize public service improvements*. Both developers and academics felt *local government cooperation* was third in importance, unlike the sample as a whole, which voted for *the power to issue bonds* as their third priority choice.

Comments stressed that no single power in isolation could prove very effective. Only with a combination of powers could much success be attained in developing central city areas.

Summary of Responses to Round II
The second (and final) round of the Delphi was distributed to 66 persons especially knowledgeable in the area of central city revitalization. The

Table 8–1. Future Priorities for Central City Development Programs: Priority Choices by Group

BASED ON OUR EXPERIENCE IN URBAN RENEWAL, MODEL CITIES, AND OTHER LARGE SCALE URBAN DEVELOPMENT EFFORTS, PUBLIC CENTRAL CITY DEVELOPMENT PROGRAMS SHOULD EMPHASIZE:	Priority Choices by Group			
	Total Sample	Academicians, Researchers	Developers, Builders	Local Government Officials
	(n = 37)	(n = 14)	(n = 8)	(n = 9)
1. Upgrading the public and private services available to central city residents	FIRST	SECOND	FIRST	SECOND
2. Increasing the supply of housing in general				
3. Increasing the supply of housing for the disadvantaged				
4. Creating employment opportunities in general	Third* tie	Fourth* tie	SECOND* tie	Third
5. Creating employment opportunities for the disadvantaged	Third* tie	FIRST	SECOND* tie	
6. Financing net additional private development in the central city (beyond what would be the case otherwise)				
7. Arresting the physical decline of the central city	SECOND	Third		FIRST
8. Attracting higher income families back to the central city				
9. Achieving a high level of racial mix				
10. Achieving a high level of income mix			Fourth	
11. Encouraging the dispersal of the disadvantaged of the central city to other areas of the region				
12. Improving the fiscal position of the central city government	Fifth	Fourth* tie	Fifth	Fourth

Table 8–2.   Future Priorities for Funding Central City Development Programs: Priority Choices by Group

BASED ON OUR EXPERIENCE IN URBAN RENEWAL, MODEL CITIES, AND OTHER LARGE SCALE URBAN DEVELOPMENT PROGRAMS, THE MOST IMPORTANT SOURCES OF FUNDS FOR *PUBLIC* CENTRAL CITY DEVELOPMENT PROGRAMS SHOULD INCLUDE:	Priority Choices by Group			
	Total Sample (n = 37)	Academicians, Researchers (n = 14)	Developers, Builders (n = 9)	Local Government Officials (n = 8)
1. Federally insured low interest rate loans	SECOND	Fourth	SECOND* tie	SECOND
2. Direct federal subsidies (grants for land purchase, facilities, etc.)	FIRST	FIRST	SECOND* tie	FIRST
3. Federal loans				
4. Loans by private lending institutions				
5. Private equity investment				
6. Municipal bonds				
7. Special tax assessments				
8. Tax increment financing				
9. General revenue sharing				
10. Special revenue sharing	Fifth	SECOND* tie		
11. Financed by corporations				
12. Property tax incentives	Fourth		FIRST	Fourth
13. Income tax incentives				
14. Direct state subsidies (grants for land purchase, facilities, etc.)	Third	SECOND* tie		Third

Table 8–3. Priorities of Alternative Institutional Arrangements for Central City Development Programs: Priority Choices by Group

BASED ON OUR EXPERIENCE IN URBAN RENEWAL, MODEL CITIES, AND OTHER LARGE SCALE URBAN DEVELOPMENT EFFORTS, THE MOST EFFECTIVE INSTITUTIONAL ARRANGEMENTS FOR *PUBLIC* CENTRAL CITY DEVELOPMENT PROGRAMS ARE:	*Priority Choices by Group*			
	Total Sample (n = 37)	*Academicians, Researchers* (n = 14)	*Developers, Builders* (n = 8)	*Local Government Officials* (n = 9)
1. A locally based *public* development corporation	FIRST	FIRST	FIRST	SECOND
2. A locally based *private* development corporation	Fourth		Fifth	FIRST
3. The local public renewal authority				Fourth
4. The local city government		Fourth		
5. The local county government				
6. The state government				
7. A state development corporation	Fifth	Fifth	Third	
8. A federal agency				
9. A combination of a private development corporation working with a local governmental agency	SECOND	SECOND	SECOND	Third
10. A state development corporation working with some private or public local unit	Third	Third	Fourth	

Table 8–4. Priorities of Legal and Financial Powers for Central City Development Programs: Priority Choices by Group

BASED ON OUR EXPERIENCE WITH URBAN RENEWAL, MODEL CITIES, AND OTHER LARGE SCALE URBAN DEVELOPMENT EFFORTS, THE MOST IMPORTANT LEGAL AND FINANCIAL POWERS FOR *PUBLIC* CENTRAL CITY DEVELOPMENT PROGRAMS ARE:	*Priority Choices by Group*			
	Total Sample	*Academicians, Researchers*	*Developers, Builders*	*Local Government Officials*
	(n = 37)	*(n = 14)*	*(n = 8)*	*(n = 9)*
1. The power of eminent domain	FIRST	FIRST	FIRST	FIRST
2. The ability to write down the cost of land	SECOND	Fourth* tie	SECOND	SECOND
3. The power to issue bonds	Third	Fourth* tie	Fourth	Third* tie
4. The power to tax				
5. The power to override local zoning ordinances				
6. The power to override local building codes				
7. The ability to subsidize public service improvements	Fourth* tie	SECOND		
8. The power of tax increment financing				
9. The power to assure cooperation from local government agencies		Third	Third	
10. The power to assemble and hold land for future use	Fourth* tie	Fourth* tie		Third

sample included persons contacted during the first round (whether they had actually responded or not) in order to get as representative a reaction as feasible. Thirty-one questionnaires had been returned in usable form by the cutoff date. As was the case in Round I, sufficient replies were received to justify compilation of the responses of three subgroups within the sample: academicians (and researchers), local government officials, and private developers (including builders and private consultants). The returns for each subgroup follows:

Subgroup	No. Distributed	No. Returned
Academicians and Researchers	22	11
Local Government Officials	14	6
Private Developers, Builders, Consultants	17	12
Others[d]	13	2
Total Sample	66	31

The first round Delphi had identified many major areas of concern among those sampled. The second round was designed to measure the degree of concensus regarding a series of (hypothetical) policy statements directed at HUD, based on the areas of concern singled out by the Delphi Round I responses and other sources.[e] Respondents were asked to evaluate each statement on a five point scale ($+2$ = Strongly Agree to -2 Strongly Disagree) and then to justify their evaluation. Table 8—5 summarizes the results, noting the numerical spread of the responses, the mean response, and the standard deviation about the mean, for the total sample and the three major subgroups. A representative sampling of justifications and other comments relating to each policy statement are contained in Attachment A.

Summary of Responses

A. Program Objectives
(1) "Primary Objectives of a New Towns Intown Program"
Based on the response to Round I, three objectives were most often identified as deserving a high priority in publically supported programs of central city revitalization: a) upgrading public and private services; b) arresting physical decline; and c) creating employment opportunities. The importance of these objectives to the sample group was substantiated in Round II. The vast majority of the respondents in all subgroups support these programs objectives, although the creation of jobs was seen as somewhat less important judging by the some-

d. Includes state and national officials, and those not readily classifiable.
e. Primarily lengthy, private interviews, both with some of those belonging to the Delphi sample as well as other experts.

what less positive "vote." One academician argued creation of employment should be viewed as a "concomitant rather than a primary objective."

Among those disagreeing with the primacy of these three objectives, most did not appear to oppose them so much as they argued in favor of a wider, more flexible interpretation of the role of the new town intown program. As one private developer remarked, "The NTIT program must be full and flexible enough to respond to your three needs and many others, the priority varying from place to place and time to time."

(2)   "Role of Housing in the New Town Intown Program"

Increasing the supply of housing, either in general or specifically for the less advantaged, was assigned little importance as an NTIT objective in the first round of the Delphi. To test the apparently low value placed upon housing among the sample groups, a hypothetical recommendation to HUD, suggesting that housing not be assigned first priority in the NTIT program of central city revitalization, was included in Round II. A sizable majority of all subgroups supported this negative statement although a significant minority registered their disagreement. Comments associated with this recommendation indicated opinions regarding the importance of housing were more a matter of intuitive feeling rather than any sort of reasoned argument, with some arguing housing "had to be" the first priority objective while many others maintained other goals were more desirable.

Several comments indicated the question was not so much whether housing was, or was not, a desirable objective; rather, opposition was based on the realization that a more broadly based definition of NTIT objectives may be called for. Rather than "just another housing project," the role, and potential, of the new towns intown program was rated much higher. As one local government official argued "Housing is one of the 10 or 11 crucial life support systems of a community—NTIT should aim at all of them." Concurring with this, an academician noted, "[housing] is a next to the top priority—top item is initiation of comprehensive development *process.*"

B.   Funding Sources
(3)   "Potential of Title VII Loan Guarantees"

A key issue addressed in the evaluation of the new town intown program was the overall usefulness of Title VII loan guarantees as a means of funding revitalization efforts. Since so many of the individuals contacted in the course of our research questioned the worth of this approach (when unsupported *by other public funding*), the following (hypothetical) policy statement was posited in the Round II Delphi:

> At best, a new town intown program of inner city revitalization involving only federal loan guarantees (that is, no housing subsidies,

no capital grants, and so forth) will be only a minor or peripheral element in the revitalization of America's central cities.

There was practically unanimous agreement among all subgroups that this is indeed the case. Only two (one a private consultant and one local government official) of the 31 participants who responded expressed a negative opinion, apparently arguing that "every little bit helps." Twenty-two persons indicated strong agreement with the statement while another 7 indicated mild agreement.

(4) "Need for Direct Federal Subsidies"

As a followup to policy statement No. 3 (discussed above), the role of direct federal transfers of funds in the financing of central city revitalization efforts was explored in policy statement No. 4 which made the following claim:

A successful national program of central city revitalization cannot be carried without direct federal subsidies.

There was general agreement that this statement was a valid evaluation, with 22 persons expressing strong agreement and another 3 indicating mild agreement. Every local government official responding expressed strong agreement with the statement. Again, there were 2 dissenters, both private developers, who argued private or some other funding might take the place of federal subsidies. In essence, it was agreed effective central city revitalization requires considerable public funds and that the federal government was the most logical source of these funds.

C. Institutional Arrangements

(5) "Effectiveness of a Locally Based Public Development Corporation for Administering NTIT Programs"

Based on the priority choices made in the Round I Delphi, the single most effective institutional arrangement for the administration of a NTIT program of central city revitalization is a locally based public development corporation. Statement No. 5 of the Round II Delphi allowed participants to reassess this evaluation. Results indicated the majority of the sample still supported this conclusion although a significant number voiced uncertainty.

There was an interesting reversal between Round I and II. Local government officials, who had assigned first priority to the local renewal authority as the most desirable NTIT lead agency in Round I, generally changed their opinion, switching their support to the locally based public development corporation approach. The exact reasons for this reevaluation were uncertain since their positive "vote" was unsupported with comments or qualifications.

Although few actually reacted negatively to this policy statement, a sizable minority within the sample voiced uncertainty (7 out of 28). Comments by some of those who indicated "uncertainty" suggested definitive statements were not appropriate here because the "most effective institutional arrangement" would vary from locality to locality. Several others suggested there would be considerable political difficulties in most metropolitan areas in actually implementing an effective locally based public development corporation.

Three of the sample (a private consultant, a developer, and a local government official) disagreed with this statement. They suggested that other existing institutions, both public and private, were more desirable and more politically feasible.

(6) "Regional Approach Involving Linked Projects"

The value of, and need for, a programmatic, as opposed to a project oriented, approach to central city revitalization was discussed by many of the experts contacted, through the Delphi and via other channels. Policy statement No. 6 was included to sample group opinion as to the merits of a "programmatic, regional approach to development of a new town intown, involving linked, mutually interdependent projects." As can be seen in Table 8–5, Statement No. 6 evoked a mixed response, with a sizable minority indicating either uncertainty or dissent. Opinions were equally divided in each of the subgroups.

For those who favored the idea of a regional, programmatic approach, their evaluation often included the question of scale. Comments included:

> Very small areas are "too" open to be able to transmit much growth internally (low multipliers) or to be able to support a diversity of activities. . . . Interdependence increases local multiplier effects and strengthens sense of community (Academician).

> The solution must be in scale with the problems (Private developer).

> The public investment portfolio must contain at least five major investment categories: 1) reclamation of the ghetto; 2) rehabilitation and conservation of gray areas; 3) containing and reordering suburban growth; 4) expanding the job base; and 5) equalizing tax burdens (Private consultant).

In stating the case against this policy recommendation, dissenters emphasized the political and administrative difficulties of actually carrying out a regional programmatic NTIT program, and/or the dangers of diluting the effort. Typical comments included:

> Too complicated for American Institutions (Academician).

> A very long term solution! There are few governments capable of a regional approach (Private developer).

> . . . the required time for completion will amount to several years. It

is unrealistic to expect continuing support . . . (Local government official).

If by 'regional' you mean suburban, forget it. This gives the game away, and, in my experience is a thin disguise for antiurban and anticentral attitudes (Private consultant).

(7) "Regional Focus, re Impacts"
(8) "Regional Focus, re Linked Projects"
(9) "Regional Focus, re Regional Development Corporation"

Statements No. 7, No. 8 and No. 9 were included to further define attitudes among the sample population regarding the appropriate regional focus for a major NTIT effort. There was generally wide agreement among the sample and the various groups with policy statement No. 7, which concerned the need for careful consideration of the relationships existing between a NTIT and surrounding region. However, the practical applicability of the assertion was questioned at times, with some respondents claiming "truism " "platitude," and the like.

There was considerable disagreement about the validity of policy statements No. 8 and No. 9. Recommendation No. 8 dealt with the concept of "linked projects." While more respondents agreed than disagreed with this statement, the largest number of "votes" was registered in the "uncertain" column (see Table 8–5, Statement No. 8). Most of these apparently felt generalizations in this area were not appropriate—that the local context was the key element.

Among those supporting Statement No. 8, their opinions were generally again related to the question of adequate scale, critical mass, and so forth. Those who rejected the statement argued against "simplistic" answers.

The general utility of a strong regional development agency or corporation to administer a new town intown program was assessed in Statement No. 9. The view was disputed by the majority of those who responded. Comments on this issue were surprisingly few, with the chief concern again being with the need to consider the "local context." There were also fears expressed concerning diluting overall effort, the central city losing out to the suburbs, and doubts about the political feasibility of such an institutional arrangement.

D. Powers
(10) "Necessary Powers for NTIT Development Entity"

Statement No. 10 was included to allow participants to reassess the priorities they assigned to legal and financial powers in Round I of the new town intown Delphi. In the first round, the three most important powers identified were "the power of eminent domain, "the ability to write down cost of land," and "the ability to lower other capital and operating costs to competitive levels." As can be seen by the Round II results (see Table 8–5, Statement

Table 8–5.   Summary of Responses to Policy Recommendations*

A.   Program Objectives

Statement No. 1:   The primary objectives of a New Town Intown program of inner city revitalization should be to:

a)   upgrade public and private services available to inner city residents

	Agree +2	+1	Uncertain 0	−1	Disagree −2	Mean	Standard Deviation
Total Sample	14	11	–	1	2	+1.2	1.1
Academicians Researchers	6	5	–	–	–	+1.6	.5
Local Government Officials	–	3	–	1	1	0.0	1.4
Private Developers Builders, Consultants	7	2	–	–	1	+1.4	1.3

b)   arrest physical decline of the inner city

	Agree +2	+1	Uncertain 0	−1	Disagree −2	Mean	Standard Deviation
Total Sample	14	11	3	1	2	+1.1	1.1
Academicians Researchers	3	7	1	–	–	+1.2	.6
Local Government Officials	5	–	–	–	1	+1.3	1.6
Private Developers Builders, Consultants	5	4	1	1	1	+ .9	1.3

c)   create additional employment activities

	Agree +2	+1	Uncertain 0	−1	Disagree −2	Mean	Standard Deviation
Total Sample	14	7	3	3	2	+1.0	1.3
Academicians Researchers	6	2	1	2	–	+1.1	1.2
Local Government Officials	1	2	1	–	1	+ .4	1.5
Private Developers Builders, Consultants	6	3	1	–	1	+1.2	1.2

Statement No. 2:   Although of importance, increasing the supply of housing should *not* be a first priority objective of a New Town Intown program of inner city revitalization.

	Agree +2	+1	Uncertain 0	−1	Disagree −2	Mean	Standard Deviation
Total Sample	12	10	–	2	7	+0.6	1.6
Academicians Researchers	3	3	–	1	4	0.0	1.8
Local Government Officials	4	1	–	–	1	+1.2	1.6
Private Developers Builders, Consultants	4	6	–	1	1	+0.9	1.2

*Totals include responses from "other group" not included in categories indicated. Therefore, items shown sometimes do not add to "total".

B. Funding Sources

Statement No. 3: At best, a New Town Intown program of inner city revitalization involving only federal loan guarantees (that is, no housing subsidies, no capital grants, etc.) will be only a minor or peripheral element in the revitalization of America's inner cities.

	Agree +2	+1	Uncertain 0	−1	Disagree −2	Mean	Standard Deviation
Total Sample	22	7	–	–	2	+1.5	1.0
Academicians Researchers	9	2	–	–	–	+1.8	0.4
Local Government Officials	3	2	–	–	1	+1.0	1.6
Private Developers Builders, Consultants	8	3	–	–	1	+1.4	1.2

Statement No. 4: A successful national program of central city revitalization cannot be carried out without direct federal subsidies.

	Agree +2	+1	Uncertain 0	−1	Disagree −2	Mean	Standard Deviation
Total Sample	24	3	1	1	1	+1.6	1.0
Academicians Researchers	9	2	–	–	–	+1.8	.4
Local Government Officials	6	–	–	–	–	+2.0	0.0
Private Developers Builders, Consultants	8	1	1	1	–	+1.5	1.0

C. Institutional Arrangements

Statement No. 5: In general, a locally based *public* development corporation would be the most effective institutional arrangement for the administration of a New Town Intown program of inner city revitalization.

	Agree +2	+1	Uncertain 0	−1	Disagree −2	Mean	Standard Deviation
Total Sample	13	7	7	3	1	+.9	1.2
Academicians Researchers	4	5	2	–	–	+1.2	.8
Local Government Officials	2	1	2	1	–	+ .7	1.2
Private Developers Builders, Consultants	6	1	2	2	1	+ .8	1.5

Statement No. 6: In general, a programmatic, regional approach to development of a New Town, involving linked, mutually interdependent projects, will be more effective than a single project covering a limited contiguous area or a series of isolated projects.

	Agree +2	+1	Uncertain 0	−1	Disagree −2	Mean	Standard Deviation
Total Sample	13	4	7	6	1	+.7	1.3
Academicians Researchers	4	2	3	2	–	+.7	1.2
Local Government Officials	2	–	2	2	–	+.3	1.4
Private Developers Builders, Consultants	5	2	2	2	1	+.7	.5

Statement No. 7: In planning a New Town Intown program, careful consideration should be directed to the impacts the program will have upon the surrounding region and the impacts the region will have upon the New Town Intown.

	Agree +2	+1	Uncertain 0	−1	Disagree −2	Mean	Standard Deviation
Total Sample	18	8	2	1	1	+1.4	1.0
Academicians Researchers	4	3	2	−	1	+ .9	1.3
Local Government Officials	4	1	−	1	−	+1.3	1.2
Private Developers Builders, Consultants	8	4	−	−	−	+1.7	.5

Statement No. 8: A successful New Town Intown program of inner city revitalization should involve linked projects, some in town and some in other areas of the region.

	Agree +2	+1	Uncertain 0	−1	Disagree −2	Mean	Standard Deviation
Total Sample	9	1	12	5	4	+.2	1.4
Academicians Researchers	3	−	6	−	2	+.2	1.4
Local Government Officials	1	−	3	2	−	0.0	1.1
Private Developers Builders, Consultants	5	1	1	3	2	+.3	1.7

Statement No. 9: For greatest effectiveness, a New Town Intown program of inner city revitalization should be under the administration of a strong regional development agency or corporation.

	Agree +2	+1	Uncertain 0	−1	Disagree −2	Mean	Standard Deviation
Total Sample	6	4	6	9	5	−.1	1.4
Academicians Researchers	1	1	4	3	1	−.2	1.1
Local Government Officials	3	−	−	2	1	+.3	1.9
Private Developers Builders, Consultants	2	2	1	4	3	−.3	1.5

D. Powers

Statement No. 10: In order to successfully carry out a New Town Intown program of inner city revitalization, the development entity should possess:

a) the power of eminent domain

	Agree +2	+1	Uncertain 0	−1	Disagree −2	Mean	Standard Deviation
Total Sample	25	2	−	1	−	+1.8	.6
Academicians Researchers	11	−	−	−	−	+2.0	0.0
Local Government Officials	5	1	−	−	−	+1.8	.4
Private Developers Builders, Consultants	10	1	−	1	−	+1.7	.9

b)   the ability to write down the cost of land

	Agree +2	+1	Uncertain 0	−1	Disagree −2	Mean	Standard Deviation
Total Sample	21	5	1	1	−	+1.6	.8
Academicians Researchers	5	3	1	1	−	+1.2	1.0
Local Government Officials	5	1	−	−	−	+1.8	.4
Private Developers, Builders, Consultants	9	2	−	−	−	+1.8	.4

c)   the ability to lower other capital and operating costs to competitive levels

	Agree +2	+1	Uncertain 0	−1	Disagree −2	Mean	Standard Deviation
Total Sample	17	8	3	−	−	+1.5	.7
Academicians Researchers	5	4	−	−	−	+1.6	.5
Local Government Officials	5	1	−	−	−	+1.8	.4
Private Developers Builders, Consultants	6	2	3	−	−	+1.3	.9

E. Other Recommendations

Statement No. 11:   The current HUD guideline requiring that the on-site resident income mix approximate the income mix of the population of the surrounding SMSA is too rigid and should be replaced with a more flexible set of criteria.

	Agree +2	+1	Uncertain 0	−1	Disagree −2	Mean	Standard Deviation
Total Sample	15	6	3	3	3	+ .9	1.4
Academicians Researchers	3	1	2	1	3	0.0	1.7
Local Government Officials	4	1	1	−	−	+1.5	.8
Private Developers Builders, Consultants	6	4	−	2	−	+1.2	1.1

Statement No. 12:   Development of income class-integrated New Town Intown communities without housing subsidies is not feasible, except under unusual or extremely fortunate conditions.

	Agree +2	+1	Uncertain 0	−1	Disagree −2	Mean	Standard Deviation
Total Sample	25	2	2	1	1	+1.6	1.0
Academicians Researchers	9	1	−	−	1	+1.6	1.2
Local Government Officials	5	1	−	−	−	+1.8	.4
Private Developers Builders, Consultants	9	−	2	1	−	+1.4	1.1

Statement No. 13:   Utilization of innovative building techniques is *not* an effective means of lowering housing costs to levels where housing subsidies would not be required.

	Agree +2	+1	Uncertain 0	−1	Disagree −2	Mean	Standard Deviation
Total Sample	19	5	4	3	—	+1.3	1.0
Academicians Researchers	8	2	1	—	—	+1.6	.7
Local Government Officials	5	—	—	1	—	+1.5	1.2
Private Developers Builders, Consultants	4	3	3	2	—	+ .8	1.1

Statement No. 14:   Given the high cost of land in the inner city, a New Town Intown program of inner city revitalization should contemplate unusually high densities.

	Agree +2	+1	Uncertain 0	−1	Disagree −2	Mean	Standard Deviation
Total Sample	8	7	3	8	4	+.2	1.5
Academicians Researchers	4	3	—	2	1	+.7	1.5
Local Government Officials	2	—	—	2	2	−.3	1.9
Private Developers Builders, Consultants	2	4	3	3	—	+.4	1.1

Statement No. 15:   Given the limited amount of open or vacant land in most cities, a New Town Intown development program should contemplate projects which rely strongly on housing conservation and rehabilitation in lieu of construction of new units.

	Agree +2	+1	Uncertain 0	−1	Disagree −2	Mean	Standard Deviation
Total Sample	3	9	7	6	4	0.0	1.3
Academicians Researchers	1	4	4	1	—	+.5	.8
Local Government Officials	—	1	—	2	3	−1.2	1.2
Private Developers Builders, Consultants	2	3	2	3	1	+.2	1.3

No. 10, a, b, and c), there is wide agreement among all the subgroups that these three powers should be possessed by the NTIT development entity.

The dissenting vote (cast by a private consultant) was based on the argument that one should know more about which agency would be attempting the revitalization and for what purposes before an assessment could be made as to appropriate powers.

E. Other Recommendations   In the course of our research efforts, certain issues were raised again and again by the public and private experts. To estimate the consensus or spread of opinion within these areas, the most important of the issues were put forth as policy statements, to be assessed by the Delphi sample group.

(11) "HUD Guidelines"

The first of these policy statements dealt with the HUD guidelines regarding the income mix among on-site residents. The majority of the Round II sample felt the current HUD standard (that the on-site mix approximate the mix of the surrounding metropolitan area) was too rigid and should be replaced by a more flexible set of criteria.

It is interesting to note that, although a majority favored greater flexibility, very few respondents made any comments supporting their opinion. The one private developer who commented (favorably) argued not for a change in the ultimate mix, but for greater flexibility in the timing of rental or sale of housing to lower income groups (that is, later in the development process after the project is established with middle and upper income residents).

Opponents of this policy statement, on the other hand, were quite verbal. Their concern was chiefly that, without a fairly rigid guideline, the ratio of low income families in new towns intown would decline. One academician argued, "This is about the only equitable provision in the guidelines! Without it, or something similar, NTITs will surely become upper middle class and light industrial park preserves." Several respondents (all academicians) argued in fact for stricter guidelines, favoring larger proportions of housing priced for low and moderate income families and individuals.

(12) "Need for Housing Subsidies"

There was almost unanimous agreement that development of income class integrated new towns intowns is not feasible without housing subsidies except under unique conditions. The consensus of opinion was quite striking, with 25 voicing "strong agreement" and 2 others expressing "mild agreement." Two were "uncertain," 1 indicated "mild disagreement," and 1 "strong disagreement" (see Table 8–5, Statement No. 12).

Arguments in support of this policy statement reflected the belief that it is an "economic reality" that cannot be ignored. The one individual voicing strong disagreement (an academician) argued that income subsidies or expanded job opportunities would also serve, because the poor could better afford market price housing if their income levels rose.

(13) "Role of Improved Building Techniques"

Most respondents felt that utilization of innovative building techniques is *not* an effective means of lowering housing costs to levels where housing subsidies would not be required. As one developer noted, "If you don't believe this yet, forget the rest: you're still up on some cloud."

Of those who withheld their support for the above conclusion, several argued more time and information was required before honest evaluation could be made.

Opponents of this policy statement offered few comments in support of their opinions. They were possibly fearful of poorly designed, high density projects.

(14) "Density and the New Town Intown Program"

One of the most controversial issues of new town intown development is the question of appropriate or acceptable residential densities. The responses to policy statement No. 14 substantiated this lack of consensus, with almost equal numbers arguing for and against considering "unusually" high densities as a means of overcoming the high cost of land in the inner city. Most comments were made by those who supported higher densities which involve good design. Typical comments included:

> Higher densities, *when well planned,* will bring many advantages, lower relative costs being one of them (Academician).

> Densities can be much higher and still satisfy family requirements and preferences—but with much greater design sensitivity than is typical at this time (Private consultant).

> . . . Remember the old developer's saying: "It's not how dense you make it, it's how you make it dense" (Private developer).

(15) "Role of Housing Conservation and Rehabilitation in NTIT Program"

Policy statement No. 15 was included in the Round II Delphi to sample opinion about conservation and rehabilitation to overcome the high cost of relocation which results from any large scale clearance of residential areas. There was virtually no consensus whatsoever on this suggestion, with the mean response exactly 0.0 ("perfect" uncertainty!). Academicians tended to favor this approach somewhat; local government officials were almost completely opposed. Private developers, builders, and consultants were fairly evenly split (see Table 8–5, Statement No. 15).

Comments also varied widely. Proponents suggested it was wrong to destroy salvageable housing or to ignore the role of conservation and/or rehabilitation as a possible strategy. Those less favorably inclined towards this approach noted practical difficulties (economic and otherwise), the need to consider local context, and need of new units for marketability.

Additional Policy Recommendations to the Department of Housing and Urban Development

Respondents were given the opportunity to suggest the policy recommendations they would make to HUD if given the chance. This was perhaps one of the most interesting sections of the Round II Delphi, for the richness and detail of the responses indicated the level of interest in the new town intown program among the Delphi respondents and their desire to make the program function more effectively.

All recommendations (and other comments made in connection with this section) are quoted verbatim in Attachment A. A summary of the suggestions is provided below:

1. Development Agency. By far the most common policy recommendation concerned creation of a locally based community development corporation to administer the NTIT program in a given metropolitan area. Although described in various ways, this development entity was generally viewed as having relatively wide powers, with sufficient political and financial strength to "get the job done." Probably the clearest description was made by a private developer who suggested:

> Create—or sponsor—"independent" development corporations with sufficient powers to get the job done and with workable but broadly based boards of directors: typical city or other public agency mentality/structure and general capability *cannot* do job.

Other suggestions included the following:

> Autonomy in Administration: A NTIT program will only succeed if it is governed by a largely autonomous local agency which will use federal policy regulations as an excuse to influence both economic and welfare objectives upon local governments even when the mayor and local government are unwilling to do so . . . (Academician).

> Be sure that CDCs are given a real role in whatever public or quasi-public development authorities are set up (Academician).

> . . . It is perhaps something beyond coordination that is needed, perhaps a development agency that has from the start a delegation of authority from all affected jurisdictions that is sufficient to insure the development agency's capability to see the program through (Academician).

> Combine a strong *management* approach (probably a COMSAT or TVA semipublic corporation) with a comprehensive *program* approach (à la Model Cities) . . . (Academician).

2. Programmatic, Multifocus Approach. In addition to a strong institutional framework, many respondents argued for a much wider definition of program objectives than has been the case in past HUD supported central city efforts. Rather than concentrating on a single function or two, those making these recommendations seemed to suggest that the NTIT program at least be flexible enough to involve whatever functions are most important in a given metropolitan area. Typical recommendations were as follows:

Broaden the scope of goals that are set so they are not limited to or dominated by housing for a special group, at the expense of economically sound community development or some other local goals such as public works (Local government official).

Consider HUD program as only one part of encouraging multiagency multifocus new *cities* (Private developer).

No program can succeed without being part of a larger policy formulation towards our metropolitan areas (Private consultant).

Fund only comprehensive renewal approaches (except for public works and emergencies). Though "individual" needs may suffer, renewal need to create a "critical mass" to have neighborhood impact (Private developer).

3. Streamline HUD Decision Making Process. Several recommendations were made addressing the need to overhaul the federal bureaucracy due to its apparent inability to act efficiently and effectively. Suggestions included the following:

HUD should quit its perpetual reorganizing and direct its energies to administering its existing programs. It doesn't seem that Title VII was ever given a chance. HUD always seems to prefer planning to action. It is always easier to obtain HUD funds for surveys and 701 plans than for implementing such plans . . . HUD should acknowledge that subsidization in housing is inseparable and then do it properly—probably directing subsidies more to people than to construction. Then with no more agonizing over that, HUD should administer its other programs in business-like fashion (Local government official).

Increase authority and responsibility of local and regional HUD offices—application processing times are inexcusable (Private developer).

Provide a clear-cut mechanism for the planning, building and managing of the program—a mechanism that joins public and private effort. More attention must be given to the methods whereby private developers can be brought into development and assured of cooperative governmental support. I think a key problem is the multiplicity of agencies—city, county, special purpose, state—that are involved in New Town Intown planning. HUD policies must provide a more effective mechanism for coordinating all these governmental interests . . . (Academician).

Since you cannot expect HUD to keep a trained staff, design programs so that they can be administered by reasonably intelligent, but uninformed staff. Design a record system to provide background information about local activities to serve a staff that changes periodically (Local government official).

4. Development Bank. Obtaining sufficient financing was frequently identified as a major hindrance to central city revitalization. The most common solution proposed was some sort of urban development bank (possibly on a national level) "which would provide low cost loans for public and private development projects of higher priority" (as one local government official described it). One consultant suggested the Rockefeller proposal for a development bank as a prototype of this institution.

ATTACHMENT A

ADDITIONAL POLICY RECOMMENDATIONS TO THE DEPARTMENT OF HOUSING AND URBAN DEVELOPMENT

Assuming you were in a position of advising HUD about their future involvement in programs of inner city revitalization, what recommendations would you make to aid them in their administration of such programs? Indicate your suggestions below, with a brief justification or explanation:

Academicians' Recommendations

Combine a strong *management* approach (probably a COMSAT or TVA semipublic corporation) with a comprehensives *program* approach (à la model cities). Within this framework, concentrate on a limited number of objectives (say economic development, low and moderate income housing, and safety) for a limited geographic area or population group.

More low and moderate income housing is required, not only as a humanitarian measure, but also to allow survival of communities which can maintain a labor force or competitive industry. Adequate public investment in (or subsidy for) low cost housing is a clear priority.

Adequate nonautomobile (low cost public) transport is an additional priority which is being badly planned or delayed in some recent developments (for example, Columbia Point, Welfare Island).

Political power and self-government of residents.

Provide a clear-cut mechanism for the planning, building, and managing of the program—a mechanism that joins public and private effort. More attention must be given to the methods whereby private developers can be brought into development and assured of cooperative governmental support. I think a key problem is the multiplicity of agencies—city, county, special purpose, state—that are involved in New Town Intown Planning. HUD policies must provide a more effective mechanism for coordinating all these governmental interests. It is perhaps something beyond coordination that is needed, perhaps a development agency that has from the start a delegation of authority from all affected jurisdictions that is sufficient to insure the development agency's capability to see the program through.

Develop a typology of communities in terms of specific life cycle/relationship to government mechanisms.

Project a model of future jobs in the central city.

Project a model of future functions in the central city.

Decide on national priorities.

Major support to *existing* community development corporations, many of which are now *doing* commercial, industrial, housing, social, and land development. (I know that looks like a baseless academic laundry list, but its *not* Harlem Commonwealth and Bed–Sty restoration for example are doing all of these things).

Be sure that CDCs are given a real role in whatever public or quasi-public development authorities are set up.

Local Government Officials' Recommendations

Less stringent requirements on densities, open space, and so forth. Each city and administration *should* be aware of the intensity of usage and impact which its central core requires.

Programs urgently needed include:

Loan Insurance and grants for fix-up of existing housing;
Subsidies for new housing for the elderly and other low and moderate income families;
Financing of land acquisition, building demolition, family relocation and redevelopment in inner city neighborhoods;
An Urban Development Bank to provide low cost loans for public and private development projects of high priority;
Housing allowance tied to fix-up.

Communities must be reasonably free to choose their own path without fighting guidelines written in infinite detail that fail to reflect the local circumstances. With the closest cooperation that anyone could have from a HUD area office and the finest technical personnel, our situation is a constant fight to progress even some. . . .

Annual financing is a bomb that prevents communities from decent planning. Constant, continual reworking of the rules and regulations force cities to bend, break, and ignore the guidelines that should help them. Technical assistance, not dogma, is what we need, with a total national commitment to the inner city. General rules, yes . . . specific steps, no! In other words: *Anything that is universal fits nothing!*

Title VII should be very nearly a break-even program. But it will be a slow repayment program. HUD should give it a chance. It should encourage use of Title VII with other proven techniques such as federally assisted code enforcement and urban redevelopment. Forget operation breakthroughs which is like the plaintive hope that planning can be used to eliminate the need for acting. Forget model cities in towns over 100,000.

Private Developers' Recommendations

Increase funding of basic research and development in the housing industry (such as breakthrough)—housing needs its Rand Institute;

Increase authority and responsibility of local and regional HUD offices—application processing times are inexcuseable;

Use only MAI (independent) appraisers. Partially get around (corrupt) FHA system;

Create a national land bank. Allow the public sector to reap the benefit of "unearned increment;"

Fund only where there is reason to believe chance of success exists. Special revenue sharing and other guaranteed sources of money tend to tolerate local disunity, which is a clear source of project failure;

Use, as a criterion for identifying chance of success, the presence of a local coalition of interests behind the project;

Find ways to utilize effective regional planning and controls in support of NTIT; for example, regional controls may be able to direct industrial location to help insure viability of NTIT;

See to establishment of Rockefeller proposed development bank: if private sector won't do it, have it done by federal government organized along the lines of OPIC;

Be certain the scope of the "project area" is large enough to have something in it for *everyone* to want—including the potential for real newly created amenities of value to the new residents, the old residents, and the region—that is, new parks, water recreation, culture, shopping, or other missing ingredients in the region. The resulting plans have to create an "everyone wins" area— everyone must benefit from his own personal trade-offs;

Develop cross-agency, public response; that is, HUD, HEW, and so forth, with enough money to invest and even some to risk;

Consider HUD programs only one part of encouraging multiagency multifocus new cities.

I am not in a position to advise HUD about programs for the inner city revitalization. I think it is important that we all work together and assist HUD in reorganizing the present programs which Congress has approved, but [for which] the administration has failed to appropriate funds or has cut back funds which were appropriated to these programs. At the present time we have some excellent programs which can help our cities reestablish themselves but, unfortunately, these programs are not being administered properly or supported by the federal government and city administration. I do not think it is time to start writing up new programs but I do think it is time that private enterprise and public bodies find a mutual meeting place to start to work on rebuilding our present cities so that the people of this country can be proud and secure in walking down the streets of today's cities. Federal programs will not solve the problems of today's cities. It will take the people and the leaders of those cities working together with a willingness and a strong desire to reach down and pull up their boot straps in order for the city to rebuild and reestablish itself as a decent and secure place to live. Building cities or satellite cities only serves as a hiding place for those people who refuse to face reality and get involved with the problems of the inner city. Eventually, the social problems that were created in the inner city will also creep into the new satellite New Towns and they will be faced with the same unresolved problems that they were faced with in the inner city. In reality when you build a New Town or a satellite city, you are only creating new facilities because the same everyday problems are there. They have just been temporarily covered up with the glamour and the marketing propaganda that surrounds these New Town developments.

Private Consultants' Recommendations

Many cities now find themselves in a position of: a) substantial new investment taking place in their own areas; b) this growth is uncoordinated; c) early plans have been indifferently carried out; d) new access is or is about to happen; e) areas around downtown are still "grey," and have not been able to take advantage of the latent strengths in the central area; f) and a new, often Black, clientèle has or is about to take over city hall. What is now needed is reexamination of old goals, strategy, and philosophy, with the result being the development of a "growth management" capability, not more plans. This means that HUD must get a clearer philosophy about urban areas and fund programs to support them. NTITs should be conceived as part of this kind of strategy in the regional context only in the sense of seeing how regional forces and factors can be made to work for the central area or at least [be] nullified. We must not lose sight of the fact that this is *war;*

Other Recommendations

Don't set "national goals," as in the past, by forcing a project or a city to meet them when a region should be responsible;

Provide more information and general consulting (under contracts with experts) and less procedural supervision;

Treat local government and authorities as responsible partners, then audit them carefully and publicize the results, after local consultation and clarification.

ATTACHMENT B

UCLA–NTIT CENTRAL CITY DEVELOPMENT
DELPHI: LIST OF PERSONS CONTACTED

Mel Adams
Director
Renewal and Housing Authority
Dade County, Florida

James G. Banks
Special Assistant to the Mayor
for Housing Programs
Government of the District of
Columbia, Washington, D. C.

Howard Baptista, Director
Urban Renewal Authority
New Bedford, Massachusetts

Joel Bergsman
The Urban Institute
Washington, D. C.

Robert Bliss, Director
Community Redevelopment Agency
Hartford, Connecticut

Ernest R. Bonner, City Planner
Cleveland City Plan Commission
Cleveland, Ohio

Professor Leland S. Burns
School of Architecture and Urban
Planning
University of California, Los Angeles

Isadore Candeub, President
Candeub, Fleissig, and Associates
Newark, New Jersey

James L. Carney, Vice President
Charles F. Curry Real Estate
Company
Kansas City, Missouri

Howard Cayton
Washington, D. C.

Reuben Clark
Wilmer, Cutter and Pikering, Assoc.
Washington, D. C.

John F. Collins
Massachusetts Institute of
Technology
Cambridge, Massachusetts

Carl Coan, Sr.
Congressional Staff
Washington, D. C.

Kathleen Connell
Cedar–Riverside Associates, Inc.
Minneapolis, Minnesota

John V. Crimmins
Minneapolis Housing and
Redevelopment Authority
Minneapolis, Minnesota

Robert Devoy
Real Estate Research Corporation
Chicago, Illinois

Professor Matthew Edel
Queens College
City University of New York
Flushing, New York

Hilbert Feffermann
Tulip Hill, Maryland

Michael Fischer
San Francisco Planning and Urban
Renewal Association
San Francisco, California

Charles Q. Forester
Department of City Planning
San Francisco, California

Marc Fried
Professor of Psychology
University of Boston
Boston, Massachusetts

The Honorable Hortense W. Gabel
Judge
Civil Court
New York, New York

Morton Hoppenfield, Consultant
Hartford Process, Inc.
Hartford, Connecticut

Ada Louise Huxtable
New York Times
New York, New York

John Martin Jones
Piper and Marbury
Baltimore, Maryland

Talbot Jones, Director
Minneapolis Housing and
Redevelopment Authority
Minneapolis, Minnesota

Norman Korumholz
Director of Planning
Cleveland, Ohio

Peter Kory
Urban Development Corporation
New York, New York

Charles E. Lamb
Rogers, Taliaferro, Kostritsky,
Lamb, and Partner
Baltimore, Maryland

Lawrence Lawless
Illinois Center Corporation
Chicago, Illinois

Professor Julian Levi
School of Law
University of Chicago
Chicago, Illinois

Nathaniel Lichfield
University of London
London, England

Warren Lindquist
Rockefeller Plaza
New York, New York

Peter Lobasi
Greater Hartford Process
Hartford, Connecticut

Vince Gallagher
First Boston Corporation
New York, New York

Alexander Ganz
Director of Research
Boston Redevelopment Authority
Boston, Massachusetts

Robert Gladstone
Gladstone and Associates
Washington, D. C.

Michael B. Glick
Richard P. Browne Associates
Columbia, Maryland

Professor Leo Grebler
School of Management
University of California, Los Angeles

Robert Groberg
National League of Cities
Washington, D. C.

George Gross
Office of Honorable Thomas Ashley
House of Representatives
Washington, D. C.

Bennett Harrison
Economics Department
Massachusetts Institute of
Technology
Cambridge, Massachusetts

Chester W. Hartman
National Housing and Economic
Development Law Project
Earl Warren Legal Institute
Berkeley, California

Frederick Hayes
The Urban Institute
Washington, D. C.

Keith Heller
Cedar–Riverside Associates, Inc.
Minneapolis, Minnesota

Morton Hoffman
Morton Hoffman and Company
Baltimore, Maryland

Robert Maffin
Executive Director
National Association of Housing
and Redevelopment Officials
Washington, D. C.

Winston Martin, Director
San Antonio Development Agency
San Antonio, Texas

William L. Marvel
San Antonio Development Agency
San Antonio, Texas

William Mason
San Francisco Redevelopment
Agency
San Francisco, California

Arnold Mays
Redevelopment Land Agency
Washington, D. C.

Robert McCabe
Detroit Renaissance
Detroit, Michigan

Hugh Mields, Jr.
Linton, Mields and Coston, Inc.
Washington, D. C.

Richard Mitchell, Director
Community Renewal Agency
Los Angeles, California

Leo Molinero
American Cities Corporation
Columbia, Maryland

Professor Roger Montgomery
Dept. of City and Regional Planning
University of California, Berkeley

Marion E. Morra
Hartford Process, Inc.
Hartford, Connecticut

Norman Murdock
Director of Planning and
Development
City Planning Commission
St. Louis, Missouri

Professor Arthur Naftalin (former
Mayor of Minneapolis)
University of Minnesota
Minneapolis, Minnesota

Jay Nathan
Franklin Town
Philadelphia, Pennsylvania

Paul Neumann
Director of General Research
Minneapolis Housing and
Redevelopment Authority
Minneapolis, Minnesota

Thomas O'Brian
Research Department
Boston Redevelopment Authority
Boston, Massachusetts

David A. Ornstein
Director of Urban Development
Peekskill, New York

David L. Peterson
Development Research Associates
Los Angeles, California

Delroy C. Peterson
Director of Development
Minneapolis Department of Planning
and Development
Minneapolis, Minnesota

Diane M. Porter
Chief Planning Officer
Welfare Island Development
Corporation
New York, New York

John Portman
Portman and Associates
Atlanta, Georgia

Dolph Prothrow
Krooth and Altman
Washington, D. C.

E. R. Quesada
Project Director
L'Enfant Plaza Corporation
Washington, D. C.

Jerome L. Rappaport
General Partner
Charles River Park
Boston, Massachusetts

George Raymond
Raymond and Mays, Associates
New York, New York

E. M. Risse
Richard P. Browne Associates
Columbia, Maryland

Anne Roberts
William L. Pereira Associates
Los Angeles, California

Marty Roberts
Executive Vice President
Pontchartrain Land Corporation
Dallas, Texas

Professor Lloyd Rodwin
Department of Urban Planning
Massachusetts Institute of
Technology
Cambridge, Massachusetts

Robert L. Rumsey
Executive Director
San Francisco Redevelopment
Agency
San Francisco, California

Honorable James Scheur
House of Representatives
Washington, D. C.

Alvin L. Schoor, Dean
New School for Social Research
New York, New York

Lewis I. Schwartz
Project Director
University Circle, Incorporated
Cleveland, Ohio

John Shrively
The Brookings Institute
Washington, D. C.

William Slayton
Executive Vice President
American Institute of Architects
Washington, D. C.

Hans Spiegel
Hunter College
City University of New York
New York, New York

William J. Spring
U. S. Senate Subcommittee on
Employment, Manpower and
Poverty
Senate Office Building
Washington, D. C.

Professor George Sternlieb
Center for Urban Policy Research
Rutgers University
New Brunswick, New Jersey

David Wallace
Wallace, McHarg, Roberts and Todd
Philadelphia, Pennsylvania

Professor Robert Weaver
Department of Urban Affairs
Hunter College
City University of New York
New York, New York

Dean William L. C. Wheaton
School of Environmental Design
University of California, Berkeley

Dean Paul Ylvisaker
School of Education
Harvard University
Cambridge, Massachusetts

Chapter Nine

The Hartford Process:
A Programmatic Approach
to Development

Summary

Plans for the revitalization of Hartford involve some of the most ambitious proposals now under discussion, and suggest what a programmatic approach to central city development might encompass.

Essentially a regional development program, the Hartford Process proposal encompasses an area of 750 square miles and 700,000 people, and includes the City of Hartford as well as 28 other jurisdictions. Initiative for the effort lies with the Greater Hartford Process, Inc., an organization formed by Hartford's major business interests to reverse downward trends in the region's economy and environment. The Process serves as a source of, and a forum for, new ideas on how to improve the region. Most major interests, public and private, are now represented on its board.

The Process has a development arm in the Greater Hartford Community Development Corporation (DevCo). The Process analyzes and makes proposals; DevCo exists to implement these proposals.

Current plans for Hartford proper call for a two-stage program with Phase I involving the entire northern half of the city, with 40 percent of the population and some 75 percent of the commercial base. Planning for Phase II, involving the remainder of the city, would begin as Phase I is implemented. Concurrent with these intown activities, other projects and programs would be undertaken elsewhere in the region.

Process planners envision a development program that would impact a wide array of Hartford's physical, economic, and social problems. The housing plan, for example, is ambitious in calling for clearance of 5,000 units, rehabilitation of another 10,000, construction of 6,000 new units plus conservation of at least 9,500 units. Homeownership would be encouraged. To assure equity, all low and moderate income housing units lost through clearance or rehabilitation would be replaced on a one-to-one basis.

A major issue raised by the housing plan is that up to 2,000 lower income families may have to be relocated outside the city. This arises because proposals for the new town intown in north Hartford call for an income mix similar to that of the region. Project planners want to ameliorate the impact of relocation by staging it over the 15-year development period, with only about 150 families relocated per year. While some believe relocating lower income families to suburban homes may require a regional "fair share" housing plan, the Process is exploring alternatives such as a city funded housing allowance, a second mortgage plan, and similar financial mechanisms. In addition, the Process is working closely with the Capital Region Council of Governments (CRCOG) which is developing a regionwide housing strategy for the next ten years.

Supportive social programs are assigned high priority. Most services would be focused around a neighborhood unit consisting of approximately 10,000 persons. Each neighborhood would be defined according to existing residential and social patterns in the city. The local school would be the focal point for a cluster of facilities designed to meet specific neighborhood needs. In most, if not all instances, local development activities carried out by DevCo would be in close cooperation with a neighborhood development corporation representing local interests, so as to assure local service needs are defined and met.

Process, Inc., is proposing many innovative—to some people's minds, almost utopian—changes in community social systems. Among others, it wants greater flexibility and accessibility in the educational system, prepaid health plans and a regionwide organization to serve as a consumer advocate for health care; a police force more oriented and responsive to community needs; greater community involvement in rehabilitating former criminals; and creation of "Neighborhood Life Centers" to provide community social and recreational services.

Economic development also plays an important role in Process proposals for the region. In Hartford, major emphasis would be on modernizing the downtown and creating an industrial park on a vacant site (North Meadows) close to the downtown. Emphasis would include stimulating Hartford's office based service industries as well as retaining its manufacturing base.

Much of the responsibility for economic development has been taken over by the Greater Hartford Chamber of Commerce. It hopes to attract 25,000 new jobs to the region by 1976. It works closely with Process, Inc. and DevCo to coordinate economic development and job creation.

The Process will rely on a wide variety of financial sources to support the modernization program. On the public side, the Process believes federal and state development funding (at the same levels as recent years), combined with normal city capital investment and tax increment financing, can provide sufficient governmental support. Private investment would also be significant.

One estimate of the cost of Phase I projects an investment outlay of $800 million (of which $200 million would be public and $600 million private).

History of the Development

The Hartford Process originated in the 1960s when many of the city's major businesses began to realize the need for a regional modernization program. They decided to work together to try to arrest the region's social, economic, and physical decline. Several factors prompted this effort. Hartford was rapidly losing its manufacturing industries, and employment in the remaining plants was threatened as many were becoming more capital intensive. Furthermore, the city's social and physical decline was beginning to threaten the downtown's finance and insurance industries. Last, but probably not least, was the feeling that the business community could and should do something about the region's problems. One observer noted that some business leaders "got religion" after attending a conference on urban problems at which James Rouse spoke.

To accomplish their aims, these firms formed the Greater Hartford Corporation. Its board of directors represents insurance companies, financial institutions, public utilities, and newspapers. From its incorporation in 1969 the corporation has supported the regional effort financially by raising over $5 million by 1973. Initially the American City Corporation, a subsidiary of the Rouse organization (responsible for Columbia, Maryland) was retained to analyze Hartford's problems and propose solutions. Out of its work arose Greater Hartford Process, Inc., a nonprofit corporation formed in 1970 to catalyze urban and regional modernization. It is charged with examining the region, setting forth goals, and then developing strategies to attain these goals. Its board of directors was structured to represent a board coalition of business, labor, local government, community, and other regional interests.

As a result of intensive planning involving many community groups and public bodies, the Process issued a major report in 1972. The report describes in considerable detail the region, goals for development, implementation plans, necessary funding, and possible funding sources. It has engendered extensive discussion, within and outside the region, due to its many innovative (to some, almost radical) proposals. The Process staff concentrated on developing a workable program for financing the first phase (The New Hartford NTIT) and on organizing a development corporation with the powers and political support to be successful.

The Greater Hartford Community Development Corporation (DevCo) is the development arm and subsidiary of the Process. DevCo's role is to acquire land, obtain financial support, and plan and implement Process proposals. It will work closely with interested parties to execute the development program.

The Process has been increasingly successful in lining up support for its programs and proposals. The Chamber of Commerce is providing support and leadership for the city's economic development while the city government is supplying additional backing. Working relationships between DevCo, Process, and the city are being established. A preapplication for $50 million in Title VII guarantees has been submitted by the city to HUD.

There are political problems. Some factions of the city council would like the council itself to function as the development entity. There is some opposition from suburbia concerning location of subsidized housing for relocatees from Hartford. Significantly, some progress has been made by DevCo and the Process. In addition to the city's request for HUD financial support, work has begun on other fronts:

> The Department of Health, Education, and Welfare has made a first-year grant of $225,000 for planning and implementing a prototype Neighborhood Life Center to deliver community social services in areas such as health, employment, recreation, child care, and police/community relations. HEW is committed to fund the second year of the three-year effort.
>
> Process/DevCo has established a working relationship with the South Arsenal Neighborhood Development Corporation (SAND) to construct and renovate housing, expand educational services, facilitate creation of a Neighborhood Life Center, and engage in related activities.
>
> Similar agreements have been reached with the upper Albany Community Organization and other groups. A joint planning-management team involving Process/DevCo and community leaders has been created to evolve a development program for their area. Initial costs have been partially covered by a $75,000 grant from HUD and $10,000 from the Ford Foundation.
>
> Another community group, Asylum Hill, Inc., is preparing a community development plan for its neighborhood. HUD support has been applied for.

In essence, Process wants to modernize the Hartford downtown and region by mobilizing all relevant public and private organizations. While DevCo lacks some powers of other public development corporations such as UDC (that is, the power to condemn land), Process planners believe the quality of their product will assure success.

Unique Nature of the Process

The Process is guided by several principles which, taken together, make it significantly different from approaches tried in the past:

1. **Bring the essential parties to the table.** The Process has made a heroic effort to incorporate all regional leadership elements into the planning process. These include local government, private sector, and citizen groups. Whether the Process can mold an effective coalition from such diverse groups remains to be seen. It is supported by the business community and some suburban governments; Hartford's city government recently also gave its much needed support.

2. **Set forth a believable image of the region that works.** The Process report presents a believable, albeit slightly utopian, image of how the region might be changed to provide a better life for its inhabitants. The language and graphics of the 1972 report are understandable by the general public; its analyses of costs and methods of financing add to its credibility.

3. **Unite planning and development with a commitment to carry out the plans.** The Process favors use of its development arm, DevCo, to implement its proposals in cooperation with public and private groups. Near the outlying community of Coventry, 15 miles east of Hartford, DevCo has assembled close to 2,000 acres for a suburban new community. In town, DevCo is involved in joint ventures with several inner city neighborhood corporations to physically and socially modernize their areas.

4. **Recognize the inseparability of social, economic, and physical planning and development.** In the 1972 report, various areas were analyzed in terms of the life support systems needed (that is, employment, transportation, education, recreation, security, and housing). A life support system was defined as "all of the opportunities, services, and programs that people use in the everyday pursuit of their lives" (American City Corporation, *The Greater Hartford Process,* p. 70).

5. **Use physical development to leverage positive social change.** The Process believes that physical renewal is a means of accomplishing desired social change rather than as an end in itself.

6. **Work at a sufficiently large scale.** Nationally, it is clear that small, single purpose, (for example, urban renewal or public housing) projects are not successful in reversing trends towards accelerating social disintegration and net disinvestment in urban areas. A programmatic approach is required to marshal regional resources to meet regional needs. The Process operates at such a scale.

7. **Create and capture economic values.** Process planners are stressing recapture of economic values created by the development process to pay

back public investment and finance social programs. In other words, they believe a city can generate sufficient revenues by investing in physical and human resources to recover its capital investment. The key linkages in the development strategy connect investments in the city's life support systems and an income development program. The linkages run both ways. On one hand, an income development program would raise incomes, thereby increasing effective demand for output of life support systems (and reducing the subsidy necessary to bring consumption up to desirable levels). On the other, the investments in life support systems (such as education, health, and so forth) can be viewed as part of an income development program.

8. Establish a continuing process. After several decades of intensive but fragmented urban programs, it is obvious that our national urban problems are not going to be solved once and for all. Producing more viable cities and regions requires continuing attention. The Process is designed to provide that attention.

DEVELOPMENT PLAN

Introduction

The Greater Hartford Process is evolving a development strategy for the entire 750 square mile region surrounding the City of Hartford, an area with 670,000 people and 29 local governments. Although one major developmental thrust would be directed at Hartford itself, activities would be encouraged throughout the region to contribute to the overall revitalization effort.

Renewal of Hartford is a major objective of the Process. The capital of Connecticut, Hartford is the major center of the region. Despite the strong image associated with its insurance industry, Hartford has long been primarily a manufacturing center (Stanback and Knight 1970). And like most such centers, it has had problems in generating sufficient jobs to replace those lost to automation, migration, and foreign markets. Part of the development strategy is to change Hartford from a declining manufacturing area to a nodal center specializing in services for regional, national, and international markets.

Hartford's revitalization would occur in two phases. The first phase emphasizes development of the entire northern half of Hartford. This area encompasses 40 percent of the city's population and 75 percent of its commercial and office base as well as its Black and Puerto Rican ghettos. The second phase would concern itself with the remainder of the city. Definitive proposals for this phase have not been made.

Because the New Hartford NTIT would be integral to the regional development strategy, it is nearly impossible to evaluate it independently. Many policies in the NTIT assume the existence of regionwide programs. For example, it may be that development of balanced intown neighborhoods can be accomplished only if suburban communities agree to accept some of the displaced minority and lower income people. The job and income development programs are also to be regional in scope, as is transportation planning. However, since evaluation of the entire Process is beyond the scope of this case study, attention here will be focused on Phase I of New Hartford NTIT and the critical linkages between it and the regional Process.

The northern portion of Hartford was selected for primary attention in Phase I because it contains major problem communities as well as several major sources of development strength. The choice was predicated upon three major considerations as to scale:

a) Large enough for planning a whole community—to insure the population is sufficiently large (70,000 in this case) to allow planning and provision of appropriate housing, employment, and life support systems;

b) Large enough to deal with development spillover effects—to insure that problems and households are not merely shifted to some other location in the city;

c) Large enough to create and capture economic values—to insure that gains stimulated by public investment accrue to the public sector.

Within the Phase I initial planning and development, activity would focus in on four "highest priority" areas (see Figure 9–1):

1. North Hartford contains the major problem communities of the city. It was selected for two reasons. First, North Hartford is the site of the city's, and region's, worst physical, social, and economic conditions. Thus, since it places the greatest strain on the system in terms of unemployment, crime, housing deterioration, social unrest, and economic disinvestment, it is the area most needing effective public and private intervention.

Second, it is argued that improvement of North Hartford, rather than some other portion of Hartford, would have the greatest impact on the region. Success here could produce the greatest positive effects because it currently has the greatest negative effects:

Philosophically, an urban region in which the quality of life is declining for some is a region in which the quality of life will, in the long run, decline for all. Thus, it is of vital importance to initiate efforts to improve the quality of life where it is presently declining, and that area is North Hartford (Greater Hartford Process, Inc., *The New Hartford*, p. 15).

2. The downtown was selected because it is, in every sense of the word, the major regional center. A decline would be felt throughout the region,

Figure 9-1. The New Hartford (Phase I): Project Boundaries and Major Activities

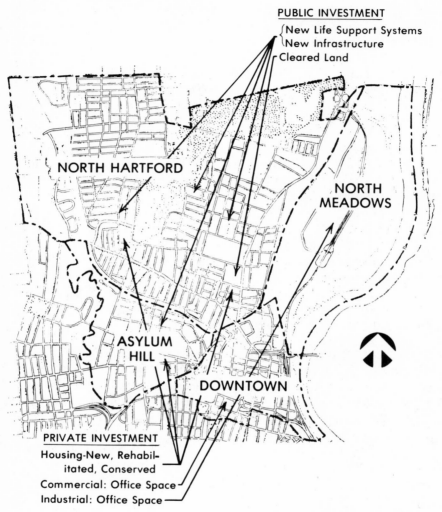

PUBLIC INVESTMENT
New Life Support Systems
New Infrastructure
Cleared Land

NORTH HARTFORD

NORTH MEADOWS

ASYLUM HILL

DOWNTOWN

PRIVATE INVESTMENT
Housing-New, Rehabilitated, Conserved
Commercial: Office Space
Industrial: Office Space

Source: Greater Hartford Process, Inc., *The New Hartford (Phase I): A Community Development Model,* Hartford, March 1972, p. 17

and downtown Hartford appears on the threshold of just such a decline. Revitalization would stress strengthening finance, insurance, and other industries; stimulating growth of additional office based, service activities; and improving the downtown environment through enhanced accessibility; beautification efforts; increased nighttime activity; improvement of civic, cultural, and social attractions.

3. Asylum Hill was selected because it, too, may be at a critical threshold: a largely white, high income community with healthy institutions and significant office employment base is faced with blighting influences from surrounding neighborhoods.

4. North Meadows was selected because of its rich potential for major new development. It is a largely vacant site only one mile from the downtown. Current plans call for its development as an employment park.

Process planners stress that planning for each area is closely interrelated with others. Success in any would depend on success in all four. Moreover, efforts in these four areas are to be linked with broader regional efforts to improve transportation, education, law enforcement, and health care.

Program Components: Housing

The housing plans for the Phase I New Hartford NTIT envision:

Clearance of 5,000 substandard housing units in North Hartford and Asylum Hill;

Construction of 5,000 new units in North Hartford and Asylum Hill, and 1,000 new units downtown;

Rehabilitation of 10,000 existing units in Asylum Hill and North Hartford;

Conservation of 9,500 units.

The new units would seek to establish the "newness" of each neighborhood. To promote neighborhood stability, homeownership will be encouraged. To prevent a net reduction of low and moderate income units, any housing demolished or lost through rehabilitation would be replaced on a one-to-one basis. The Process wants to use 60 acres around the edges of an underutilized park for housing. If this is feasible, it could eliminate many relocation problems arising with the demolition of 5,000 units.

Rehabilitation of entire neighborhoods would be undertaken with the aim of: (a) increasing opportunities for homeownership, (b) improving the total package of "residential services" available in each area, and (c) upgrading individual housing units. Rehabilitation funding was to have come primarily from the currently suspended Sections 235, 236, and 202 housing programs. Funding of housing programs, and indeed all elements of the Process' proposals, however, will be highly flexible. As noted above, the "eighth principle of the Process" calls for establishment of a continuing process. Since development would occur over a 15- or 20-year time frame, its effectiveness will depend on the program's ability to adapt to the changing political and financial environments.

Similar flexibility would typify planning to implement the housing programs. While a development entity (for example, DevCo) working in conjunction with a community group is one workable combination, ultimate arrangements for a given area would depend on local needs. At South Arsenal (a neighborhood within North Hartford), for example, a joint venture between DevCo and the South Arsenal Neighborhood Development Corporation is under way. Commitments for 270 housing units had been secured as of August, 1973. In Upper Albany (another North Hartford community), different arrangements appear necessary since rehabilitation, rather than clearance and rebuilding, is required.

Racial and Income Integration

The Process report proposes a major shift in the distribution of income and minority groups within the region. As with other NTITs, the plan provides for open occupancy for racial and ethnic groups (with no specific target for mix given) and aims for an income mix reflecting regional income levels:

> The number of households in the renewed area will be approximately the same as the number of families in the area today, but the range of housing price—and therefore the required family income—will reflect income levels of the region as a whole (*Greater Hartford Process*, p. 50).

By this definition, a balanced distribution for the New Hartford NTIT would include:

Income for Family of Four	*Percent of Total Families*
$6,999 or less	20%
$7,000 to 11,999	20%
$12,000 and up	60%

In order to attain this mix, up to 2,000 families may have to be relocated outside of the NTIT area. For this reason, some believe development of the NTIT would require a regional fair share housing plan whereby suburban communities agree to accept part of the displaced population. Another prerequisite may be housing subsidy funds to enable displaced families to relocate in decent housing. However, Process planners feel other alternatives exist such as a city housing allowance and improved second mortgage plans.

Program Components: Services

Process attaches great importance to life support systems in the renewal of deteriorating communities. Neighborhood improvement and enhancement of social cohesion are viewed as basic concepts underlying physical and social development plans.

All neighborhood services would be centered around the "neighborhood unit"—an area of about 10,000 persons based on existing residential and social patterns. Each unit would be served by a cluster of facilities centered around a local elementary school. In addition to the school, each cluster could include the following (depending upon neighborhood needs):

Improved commerical areas;
Major new shipping centers;
An adult learning center;
A health care facility;
A Neighborhood Life Center.

Education is viewed as especially important. Each neighborhood would have at least one elementary school designed to serve other community uses as well. In addition, early childhood development, adult learning, and child care facilities are proposed. Innovation is the watchword with Process planners seeking the most up-to-date teaching techniques and programs.

Another innovative proposal is the Neighborhood Life Center concept. Each neighborhood would have a Center which would provide public and private services. A Center would be operated by the Community Life Association, a citywide, nonprofit corporation which would channel public and private social services to neighborhoods. The association would have "the power and responsibility to meet all kinds of personal/social problems and provide recreational activities for all residents" (*The New Hartford,* p. 56).

Key social services based in each Neighborhood Life Center would include family services, rehabilitation counseling for lawbreakers, recreational services, community meeting rooms, hobby and craft rooms, and possibly a police community information desk. The ultimate goal is to create a responsive, "destigmatized," social and recreation center at a scale and level most receptive to local needs.

The first Neighborhood Life Center is already operating in the South Arsenal neighborhood of North Hartford (funded by a $225,000 HEW grant). Its current emphasis is on job training and placement, home care, health care, and related social services. Similar centers will begin operations in two other neighborhoods within two years to pilot test the concept in a real life situation. The Community Life Association is also functioning, and state and private support for the experiment is present and expanding.

The Hartford Process has put forth proposals in almost every service area imaginable. In terms of health care, it discusses the desirability of a prepared health insurance plan for the entire region. Each neighborhood unit would have a medical facility. The importance of transportation has also been addressed, with planners suggesting improved movement systems, facilities for pedestrians, more intensive use of parking, and rapid transit.

Even police community relations are discussed—an area little mentioned in other new town intown proposals. Some proposals include fairly drastic changes in police methodology:

> Police officers will be the advocates of the community, seeking changes in other life support systems so as to reduce crime . . . ,
>
> Since many emergencies will be handled by social services and other systems, the police will have more time to spend on crime prevention—advising property owners, participating in community planning decisions, and working with representatives of other life support systems . . . ,
>
> In their new community patrols, the police officers will be given new responsibility and will have new interaction with the neighborhoods. They will be viewed as friends and neighbors, not as an occupation force . . . (*The New Hartford*, p. 57).

Since no one knows how to bring about such innovations, Hartford Process' proposals can be seen essentially as calls for "social experimentation."

It should be noted that many ideas discussed by the Process were proffered primarily to generate feedback and discussion. They consistently imply that the most important consideration in discussing social services is meaningful community involvement in decision making and a continual dialogue between residents and the suppliers of services. Neighborhood social service needs change over time; maintenance of an adequate quality of life requires continual renewal of social service systems as the surrounding physical, social, and economic environments evolve. Provision of services is thus not a one-time planning effort. It is a never ending, ongoing adaptation to changing local requirements.

Job Creation and Economic Development

As with other Process's proposals, job and economic development can be divided into regionwide and Phase I new town intown efforts. Initial proposals for a regionwide program included the following:

> *Greater Hartford Full Employment Commission:* To manage the region's manpower training and public job creation programs. This body would allocate all public funds for these programs as well as enforcing affirmative action requirements;
>
> *Greater Hartford Economic Development Group:* To seek new industries for the region and provide venture capital to support such industry;
>
> *Computerized Job Information System:* To match job vacancies and job seekers;
>
> *Minority Economic Development Program:* To provide financial and technical assistance to Black and Spanish-speaking workers.

In addition, the Process encouraged ongoing analysis of manpower and economic development programs so as to increase incomes for families and revenues for governmental agencies.

In actual practice, the Greater Hartford Chamber of Commerce has taken on a program of regional economic development. In cooperation with the Process, city, and private interests, the Chamber has proposed, and has partially implemented, a four-point program.

1. Retain Existing Businesses and Industries. The chamber plans to contact every manufacturing firm with 25 or more employees to determine their problems and identify possible solutions. It hopes to encourage better communication between the city and business community in order to expedite resolution of major issues that currently divide them;

2. Recruit New Businesses and Industries. Based on a recently completed study, firms throughout the nation have been identified as especially suited for operation in the Hartford region. Five hundred of the most likely will be contacted directly in order to encourage relocation;

3. Inventory of Sites and Facilities—Create Jobs. In conjunction with Process and DevCo, the chamber wants to encourage creation of jobs required by the city's work force. It plans to identify all facilities and sites within the region that might provide such jobs. The chamber also hopes to develop, either independently or in a joint venture, one or more industrial parks;

4. Support for Job Training and Other Manpower Programs. In cooperation with the Process and the city, the chamber plans to press for state and federal support for manpower training, management development, and similar programs (Greater Hartford Process, Inc. "Work in Progress," p. 2).

Economic development within the New Hartford NTIT would be centered in a North Meadows Employment Park and downtown. North Meadows is located one mile from the downtown and has excellent access to the region's interstate highways, railroads, international airport, and the Connecticut River. A recently constructed flood control levee permits development. Uses for the 250-acre site include office buildings, a motel-restaurant, the city incinerator, and a 25-acre postal facility. The Process report (p. 62) states that:

> The city is currently applying to the state for the final $2 million of the $8 million project. The intention is to purchase or condemn land, develop infrastructure and sell to one or more developers, absorbing some of the costs of land preparation to make North Meadows economically competitive with other areas.

In other words, there will be some land write-down.

Development of downtown Hartford would emphasize the area's natural potential for growth of office employment, state and local government employment, and retail activities. Table 9–1 shows the potential growth of downtown employment, office space, services, and housing. Key to the downtown development strategy will be stimulation of both public and private office based employment:

> The major insurance company headquarters will be joined by the headquarters of other national corporations; the New Hartford will be a natural alternative to overcrowded cities like New York. Nearly 10 million square feet of office space (up from five million at present) and nearly 50,000 office workers (up from 30,000) will provide a resource for various business services—advertising, maintenance, legal services, and so forth. Retail shops, restaurants, and other activities will cater to this large market (*Greater Hartford Process*, p. 63).

Employment in the state government is also projected to rise sharply.

The action program proposed to address the problems inhibiting the downtown from developing to its full potential, would involve:

Table 9–1. The Potential Growth of Downtown

	1970 *Existing*	*Addition* *1970–1980*	*1980*
Employment	47,000	15,000	62,000 jobs
Office Space (Million sq. ft.)			
Headquarters	1.5		
General	3.3		
Government	1.2		
Total	6.0	2.0	8.0 million sq. ft.
Retail Space (Million sq. ft.)			
Shopping Goods	1.9	1.7	3.6
Convenience Goods	.3	.5	.8
Total	2.2	2.2	4.4 million sq. ft.
Parking Spaces	14,000	10,000	24,000 spaces
Miscellaneous			
Hotel Rooms	1,215	785	2,000
Restaurants	11	14	25
Movie Theaters	1	3	4
Housing Units	500	1,000	1,500

Source: American City Corporation, *The Greater Hartford Process*, Report prepared for the Greater Hartford Corporation and Greater Hartford Process, Inc., Hartford, April 1972, p. 63

a) Building a high quality shopping center;

b) Improving access to the downtown by all means of transportation—particularly public systems such as bus and rail;

c) Integrating new projects with existing downtown facilities through physical design methods;

d) Emphasizing the unique advantages of the downtown by drawing high quality and specialized retail trade, and by keeping and improving civic, cultural, and social attractions;

e) Extending use of the downtown by emphasizing night time activities and by carefully controlling the timing, quality, and mix of new activities;

f) Attacking the specific problems that inhibit downtown visitors and business, especially fear of crime, but also including beautification and other environmental efforts (*Greater Hartford Process,* p. 65).

The city thus could participate more fully in the national boom in office based, service industries in central cities.

Financing and Managing the Hartford Process

Financial and management plans are as yet little developed. Most proposals put forth to date were primarily geared to stimulating discussion and analysis of problems by the major community interests. Planners did emphasize the need for flexibility and innovation, however, by arguing:

> Building the New Hartford—achieving its economic, physical, and social objectives—will be an enormous long-term task. The job will require new kinds of relationships between public and private sectors. Not only will private capital be required to supplement public expenditures, but private entrepreneurship and the ability of private entities to make agreements and arrangements across jurisdictional barriers will also be essential. The unification of public and private interests will be necessary (*The New Hartford,* p. 68).

All concerned agree the Process will require sizable outlays of private and public funds. One recent working paper suggests the Phase I redevelopment in Hartford will require $780 million, of which $580 million[a] would be private investment and $200 million public investment. Details of expenditures under this proposal are outlined in Table 9–2.

One interesting feature is the argument that much or all of the initial public investment can be recovered by capturing the economic values created by the development process. Not only could physical and economic development

a. Only $480 million of the private sector's investment would be "new," since around $100 million of private investment is anticipated even if there is no public program.

Table 9–2. Investment and Payback Schedule: The New Hartford (Phase I) *(1970 Dollars in millions)* *

	1972–75	1975–80	1980–85	1985–90	Total
Private Investment					
Housing (New, Rehabilitated and Conserved)	—	—	—	—	350
Commercial and Office (Downtown and Community Focused)	—	—	—	—	160
Industrial Space	—	—	—	—	70
Subtotal	—	—	—	—	580
Minus Trend Investment	—	—	—	—	–100
Minus Clearance	—	—	—	—	–120
Net Added Investment (Market Value)					360
Average Net Added Assessable Base: Resultant Cumulative Average Assessable Base Available for Tax and Payback	—	50	100	235	235 million/year
Public Investment					
Acquisition, Clearance, Relocation	—	—	—	—	60
Road, Water, Sewer and Utility Systems	—	—	—	—	30**
Life Support System Development	—	—	—	—	50
Management, Interest and Taxes	—	—	—	—	60
Total	70	110	20	—	200 million
Payback on Public Investment					
Land Sales	2	10	8	—	20
Federal, State, and City Grants and Contributions	30	75	45	—	150

Tax Revised from Increased Assessable Base	—	20	40	94	154
Total	32	105	93	94	324 million
Payback Minus Investment (Cumulative Total)	−38	−43	30	124	124 million

*Totals shown are based on rough estimates and are not subject to refinement until elaborations of plan and development activity are undertaken

**This figure could be considerably higher depending on the extent of sewer and utility improvements

Source: American City Corporation, *The Greater Hartford Process*, Report prepared for the Greater Hartford Corporation and Greater Hartford Process Inc., Hartford, April 1972, p. 67

generate new tax revenues, planners also anticipate considerable return from investments in social and life support systems. They believe improvements in life support systems, (that is, investment in "human capital") would increase demand for, and hence value of, intown real estate. Although not enumerated in the financial plan summarized in Table 9–2, planners believe neighborhood improvements would produce other returns such as increased income tax revenues, increased sales tax revenues, decreased support payments (for example, welfare and housing subsidies) and so forth.

Current thinking on Phase I suggests the public sector could anticipate a "payback" net surplus of $124 million beyond the $200 million invested initially. This term payback is in a sense misleading since it may connote "profit" to some readers. In actuality, payback encompasses two different kinds of financing. On the one hand, it includes "grants and contributions" which the public sector must provide without reimbursement; on the other, it lists land sales and increased tax revenues to be generated by (and hence available to reimburse) initial outlays of public funds.

Interestingly, the "grants and contributions" entry of $150 million represents the level of public investment which will be spent in the project area if funding continues at current levels. The innovation introduced by the Hartford Process is the proposal that these funds, now dispersed among unconnected programs, be channeled into one account to support the development program.

It is useful to look at these payback expenditures from a cost-revenue perspective and to compare the status quo situation (without a NTIT) against the situation with a NTIT effort. With the status quo, the public investments would be expected to maintain, but not increase property values. Hence, the $150 million normally invested in the area would produce relatively little additional tax revenue. By investing an additional $50 million for the New Hartford, the project could generate $154 million in extra tax revenues and $20 million from land sales that would flow into the city's coffers. Obviously, the marginal return on the additional public investment for the NTIT would be quite high (about $3.50 in public revenue for every dollar of public funds).

Financial data for Phase I are still rough approximations put forth to highlight problems and propose solutions. A New Hartford Finance Committee was created to prepare more specific figures. Table 9–3 summarizes initial estimates of the public investment (and recapture) features of a 20 year development program for two of the four project areas, North Hartford and Asylum Hill. The downtown and North Meadows are excluded and will proceed under a separate, yet to be worked out, financial program. Development of North Hartford and Asylum Hill would include the following:

> Clearance of 5,000 substandard units;
> Construction of 5,000 units;
> Rehabilitation of 10,000 units;

Development of supporting shopping and office space;
Development of economic and social system programs.

Accomplishing these goals will be quite expensive, especially as compared to the North Meadows Employment Park and downtown (where the economic development should generate considerably higher marginal returns). Nonetheless, financial planners believe the program would generate a positive net public payback even under the most conservative of assumptions. As can be seen in Table 9-3, omitting public development funding (federal, state, and local grants and contributions), revenues generated would fall $118.2 million[b] short of total costs. However, when public development funds are included ($120 million under the most conservative estimate[c]), a positive net payback of $1.8 million could be realized. Under a more liberal projection, the estimated net payback exceeds $127 million.

The specific sources of the public sector's investment remain to be worked out. The city has submitted a preapplication to HUD for federal loan guarantees of $50 million.

Table 9-3. Summary: Twenty-Year Investment and Payback Characteristics (North Hartford and Asylum Hill) *(Thousands of Dollars)*

Conservative Estimates			Likely Estimates	
Investment	*Payback*		*Investment*	*Payback*
232,800	–	Public Investment	232,800	–
–	56,700	Public Project Revenue	–	56,700
–	150,000 .	Additional Property Tax Revenues	–	150,000
26,100	–	Deficit Before Interest and Public Development Funds	26,100	–
92,100	–	Interest*	40,000	–
–	120,000	Public Development Funds	–	194,000
–	1,800	Net Public Payback	–	127,400

*Note: Interest costs are calculated assuming an appropriate public borrowing rate of 5 percent and based on the initial cost flow proformas in Working Paper No. 5. Interest costs vary directly with the total cash flow over time and thus interest costs would be substantially higher with the conservative public development funding projections

Source: Personal Correspondence, Marion E. Morra, Director of Communications, Greater Hartford Process, Inc., to Harvey S. Perloff, September 6, 1973.

b. Deficit plus interest cost.
c. Conservative estimate assumes federal investment at one-half the levels experienced in the recent past and no state financial support at all. The higher estimate assumes public support at, roughly, current levels.

Financial plans for New Hartford are closely linked with proposals for program management. While still in the discussion stage, the general outlines are fairly clear. The Process has proposed a community development management entity be established to function as project manager for the entire program. This organization would enter into an agreement with the city concerning the respective responsibilities and functions. The Process has stated:

> To create a totally renewed community, it will be necessary to integrate social, economic, and physical development programs in a single management system. This unitary system will be based on the idea of a well-defined partnership arrangement between the city and a single prime contractor-manager.
>
> The single project manager—the Community Development Management—will have a comprehensive social, economic, and physical development staff. The CDM will carry out the development plan approved by the City Council after appropriate public hearings. The City Manager will enter into the contract on behalf of the City with Council approval and will supervise the work of the CDM . . . . (*The New Hartford*, p. 68).

How the community development management would operate in practice and what its powers would be have yet to be worked out. Its success will require the city's active involvement in all stages and long-term commitments by public and private sectors to the Hartford Process, its development policies and programs.

Chapter Ten

Organizing a Modernization
Program for a Major City:
The Case of Los Angeles

If a large community, like the City of Los Angeles, wanted to carry out a thoroughgoing modernization program, aimed at revitalizing the central city and improving the quality of life and range of opportunities available to the less advantaged of the central city, how might it best proceed and what would it need to do? This chapter records the results of an in-depth study seeking to answer that question.

What we did specifically was to test out, within the Los Angeles context, the problems and potentialities of the two model approaches already identified as the major alternatives for new town intown development, and to analyze the major developmental requirements. We made one major assumption: namely, that our initial "client" was the government of the City of Los Angeles rather than a private developer or some other governmental entity. (This did not prevent the use of a private developer or of private developers, nor of a combined public-private approach nor even of a countywide or larger public effort). We made this assumption simply because it provided sufficiently broad scope for considering various alternatives; also, realistically it was the most plausible scale for a major development program in the Los Angeles area at this time.

INSTITUTIONAL MODERNIZATION:
THE STARTING POINT

The capacity to modernize the physical, economic, and social facets of a central city—in order to achieve greater efficiency and equity as well as higher quality of life in the city—depends on modernizing the appropriate governmental and private institutions. The fact is that such institutions—particularly the city government—are themselves obsolete in terms of their ability to promote and/or execute central city development. The general inadequacies of city governments in the United States are widely publicized and broadly understood, but there is

249

much less appreciation of the extent to which city governments are currently handicapped in dealing with developmental problems. Municipal governments can deliver a limited number of public services and provide some basic facilities but are generally incapable of dealing effectively with physical, economic, and social *development* problems. Although a few of their renewal authorities have scored some development successes (as in Boston), in general the institutional frameworks have not been adequate for extensive development and redevelopment tasks, due to confusion over objectives, inability to attract appropriate leadership and isolation of action agencies from political decision makers, as well as having insufficient funds, and other problems.

Clearly, institutional capability should be a key concern of a "Stage II" new town intown program. Stage I (Title VII) new towns intown which have been launched or planned have viewed institutional change narrowly, largely to ease implementation of their plans. It is well to note that, in this regard, new towns intown share common ground with outlying new towns; in fact, this is a core feature of the "new town" approach.

The common institutional principles underlying new towns are worth noting. In essence, new town development should be defined functionally, not locationally. A new town should be understood as organizing complex functional relationships to produce a particular kind of urban environment. Such an environment is not place-bound and, potentially, could be replicated anywhere within a region, because the core principles of a new town can be applied equally well to the already built-up sections of a central city. Similarly, new town development must seek to meld economic, social, physical, *and* institutional forces in order to institute a superior organization of growth and development, whether suburban or central city.

1. Organizing for Development.   Institutional objectives need to be clearly stated so as to effectuate basic new town principles of development: namely;

a) To achieve a superior organization of growth and change—physical, economic, social, and locational—by overcoming dysfunctional suburban and central city development patterns through a superior organization of institutional capabilities;

b) To achieve carefully integrated and staged development of communities having multiple objectives—physical, economic, and social; institutionally, to be able to "orchestrate" such complicated and highly interrelated development;

c) To enable planning and development at "town" or "community" scale so as to achieve the large programmatic objectives; institutionally, to optimize both the territorial and functional considerations within the project or program area;

d) To provide for an entrepreneurial function, whether initiated in the private or public sector, because new town development *requires* an entrepreneurial function to maximize the leverage of limited capital and to minimize the costs and risks of long-term development.

The application of these principles has involved a good bit of experimentation—and blundering about—and it is still very far from clear as to what is the best institutional embodiment. All sorts of trade-offs have to be considered in trying to set out relative advantages and disadvantages of alternate institutional forms.

Table 10–1 brings together a substantial amount of information, including the powers and other features of different institutional arrangements that have carried out and/or are planning suburban or central city new towns. Three major types are identified: public, public-private, and private; each has an entrepreneurial capability, but of a different kind. They all share the corporate form so as to achieve organizational and financial flexibility and to limit corporate liability. The public and public-private types also may establish subsidiary units or special cooperative arrangements. Accordingly, there can be substantially different powers, organization, and functions of the umbrella (parent) entity as contrasted with subsidiary or joint units. The descriptions in the chart do not try to distinguish between the two, but encompass the powers and capabilities of the ultimate institutional combination.

Reviewing the situation in Los Angeles against the background of other urban development experience and proposals, we conclude that a new town intown can succeed only if sponsored by a new and powerful development corporation. The sponsoring unit could be either (a) a public corporation with operating subsidiaries, or (b) a joint public-private corporate arrangement. With little American experience to draw upon, relative advantages and disadvantages of either form are not clear. Nonetheless, it is important to combine the public-mindedness and powers of a public entity with the operational capacity and relative independence of a soundly organized private corporation (or set of corporations). If one were to idealize the good features of either entity abstractly and overlook real world weaknesses, a strong case can be made for either form of institutional sporsorship. In the real world, the actual "cast of characters" who would "run the show," and their relative effectiveness, cannot be predicted in the abstract. Without substantial experience to generalize on, each situation has to be judged on its own merits, including the specific case of Los Angeles. A great deal depends on who, if anyone, wants to undertake the job of thoroughly modernizing the central city.

By contrast, we are more certain about specifying needed powers, financial requirements, and other related institutional features. If Los Angeles were to attempt a Model II type of development directed at the twin objectives,

Table 10–1. Various Features of Institutional Sponsor

	(A) Public		(B) Public-Private
Features	British	N.Y. UDC	Two Entity Type "Super UR" Cedar–Riverside
Entrepreneurship:			
1. Initiative	Public	Public (but also involving private)	Private
2. "Last Resort" Developer	Yes	Yes	No
Public Sector Finance			
1. Long Term Below Market Interest Rate Loans	Yes	No	No
2. Housing Loans or Grants from Higher Level of Government	Yes (loans)	Yes (Mitchell–Lama, 235, 256, public housing)	Yes (235, 256, public housing)
3. Public Leasehold System	Yes	Yes	No
4. National Development Grants (other than housing)	No	No	Yes
5. Public (national or state) Mortgage Guarantees	No	Yes	Yes (Title VII)
Land Use Power			
1. Eminent Domain Land Assembly Land Banking	Yes	Yes	Yes (within project area only)
2. Code Override	Yes	No (removed in 1973)	No
3. Planning Override (supersedes local agency) planning programs	Yes	Yes (within project)	Yes (within project)
4. Public Investment Coordinator (supersedes local agency investment programs)	Yes	Yes (within project)	No
Other Features			
1. Single Project Capability	Yes	Yes	Yes
2. Multiple Project Capability	Yes	Yes	No
3. Independent Financing (self-financing capability)	Yes (public) Yes (private)	Yes (public) Yes (private)	No (public) Yes (private)

(B) Public-Private	(C) Private		(D) Proposed for Los Angeles
Joint Public-Private Pontchartrain	HUD Title VII Suburban New Towns	Nonfederally Supported Private	Public-Private
Joint public and private	Private	Private	Public (but also involving private)
No	No	No	Yes
No	No	No	Yes
Yes	Yes (235, 236)	No	Yes
Yes (?)	No	No	Yes
No	No (in legislation but not yet used)	No	Yes
Yes (Title VII)	Yes (Title VII)	No	Yes
Yes	No	No	Yes
No	No	No	Yes (with mayor/council approval)
Yes (within project)	No	No	Yes (with mayor/council approval)
No	No	No	Yes (with mayor/council approval)
Yes	Yes	Yes	Yes
No	No	No	Yes
Yes (public) Yes (private)	Yes	Yes	Yes (public) Yes (private)

central city modernization and improving the situation of less advantaged families, it would require all the powers and capabilities attached to existing development corporations. After studying the national experience with urban renewal, model cities, and Title VII new towns intown, we are impressed with the difficulty of carrying out the really significant tasks of central city modernization and assisting the less advantaged—as contrasted, for example, with the much less difficult (and important) task of building small "balanced" residential communities on vacant land. If the twin objectives are to be met, a development corporation must have the power and capability equal to the endeavor.

2. **A Development Corporation for Los Angeles.** The case for a development corporation to direct a new town intown effort in a major city like Los Angeles can be readily made:

a) Private enterprise and conventional economic forces *by themselves* cannot be expected to undertake and carry out the modernization of the central city over a generation or more; and

b) Existing city agencies such as the Community Redevelopment Agency, the city's LPA, Los Angeles Housing Authority, or Model Cities agency cannot, as presently organized, sufficiently (1) mobilize the requisite public authority and resources, (2) stimulate the private sector to ensure large scale development—physical, economic, and social, and (c) thereby achieve the twin objectives of central city modernization and assisting the less advantaged. Parenthetically, CRA could be the base for reorganization into a general development corporation.

The advantages of corporate entrepreneurship and flexibility could be expressed in the legislative policy section of the entity's charter.

> *Example:* Because the development actions to be undertaken will be predominantly of a business nature; because this new entity is expected to produce revenue and have the potential at some point to be self-sustaining; because its action as contemplated by this Act will involve large numbers of business transactions with the public; and in order to properly undertake all actions contemplated to be necessary, the entity will require much more flexibility than would be normally permitted a department of city government, it is found that a public development corporation provides the most appropriate institutional approach to the needs and problems of the city as contemplated by this act . . . . (Adapted from "Statement of John Gunther, Chairman of the Board of Directors of the District of Columbia Redevelopment Land Agency, June 11, 1973, and from other materials supplied by the Agency relating to a proposed Washington, D. C. development corporation.)

These advantages of entrepreneurship and flexibility can be achieved through several organizational scales. These need to be contemplated at two levels: (1) the "umbrella" level, or parent agency, administering the general development *program,* and (2) the subsidiary level, normally related to a single development project, community, or specialized development functions.

(1) The parent agency could be a public agency such as the New York Urban Development Corporation (UDC) or a joint public-private form with private interests serving on the board of directors along with publicly appointed members.

Also, it is evident that the development corporation could be organized by the state, a regional entity, or the city government. If sponsored by the state, the local development corporation (in this case, the entity responsible for the development of central Los Angeles) would itself be a subsidiary, and it, in turn, could launch other subsidiaries to execute individual projects. While we discuss here a corporation sponsored by the city, it should be understood throughout that the city entity might itself be a subsidiary of a state or regional corporation.

(2) At the executing level, various institutional forms are possible. Thus, a subsidiary unit at the "development sector," individual project, or single function level, could be a private corporation, a private-public arrangement, or a public corporation (such as a community development corporation). One form already employed in Title VII new towns intown, is to have two entities contractually organized as a joint venture. The public entity, assuming it possessed general development powers, would play essentially a facilitative role enabling the other entity, a for-profit developer, to undertake new town development within a given project area. Thus, it would replicate the LPA-private developer model for urban renewal projects. In the case of larger projects, there might be resort to assembling (and maintaining) a consortium of private investors and developers. Joint ventures for project development, such as those utilized by UDC, could be spun off by a parent development corporation with few disadvantages and considerable corporate dexterity (Reilly and Schulman 1968).

Interviews with developers, bankers, and builders in Los Angeles indicated a potentially lively interest in inner city development and redevelopment—assuming that the institutional and financial context was reasonably attractive. A number of this group expressed the view that not only was inner city modernization urgently needed for both economic and social reasons, but that the time seemed propitious for a major effort to revitalize the inner city of Los Angeles.

In a Model II new town intown development of the type contemplated for Los Angeles, somewhat similar to the Boston renewal program and the Hartford, Chicago, and Cleveland NTIT proposals, we would anticipate establishing various executing entities to meet the different developmental problems to be overcome by a NTIT general development program for the central city and less advantaged groups. This would not only provide optimum flexibility, but would permit using the best features of private enterprise on one side and of public (or community) authority on the other.

It seems evident that it will take a long period of experimentation before an optimum institutional form, if possible, will become known and widely adopted. The basic features of a parent development corporation for Los Angeles, however, can be outlined at this stage. Thus, we believe that a "model" parent development corporation would possess certain features: (We use the city sponsored corporation as the most convenient for establishing the key points.)

a) The Central City Development Corporation (CCDC) would be chartered by special enabling legislation as a multipurpose, public benefit corporation legally independent of the City of Los Angeles in all matters of operation and liability *except* for appointment of the board of directors; general review and approval of *major* policies, programs, and projects; issuance of long-term obligations; and maintenance of a contingent debt reserve fund.

b) To the degree feasible, existing physical, economic, and social development activities of CRA, the housing authority, model cities, and other development agencies would be absorbed by the new corporation, and the agencies phased out of existence, except as possible subsidiaries of CCDC.

c) The corporation would have citywide jurisdiction augmented with full powers for land condemnation, banking, assembly and write-down; for developing, operating, holding, and leasing land and improvements; and for undertaking physical, economic, and social development without restriction to "blighted" areas or "low income" housing units.

d) With prior approval of the mayor and city council, the CCDC would have primary responsibility for planning, zoning, building, and land use controls within authorized development sectors (relating its activities to city, state, and regional planning and control agencies); and for coordinating and staging city, and, where feasible, other public improvements within such sectors.

e) The corporation would have a capital borrowing authorization of several hundred million dollars and authority to issue revenue and tax allocation obligations based upon revenues generated within development sectors.

f) The corporation would have the authority to instigate public or public-private subsidiaries and to undertake joint ventures with existing corporations. Through its programs and subsidiary corporations, the CCDC would attempt fully to involve private investors and developers as well as citizens, neighborhoods, and nonprofit community development corporations.

3. General Corporate Functions. A general development corporation established in a major city like Los Angeles should encompass four general functions: entrepreneurial, developmental, financial, and coordinative.

a) The Entrepreneurial Function. The distinctive feature of a development corporation, setting it apart from single purpose line departments or agencies, would be its entrepreneurial *mandate.* Except for the New York UDC, operating at state level to develop new towns, there are no adequate American governmental models:

> ... the truly innovative character of the corporation (UDC) is its power to initiate and carry out its own enterprises. This is a capability that has not been seen before in America—a multipurpose public authority empowered to act out any or all of the roles associated with urban development from acquisition to management (Reilly and Schulman, 1968, p. 136).

At the federal level new communities were developed as part of a World War I mobilization program, New Deal experiments with greenbelt cities, or as spin-offs of Tennessee Valley, Hoover Dam, or Atomic Energy Commission projects. (Advisory Commission on Intergovernmental Relations, 1968, p. 73.) Accordingly, a city dissatisfied with its traditional passive reactive stance to development must necessarily synthesize entrepreneurial aspects associated with both public and private development corporations. This "synthetic" model was summarized by Bain:

> The agency should play the role that would be expected of the private developer of a new community *if all the land were in a single ownership.* Entrepreneurship includes taking the initiative to call forth the many public and private activities needed to create new or expanded communities, coordinating these in space or time, providing the drive to overcome obstacles and the follow-up to keep every phase of the process moving along on schedule, assuming responsibility for the whole undertaking so that no necessary element is overlooked or neglected, and performing or securing the performance of any functions that would otherwise be lacking (Emphasis supplied.) (Henry Bain, 1969, p. 187).

Moreover, since entrepreneurship is not readily built into organizational structure, especially in public institutions lacking for-profit motivations, design of a development entity must be approached indirectly by removing impediments characterizing urban renewal, public housing, and model cities programs and agencies. These would include limitations associated with scope of authority, funding, powers, and civil service.

In addition, the preamble to the entity's charter should make clear the entrepreneurial mandate.

Example:
In order for the City (here Los Angeles) to deal properly with the areas of the City in need of substantial revitalization; to effectively

undertake comprehensive development initiatives to overcome recognized physical, economic, and social deficiencies of the City's continuing development; to provide adequate levels and types of public facilities and services; and to enhance economic opportunities and well-being of citizens, neighborhoods, and private enterprise, a new developmentally oriented governmental entity is necessary and desirable; and

In order to deal effectively with the wide range of development opportunities and problems which must be addressed to maintain and conserve the entire City as well as selected target areas and groups, such an entity must be able to act on behalf of the city government, on a city-wide basis, and in a manner fully utilizing the capabilities of private enterprise where feasible but also, where necessary, undertaking such developmental activities for which private developers lack interest or capability. (Adapted from Gunther, 1973, note 4).

b) The Developmental Function. The entity would have two developmental roles: public developer of last resort, and facilitator and catalyst of substantial private sector involvement. The New York UDC has exploited both roles to overcome conventional administrative and statutory impediments, to form subsidiaries and public-private ventures, and, progressively, to blur popular stereotypes of "public" and "private" sector activity.

(1) Developer of Last Resort: The type and rate of central city development is generally determined by: (a) the nature and availability of private and public financing, and public subsidies for land write-down and housing construction and rehabilitation; and (b) private sector willingness to make long term commercial and industrial investments yielding subregional rates of return at superregional risk and uncertainty. Private reluctance may be accentuated by deteriorating public services and reduced capital investments.

"Last resort" public development authority does not substitute public for private development, but instead assumes the initiative and initial investment risk to create a "critical mass" for reversing private disinvestment. This appears essential for new town development which has heavy front end capital costs followed by long-term "patient money" and critical mass requirements. In addition, low and moderate income housing cannot be adequately supplied by for-profit developers without some form of subsidy.

Example:
In 1970, UDC reported to the Governor of New York that although private developers had built 85 percent of the state's housing since 1950, they found it increasingly difficult to provide housing for any except upper middle and upper income groups. Private housing development in new towns was even more difficult. The obstacles included: (1) difficulty and cost of land assembly;

(2) unwillingness or inability to make the heavy investments required for capital improvements; (3) high interest rates and shortage of mortgage funds; (4) restrictions created by zoning, land use controls, and building codes; and (5) inability to achieve market aggregation needed for new building technology.

In contrast, UDC in 1970 and 1971 began construction of 18,211 housing units in 55 projects, nearly all of which were for low-moderate income families and the elderly. Total development costs approximated $600 million (New York State Urban Development Corporation, 1970, p. 37).

(2) Facilitative: A second related developmental function would be to stimulate private investment opportunities in conventional and subsidized development according to plans and programs devised by the development entity. By providing an active, early participatory role for the private sector, substantial funding could be made available from insurance companies, commercial banks, savings and loan institutions, retirement and other pension funds, and nonprofit community and religious organizations. Another innovation could be UDC-style "packaging" of physical and housing development.

Example:
... The initiative power casts UDC in the role of promoter, financier, consultant, and developer. To be successful it requires that resources and talent be concentrated so as to alter patterns of government instigated renewal in a number of important ways.

... First, the corporation itself has a highly competent and experienced staff capable of making market projections. . . . All of the other developmental activities—the search for a developer, the hiring of architects, the planning of the site, the applications for federal or state assistance—may commence as soon as the decision about marketability has been made. The seed money necessary to sustain these endeavors may be advanced immediately by the UDC. . . . The building contractor may even begin construction before a developer has been found. *Thus, operations which are conventionally sequential become simultaneous.*

Finding a developer to undertake a project on which so much has been done for him is likely to be vastly simpler than merely offering the vacant land for proposals. Moreover, for the developer, dealing with a powerful state authority with ready means of financing is certain to be attractive. The confidence of developers and financiers—to say nothing of federal housing officials—should be assured to any authority willing to make the detailed analyses, take the early risks, and process the necessary approvals. In effect, the UDC is equipped to "package" a project (Emphasis supplied.) (Reilly and Schulman, 1968, pp. 136–38).

c) The Financial Function. The financial theory of public new towns in New York and England (Evans 1972) presents a sharp alternative to American experience with urban renewal and model cities: the new town is financed principally by publicly issued notes which eventually fall due for repayment. The public (and private) new town is conceived as a long-term, potentially high risk investment opportunity. Although some governmental subsidies are utilized, they are restricted generally to reduced interest rates for long term bonds or advances, and to making feasible construction of low and moderate income housing units. The policies, plans, and programs of British and New York development corporations are accordingly so guided. Not surprisingly, these entities have common financial goals:

(1) To undertake new town development eventually capable of net positive cash flows and other revenues so as to retire the entity's capital indebtedness. This potentially enables a public entity to structure development of a single program within which internal subsidies are distributed to selected projects and activities. It could prove feasible to provide land write downs, rent reductions, or BMIR (below market interest rate) loans to community organizations and local nonprofit development corporations;

(2) To generate sufficient short term revenues so as to become financially independent of the government for annual operating appropriations. Financial self-sufficiency is associated with corporate entrepreneurship, and presently is being sought by UDC for political reasons as well.

Financial self-sufficiency for the developmental entity over the near and long term presupposes adequate borrowing and revenue authority. To have the desired type and scale of developmental impact upon the central city, the entity would be authorized:

a) To issue bonds and notes in the general capital market secured principally by anticipated tax increments and revenues from various sources. Issuance of revenue and tax allocation bonds would require prior city council approval. Because the entity would be formally independent of the city government except for policy making, its obligations would not affect the city's capital debt ceiling or credit rating in bond markets. The obligations could be guaranteed, in the unlikely event of default, by a contingent liability provision similar to UDC's in which the municipality promises to maintain a debt reserve fund equivalent to annual outstanding amortization and interest payments.

b) A capital debt authorization in the order of several hundred million dollars. Although the exact amount of its borrowing authority cannot, of course, be prespecified, anything substantially less would seriously restrict the entity's effectiveness and thus make less credible the city's commitment to central city revitalization within, say, two generations.

The essential soundness of the entity's financial structure would be evidenced by a principal source of revenues: long-term ownership of developed land, attendant revenues generated by land value appreciation, and by leases of commercial, residential, or industrial facilities. Similar leasehold methods are used in British, New York, and some suburban new towns; in Los Angeles County (Marina del Rey); and elsewhere in the form of government franchises such as airport and harbor facilities. In addition, the entity should be entitled to new tax increments—as are California LPAs and rapid transit districts—throughout the new town intown sector. This implies the need for specific designation of the sector which, when coupled with intensive public development, can be expected to generate substantial gains in land values and assessments. The entity should be entitled to the fruits of its efforts.

> *Example:* Canberra, Australia:
> Canberra, the capital of Australia, well illustrates a large scale leasehold system such as later adopted by British and New York new towns. Planning, development, and financing for Canberra are based upon a public land and leasehold system in which the national government, acting through a development commission, owns the land, undertakes land use planning, provides the infrastructure, and then allocates improved sites for public and private development. The accomplishments indicate that a leasehold system coupled with private and public development, can: (1) control the type and phasing of private and public development without impairing operation of private markets; (2) stimulate extensive private development, investment, and loan financing; (3) encourage private housing development by designation, staging, and pricing of residential sites; (4) generate substantial lease revenues to help finance public capital investment in infrastructure; and (5) capture increases in land values (particularly business sites) brought about by public development and apply to finance further public development (U. S. Department of Housing and Urban Development, May, 1973, pp. 13–14).

d) The Coordinative Function. The rationale for a single entity having primary responsibility for planning, staging, and coordinating major public and private investments rests upon necessity, efficiency, and equity in the development enterprise. It is reinforced by the broader scale and comprehensiveness of a new town intown in which more things can misfire to diminish leverage opportunities of limited public funds. In addition, the effect should be to give coherence to policies and programs of single purpose municipal agencies, and in Los Angeles, *de facto* to reorganize certain city functions so as to provide stronger accountability and responsiveness to the mayor and city council. Objectives of strong, central coordination of public and private development include:
(1) Assurance of the development plan. New towns inevitably

require heavy front end capital expenditures followed by long periods of anticipation of positive cash flows. The type and staging of development is closely integrated to assure scheduled "take out" and eventual retirement of long term bonds or mortgages.

(2) Reliance interests. Families, businesses, industries, and local agencies invest in new towns in reliance upon realization of the development plan.

(3) Public sector economies. Coordinated, synchronized public improvements tend to enhance investment efficiency by economies of scale and agglomeration. They also can stimulate and guide subsequent private development.

4. Organizational Relationships. A development corporation of the type outlined here would be a major force for centralizing municipal development functions as well as overcoming obsolete city charter provisions which diffuse power and responsibility to independent agencies governed by citizen commissions. Like CRA and the housing authority, the CCDC would be organized as a public benefit corporation independent of the formal structure of city government. It would differ from these agencies (and model cities) primarily by incorporation of physical redevelopment, housing development, and social and economic development functions into a single corporate entity, and by vesting a single board of directors with responsibility for multiple-purpose, large scale development implied by new towns intown. Thus, the CCDC would break sharply with the New Deal tradition of separate single-purpose agencies and categorical programs, and it would instead espouse principles of unified control and responsibility found in private corporations and in public development corporations in New York State, England, and Europe. By making municipal development functions more directly responsive to the elected representatives of the people, the corporate form also enables city government to be more responsive to major private investors and community organizations. This is because the CCDC could readily spin off public-private joint ventures, subsidiaries, and non-profit corporations undertaking neighborhood level development activities.

Although the CCDC would be the city's development arm, it need not be a "pure" public corporation because of the need and desirability of incorporating, to the fullest degree feasible, private investors, builders, and developers. It could be a public-private entity to maximize and combine attractive features of public and private development, but in a manner which supports a credible implementation strategy for new towns intown. The exact shape of private involvement in joint ventures, partnerships, project and site sponsorship cannot be specified at this point. Similarly, the roles of the mayor, city council, and board of directors can be only generally outlined.

The mayor and city council would have powers and responsibility befitting generalized policy making and coordination of city development.

a) Appointive. The mayor would nominate, and the council approve, a board of directors of staggered terms that would be broadly representative and internally harmonious;

b) Financial. Since the city council would indirectly guarantee the CCDC's capital obligations through a contingent liability arrangement, it logically would want to ratify revenue and tax allocation bond issues first approved by the board of directors;

c) Policy. The mayor and council would be required to approve major policies, programs, and plans adopted by the board. This feature would be critically important because the CCDC, having primary legal and financial responsibility for new town intown development, would need to supersede conventional municipal planning and investment functions impacting a development sector. The CCDC's planning and investment programs necessarily would assume precedence over similar activities of other city departments. Since there would be ample opportunity for interagency conflict, the mayor and council could (a) instruct the corporation to pursue strategies of cooperation and coordination wherever feasible, while (b) reserving authority to arbitrate and resolve interactable disputes.

d) Patron. An important lesson of UDC's formative years in New York State is that a potentially effective development corporation is heavily dependent upon the government executive for support and protection until its existence becomes generally accepted.

The board of directors would, of course, exercise overall control and responsibility for the corporation, subject to financial and policy review by the mayor and city council.

The board would face a formidable organizational challenge in absorbing, reorganizing, and integrating the urban renewal, public housing, and social welfare functions of CRA, the housing authority, and model cities. A transitional strategy would need to be developed first by the mayor and council concerning, for example, (a) designation of programs and projects to be reorganized, (b) retention of personnel and employee rights, and (c) reconstitution of commissions as advisory bodies. Reorganization of the city's development functions, although obviously an intricately wrought legal and administrative endeavor, could however be most readily brought about during a period of federal retrenchment in urban renewal, public housing, and model cities, and a corresponding period of relative inactivity for the city agencies involved.

The board would face an equally difficult challenge in working out effective arrangements with municipal agencies as well as with county, state, and federal governments, for provision of the basic public services supportive of an ambitious development program. Securing the continuing support of other governmental entities will require considerable skill and involvement by the mayor and other officials. Other governments will be constantly making resource allocation decisions vital to the social, physical, and economic development of the NTIT.

Also, the corporate form would enhance the ability of the board of directors to innovate and assure effective citizen and neighborhood participation in community development. The latter responsibility, with some notable exceptions, has consistently escaped the capabilities of most LPAs, LHAs, and economic development units. UDC has demonstrated that viable participatory mechanisms, typically operating as UDC sponsored nonprofit subsidiaries, can be made effective.

> *Example:*
> . . . the devolution of some regulatory and implementational authority to constituencies smaller than the traditional large city is more likely to be effective in avoiding the bureaucratic standardization, red tape, and depersonalization one associates with city administered affairs.
>
> The Urban Development Corporation is equipped by its legislation to respond to the demand for local participation. In addition to the usual and often perfunctory provision for local advisory committees, the UDC is empowered to act through subsidiary corporations in which it retains majority control. It may yield all its power to such corporations, loan or give them money, assign them leases, designate them to construct and manage properties. Effective use of this technique for including the local civic and church groups, labor affiliates or simple neighborhood improvement associations would confirm the genius of the drafters of the UDC bill (Reilly and Schulman, 1968, pp. 142–43).

The development corporation's ability to deeply involve communities and business interests of the central city undoubtedly would be a major factor of its initial and ultimate success. Institutional modernization involving new forms and functions of community organization is as critical as modernizing city government and the functional structure of the central city.

Chapter Eleven

Financing New Town Intown Development (Los Angeles)

Financing a new town intown program in a major city like Los Angeles is a formidable task, requiring substantial innovation and support from higher levels of government. A development corporation should be able to raise capital through various methods including bonds, conventional debt, equity capital, and other forms available to private corporations. General and special revenue sharing can provide part of the capital needed. In addition, new methods of public financing must be devised. In some cases, new institutions such as urban development banks may be required to channel funds from existing capital markets into urban developm nt uses. In other cases, the credit of state and local governments may be pledged without jeopardizing their credit standing.

The ultimate success of NTIT programs depends on the ability to attract substantial private investment and activity. Public expenditures should be directed so as to maximize leverage in attracting private capital consistent with the twin objectives of central city modernization and assisting the less advantaged.

NTIT development programs require large capital outlays over a period of years before substantial visible results are obtained. The magnitudes of these costs have been discussed elsewhere and are well documented in the financial literature (Wilburn and Gladstone 1972; Heroux and Wallace 1973). Model IA and IB proposals under Title VII suggest that front end costs of $1–2 million are incurred during the project planning stage and a peak debt on the order of $50 million. These figures are probably influenced by statutory and administrative limitations of the Title VII program and would be unrepresentative for a Model II NTIT proposed for Los Angeles.

1. **Timing of Costs and Revenues.** Timing of costs and revenues is as important as magnitudes, since timing affects debt service costs and the availa-

bility of revenues. The problem has come to the forefront in the case of suburban new towns and the basic principles seem to be similar for all large scale development. Figure 11–1 shows the timing of outlays and revenues for a hypothetical suburban new town. The annual expenditures are high in early years when planning and land acquisition occurs. Expenditures remain high for several more years as infrastructure and site improvement costs accrue. Positive annual cash flows are not experienced until about the ninth project year when land sale or lease revenues exceed continuing development costs. It is at this point when peak debt (peak investment) is reached. Cumulative cash flow does not occur until late in the project (the sixteenth year in the figure).

The long investment period has two important implications. First, the greatest capital outlays in any given year parallel land acquisition and major infrastructure expenditures; in other years, outlays are at much lower levels. This allows the development corporation to schedule capital acquisition according to project needs rather than having to face the peak debt in a single year. The second, and converse, implication is that capital expenditures must be programmed before project development begins. Positive cash flows result only

Figure 11–1.   Cash Flow—Private New Community
(Does not include public facilities)

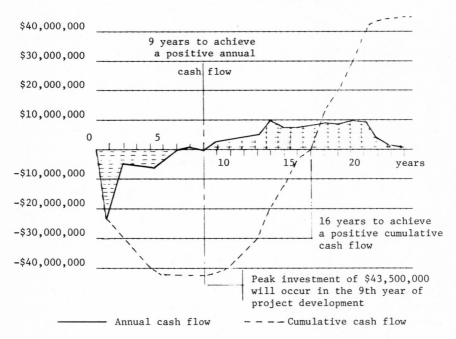

Source: New York State Urban Development Corporation. *New Communities for New York,* New York, December 1970

because private investment capital begins to flow into the project area through land purchases, leases, building construction, and the like. But private capital would not be attracted without assurance that the development program would be completed as planned. Delays, reconsiderations, or other deviations could diminish the confidence of the private sector, reduce or delay positive cash flow, and seriously jeopardize project success.

2. Long-Term Commitment Required.

The programmatic stability requirements underscore the need for a long term commitment by a development corporation not subject to annual appropriations and similar governmental budgeting constraints. The total financial plan, designed around the timing of capital outlays, must be established before project development. Governmental agencies, however, do not commit capital outlays over the long time horizons required for a NTIT program. Capital outlays by state and local governments are budgeted in one of two ways: annual capital budgets or long term bonding.

Annual capital budgets typically comprise three to six percent of the government's total expenditures and are for projects usually completed in one or two years. The projects are selected from a list of projects having a short time horizon; for example, the Los Angeles capital improvement program has a five year time horizon.

A second undesirable aspect is that expenditures must be authorized annually. Items "budgeted" for future years are tentative upon approval in those future years. Events such as a reduction in revenues resulting from economic conditions or federal programs could cause some items to be deleted in future years, jeopardizing any long term programs.

Revenues for annual capital budgets come from several sources: local taxes, intergovernmental transfers, special funds, and others. Oftentimes revenues, especially highway users' funds and state and federal transfers, are earmarked for specific uses. This process precludes firm commitment of capital funds in future years unless a local government is willing to raise its tax rates in anticipation of possible decreases of capital fund sources; local governments are naturally unwilling to do so. For example, Los Angeles had a capital budget of $36 million in 1972–73; of this, $22 million (61 percent) was highway users' funds and spent on highway related projects. Capital funds from general revenues totalled only $2.9 million or 8 percent of the total capital budget.

Bonds are an attractive way to make the long term commitment needed for central city development. Just how attractive depends in no small part upon how cheaply or dearly money can be borrowed and upon repayment provisions. The fixed interest rate on a capital debt is a major problem in large scale development. It has been pointed out that much investment must be made years before substantial revenues are generated. Nonetheless, interest on the debt must be paid in those early years. The developing entity thus may find itself borrowing more money or diverting resources from long term problems to meet short term amortization needs.

Certain disadvantages of borrowing can be overcome by use of equity capital where investors are willing to wait a number of years before realizing investment returns. Equity capital allows the developing entity to concentrate on maximizing long term gains rather than meeting interest payment deadlines.

A third shortcoming of debt financing is that the debtholder receives none of the federal income tax advantages of real estate ownership. Federal gains and depreciation provisions create strong incentives for high income individuals and corporations to invest in real estate. These tax advantages allow such persons to accept lower returns on real estate than for other investments of equal risk. The ability of the Cedar–Riverside NTIT developers to attract substantial private equity capital is one case in point.

Other disadvantages of bonded debt financing include uncertain voter approval of general obligation bonds (which require two-thirds majority for California local governments). Revenue bonds avoid this problem but have problems of their own. Sale of revenue bonds depends on investors' confidence in the bonding agency to raise revenues for debt service. There is no indication that investors would be attracted to new community developments without some form of guarantee. Title VII provides a mortgage guarantee not exceeding $50 million per project; however, the high cost and long delays incurred in meeting HUD requirement may probably offset whatever limited attractiveness Title VII may have for most potential NTIT developers.

3. New Sources of Financing. New community developments require several types of financing, with specific risk levels and length of commitment associated with each.

The first expenditures are "seed money" expenses incurred in defining a possible project area and establishing its feasibility. Costs include preliminary planning, locational analysis, determining land ownership and probable land acquisition, and related efforts which tentatively measure project costs and benefits. Seed costs are risky investments; many contingencies may prevent a feasible project from ensuing. Front end costs are lost and then written off as nonrecoverable.

In the private sector, seed costs are usually borne by the entrepreneur, often in the form of donated services rather than actual cash outlays. The entrepreneur receives the return of his front end investment through his ownership interest in the ensuing project. Returns of seed investments must be very great in order to compensate for the high risk involved.

Seed money for Stage 1 private NTIT developers follows the pattern described above. For example, owners of land on which Pontchartrain is proposed made cash and personnel services available for conceptualizing the project. At San Antonio, personnel from San Antonio Ranch performed most of these tasks using capital contributed by equity participants.

Seed money for public developers is more difficult to obtain. Such costs ideally should be borne by those who would benefit most from a successful project—the local government. Outright grants are the most appropriate funding method while loans generally are not: first, since many seed money expenditures will not yield feasible projects, no revenues could be generated to offset the loans. Second, loans necessitate interest payments long before revenues may be available. An acceptable compromise would be loans which are interest free and forgiven if no development project ensues. UDC makes interest free loans for high risk studies.

Other possible sources include grants from foundations, community interest groups, and developers or corporations with special interests in a development area. For example, the Ford Foundation has provided seed money grants to some local economic development corporations and is to provide front end money for establishing a community development corporation in New Orleans. Church, labor, and other community organizations may possibly provide seed money, especially for developing housing (The Practicing Law Institute, 1970.).

Venture capital would be the next phase of development financing. Venture capital is needed to finalize planning, acquire land, obtain building permits, and other activities which bring a proposed project to the certainty where risk evaluation by conventional analysis is possible. For private developments, venture capital is usually provided by syndications of private investors, joint ventures, or equity participation by corporations or financial institutions. Loans are not usually available at this stage, because risks are too high to be compensated by interest rates alone.

Venture capital raised through equity participation, as opposed to loans, has several advantages for a NTIT development corporation and investors. The corporation would benefit by the absence of debt service costs, especially in early project years when no revenues are produced. Investor benefits include income tax shelter as a part owner of the real estate involved and capital gain returns in later project years. These tax considerations have enabled Cedar–Riverside and San Antonio new towns to attract venture capital from private investors.

Construction or interim financing is temporary capital borrowed to cover materials and labor for site improvements and structures. Construction financing is temporary and repaid when the eventual owner of the building takes title; permanent financing is then acquired, and the construction loan is paid off. Construction financing does not cover land acquisition costs which are part of the owner's equity.

Construction loans are available from institutional lenders where a demand for the product can be demonstrated. Institutions may not be convinced of the demand for the product in early NTIT development phases. In those cases, the corporation may have to secure financing from sources described below.

Permanent financing is by far the largest capital requirement of development projects. In a conventional real estate development, permanent financing covers 60 to 90 percent of total project costs, the remainder being equity contributions for front end costs and venture capital. Permanent financing is long term (25 to 40 years) and includes repayment of principal over the term of the loan. Like construction financing, permanent financing is available from lending institutions for conventional projects with acceptable levels of risk. Many NTIT projects, especially during early phases, may have difficulty in obtaining such loans and have to seek financing from new sources.

Many well-established financial sources will not be available or suitable for NTIT development activities, at least in early years. First, the reluctance of most financial institutions to lend for inner city activities has been well documented (United States Congress, Senate. Hearings, 1968). Institutions make loans for office buildings and hotels in preferred CBD locations, but in small amounts compared to loans made in suburban areas. Further, almost no funds from institutions have been available for inner city housing, except through federally insured or guaranteed programs.

Second, NTIT development requires a long interim period (as long as five years) between initial outlays (for land acquisition, relocation, and infrastructure construction) and revenues (from land sales or building leases). During this time, it is not possible to evaluate the project's success, yet it is essential that outlays continue on schedule. Financial institutions are generally not willing to take debt positions on long term projects with this degree of uncertainty and depth of exposure.

Finally, the evaluation of risk by the financial community depends heavily on the experience of the developer, market for the product, and size of the loan needed. A NTIT may get negative ratings on all three: there are almost no developers with demonstrated ability to do large scale in-town projects involving commercial, industrial, and residential activities; the market for projects with integrated development, incomes, and races is unproven; and the financing needed is extremely large. A conventional evaluation of the risks will not encourage financial institutions to extend credit until a successful track record is established (Kelley, Campanella, and McKiernan, 1971.).

New methods and sources of financing, therefore, will have to be established for urban development. In the following sections, some promising methods are discussed. Not all of the methods are possible within existing legal and institutional restrictions and practices, however.

a) Tax Increment Financing. Tax increment financing can supply some of the necessary capital. The underlying premise is that some or all of the increased tax revenues generated by public development should be returned to the developing entity for retiring its development debt. Property tax revenues are the most easily identifiable increments resulting from development activity—

although sales, business, and personal income taxes theoretically could be included.

Several issues arise in setting the agreements between developing entity and taxing agencies. If the tax base is frozen substantially before NTIT development, revenues from normal growth (unrelated to development activity) would accrue to the developing entity. The entity then would enjoy a cash flow prior to major capital outlays and a valuable source of front end funding. By freezing the tax base prior to major nondevelopment public expenditures such as rapid transit, hospital or college construction, *all* front end and venture capital needed for NTIT development could be generated. UDC used this device at Amherst, New York, in conjunction with state university construction.

Although tax increments can provide some revenues, it must be supplemented by large amounts of capital raised in other ways. The example below will show that total real value of a project must be several times greater than the amount of the tax increment bond.

> *Example:*
> The Los Angeles property tax rate in 1973 was approximately 3.15 percent of market value of real estate. A tax increment which captured the entire increment for the developing entity could therefore provide only about 1/33 of the tax base per year for retirement of tax increment bonds. The debt service requirement on 20 year bonds having 5 percent interest rate was just over 8 percent. Thus for every dollar of debt which could be liquidated by a 3.15 percent tax rate, total taxable property of 8/3.15 or $2.50 was required. Further, this example assumes the $2.50 in added taxable property comes into existence in the first year of the 20 year period. If development proceeds slowly in initial years, the multiplier of required tax base increase to bond amount increases sharply. Moreover, public improvements made by the development entity would be nontaxable.
>
> Accordingly, it follows that capital raised in other ways would have to finance most of the $2.50 for every dollar raised by tax increments.
>
> The required ratio of other capital to tax increment capital is reduced if the term of the tax increment bond is increased; a 40 year, 5 percent bond requires only 5.83 percent annual debt service.
>
> Increases in the tax rate also make bond repayment easier for a given level of tax base increment; on the other hand, tax rate increases discourage private investors and tenants, thus reducing the pace of development. The required tax base increment of 2.5 times the bond amount can consist of increases in land value and new construction (which is assessed at cost). There is, therefore, a trade-off between land value increases and the amount of other (nontax increment) investment required.

The amount by which *small*-scale urban development projects can increase land values is not known; Wilburn and Gladstone (1972, p. 23) suggested that increases in urban areas are less than suburban development. This is consistent with Netzer (1966) and others that much urban land in its current use may be priced above its economic value.

It would be especially difficult to generate large increases in value if land uses are constrained by requirements for low cost housing, job generating industries, and other uses which may be below the highest economic use of the land. It will therefore be necessary for most of the tax base increment to be provided by new buildings, with capital raised through nontax increment sources.

The development pace will be a critical factor in the ability of the community developer to liquidate tax increment bonds. Investments made by the development entity lead private investment by several years. Private developers will usually not commit substantial amounts of capital until land acquisition and clearance, infrastructure improvements, and other development activities are essentially complete. As a result, most of the tax increment does not occur until several years after debt service on tax increment bonds has begun. Delays in attracting private investment would magnify this problem.

This is similar to the problem faced by private developers with large development loans and few revenues in early project years. In some cases, projects with extremely high eventual payoffs occurring many years after the initial investments are nevertheless not feasible investments when cash flows are properly discounted.

In conclusion, then, tax increment financing cannot provide the major source of financing for community development; substantial amounts of capital from other sources are required. The ability of a project to generate enough tax increments to liquidate tax increment bonds depends directly on two elements: (1) increases in land value created by the project, and (2) new construction not financed by the tax increment bonds. A third, but less direct factor, is the timing of development which determines how early in the liquidation period the tax increments are generated.

Investments in successful development generate a large variety of returns including:

1. Land value increases;
2. Opportunities for new residential, commercial, and industrial investments;
3. Employment opportunities in new economic activities:
4. Quality of life increases for residents.

Some of these returns are captured by taxes; tax increment financing taps part of a small flow of returns and channels it back to the developing entity. It is unrealistic to expect this small part of generated returns to provide a major part of the capital investment needed for large-scale development activities.

b) Special Revenue Sharing. Special revenue sharing can provide front end money and venture capital for NTIT projects. The "hold harmless" level of special revenue sharing for Los Angeles has been estimated at between $38 million and $50 million per year for five years or a total of roughly $230 million.

A set of guidelines for allocating *general* revenue sharing funds has been proposed by the Los Angeles County supervisors:

1. One-time expenditures to improve financial and operating capability;
2. Measures directed at long term cost avoidance;
3. Substitute financing for prior federally supported programs;
4. New programs which will increase the effectiveness of government.

The guidelines emphasize administrative purposes of long range benefit to local government.

The national experience with urban renewal and model cities suggest additional criteria for Los Angeles City's use of special revenue sharing:

5. Funds should be concentrated in limited geographical areas where real impacts can be made rather than spread thinly;
6. Funds should be spent in a coordinated way rather than on isolated single purpose projects and agencies;
7. Funds should be spent in areas with substantial development opportunities already existing, or to support existing trends, rather than trying to help the worst areas;
8. Funds should be spent so as to stimulate complementary capital from other sources, especially private sources.

The eight criteria can be summarized as advocating that special revenue sharing funds be allocated to true public investments, so as to maximize long run benefits to the *community*.

Special revenue sharing funds *per se* could not finance a major NTIT program. Instead, these funds should be allocated to maximize leverage in attracting private capital investments. There are several ways of potentially achieving such leverage. One would be a revolving loan fund from which front end costs could be borrowed. Whenever a financially successful development project emerged, these front end costs would be repaid to the fund. Also, revenue sharing funds could backstop development lending programs. Using these funds as reserves, a development corporation or urban development bank could raise as much as five times the reserve amount by issuing bonds backed by mortgages or other loans.

c) An Urban Development Bank. A development bank could assist local development entities having trouble selling revenue or tax increment bonds.

This could occur where the financial community initially lacked confidence in the ability of a development entity to carry out its programs and projects. Such a development bank would purchase an entity's bonds from funds raised through bonds issued by the bank.

A bank could *conceivably* have greater acceptance by the financial community because of:

1. A large security fund, made up of capital contributed by federal, state, and local governments (for example, special revenue sharing could provide a source for such a fund);
2. Contingent liability on the revenues of some level of government, especially federal or state;
3. A loan guarantee program, such as Title VII or the FNMA mortgage backed security program.

The historical model for development banks is the international banking system which emerged after World War II for reconstruction and, more recently, economic development of underdeveloped nations. Development banks typically receive a large capital contribution from the World Bank and/or the nation involved. A bank is empowered to issue bonds 5 to 20 times the capital contribution, with the contributed capital serving as the primary security. Loans and equity contributions are then made to industries, utility companies, housing agencies, and even small businesses which contribute to desired economic development.

In some nations, development banks go beyond the pure banking function by (a) seeking out entrepreneurs to undertake activities needed to further development plans, and (b) in some cases, becoming entrepreneurs of last resort by initiating development projects with staff and money provided by the bank itself.

Equity participation by the bank in emerging industries is usually necessary to provide the venture capital needed. Equity participation—as compared to lending—has three major advantages: (1) it does not burden the emerging industry with interest payments in early years when liquidity demands are not offset by revenues; (2) equity participation allows the bank to participate in profits once the developing industry achieves success; these profits can then be used to get other industries started; and (3) the bank is in a position to advise or even participate in management of the development activity if it seems necessary (Diamond, 1957).

A variety of legislative proposals have been made recently in the United States for the establishment of urban development banks (Jacobs, May 1973). Many are based in part on the early proposals by David Rockefeller. (Financial Institutions and the Urban Crisis, 1968.) For example, the National Growth Policy Planning Act (S. 1286, 93rd Congress, 1st Session) proposed a national development bank empowered to raise $5 billion through issuance of bonds backed by the full faith and credit of the United States. The bank would use this capital to make loans or to purchase bonds of state and local governmental agencies.

A Federal Financing Bank, which has some development bank features, was established in 1974 and can be used in conjunction with the Title VII to satisfy certain of the needs for Federal banking assistance in developing new towns intown. One feature is that it can provide lower interest rates after the requirements for Title VII have been satisfied. A federal urban development bank would be even more desirable as it could make direct loans to promising development projects earlier in the program's life and before Title VII requirements had been met.

There is interest in development banks at the state level as well. In California, Senate Bill No. 650 proposed a community development bank to make loans to or purchase bonds issued by local governmental agencies. This proposal would not create liability on the credit of the state; instead, if a local government defaulted on its loan or bonds, the bank could attach revenues due to the local government from the state treasury such as state income and sales taxes or federal programs passed through the state. Thus, revenue bonds issued by local agencies would create a contingent liability on general revenues due the local government so that the bonds would have a much lower risk level.

These proposals point out the need for an institution which can issue bonds acceptable to the financial community and channel the capital into community development activities whose credit may not be initially acceptable to the financial community. This requires some liability on higher levels of government or a guarantee program of some sort.

Both proposals cited have the shortcoming of being restricted to debt instruments only. Venture capital is still a major problem for community development activities. Development banks should be allowed some equity participation in development activities. An alternative would be a special category of interest free loans for venture capital, to be repaid only if a project progresses far enough to repay the loan from long term financing or generated revenues. Loans of this nature are made to UDC by New York State.

The urban development bank could also be empowered to make loans and equity contributions to private developers and businesses whenever such activities are in the best interest of a development program. An especially promising approach would be providing equity and loan capital to small businesses through a Small Business Investment Company (SBIC). Small businesses, aided by the development bank's financial and advisory services, could provide services, employment, and community participation in the development sector.

In the absence of an urban development bank, the credit of state or other governments can be pledged to generate capital for new town development. The Housing Finance Agency (HFA) of New York State exemplifies how a state's borrowing capacity can stimulate urban development. State bonds are issued by HFA to raise capital for housing construction for middle income families under the Mitchell–Lama Program. Loans for housing finance are made available at the interest rate which HFA bonds bear, about six and one-half percent, rather than at mortgage interest rates, which were at nine percent in mid–1973. The interest rate saving can have a substantial effect on housing costs and at no cost to the state. A federal income tax exemption on state and local government bonds provides the subsidy. A similar but more limited program is California's Veterans Farm and Home Bond Program under which state general obligation bonds finance loans to veterans for farm and home purchases at reduced interest rates. General obligation bonds require voter approval in California. However, their self-liquidating features avoid increases in tax levels and make voter approval easier to obtain.

d) Need for Private Participation. It would be a mistake to over-emphasize the public sector role in financing new urban development. The public role should be to plan and leverage public investments which attract a maximum amount of private capital from existing sources and institutions. For example, in the Pontchartrain NTIT it is estimated that $50 million of public developer investments would generate an eventual $1.5 billion in private investment. Early developments by UDC in New York relied heavily on public financing and have already generated over four dollars in private investment for every public dollar invested by UDC. As noted previously, a high ratio of private to public investment is required to make tax increment financing feasible.

Private investment can be attracted into NTIT projects and programs through two channels: (1) loans and investments in NTIT land and buildings; and (2) investment directly in a development corporation(s) at subsidiary or umbrella (parent) corporation level. UDC stimulates private equity investment in its developments by direct equity participation in its subsidiary corporations. Equity investors usually are developers with major activities in project areas.

Private equity participation in NTIT activities has a number of very desirable features. Equity capital avoids the problem of meeting debt service payments in early years when no revenues are being generated. Another advantage are tax shelters for equity contributors; the success of Cedar–Riverside in attracting private equity capital demonstrates the importance of this feature.

A disadvantage is the very real problem of structuring private involvement in a way which avoids any taint of wrongdoing and conflicts of interest. A second disadvantage could be public disclosure of returns to equity contributors. Although the contributors can show tax losses in early years, it will be necessary sooner or later to return substantial gains to the contributors.

Private developers are potential contributors of equity capital. Participation by such developers has the feature that returns on equity can be concealed from public view through transfer pricing (for example, Cedar–Riverside), below market leases (Roosevelt Island), and other methods. The potential for public misunderstanding or misrepresentation of such schemes may make such methods risky, however.

e) Need for Federal Financial Assistance. A new town intown program in Los Angeles similar to that proposed could not be financed from local sources with no more federal assistance than Title VII loan guarantees. A reasonably well funded development corporation could undertake a program of central city modernization in Los Angeles. Nonetheless, it would still require federal financial assistance to generate local public and private investments.

It would be necessary to have a more definitive development plan so as to estimate total cost and the needed federal share. Even without detailed estimates, however, it seems evident that the latter would exceed the $50 million limit to federal loan guarantees per NTIT project—unless HUD (a) construed Title VII to apply to each individual project within a multiproject NTIT program in Los Angeles (or as proposed for Hartford, Cleveland, and Chicago), and (b) was willing to support several of such projects within a short period of time within a single city.

Chapter Twelve

The Los Angeles New Town: A Scenario

In the past, intown development emphasized problem areas and situations often seen in limited and isolated perspective—rundown neighborhoods, declining central business districts, the most extreme poverty areas, and the like. The character and territorial scale of these efforts tended to be defined in terms of physical decay and in relative isolation from the basic socioeconomic fabric of the city as a whole (and the metropolitan region). What clearly emerged from our study of the national experience is the inadequacy of partial, isolated approaches and the corresponding need to relate development to: (a) the overall socioeconomic pattern of the city and region, and (b) developmental opportunities available in the city, particularly those that can be "leveraged" at the margin to achieve multiplier effects.

More specifically, our national experience underscores the need for combining—within a single, multifunction development program—city strengths and development opportunities on the one hand and problem areas and situations on the other. While the notion of using sources of urban strength to help overcome problems is hardly startling, nevertheless it is a fact worth stressing that this has *not* been the national approach to intown development and that it *should* be the approach employed in the future. The difficulty that remains is how to make this concept operational.

Components of a NTIT Program
in Los Angeles

As to Los Angeles, we have identified two general kinds of areas: (a) high potential "resource and opportunity areas," that is, areas with substantial development strength or potential; and (b) "primary impact areas,"—areas with high levels of need but also with high marginal potential to benefit from appropriate public intervention. These resource and opportunity areas, while representing significant sources of developmental strength, typically also have

279

serious problems and sections needing improvement, while the primary impact areas contain some sources of strength that could be exploited and built upon. We are not dealing with "pure" types but a spectrum of conditions with different mixtures of developmental strengths and weaknesses.

   1. Resource and Opportunity Areas. Resource and opportunity areas are those leverage points within the urban system with sufficient developmental potential to modernize the central city and, in the process, to assist the less advantaged. For purposes of identification, selection, and feasibility analysis of a new town intown, a resource and opportunity area is characterized by one or more of the following criteria:

a)   Areas to which private business investment is already attracted and likely to continue;
b)   Areas where cooperative investment arrangements appear particularly feasible (for example, through unions or community organizations);
c)   Areas in which urban renewal and other public development or service funds are already invested;
d)   Areas which have unusually strong attractions for cultural, historical, recreational, and medical facilities, and are capable of attracting additional public and private investment;
e)   Areas with development potential that can be marginally leveraged to a significant degree through public intervention.

Resource and opportunity areas can be generally classified into three types:

1.   Nodal Points. These encompass existing centers of economic activity as indicated by concentrations of retail/wholesale trade, employment opportunities, office/commercial rentals, and so forth. Chief among these areas in Los Angeles is the central business district. Others include sections along the Wilshire Boulevard corridor, industrial corridor, Port of San Pedro, and Los Angeles International Airport;
2.   Unique Facilities. These include public and private facilities providing opportunities for surrounding communities—employment, job training, education, recreation, health services, and the like. Such smaller, more specialized clusters in Los Angeles include the University of Southern California (USC), the Martin Luther King Hospital complex, UCLA—Westwood Village, and Century City.
3.   Transportation Nodes. These include well-located transportation nodes which because of enhanced accessibility have exceptional developmental advantage. Los Angeles appears likely to undertake major changes in its urban transportation system in the near future. The resulting changes in relative accessibility of some centers would create considerable development potential.

The anticipated changes in transportation systems within the metropolitan region would substantially impact all resource and opportunity areas since relative accessibility influences land uses and values. In large part development leverage of an area is a function of its accessibility.

2. Primary Impact Areas, One of two key objectives of Stage 2 new town intown development should be to help less advantaged groups to live better lives. Accordingly, it is necessary to identify those groups and areas that should be encompassed. After a mixed, and in many cases unhappy, national experience with efforts to assist the less advantaged in the 1960s—particularly with the poverty and model cities programs, it is evident that we do not yet have appropriate guidelines.

It is important to distinguish between direct people oriented, nonplace public programs (for example, social security and family allowances) and programs essentially developmental and place related (new town intown development). Many people in the inner city can be substantially assisted by the former and helped only peripherally by the latter. However, other groups and areas can be significantly impacted by developmental place related programs. This is not to suggest that these groups and areas would not need the direct people oriented programs, but merely to identify them as particularly receptive to programs strengthening specific neighborhoods of the city and employment opportunities.

Another important lesson is the apparent ease with which the poor can be overlooked.

Too often, programs aimed at expanding opportunities for the less advantaged were limited and ineffectual. The federally sponsored renewal and housing programs—despite an apparently clear legislative intent that significant benefits accrue to less advantaged groups—in practice distributed far less of the ultimate "share" to the poor. Such outcomes can be avoided by a well-organized, broad-scale new town intown development program of the type proposed.

To guard against "overlooking" the less advantaged, certain communities or areas should be singled out by a development corporation for first order priority. These primary impact areas would be selected according to two broad criteria:

a) They must clearly be "need" areas beset with a wide array of social, economic, housing, or physical problems;

b) In addition, they must possess innate advantages to marginally benefit from public efforts to enhance opportunities in their locale. Such advantages would include effective community organizations, ongoing public or private efforts, an existing commercial base, sizable existing standard housing, locational advantages, and the like.

Thus, a development corporation would focus on inner city problem areas, especially amenable to marginally significant improvements, where existing strengths can be built upon and developed by a new town intown program. Watts, East Los Angeles, Venice, and the entire Normandie/Hoover/Pico–Union area would all qualify as such communities.

3. Development Sectors. Experience has clearly shown that limited, isolated projects cannot effectively modernize a central city while at the same time assisting less advantaged groups. Does that mean that revitalization should be aimed at the entire urban region? Ideally yes, since an urban region is a highly integrated socioeconomic-physical system. At the same time, we are faced with realistic (and normally, quite severe) limits on the human, financial, and political resources which can be made available. This suggests two requirements: (a) NTIT planning and implementation should be within the context of *regional* analysis and regional planning so that central city development makes sense in terms of the region as a whole, and (b) project staging should be designed to be simultaneously viable *and* feasible. The former, at least in principle, is clear enough not to require further elaboration. The latter, however, calls for new thinking on the very complex problem of staging development.

Our analysis to date suggests the solution lies in identifying a series of development sectors within the city. These would be "planning and action" areas with their own unified management and time frame for development programs of manageable size and complexity. Specification of a development sector would not exclude improvement in other areas of the city either simultaneously or subsequently. It would be designed, however, to maximize marginal returns from limited staff and financial/political resources directed at clearly stated development priorities.

Each development sector would encompass both resource and opportunity areas and primary impact areas. A citywide development corporation would organize a series of projects (of various scales) which link a sector's resource and opportunity and primary impact areas. Many sector projects and programs could be then carried out by subsidiary corporations.

In Los Angeles, while each sector can be viewed as possessing unique features of citywide importance, there is one sector which stands out as of special importance. This sector would have as its focus the central and older parts of the city—an area where the city's resources *and* problems are most concentrated. Success or failure here would ultimately impact the entire Los Angeles new town intown program. Because of its leading role, we would single out the downtown and surrounding area as the NTIT core development sector. The remaining sectors would be subject to concentrated development activity *at some point in the future* after core sector development was well under way.

Detailed identification of the core development sector would be based on two considerations: (a) its potential to combine both central city revitalization and major enhancement in the quality of life for the less advantaged as the primary accomplishment of the program and (b) its capacity to serve as a *platform* for further development. Thus, the core sector should embrace both the major resource and opportunity and primary impact (or need) areas of the central city in a viable development combination so as to achieve the dual objectives of a new town intown program. At the same time, development of the core sector, by the logic of its place in the regional system, should be able ultimately to revitalize the central city as a whole—mainly by leveraging the impact of initial development on other central city sections in sequential stages.

A LOS ANGELES NEW TOWN INTOWN: AN ILLUSTRATION

One of the first decisions facing a development corporation would be where and how to begin. Its initial actions would be crucial, since it would doubtless be under considerable pressure to produce visible results early on in its existence. Moreover, because it probably would be operating under severe financial constraints, its investment/involvement decisions should be strategized to insure maximum impact.

We believe a workable solution would be staged development of specific sectors of the city over a long period of time, such as a 25-year capital budget horizon. Available resources could then be marshalled for concentrated attack on social and economic problems of various sectors of the city in sequence. By staging development, gains realized in one sector could stimulate subsequent development efforts in other sectors.

As discussed above, each development sector would encompass both resource and opportunity and primary impact areas in order to strike a balance between strengths and needs. Thus, programs and projects within each sector would build upon positive development features and trends so as to overcome problems manifested in decaying housing, infrastructure, economic and employment bases, educational opportunities, and services. For purposes of clarifying these concepts, we can outline below a scenario for the first phase of the development corporation's activities.

Spatial Characteristics of the Core Development Sector

In general, we assume a development corporation would be most effective if it operates initially where developmental resources and needs are most concentrated. In Los Angeles, as with most urban areas, resources and needs are most concentrated around the central business district. Thus, we have identified a core development sector to serve as the platform for subsequent efforts in other sectors.

Although various sizes and shapes might be envisioned, the core sector would clearly involve the central business district. As the single most important governmental, financial, cultural, and employment center of the city and region, the CBD would be pivotal for any major revitalization program in Los Angeles. Given the CBD as the major anchor, the core development sector would then extend outward to encompass problems and opportunities represented by nearby central city resource and opportunity and primary impact areas.

1. **Primary Impact Areas.** In terms of economic and social need, central Los Angeles stands out as the high priority area of the city (and county). With the exception of small pockets in the San Fernando and San Gabriel Valleys, the major poverty and unemployment areas in Los Angeles consist of two sectoral extensions of the central business district. One runs southward through eastern portions of the South Central area to the harbor areas of San Pedro and Long Beach, while the other branches westward to Venice in a series of enclaves south of the Wilshire Corridor. These two sectors are broadly, but not totally, coincident with the predominant minority areas. A third major concentration of poverty and unemployment is located east of downtown, extends into Los Angeles County, and contains the main concentration of Spanish-speaking populations. *Taken together, these areas represent what may be the most geographically extensive zone of urban poverty in any American city.*

To represent the centrality of poverty and unemployment,[a] the Los Angeles areas of highest concentrations in 1970 are noted on Maps 12–1 and 12–2.[b] The density of poverty is clearly highest at the center. Distributions of major minority populations (Black and Spanish surname) are indicated for comparison on Map 12–3. As can be seen, there is considerable, but by no means complete, overlap between areas of minority populations, low income, and high unemployment, but there are also substantially middle class minority areas (see Tables 12–1 and 12–2 for comparative data by race for the city and county).

A further indication of the concentration of "needs" in Los Angeles is demonstrated by Map 12–4, which portrays the location of the most aged of the city's housing stock. Not surprisingly, the oldest housing tends to be found at the center of the urbanized area. Other structures, streets, utilities, and related infrastructure are correspondingly old. Thus, although Los Angeles may be somewhat younger than most eastern cities, much of the housing and infrastructure at its center is near, or past, the limits of expected usefulness. Since improvement or replacement is necessary in central Los Angeles, public intervention would be most warranted here. Certainly the less advantaged would gain

a. The unemployment figures in the middle range for 1970 (seven to ten percent) are somewhat misleading. Unemployment in the aerospace industry was at an unusually high level in 1970. The highest category (over ten percent) is more representative of the typical Los Angeles spatial pattern with regard to unemployment.

b. Note: The shaded areas which appear on all maps represent the territory contained within the boundaries of the City of Los Angeles.

Map 12–1.   Distribution of Low Income Families, 1970

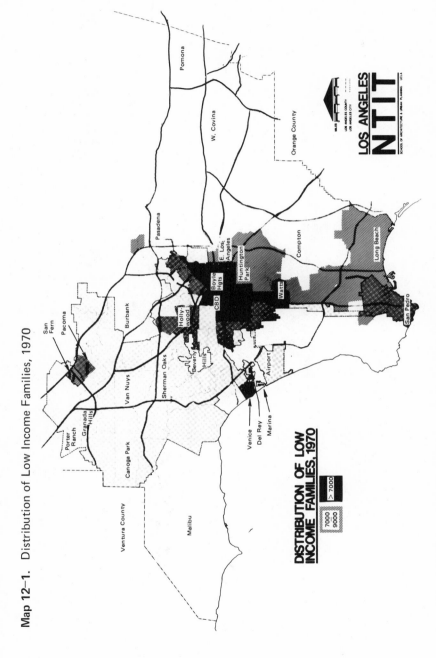

DISTRIBUTION OF LOW
INCOME FAMILIES, 1970

SOURCE: U.S. CENSUS (1970) MEDIAN FAMILY INCOME, BY ZONE

Map 12–2. Unemployment in Los Angeles, 1970

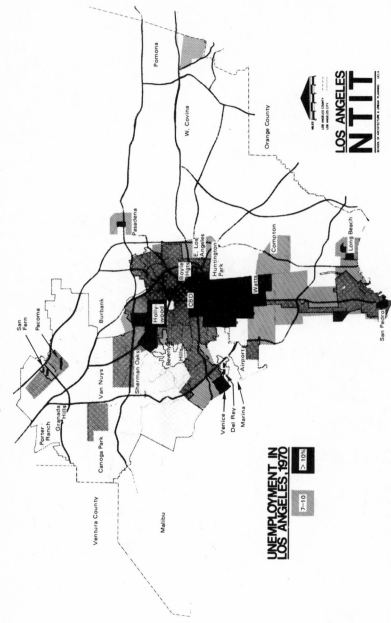

SOURCE: U.S. CENSUS (1970)

Map 12–3. Spanish Surname Percent, Black Percent, 1970

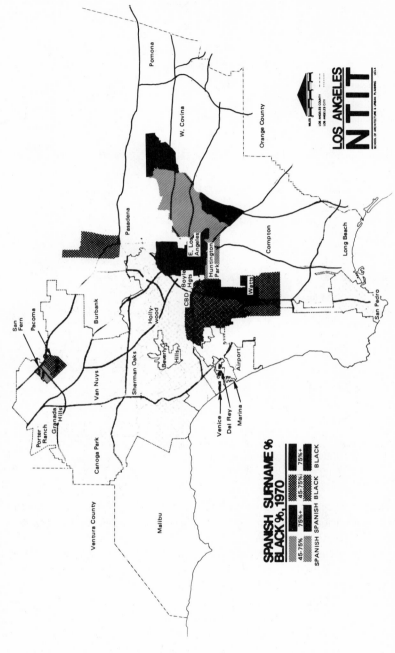

SPANISH SURNAME %
BLACK %, 1970

45-75%   75%+   45-75%   75%+

SPANISH   SPANISH   BLACK   BLACK

LOS ANGELES
NTIT

SOURCE: U.S. CENSUS (1970)

Table 12–1. Population Trends by Race, Los Angeles, 1960–1970

	1960	*1970*	*% Change*
Los Angeles County			
Black	461,546	762,844	
	7.6%	10.9%	+65.3%
Spanish Surname	576,716	1,289,311	+123.6%
	9.6%	18.3%	
Other White	4,877,150	4,717,188	−3.3%
	80.8%	67.1%	
Other Non-White	123,359	262,732	+113.0%
	2.0%	3.7%	
Total Population	6,038,771	7,032,075	+16.4%
	100.0%	100.0%	
City of Los Angeles			
Black	334,916	503,606	+50.4%
	13.5%	17.8%	
Spanish Surname	260,389	518,791	+99.2%
	10.5%	18.4%	
Other White	1,801,419	1,654,746	−8.1%
	72.7%	58.9%	
Other Non-White	82,291	138,855	+68.9%
	3.3%	4.9%	
Total Population	2,479,015	2,815,998	+13.6%
	100.0%	100.0%	

Source: United States Bureau of the Census
  1960: *U.S. Census of Population and Housing: 1960, Census Tracts, Los Angeles–Long Beach Standard Metropolitan Statistical Area,* Table P–1, p. 25
  1970: *U.S. Census of Population and Housing: 1970, Census Tracts, Los Angeles–Long Beach Standard Metropolitan Statistical Area,* Table P–1, pp. p–1, p–3; Table P–2, pp. p–136, p–138

most from projects and programs in areas most accessible to them; this is an important rationale for locating the initial core sector at the center of Los Angeles rather than elsewhere.

Accordingly, several areas can be singled out as ripe for NTIT development due to their apparent marginal receptivity to public intervention. Some primary impact areas which logically could be linked with revitalization of the core sector include the following:

Watts. Perhaps the most noteworthy of all primary impact areas is Watts which could qualify as a prototype need area. Long the focus of numerous

Table 12–2. Unemployment and Poverty, by Race, Los Angeles, 1970

	Black	Spanish Surname	Other (White and Non-White)	Total
Los Angeles County				
Unemployment				
Total Civilian Labor Force	287,569	479,214	2,247,333	3,014,116
Total Unemployed	28,476	33,933	125,142	187,551
Percentage Unemployed	9.9%	7.1%	5.6%	6.2%
Poverty				
Total Families	175,208	293,124	1,300,999	1,769,331
Total Families with incomes below poverty limit	35,730	37,637	69,213	142,580
Percent below poverty limit	20.4%	12.8%	5.3%	8.1%
Los Angeles City				
Unemployment				
Total Civilian Labor Force	197,324	201,369	852,488	1,251,181
Total Unemployed	19,753	15,315	51,734	86,802
Percentage Unemployed	10.0%	7.6%	6.1%	6.9%
Poverty				
Total Families	117,959	119,607	457,153	694,719
Total Families with incomes below poverty limit	25,184	17,986	25,331	68,501
Percent below poverty limit	21.3%	15.0%	5.5%	9.9%

Source: United States Bureau of the Census, *1970 Census of Population and Housing, Census Tracts, Los Angeles–Long Beach Standard Metropolitan Statistical Area, Part I,* Table P–3, pp. p–271, p–273; Table P–4, pp. p–406, p–408; Table P–6, pp. p–568, p–570; Table P–8, pp. p–667, p–669

public and private programs, Watts possesses an increasingly effective array of community organizations and an aware, concerned resident population which could become strongly involved in a developmental program. Watts could be the logical southern boundary of a first phase core development sector.

Hoover/Normandie/Pico–Union. Farther north, residential communities around the University of Southern California and Exposition Park and northward to the Convention Center also congregate as a likely primary impact area. Already the focus of major development projects (Hoover urban renewal project, Normandie NDP, and Pico–Union NDP), this area benefits from close accessibility to surrounding public and private institutions and facilities. Like Watts, it has functioning community organizations (especially in Pico–Union) and other strengths to be built upon in order to contribute to a new town intown program.

Map 12–4. Substandard Housing in Los Angeles

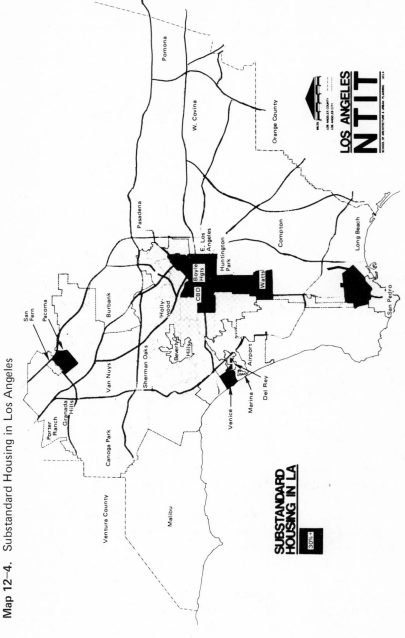

* ZONES WITH 30% OR MORE SUBSTANDARD DWELLING UNITS
SOURCE: COMMUNITY ANALYSIS BUREAU, "STATE OF THE CITY, CONDITIONS OF BLIGHT AND OBSOLESCENCE." 1970
NOTE: INCLUDES LA CITY ONLY

Crenshaw. Although the need to concentrate development resources could logically make Hoover/Normandie/Pico–Union the core sector's
western boundary, it may prove advantageous to proceed farther westward to
incorporate the communities around the Crenshaw commercial area (for
example, the Crenshaw shopping center and businesses along Crenshaw Boulevard). Although many communities here are actually middle class rather than
less advantaged, the area in general is pivotal because it is the current focal point
for upwardly mobile Black families, in terms of both employment and housing.
Unfortunately, there are disturbing signs of community decay: high unemployment rates, rising incidence of venereal disease, gang activity, increased crime,
imminent departure of major commercial firms, and so forth. Early intervention
by a development corporation and NTIT program could stabilize and enhance
the area as a viable alternative for Black and other families; failure to effectively
intervene could sanction decay and ultimately require unnecessarily massive
public outlays in the future.

East Los Angeles/Boyle Heights. Again dependent upon the availability of development resources, East Los Angeles could be targeted as a first
phase or subsequent primary impact area. Immediately adjacent to the central
business district, the area would benefit considerably from downtown modernization in terms of increased employment, services, and related opportunities.
Further, this need area (lying within and beyond the city limits) contains the
largest concentration of Spanish-speaking population in Los Angeles County.
While East Los Angeles' organizational fabric is still evolving, the growing
Chicano consciousness may prove valuable. Although the jurisdictional split
between county and city could vastly complicate planning and development,
nonetheless its unique character and resources indicate high responsiveness to
opportunities generated by a successful new town intown program.

Other Primary Impact Areas. Additional communities qualify as
potential primary impact areas but due to geographic isolation are not suitable
for incorporation into the *initial* phase of a new town intown program. The most
notable are Venice, Pacoima, and the San Pedro communities around the Port of
Los Angeles. Along with East Los Angeles, they could be targeted during subsequent development stages. The primary impact areas recommended for initial
development, that is, within the core development sector, make up the central
four of seven such areas identified in the City of Los Angeles (see Map 12–5).

2. Resource and Opportunity Areas. Although enhancing opportunity for the less advantaged would be an important objective, little would be
accomplished if a NTIT were predominantly restricted to primary impact areas
of concentrated need. Such isolated approaches (for example, under urban

Map 12–5.   Primary Impact Areas

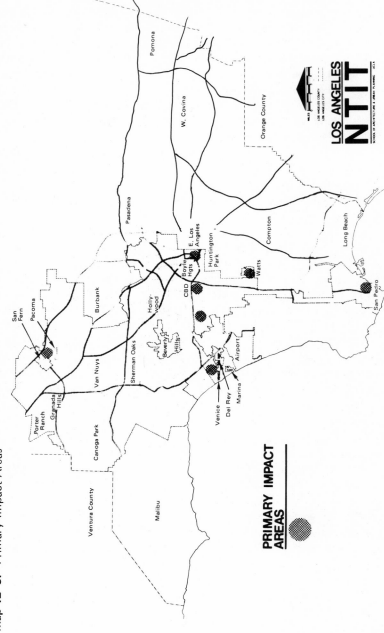

NOTE: INDICATED AREAS ARE SCHEMATIC AND ARE INTENDED AS REPRESENTATIVE EXAMPLES ONLY
SOURCE: UCLA/NTIT STUDY (1973)

renewal or model cities) almost invariably failed in the past. Instead, revitalization activity should emphasize areas of existing or potential strength, build upon existing concentrations of opportunity, and avoid the least viable environments.

As with "need," Los Angeles' strengths are most concentrated in the central city. Although numerous factors have combined to make the city's economic activities more dispersed than most other American cities, contrary to popular belief the city does not lack a clearly defined center. Los Angeles has a downtown—a major governmental, commercial, and banking center at the main freeway crossroads in the heart of the urbanized area. While there are significant competing centers, most are nearby or oriented toward the central section.

For example, in terms of office/commercial activity, the central business district is by far the largest single center of the county. Other leading commercial centers (in terms of net rentable office space) are found along the Wilshire corridor (actually, a series of centers along Wilshire Boulevard extending westward from the downtown to Santa Monica), in Hollywood, and around Los Angeles International Airport (see Map 12−6). The downtown is the largest single employment center, although the Wilshire corridor and L. A. Airport appear to be major competitors. Long Beach is a major employment center because of its proximity to Los Angeles' twin ports (see Map 12−7). Table 12−3 indicates the relative magnitude of the principal employment centers.

The county's major shopping centers are much more dispersed; their distribution is more closely related to population. Nonetheless, even these tend to be most strongly represented at or near the city core (see Map 12−8). The center city has a natural *geographic* advantage due to its relatively greater overall accessibility. Located at the "middle," it is obviously closer to more areas of the city than outlying sections. Its advantages are increased by a freeway system which links the central business district to most major centers and communities.

Impressive indicators of the strength and importance of the central city are revealed by a computer simulation of Los Angeles (Hafner and Lang, May 1973). This research effort, the Los Angeles Simulation Study (LASS),[c] utilized census and other data to depict essential features of the urbanized areas of Los Angeles County. One output of the computer model measured density of total employment for various zones throughout the county.[d] Map 12−9 depicts zones with the greatest shares of the county's total employment. As can be seen, job density is greatest in the center city.

Map 10 portrays the relative accessibility of employment opportunities. Again utilizing the LASS computer simulation, it was possible to calculate the relative number of people physically accessible to Los Angeles' jobs,

c. Source: Hafner, Bernhard and Jurg Lang. *Los Angeles Simulation Study,* unpublished working paper, School of Architecture and Urban Planning, University of California, Los Angeles, 1973.

d. Each zone was composed of a number of census tracts grouped together on the basis of their general similarity.

Map 12–6.   Primary and Secondary Office Nodes

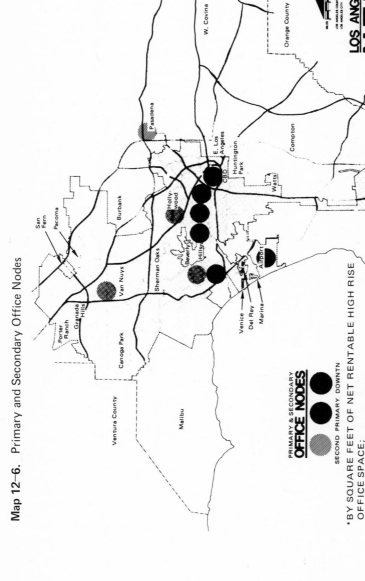

PRIMARY & SECONDARY
OFFICE NODES

● PRIMARY DOWNTN
● SECOND PRIMARY
◍ SECONDARY

*BY SQUARE FEET OF NET RENTABLE HIGH RISE
OFFICE SPACE;
DOWNTOWN - 16.5 million sq. ft.
PRIMARY - over 2.0 million sq. ft.
SECONDARY - 0.5 to 2.0 million sq. ft.

SOURCE: COMMITTEE FOR CENTRAL CITY PLANNING, INC., CENTRAL CITY LOS ANGELES 1972/1990, PRELIMINARY GENERAL DEVELOPMENT PLAN, APRIL, 1971

LOS ANGELES
NTIT

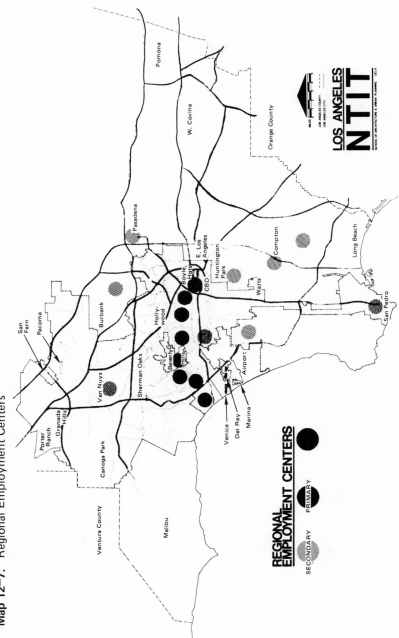

Map 12–7.   Regional Employment Centers

Table 12–3. Primary and Secondary Employment/Population
Centers: Actual (1970 and 1967) and Projected (1990)

	Population		Employment	
Centers	*1970*	*1990*	*1967*	*1990*
Primary				
Downtown	12,981	17,770	200,600	311,000
Westwood	17,806	24,910	19,350	32,487
Long Beach	19,887	17,839	30,600	50,025
Pasadena	21,030	29,297	18,200	39,972
Santa Monica	19,887	17,839	19,400	31,527
Century City	2,000	16,000	9,900	49,462
Beverly Hills	17,850	24,991	20,100	39,018
Wilshire	100,286	128,170	63,100	98,450
Miracle Mile	19,930	28,740	14,400	24,625
Hollywood	110,527	147,850	62,000	104,248
Pomona	10,680	14,844	7,600	29,632
Van Nuys	14,800	23,200	18,900	28,740
Totals	367,664	491,450	484,150	839,186
Secondary				
Inglewood	34,084	38,184	15,500	15,821
LAX	13,844	24,470	46,800	52,288
Del Amo	20,622	23,960	6,400	10,128
Glendale	31,116	35,902	18,900	38,942
Compton	25,102	29,474	4,800	9,348
Crenshaw	28,790	31,050	10,500	17,650
Whittier	10,066	11,133	3,800	7,071
Lakewood	24,343	27,015	10,200	11,218
Downey	9,285	10,732	6,300	11,821
West Covina	7,893	13,502	3,600	9,544
Warner Ranch	10,789	15,061	5,400	20,241
San Pedro	18,215	19,200	12,700	17,850
Exposition Park	27,529	30,800	5,900	16,047
Canoga/Woodland Hills	12,500	14,500	2,400	3,722
Avalon/Manchester	15,802	18,100	3,100	4,357
Totals	289,980	343,083	156,300	246,048

Source: Southern California Rapid Transit District, *Phase I Progress Report*, Los Angeles,
March 1973, p. IV–12

weighted as a function of the number and distance from jobs in various zones.
As Map 12–10 indicates, for those living in central Los Angeles the greatest
number of job opportunities are accessible (physically). It thereby suggests that
increases (or decreases) here could have significant marginal impacts. The results
also suggest the need to enhance socioeconomic accessibility, because high
unemployment rates demonstrate that mere physical proximity to jobs is insufficient in terms of actually generating employment.

To facilitate planning a NTIT of the type proposed, certain areas
with great development potential should be singled out. These resource and
opportunity areas are discussed below (see Map 12–11).

Map 12–8. Shopping Nodes

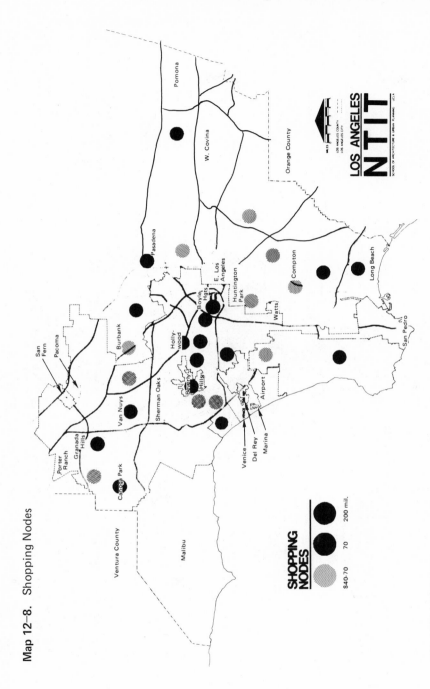

SHOPPING NODES

$40-70   70   200 mil.

LOS ANGELES
NTIT
SCHOOL OF ARCHITECTURE & URBAN PLANNING, UCLA

LOS ANGELES COUNTY
LOS ANGELES CITY

*BY ANNUAL SALES
SOURCE: LOS ANGELES TIMES MARKET RESEARCH STAFF, DEPARTMENT STORES AND REGIONAL SHOPPING CENTERS 1972

Map 12–9.   Density of Total Employment

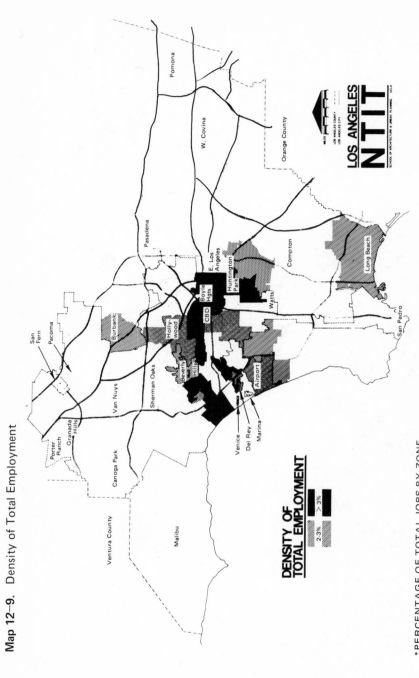

DENSITY OF
TOTAL EMPLOYMENT

2-3%   > 3%

*PERCENTAGE OF TOTAL JOBS BY ZONE
SOURCE: LOS ANGELES SIMULATION STUDY, BASED UPON LARTS DATA (1967)

LOS ANGELES
NTIT

Map 12–10. Relative Accessibility to Employment, 1967

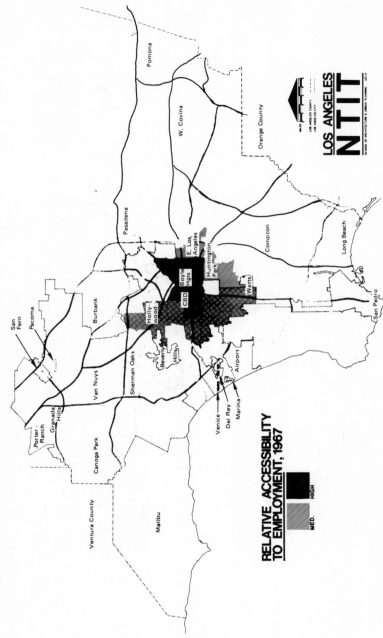

RELATIVE ACCESSIBILITY
TO EMPLOYMENT, 1967

HIGH

MED.

LOS ANGELES
NTIT

*SCALE BASED UPON WEIGHTED RELATIONSHIP OF POPULATION BY ZONE TO EMPLOYMENT BY ZONE, AS A FUNCTION OF
NUMBERS AND DISTANCE
SOURCE: UCLA/NTIT STUDY (1973)

Map 12–11. Resource and Opportunity Areas

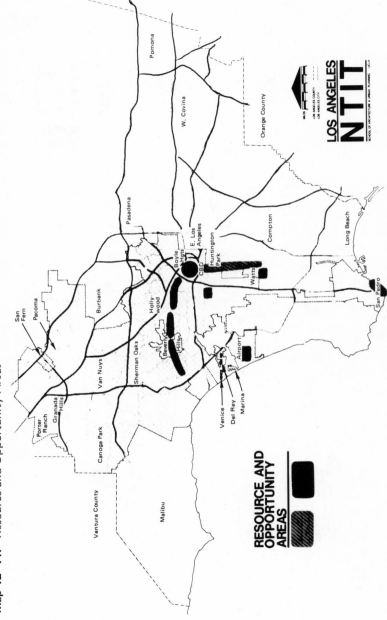

NOTE: INDICATED AREAS ARE SCHEMATIC AND ARE INTENDED AS REPRESENTATIVE EXAMPLES ONLY
SOURCE: U.S. CENSUS (1970)

The Central Business District. Of all resource and opportunity areas, the central business district is clearly the single largest economic and social asset. Logically, the core sector of a new town intown program would focus upon the CBD. Already undergoing major development, the CBD acts as a magnet for numerous service industries. Private investment in urban renewal (Bunker Hill) may ultimately exceed $1 billion. Efforts already well-advanced to produce a "Downtown Plan" could become the foundation for a more comprehensive revitalization strategy. Thus, downtown Los Angeles would anchor a citywide development program.

Eastern Wilshire Corridor. Commercial development along Wilshire Boulevard of the CBD (and south to the Convention Center) comprises a major resource for first phase inclusion in a new town intown program. Adjacent to the downtown, it is also accessible to the Hoover/Normandie/Pico–Union primary impact area immediately southward. Improvements here thus would favorably impact nearby communities. Although signs of deterioration have appeared, close proximity to the central business district should facilitate new town intown linkages aimed at preventing decay and initiating development.

USC/Exposition Park. Assuming the core development sector embraced Watts as a primary impact area, the USC/Exposition Park complex probably constitutes the single greatest resource south of the central business district suitable for development. Within, or adjacent to, this center lie a major university with its own development program; two urban renewal projects; a major park with museums, stadia, and related facilities; and a reviving commercial base. It is well located to assist the Watts and Hoover/Normandie/Pico–Union primary impact areas.

Adjacent Resource and Opportunity Areas. The three centers discussed above lie within the proposed core sector. Additional areas outside the core sector or city could influence the primary impact areas. From Watts' viewpoint, the most important local source of jobs, training, and health care might be Martin Luther King Hospital. Although a county facility on county land, it is the major public facility in terms of services provided.

The industrial corridor is also outside city boundaries. Because industries in central Los Angeles are concentrated here, improvement of skills and reduction of job discrimination barriers could vastly stimulate employment in Watts and the South Central area. Also, the Los Angeles International Airport and San Pedro/Long Beach port complexes could each contribute to initial new town intown development. These resource and opportunity areas are shown on Map 12–11.

Transportation Nodes and Linkages. Los Angeles is notorious for dependence upon private automobiles for regional transportation. The stereotype is warranted: with an extensive freeway system Los Angeles owes much of its distinctive character and development patterns to the automobile.

Planning for a core sector should not underestimate the importance the proposed mass transportation system would have on the city's future development. Such a transit network (see Map 12–12), if successfully implemented, would significantly influence the relative accessibility, and hence development potential, of certain areas of Los Angeles. These changes could create unique opportunities for a NTIT program.

3. Core Development Sector. Given this tentative listing of resource and opportunity and primary impact areas, boundaries of an initial core sector are apparent. They would be drawn to encompass or be accessible to the major centers of the central city (see Map 12–13). The northern boundary would be the central business district with its concentration of economic activities and development opportunities. The CBD should be closely linked with the East Wilshire corridor, the Hoover/Normandie/Pico–Union primary impact areas, and USC/Exposition Park. Depending on financial and political support, the core sector could extend southward to the Watts primary impact area (and to the resources and opportunities at the Martin Luther King Hospital complex and the industrial corridor).

Also, the core sector could extend westward to the Crenshaw area (with its dual attributes as a primary impact and resource and opportunity area) and eastward to the Boyle Heights primary impact area. Other areas beyond the core development sector could be scheduled for subsequent development.

If the core sector were extended as indicated above (shown on Map 12–13), it would encompass all or part of 12 central city "statistical areas" with a 1972 population of 465,000 (Table 12–4). However, the areas and population encompassed by individual development *projects*–possibly the seven project areas shown (schematically) within the core sector on Map 12–13 would be substantially smaller. Areas and populations *not* directly encompassed by individual NTIT projects would, nevertheless, be part of the development effort because they would be directly impacted.

Tables 12–4 through 12–7 provide a thumbnail sketch of some characteristics of such a core sector. Thus, it might be noted that the sector as a whole lost population over the past 12 years; losses in the downtown, central, Avalon, and Watts areas were substantial. All of the designated communities have a large proportion of minority populations (with only the Westlake and wholesale industrial statistical areas having minority populations in 1970 less than 50 percent of the total). (See Table 12–5.) The sector as a whole has over 80 percent minority population. Whether an "unbalanced" population would jeopardize the political and social viability of the proposed development is not clear. The programmatic logic of choosing these communities is underlined by the data in Tables 12–6 and 12–7. These tables show a large proportion of poverty households in these communities, the very large percent unemployed in

Map 12–12. Proposed 1973 Rapid Transit Corridors

SOURCE: SCRTD, PHASE I PROGRESS REPORT, MARCH, 1973

Map 12–13. NTIT Core Development Sector

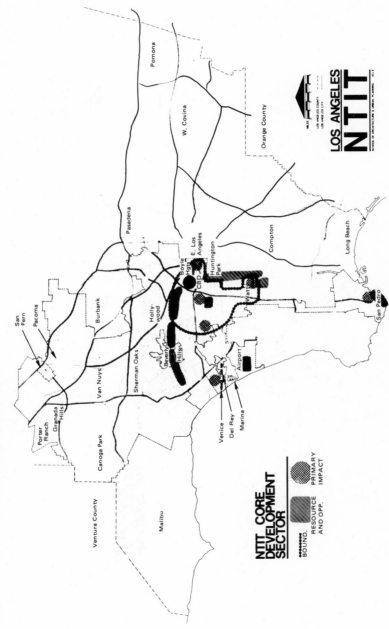

Table 12–4. Population Trends: NTIT Core Development Sector

	Population 1960/1970/1972*			
Statistical Area	1960	1970	July 1, 1972 (estimate)	% Change 1960–1972
Downtown	20,496	11,172	11,180	−45.5%
Wholesale/Industrial	19,690	10,309	10,136	−48.5
Central	23,367	16,296	16,023	−31.4
Boyle Heights	84,733	83,040	82,796	− 2.3
Westlake	58,680	58,534	58,572	− 0.2
West Adams (containing Crenshaw)	23,226	23,424	23,412	+ 0.8
Santa Barbara	59,045	61,366	61,285	+ 3.8
University	20,775	20,710	20,724	− 0.2
Avalon	52,486	45,054	44,367	−15.5
Exposition Park	70,488	77,234	76,784	+ 8.9
Green Meadows	31,198	32,702	31,355	+ 0.5
Watts	34,001	29,383	28,137	−17.2
Total Core Area	498,185	469,224	464,771	− 6.7
City of Los Angeles	2,479,015	2,809,813	2,824,622	+13.9
County of Los Angeles	6,038,771	7,040,670	7,090,452	+17.4

*Note: Data for 1960 provided by City of Los Angeles; Estimates for 1970 and 1972 based on data provided by County Regional Planning Commission

Sources: City of Los Angeles, Community Analysis Bureau, *The State of the City, 1972*, January, 1973, Volume I, pp. II–16, II–17

County of Los Angeles, Regional Planning Commission, "Quarterly Bulletin, July 1, 1972," Bulletin No. 117, July, 1972, pp. 2–4

most of them, the high proportion of old housing (although the 20-year figure shown here—the only one available to us—is not an adequate standard), and the high proportion of nonautomobile households. This is the type of population that can be assisted by a development program aimed at enlarging employment opportunities (and over a large range of industry categories) and at improving public services, facilities, housing, and environmental conditions.

Operational Policies for a Core Development Sector

Once the core development sector has been identified, a general development strategy and program would be evolved by the development corporation working closely with appropriate political, economic, and community groups. Although the process would depend upon new financial and institutional arrangements, the general principle is clear: to organize policies, programs, projects, and supplementary activities for realizing NTIT objectives.

This would in most cases imply concentrating development activities on existing strengths and positive trends and avoiding attempts to reverse those negative trends, except under special circumstances, with low marginal return on

Table 12–5. Racial Characteristics, 1970: NTIT Core Development Sector

Statistical Area	Black		Spanish Surname		Other		Total
	Number	%	Number	%	Number	%	
Downtown	1,435	12.4%	5,971	51.6%	4,166	36.0%	11,572
Wholesale/Industrial	2,680	26.0	2,330	22.6	5,299	51.4	10,309
Central	10,609	65.1	3,194	19.6	2,493	15.3	16,296
Boyle Heights	3,488	4.2	68,757	82.8	10,795	13.0	83,040
Westlake	1,697	2.8	25,827	42.6	33,102	54.6	60,626
West Adams (estimate)	17,348	73.6	589	2.5	5,630	23.9	23,567
Santa Barbara	36,427	59.0	11,175	18.1	14,139	22.9	61,741
University	2,789	13.0	11,326	52.8	7,335	34.2	21,450
Avalon	42,880	94.6	1,496	3.3	952	2.1	45,328
Exposition Park	65,661	84.5	5,750	7.4	6,294	8.1	77,705
Green Meadows (estimate)	29,512	89.7	1,546	4.7	1,843	5.6	32,901
Watts	27,051	91.2	1,750	5.9	860	2.9	29,661
Total Core Area	241,577	50.9%	139,711	29.5%	92,908	19.6%	474,196
City of Los Angeles	503,606	17.8%	518,791	18.4%	1,793,601	63.8%	2,815,998
County of Los Angeles	762,844	10.9%	1,298,311	18.3%	4,979,920	70.8%	7,041,075

Source: City of Los Angeles, Community Analysis Bureau, *The State of the City, 1972, Los Angeles*, January, 1973, Vol. I, pp. II–16, 17, pp. V–110, 111, 116, 117
 U. S. Bureau of the Census, *U. S. Census of Population and Housing: 1970, Census Tracts, Los Angeles–Long Beach Standard Metropolitan Statistical Area*, Table P–1, pp. P–1, p–3; Table P–2, pp. p–136, p–138

Table 12–6. Selected Income Statistics, 1970: NTIT Core Development Sector

Statistical Area	Median Family Income	Percent Households in Poverty[1]	Percent Unemployed[2]
Downtown	$3,003	47%	40%
Wholesale/Industrial	2,337	80	47
Central	5,416	55	16
Boyle Heights	4,931	43	18
Westlake	3,031	43	24
West Adams	7,146	38	6
Santa Barbara	4,331	44	18
University	3,401	47	18
Avalon	6,083	55	18
Exposition Park	6,262	47	15
Green Meadows	6,159	46	8
Watts	5,206	57	26
Core Total	*	43	*
City of Los Angeles	7,511	25.2%	7.0%[3]
County of Los Angeles	8,562	22.6%	6.0%[3]

[1] Proportion of households with annual incomes below $4,000; Note: figures represent CAB estimates, not 1970 census data
[2] 1971 CAB estimate
[3] 1970 Census
*Not available

Sources: City of Los Angeles, Community Analysis Bureau, *The State of the City, 1972, Los Angeles,* January, 1973, Table XII–4a, Vol. II p. XII–21; Table XII–13a, Vol. II, pp. XII–80, 81; Table XII–14a, Vol. II, pp. XII–88, 89; Table XII–16, Vol. II, pp. XII–102, 103; Table XII–17, Vol. II, pp. XII–108, XII–109

United States Bureau of the Census, *1970 Census of Population and Housing, Census Tracts, Los Angeles–Long Beach Standard Metropolitan Statistical Area, Part I,* Table P–3, pp. p–271, p–273; Table P–4, pp. p–406, p–408

public investments. By the same token, the basic program should avoid "worst first" efforts which characterized the model cities program.

In its day-to-day functioning, some activities of the development corporation might not be visibly different from existing programs and projects. The major innovation would be: (a) to integrate formerly distinct central city activities into a single program, and (b) thereby to attain the twin objectives of modernizing the central city and enhancing opportunities for the less advantaged.

The city is a complexly integrated socioeconomic system. In the past, many central city programs and projects did not make this connection and largely failed as a result. With functional responsibility limited to small fragments of central city problems, they could not exercise effective control over their programmatic domains. For example, public housing programs often yielded poor social outputs, because opportunities for employment, personal security, and other housing related needs were assumed away. Manpower train-

Table 12–7.   Selected Housing and Accessibility Statistics: NTIT Core Development Sector

Statistical Area	% Housing Units 20 yrs. or Older	% Housing Units Lacking One or More Plumbing Facilities	Median Imputed Rent[1]	% of Households With No Autos
Downtown	68%	28.2%	$ 72	97.2%
Wholesale/Industrial	92	71.1	51	92.9
Central	84	8.7	73	54.0
Boyle Heights	83	3.3	85	40.9
Westlake	82	8.1	73	61.3
West Adams	72	.7	111	30.4
Santa Barbara	73	3.6	91	43.5
University	80	12.1	75	49.4
Avalon	77	2.8	71	42.1
Exposition Park	90	1.4	91	38.0
Green Meadows	68	1.5	96	32.6
Watts	50	1.7	90	42.7
Core Total	*	*	*	*
City of Los Angeles	78%	1.9%	$145	20.1%
County of Los Angeles	75%	1.5%	*	15.1%

[1]CAB Computation: weighted average of monthly contract rent and valuation of owner occupied housing
*not available
Sources: City of Los Angeles, Community Analysis Bureau, *The State of the City, 1972, Los Angeles,* January, 1973, Table V–5, Vol. II, pp. V–32, 33; Table V–9, Vol. II,   pp. V–56, 57; Table V–20, Vol. II, pp. V–132, 133; Table IX–2, Vol. II, pp. V–12, 13
United States Bureau of the Census, *1970 Census of Population and Housing, Census Tracts, Los Angeles–Long Beach Standard Metropolitan Statistical Area,* Part II, Table H–1, pp. h–1, h–3; Table H–2, pp. h–136, h–138

ing programs sometimes failed, because creating job opportunities and physical and social accessibility to jobs were neglected. The list is seemingly endless.

Economic development, especially creation of new jobs and maintenance of existing jobs, should have very high priority. For example, the corporation should assist those businesses needing additional space for expansion in order to continue in the central city, and thus to preserve job opportunities and the city tax base. It should also recognize that attainment of a minimal level of personal security is a prerequisite to revitalization of certain areas. Effective intervention to facilitate economic development would require correction of some of the social maladies that afflict a given community.

Meaningful development also requires new kinds of relationships between private and public interests. Experience with Stage 1 NTITs clearly suggests that innovative public-private arrangements can greatly facilitate revitalization efforts.

In certain instances, the development corporation should be prepared to take over traditional private investment functions thwarted by financial uncertainty, long time frames for payback, problems of discrimination, or unprofitability. The corporation may also have to intervene to catalyze private investment or to assure adequate returns on private investment.

The development corporation would also be interested in leveraging the considerable development potential represented by the proposed rapid transit system. It should work closely with appropriate agencies and organizations to assure that urban development objectives are embedded in planning and implementation of the transit system. Development opportunities represented by new transportation nodes and changes in relative accessibility for certain areas should not go untapped.

The corporation would also be concerned with increasing housing opportunities for the less advantaged of Los Angeles. This would include more traditional approaches such as housing subsidy, rehabilitation, and conservation programs. In many respects the corporation would function as a housing agency *and* redevelopment authority working for physical development, public facilities, and low-moderate income housing in less advantaged communities.

In essence, development of the core sector under a Model II format would consist of a web of highly—and complexly—interrelated programs, processes, projects, actions, and events operating at various dimensions and scales. While this web of relationships would be place bound in many instances, these development policies would always be viewed *as components of the larger urban regional system.*

In carrying out its various programs and projects, the development corporation might find it expeditious to create subsidiary corporations to carry out specific programs, projects, and/or sectors. Development of the downtown would continue as a part of the "NTIT core development sector's" activities. However, new town intown activity in this part of the sector would now be under the direction of a development entity involving the various interests of the downtown, but subsidiary to the parent development corporation. Similar arrangements could prove useful in conducting major revitalization programs for the USC/Exposition Park region, East Wilshire, and other "resource and opportunity" areas.

Specific strategies for these "second level" executing development corporations would, of course, depend on local needs, the views of the various special interest groups, and the views of the community residents as to the priorities that should rule in any changes that are brought about. However, in order to *illustrate* the types of efforts and programs that might be launched by such corporations, we have outlined (in Attachment B) some possible strategies for each of the major "resource and opportunity areas" related to the "core development sector" and for several "primary impact areas." While merely meant to be illustrative, it should be observed that these proposed activities are based on in-depth studies of each of the areas involved.

Certain of the subsidiary corporations might take the form of *"community development corporations"* to facilitate improvements in less advantaged "primary impact areas." Such entities could serve as conduits for programs and projects aimed at expanding opportunity for the residents of these communities.

Special purpose subsidiary corporations might also prove useful in the new town intown effort in the "core development sector." An obvious possibility would be an industrial park project, where a certain area might be designated for the development (and encouragement) of appropriate industrial, service, or other needed activities. The development corporation could offer various incentives (tax advantages, improved transportation, additional public services, and so forth) to attract, or retain, businesses and firms.

Besides managing programs and projects and coordinating the activities of its various subsidiaries, the new town intown development corporation would also in a sense fulfill a "lobbying" function, working to involve the important interest groups of the city and representatives of the impacted communities in every phase of the operation. A large developmental program of the kind involved in a Model II new town intown program for Los Angeles would have little chance for success without full support of the major actors in the city.

Strong efforts would have to be made to build various kinds of organizations into the developmental scheme (labor unions, businesses, associations, cooperatives, community groups of various kinds) as partners, developers, management teams, and investors.

Ultimately, the success of any major modernization program in Los Angeles would require the full—and long-term—support of the city government. Without municipal commitment, other interests of the city would see little incentive to involve themselves. A full scale new town intown program assumes a significant reinterpretation of the role and function of city government. The city itself must begin to accept greater responsibility for its own future, recognizing the necessity for ongoing modernization to meet the changing needs and demands of its citizenry. Rather than a mere provider of basic services, the city must become the agent of its own renewal and work continuously to ensure the amenities and opportunities expected of American urban centers of the late twentieth century.

ATTACHMENT A

OPEN SPACE IN LOS ANGELES[e]

The national experience with Stage 1 new towns intown elsewhere in the country indicates that the most desirable resource is vacant or greatly underutilized land. Such urban terrain is highly sought after due to the relative ease of development (no relocation problems, avoidance of land clearance costs, and the like). This is as true in Los Angeles as it is elsewhere. Inevitably, given the high desirability of such properties, most suitably large parcels in Los Angeles have long since been developed. Those that remain are generally plagued with locational, physical, or social disadvantages that have discouraged private activity.

Vacant (or greatly underutilized) land in Los Angeles can be classified in four general categories:

1. Privately owned vacant land. Land that is completely undeveloped and in private ownership;
2. Governmental land. Vacant land (generally cleared) in public ownership. This primarily involves urban renewal, county, and state Department of Transportation land;
3. Underutilized industrial land. Land that is developed but at a low intensity or inappropriate use. Examples include oil, rail, harbor, and other industrial facilities (This is probably the most significant category in terms of available acreage.);
4. Open space. National forests and parks, public recreational areas, and so forth.

The relative availability of each type (See Map 12–14) is discussed below:

1. Private Vacant Land. Privately owned vacant land of sufficient size for a new town intown development is practically nonexistent in central Los Angeles. The private vacant land that is available tends to be in scattered parcels unsuitable for large scale development. There are considerable large vacant tracts in outlying sections of the county, but they are of little use to the central city due to geographic inaccessibility.

2. Governmental Land. Most suitable large parcels of developable vacant land in Los Angeles are currently under public ownership. A number are held by the Los Angeles Community Redevelopment Agency. Several of its

e. Based on materials prepared by Eugene Brooks, Leroy Higginbotham, and Nicki King.

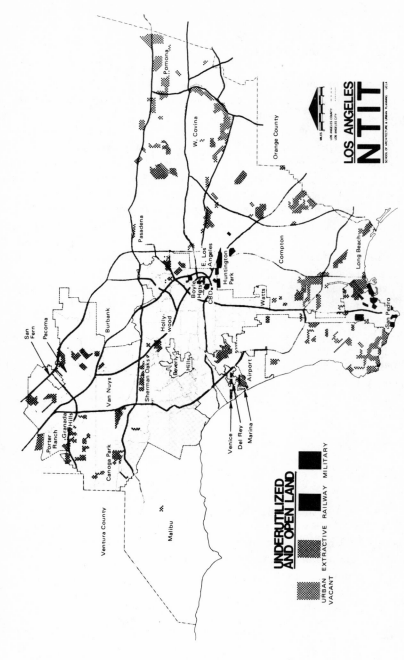

Map 12–14. Underutilized and Open Land

SOURCE: COUNTY OF LOS ANGELES

projects involve considerable acreage, the most significant being Monterey Hills (200+ acres), Watts–103rd Street (100 acres), Bunker Hill (50 acres), and Hoover/USC (50 acres). Development of the Watts–103rd Street has been held back by a variety of social, geographic, and political problems. Monterey Hills' development has been delayed due to geographic unsuitability of the land.

Other potentially developable land is held by the state Department of Transportation. The Department has placed considerable emphasis on development of freeway corridors throughout the Los Angeles basin. In addition to existing corridors, five additional freeways are in various stages of planning. The potential of the state's freeway system as an unintended generator of land for development purposes can be approached from two vantage points:

a) As the freeway system has come under increasing criticism, public opposition led to increased scrutiny and pressure to stop highway construction. Since the Department already acquired considerable acreage for freeways that now may not be constructed, alternative uses for this land seem feasible;

b) When freeways are actually planned to completion, land acquisition policies of the Department of Transportation could be coordinated with land needs of the new town intown program. (In practice, unfortunately, most of this Department of Transportation land is poorly shaped, that is, long and narrow.)

3. Underutilized Industrial Land. Probably the greatest vacant or underutilized land resources in Los Angeles are industrial sites that are becoming increasingly unsuitable for their present uses. Many of these sites lie within the industrial corridor where the heavy industry in Los Angeles is currently concentrated. The industrial corridor is currently in decline, due to the growing inefficiency of labor, intensive industries intown, and the growing attractiveness of suburban locations for new industrial development.

A recent Los Angeles County report indicates that some 900 acres of such industrial land lie scattered across the industrial corridor. Much of this is currently occupied by oil drilling areas which might be converted to other uses. The current shift of petrochemical industries to the harbor area also releases large parcels for other uses.

Another important component is the various railroad land holdings. The decline of the rail industry has led to a decline in use of the extensive shipping, maintenance, freight, storage, and passenger facilities that exist in the central city. The location of these large land areas, adjacent to the central business district and under a single ownership, suggests that development might be feasible and productive. Major railroad systems in Los Angeles include Southern Pacific, Santa Fé, Pacific Electric, and Union Pacific. It should be noted that these resources lie beyond the city's legal limits; nevertheless they represent the largest available source of underutilized land anywhere near the city. Redevelopment of this land could have significant impacts upon the level of opportunity within the city.

4. Open Land. In addition to cleared urban land, Los Angeles possesses considerable open public land outside urban areas. The Los Angeles environment, in fact, owes much of its character to the extensive National Forests which form a natural geographic barrier between the northern and southern portions of the county. These areas have been preserved and protected from the encroachment of speculative development, but they may serve as an important land and natural resource inventory under certain circumstances (and assuming environmental needs can be met). As with privately owned vacant land, however, inaccessibility may minimize or eliminate their contribution in terms of central city modernization.

Summary

With the exception of certain sizable underutilized industrial land holdings, Los Angeles' inventory of readily developable vacant land is rather meager. Most parcels that do exist are either too small or beset with social, locational, or other problems that greatly complicate development. Los Angeles' lack of vacant land reinforces the conclusion that a Stage 1 new town intown has limited applicability. New town intown developments on vacant land in the central city are only possible under unusually fortuitous conditions. In most instances, suitable sites are simply not available. However, while inappropriate for single projects, vacant land resources may be utilizable under a programmatic approach, where specific weaknesses of given sites are overcome by linkages with existing strengths elsewhere. This appears especially true of urban renewal land within the core development sector.

ATTACHMENT B

1. SOME POSSIBLE STRATEGIES FOR RESOURCE AND OPPORTUNITY AREAS

Central Business District

Resources and Opportunities
Largest of Los Angeles' regional centers
Primary financial, commercial, cultural, and governmental center of Los Angeles
Important industrial center (but partially deteriorated state)
Major employment center (around 220,000 employed downtown)
Rentable High Rise Office space: 16.5 million square feet
Contains major historical landmarks
Local business, financial, and other institutional interests seemingly interested in the possibility of major change
Commitment to rapid transit system
Existing urban renewal projects: Bunker Hill, Little Tokyo
Continuing major private investment
Some tendency for increased intown residence for middle and upper income individuals

Strategies
Need to "remodel" Downtown image, emphasizing its regional role and renewed strength
Maximize and build upon potential impacts of rapid transit plans; Enhance access to rest of city
Improve downtown circulation system: pedestrian access, parking, automobile movement, and so forth
Encourage continued redevelopment activity in Bunker Hill and Little Tokyo but with more emphasis on residences, small units, and lower income activities; also less monumental structures
Retain existing industrial activity (and employment) by facilitating expansion, favorable tax considerations, enhanced downtown environment (for example, less crime)
Encourage growth of service related activities where appropriate, by facilitating land assembly, upgrading workforce, improving accessibility via transit system
Provide special assistance to employers offering job opportunities for the less advantaged
Encourage major residential developments for all income classes
Maintain and enhance historical landmarks, enhance quality of building and

street design, and pursue viable open space suggestions and proposals to enhance quality of downtown environment

Encourage public/private cooperation; encourage public and private investment

Wilshire Corridor East

Resources and Opportunities

Major commercial development along Wilshire Blvd. (adjacent to CBD, Miracle Mile, Wilshire centers, and so forth)

Important component of a primary regional core

Rentable High Rise Office Space: 6.5 million square feet (includes West Wilshire)

Adjacent to a variety of residential communities

Temple Redevelopment Project (proposed)

Los Angeles Convention Center

Westlake Park: heterogenous residential community, center for art and related activities

Strategies

Encourage retention and expansion of commercial base by facilitating expansion, acquisition of sites, and so forth

Build upon strengths of Westlake Park: conserve housing stock, improve services to residents, encourage local art schools and related activities

Incorporate rapid transit plans; enhance accessibility to CBD, to Century City, South Central Los Angeles, and so forth

Enhance environmental considerations via improved design, better circulation/pedestrian/parking facilities, consideration of importance of open space

University of Southern
California/Exposition Park

Resources and Opportunities

Contains University of Southern California (20,000 students), Exposition Park (L. A. Coliseum, swimming stadium, L. A. County Museums, Exposition Hall, and so forth

Major education/recreational/cultural/research center

Adjacent to but isolated from numerous low income minority communities

USC in midst of major redevelopment program

Enormous existing investment in facilities and programs

Adjacent to numerous neighborhoods which might benefit from USC activities

Strategies

Closer involvement of USC and surrounding communities

Encourage USC expansion, but especially programs and activities which enhance opportunity for less advantaged

Maintain and expand recreational and cultural opportunities of USC and Expo Park

Initiate programs to counteract crime and vandalism

Enhance housing adjacent to USC, for students as well as other groups

Exploit opportunities for new hotel, office and other facilities

Martin Luther King Hospital Area

Resources and Opportunities

Contains Martin Luther King, Jr. General Hospital, Charles R. Drew Post–Graduate Medical School, Ujima Village (moderate income housing and supportive shopping facilities)

Beyond city bounds, on county unincorporated land

Major employment/job training/health facility (county administered)

Adjacent to numerous less advantaged communities

King–Drew Triangle Neighborhood Development Program

Expansion of MLK/Drew facilities

Expansion of Ujima Village

MLK/Drew—a model for successful attempt to enhance opportunity and quality of life for less advantaged

Strategies

Continued expansion of facilities and programs

Need for city/county cooperation

Use MLK/Drew as model for developments elsewhere

Industrial Corridor

Resources and Opportunities

Linear concentration of manufacturing and labor intensive industry

Major employment base—over 200,000 jobs

Physically accessible to many less advantaged communities

Beyond city boundaries, to east of city

Underutilized land (railroad, and so forth)

Need for expanded job training and employment placement programs

Need for increased "social accessibility" to employment

Strategies

Public intervention to facilitate maintenance or expansion of existing plants and firms (to prevent decline in employment opportunities)

Joint city/county action required

Expand opportunity via job training and employment placement programs

Improved transportation facilities

Development of underutilized land

Training and other programs to provide increased "social accessibility" to employment

2. SOME POSSIBLE STRATEGIES FOR PRIMARY IMPACT AREAS

Watts

Description

Watts/103rd St. community: Once incorporated city, now three square mile area of city of Los Angeles

Area of low median income, high unemployment, high crime, and so forth

Primarily Black population

Considerable deteriorated housing

Small commercial base

Strengths

Nationally known Black ghetto: Heart of Los Angeles' Black community

Focus for numerous public and private programs

Watts Urban Renewal Area: Vacant land

"Greater Watts" Model Cities Area

Watts Industrial Park

Existing community organizations, some quite strong

Physically accessible to numerous employment and service opportunities (Industrial Corridor, Martin Luther King Hospital, and so forth

Strategies

Improve housing through rehabilitation, conservation, renewal

Improve public services, notably crime prevention, education, job training, and so forth

Encourage local commercial community centers, for employment and improved private services

Promote parks and other open space proposals

Enhance accessibility to opportunities outside area

East Los Angeles/Boyle Heights

Description

Deteriorated residential community, east of CBD

Area of low median income, high unemployment, high crime, and so forth

Primarily Mexican-American population

Considerable dilapidated housing

Functioning local commercial activities

Strengths
Major center of Los Angeles' Mexican-American population
L. A. County Hospital
East Los Angeles Junior College, California State University at Los Angeles
Adjacent to Central Business District
Existing community organizations

Strategies
Concentration, and strengthening, of existing commercial activity
Improvement of housing through rehabilitation, conservation, and renewal, where appropriate
Utilize rapid transit plans to enhance accessibility to existing opportunities elsewhere and investigate possibilities of using supplementary transportation system
Improve public services, especially education, vocational training, and so forth

Crenshaw

Description
Mixed residential/commercial area
Area of low and medium median incomes, relatively high unemployment in some areas, hints of social disorganization (gang activity, rising venereal disease rates, and so forth)
Contains areas of dipapidated housing
Sizable commercial base: Unstable due to threatened departure of major firms
Population in transition from white to primarily Black, with other minorities
Important middle class Black employment center

Strengths
Sizable middle class (Black) population: Focal point for upwardly mobil Blacks, in terms of both employment and housing
Sizable stock of existing high quality housing
Major regional shopping center

Strategies
Maintain area as viable alternative for Black (and others) employment and residence
Enhance public services, notably personal security, education
Retain and expand commercial base, through concentrating existing firms, provision of land for expansion, reduction of vandalism, improved parking and access, and so forth
Incorporate rapid transit planning and planning of supplementary systems to enhance circulation within the community and accessibility to opportunities in other communities

Preserve existing housing, relying especially upon rehabilitation/conservation techniques

Hoover/Normandie/Pico—Union

Description
Series of residential communities, north of USC/Exposition Park, south of Convention Center
Primarily Black and Mexican-American populations
Area of low median incomes, high unemployment, high crime, and so forth
Scattered commercial activities
Considerable dilapidated housing

Strengths
Hoover Urban Renewal Area (university focused housing, educational and commercial facilities)
Normandie Neighborhood Development Project (extensive conservation and rehabilitation area; 2000 acres)
Pico—Union Neighborhood Development Project (conservation and rehabilitation area)
Los Angeles Convention Center
Physically accessible to numerous opportunities (USC, Exposition Park, CBD)
Existing community organizations
Considerable underdeveloped land, possibly developable for a variety of uses

Strategies
Maintain present housing stock via conservation and rehabilitation; encourage additional housing
Enhance public and private services, especially building upon strengths of USC, Exposition Park, and other existing centers
Encourage additional open space; parks, and so forth
Concentrate existing commercial activity; encourage additional commercial activity to improve shopping opportunities and enhance job base
Encourage development of Convention Center supportive activities that most favorably impact area
Provide for enhanced accessibility via rapid transit planning and supplemental transportation systems

Part III

Bibliography

Advisory Commission of Intergovernmental Relations. *Urban and Rural America: Policies for Future Growth* (Washington, D. C., 1968).

Bain, Henry. "The Organization of Growth," in National Committee on Urban Growth Policy. *The New City,* Donald Canty (ed.) (New York: Praeger Publishers, 1969).

City of Los Angeles, *Budget, Fiscal Year 1972–1973* (Los Angeles, 1972).

City of Los Angeles. *The City of Los Angeles Budget for the Fiscal Year Ending June 30, 1974* (Los Angeles, 1973).

Clapp, James A. *New Towns and Urban Policy, Planning Metropolitan Growth* (New York: Dunellen, 1971).

Committee for Central City Planning, Inc. *Central City Los Angeles, 1972–1990, Preliminary General Development Plan* (Los Angeles, April 1972).

County of Los Angeles. *County Budget, Fiscal Year Ending June 30, 1973* (Los Angeles, 1972).

Diamond, William. *Development Banks* (Baltimore, Maryland: Johns Hopkins Press, 1957).

Evans, Hazel (ed.). *New Towns: The British Experience* (London: Charles Knight and Company Ltd., 1972).

Gunther, John. "Statement of John Gunther, Chairman of the Board of Directors of the District of Columbia Redevelopment Agency," Mimeo. (Washington, D. C.: *District of Columbia Redevelopment Agency,* June 11, 1973).

Hafner, Bernhard and Jurg Lang. *Los Angeles Simulation Study,* Unpublished working paper (School of Architecture and Urban Planning, University of California, Los Angeles, May 1973).

Heroux, Richard L. and William A. Wallace. *Financial Analysis and the New Community Development Process* (New York: Praeger Publishers, 1973).

Jacobs, Eugene. *Community Development and Tax Increment Financing,* Unpublished manuscript (Los Angeles, 1973).

321

Kelley, A. J., F. B. Campanella, and J. McKiernan. *Venture Capital* (Boston: New England Industrial Resource Development Program, Boston College, 1971).

Los Angeles Community Analysis Bureau. *State of the City, Conditions of Blight and Obsolescence* (Los Angeles, 1970).

Los Angeles Department of City Planning. *Boyle Heights Community Socio-Economic Analysis,* Staff working paper (Los Angeles, 1970).

Los Angeles Department of City Planning. "Citywide Plan Programs and Available Implementation Methods, Implementation Report No. 1," City Plan Case No. 24121 (Los Angeles, February 1972).

Los Angeles Department of City Planning. *Open Space: Staff Report,* City Plan Case No. 24533 (Los Angeles, April 1973).

Los Angeles Department of City Planning, *Palms–Mar Vista–Del Rey District Preliminary Plan,* City Plan Case No. 23037 (Los Angeles, February 1972).

Los Angeles Department of City Planning. *Southeast Los Angeles District Plan, Preliminary Plan,* City Plan Case No. 22015 (Los Angeles, June 1971).

Los Angeles Department of City Planning. *Venice Community Plan,* City Plan Case No. 14311 (Los Angeles, October 2, 1969).

Los Angeles Department of City Planning. *Venice Community Plan Study,* City Plan Case No. 14311 (Los Angeles, July 1968).

Los Angeles Department of City Planning. *West Adams–Baldwin Hills–Leimert Socio-Economic Analysis,* Staff Working Paper (Los Angeles, November 1972).

Los Angeles Department of City Planning. *Wilmington–Harbor City Community Plan Study,* City Plan Case No. 17234 (Los Angeles, November 1968).

Los Angeles Department of City Planning. *Wilmington–Harbor City District Plan,* City Plan Case No. 17234 (Los Angeles, November 1969).

Los Angeles Times Market Research Staff. *Department Stores and Regional Shopping Centers* (Los Angeles, 1972).

Ludeman, Douglas. *The Investment Merits of Big City Bonds* (Boston: Financial Publishing Company, 1973).

McFarland, John R. "The Administration of the English New Towns Program," *Washington University Law Quarterly,* Vol. 1965, No. 1 (February 1965), pp. 17–55.

McPartland, Mike. "Issues in Capital Budgeting," *Implementation Analysis of Selected Components of the Los Angeles General Plan* (Los Angeles: School of Architecture and Urban Planning, University of California, Los Angeles, March 1973).

Mields, Hugh J. *Federally Assisted New Communities: A New Dimension in Urban Development* (Washington, D. C.: The Urban Land Institute, 1973).

National Committee on Urban Growth Policy. *The New City* (New York: Praeger Publishers, 1969).

Netzer, Richard. *The Economics of the Property Tax* (Washington D. C.: The Brookings Institution, 1966).

New York State Urban Development Corporation. *New Communities for New York* (New York, December 1970).

Practicing Law Institute. *The Local Economic Development Corporation* (Washington D. C.: Government Printing Office, 1970).

Reilly, William K. and S. J. Schulman. "The State Urban Development Corporation: New York's Innovation," *Urban Lawyer,* Vol. 1, No. 1 (Summer 1969) pp. 129–146.

Southern California Rapid Transit District. *Phase I Progress Report* (Los Angeles, 1973).

State of California. *1972–1973 Governor's Budget* (Sacramento, 1972).

U. S., Congress, Senate, Subcommittee on Financial Institutions of the Committee on Banking and Currency. *Hearings: Financial Institutions and the Urban Crisis,* 90th Cong., 2d Sess. (Washington D. C.: Government Printing Office, 1968).

U. S., Department of Housing and Urban Development. *Financing New Communities–Government and Private Experience in Europe and the United States* (Washington D. C., May 1973).

White, Wilson. *White's Tax Exempt Bond Market Ratings* (New York: Standard Statistics Company, 1972).

Wilburn, Michael D. and Robert M. Gladstone. *Optimizing Profits in Large-Scale Real Estate Projects* (Washington D. C.: The Urban Institute, 1972).

Part IV

Special Studies

Chapter Thirteen

Tax Increment Financing: Drawing on the California Experience[1]

One of the more promising sources of new town intown funding is tax increment financing. The materials that follow seek to deepen understanding of this method, drawing mainly upon California experience. The State of California has not only pioneered its use but has had almost two decades of rich experience. This experience includes 42 bond issues worth $178 million supported by tax increments, extensive experimentation with nonfederal redevelopment, and LPAs beginning to think and act like public investor-entrepreneurs.

California Legal Overview

In California, tax increment financing legally is an uncomplicated device which enables a local public agency (LPA) to recapture the new tax revenues generated by a financially successful urban renewal project. These gains in tax revenues, known as tax increments, are distributed to a LPA which holds them in a special fund to amortize redevelopment bonds. These bonds are known as tax allocation bonds. On the promise of anticipated tax increments assumed to result from redevelopment, the LPA may issue tax allocation bonds to finance all or part of the capital, administrative, or other costs of redevelopment.

Tax increments and allocation bonds may be used in federal and nonfederal urban renewal projects. By providing an additional source of local revenues, tax increment financing establishes a mechanism of considerable flexibility for designing and executing these projects. Most nonfederal projects are heavily dependent upon recapture of tax increments and could not be undertaken otherwise. The underlying theory of tax increment financing is that by reducing municipal out-of-pocket costs, more federal and nonfederal redevelopment activity can be stimulated. And the more redevelopment stimulated, the greater the prospect of averting center city decay and increases in long-term public sector costs.

327

In California, those tax revenues derived from assessed valuations existing in an area prior to the official redevelopment plan are "frozen" and "divided" among the "taxing agencies".[2] Typically there may be 10 to 20 taxing entities in a given locality, including the city, county, school district, and other special districts. These taxing entities are guaranteed continuance of the tax base throughout the life of the project. Any increases in assessed valuations within the project area are assumed to have been caused by the redevelopment project and are "allocated" to the LPA. The LPA is required to set them aside in a special fund for financing project costs including principal and interest of the tax allocation bonds.

The California Legislature first authorized local redevelopment in 1945. Postwar concern lay with the twin conditions of ongoing physical deterioration of center cities, and failure of conventional economic and legal processes in attracting private redevelopment capital. Now known as the Community Redevelopment Law,[3] the California act subsequently was enlarged to conform with the Housing Act of 1949[4] and later federal urban renewal legislation. A California LPA possesses the customary array of municipal powers required for participating in and executing federal renewal objectives. There is one notable exception: a LPA cannot construct, rehabilitate, or finance the construction of any building although it may provide all necessary site and capital improvements.[5]

Under California law, a LPA may suggest survey area designations, assist in selecting the project area, prepare the redevelopment plans, and proceed with project execution. In the project design and implementation process a LPA may use consultants, sponsors, and developers; exercise eminent domain, land write down, and land assembly powers; and make contractual agreements with the federal, state, municipal, and other governing bodies for grants, loans, and technical assistance. In addition, a LPA is authorized to fully participate in the federal new communities program.[6]

Although a California LPA has no direct power of taxation, it is entitled to revenues from land disposition, leases, and other sources and is broadly authorized to borrow money by issuance of notes, bonds, and other promissory obligations. As a legal creature of the municipal government and its city council, a LPA cannot administer property taxes, determine assessed valuations, or set tax rates for the project area. Its capacity to receive tax increment revenues and to issue tax allocation bonds was not legally settled until adoption of an amendment to the California Constitution in 1952.[7] The ability to harness tax increments plus extensive project and financial experience set California apart from other states, including those few states (Minnesota, Iowa, and Oregon) which also authorize use of tax increments.[8]

The basic mechanics of tax increment recapture are relatively straightforward.

After the LPA completes its preliminary studies, a proposed redevelopment plan is submitted to the city council for adoption as the official project area plan. Once the plan is adopted by ordinance, assessed valuations of existing taxable property (land and improvements) within the project are "frozen" for the project's life. The assessed valuations frozen are those "shown upon the assessment roll . . . last equalized (completed) *prior to* the effective date of such ordinance."[9] The freeze serves an accounting purpose of establishing the "base valuation" or "frozen base" to be used for calculating future gains in assessments and tax revenues within the project.

From that point forward until retirement of the tax allocation bonds, taxing entities are assured a basically stable tax base within the project. This statement requires some qualification because the assessor may subsequently change assessed valuations by periodic reviews or upon petition by a taxpayer alleging inequitable assessment. Also, the project reuse plan may cause taxable property to be reallocated to a tax exempt use such as a school, hospital, or similar public facility.[10]

The essential purpose of freezing the tax base is to protect nonmunicipal taxing agencies—county, school district, and special districts—from massive dislocation of tax revenues while redevelopment proceeds within the project area. There is no restraint prohibiting a taxing agency during the life of the project or tax allocation bonds from revising its tax rate so long as it does not discriminate, positively or negatively, as to how the project area is taxed.

Gains in assessed valuations thereafter resulting in the project area are assumed to have been generated by redevelopment. All or part of the gains in tax revenues, the tax increments, may be allocated by the city council to the LPA. With prior authorization from the city council, the LPA may pledge these revenues to repay bonds, loans, advances, or indebtedness incurred by undertaking redevelopment. In a federal project tax increment revenues may be applied against capital improvement and cash costs of the one-third local contribution. In nonfederal projects, tax increments may be used to finance all or part of the municipal net project costs. Once tax increments are allocated to a LPA, the agency typically will then issue either a short-term promissory note to provide interim financing or long-term (20 to 30 years) tax allocation bonds to provide permanent project financing.

The California act further requires that property owned by a LPA, but leased to another party, is to be assessed and taxed as if held in private ownership.[11] A LPA is thus precluded from providing tax abatements to subsidize persons or businesses holding property in the project area under a lease rather than in fee simple. However, in a federal project a LPA may apply federal subsidies to write down land resale prices, charge the write down costs against gross project costs, and thereby functionally achieve much the same end as a tax abatement.

The California legislation advances three broad purposes: supplemental financing of municipal project costs, avoidance of local referendum requirements, and exemption from municipal debt ceilings.

1. Supplemental Financing. Tax increment financing originally was nurtured in California to facilitate and stimulate community redevelopment by reducing apparent, out-of-pocket local costs of federal and nonfederal projects. The federal program distributed total capital costs by a two-to-one, federal local formula. At most, a community would be required to make a cash payment equivalent to one-third of the "net project cost"—the difference between gross project cost and land disposition revenues. But a community's cash liability could be, and invariably was, reduced by noncash credits given for municipal investment within the project areas.

Such noncash credits could be received by the LPA for site clearance work, land donations, project improvements, and supporting facilities including public buildings and other facilities. In this context, tax increment financing was an alternative method of lowering municipal, out-of-pocket cash outlays. Depending upon community renewal objectives and sufficient noncash credits from site improvements, tax increment financing enabled a LPA potentially to design a project to be self-liquidating and reduce actual local cash outlays to zero. Tax increment financing may have had a secondary redeeming grace by mitigating incentives for local gamemanship and freeing a LPA and city council to use urban renewal to pursue more comprehensive social objectives. A municipality restricted to either cash outlays or noncash improvements could be expected to, and frequently did, strategize local renewal efforts to meet federal requirements, to manipulate timing and location of on-site and off-site improvements, and accordingly, to reduce local cash expenditure.

2. Referendum Avoidance. Tax increment financing is one among numerous legal devices developed in California to circumvent a state constitutional provision[12] which is uncommonly restrictive of municipal financing of local public improvements. Only four states—California, Idaho, Kentucky, and Missouri—subject municipal general obligation bonds, the traditional method for financing public works, to referendum approval by a two-thirds majority of the local electorate. A simple majority approval is required for issuance of general obligation bonds by 32 other states for local improvements and the State of California for its public improvements.[13] The inevitable result has been a local finance field in California strewn with special district bonds, revenue bonds, leaseback arrangements, and other financial mechanisms generally needing simple or, at most, 60 percent majority approval by referendum.

Whatever the relative merits of these prolix alternate financing schemes,[14] tax increment financing requires no referendum. A simple majority vote of the city council is sufficient for allocating tax increments to a LPA as well as for authorizing LPA issuance of allocation bonds.

3. Debt Ceiling Exemption. Unlike general obligation and revenue bonds, tax allocation bonds are not issued by the municipality through its city council nor secured in case of default by pledge of real property. A municipality's capital indebtedness posture relative to its debt limitation ceiling, accordingly, is not jeopardized. Bondholders are protected essentially by covenants made by a LPA at time of issuance and ultimately by confidence that in event of default, the bonds will be refunded or other revenues will be pledged. These covenants may include promises by a LPA: not to adversely alter the redevelopment plan; not to divert tax increments until retirement of bonds; and to provide certified annual financial statements. Sometimes revenues from such other sources as land disposition and leases are pledged. The interest of bondholders is thus conditioned upon the performance of the LPA, private redevelopers, and project area to generate tax increments.

The bonds are exempt from federal and state income taxes and may be held by banks, trusts, insurance companies, and public corporations. They may be issued as serial or term obligations, the latter for a typical 20- to 30-year term, but may be retired at any time prior to maturity. The maximum statutory interest rate is seven percent, but the bonds may also be sold at a discount of five percent of par value.

Recent legislative developments in California imply that tax increment financing has been a valuable supplementary financial mechanism but a mixed blessing. The chief legislative problem is to devise a policy which provides sufficient financial incentives for redevelopment while not extracting undue subsidies from nonmunicipal entities. The basic elements of the problem may be seen by referring to the graph below.

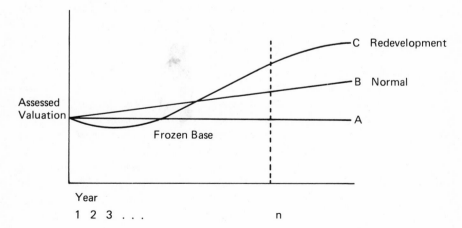

The frozen base is shown to have a constant assessed valuation over the life of the project. Assessments are frozen from adoption of the redevelopment plan in project year one until retirement of the tax allocation bonds in year n. Tax increment financing assumes a governmental finance tradeoff between municipal and nonmunicipal taxing entities and use of present and future tax revenues from the project area.

Without redevelopment, school districts, county governments, and other nonmunicipal taxing entities might expect a slow rise in assessments and tax revenues within the project area. That normal rise is shown as the difference between lines B and A. With redevelopment, the city council by simple majority vote may allocate both normal and redevelopment tax revenue gains exclusively to a LPA for defraying municipal costs. The source of intergovernmental friction is apparent, especially where school districts are competing actively for the community property tax dollar. The consequence for nonmunicipal entities has been:

a) To relinquish some or all of the normal increases in tax revenues within the project area from project year one until retirement of the bonds: and
b) To subsidize municipal redevelopment costs; while
c) Hoping that new tax revenues resulting from redevelopment after year n, when discounted back to project year one, will more than offset the losses in normal revenues which were allocated in a LPA.

At present neither the state legislation nor a subsequent court decision[15] require a city council to yield in its legislative discretion as to whether to allocate all or part of the tax increments to other taxing entities. Accordingly, the most effective recourse of school and other entities has been nonlegal remedies entailing application of pressure at political, administrative, or governmental pressure points. Despite introduction of bills in recent years to alleviate these nonmunicipal costs, the matter remains ticklish and unresolved.

Economic, Organizational, and Project Dynamics

The economic, organizational, and project dynamics of tax increment financing involve a number of complexities. In general, the California legislation and project experience can be understood as being subject to three dynamic, sometimes counterintuitive, forces. First, tax increment financing has been practiced in nonfederal and federal projects with different—but not always predictably different—results. It would be wrong to assume that the mere presence or absence of federal renewal subsidies was sufficient to determine the shape and objectives of local projects. The political and social environments of local communities also have to be accounted for.

Second, the experience cannot be appreciated without a preliminary understanding of how tax increment recapture relates to an intricate economic web—a web in which a LPA operates when it attempts to channel regional investment funds into local redevelopment. And third, there is the yet unexplored possibility that economic redevelopment objectives pushed too far could invite close constitutional scrutiny. These problems are suggested by action of some municipalities in declaring substantial portions of the city "blighted" to maximize tax increment recapture, and attempting to shift municipal redevelopment costs to nonmunicipal taxing entities.

The critical question is reached. Suppose a California LPA wanted to use tax increment financing to minimize project cash costs, what would it do? Generally, a LPA would need to immediately clarify its renewal objectives so to conform with this model; in the *limiting case* of no federal or other subsidies, a LPA, depending upon local community objectives *and* comparative investment advantages within the region, would need to perform as a quasi-development corporation; to identify and define local economic development opportunities; to facilitate competitive returns on private investment capital *not otherwise possible;* and to ensure its activities will adequately amortize its tax allocation bonds.

First and foremost, it would imagine itself standing in the shoes of a for-profit developer who can create local development opportunities through legal powers of eminent domain; land write down, assembly, and banking; issuance of tax exempt bonds; and receipt of federal and state subsidies. The LPA would then visualize itself as seeking joint venture with one or more private developers. To attract investment partners, the agency would need to ask three basic questions:

1. Where are current and future fund flows going within the region, and why are not more (or different) kinds of development opportunities being generated locally?
2. Can new development opportunities be created which are *not otherwise possible* for private capital (if private investors had the necessary array of legal powers) and are these opportunities generally compatible with community renewal objectives?
3. Can the LPA organize itself so as (a) to provide the administrative, land assembly and pricing, timing, and staging responsiveness to facilitate competitive investment returns, and (b) in a manner consistent with local social, political, and environmental objectives?

Although the above best describes the *limiting case* of nonfederal projects, it also shows the kinds of economic thinking which undergirds use of tax increment financing under the federal renewal program as well. The effective difference, then, between practice of tax increment financing in federal and nonfederal renewal projects is more a matter of degree than of kind.

Also, it is clear that use of tax increment financing necessarily extends well beyond simple considerations of designing a local redevelopment program and project for high marketability. Whereas a private developer is guided by a single objective, an investment return similar to that for comparable investments for his industry, a LPA must pursue and balance off multiple objectives. These sometimes conflicting objectives include: ensuring the project generates competitive investment returns for private developers; achieving a self-liquidating project; and meeting political, social, relocation housing, and environmental objectives.

Tax increments can be optimized by maximizing generation of new assessed values; minimizing local project costs—capital improvements, relocation, administrative, political, and social operating costs; or both. In addition, since it is probable that several locations within the community could produce favorable tax increment returns, project(s) location should elicit policy decisions by the city council and LPA. The more common policy questions would include the relative desirability of different social impact, organizational capability of the LPA, how many projects to undertake at one time, and synergistic benefits accruing from pairing two or more projects. In short, marketability entails more than maximizing tax revenues—especially where the LPA is pursuing multiple performance objectives.

In the sole study of urban renewal financing in California, Ratcliff identified seven variables important for optimizing public (LPA and community) and private (redeveloper) investment returns. Although he looked at clearance type redevelopment under the federal program, his observations are generally consistent with the financial mechanics of national urban renewal projects and nonfederal projects.

Successful financial implementation was defined as a function of project location, boundaries, reuse plan, disposition timing, sales method, land pricing, and risk and uncertainty.[16] Of these, project location, timing, and boundaries have proven significant.

1. Project Location. More than any other single variable, project location determines marketability because it heavily influences implementation strategies for defining project boundaries, reuse, timing, and land pricing. "The location of the project area determines the use, and the use, in that location at that time, largely establishes the investment quality...."[17] Since generation of tax increments is best optimized by a project location maximizing tax and investment revenues per dollar of community and LPA cost, this means that total *and* marginal revenues and costs need to be considered. Table 13-1 distills the California project finance experience and economic theory into an operational rule of thumb for where to locate a project. It should be noted that "favorable," "marginal," and "unfavorable" location are measured against a standard of how well anticipated tax increments cover local costs and marginally

Table 13-1. Redevelopment Project Locations and Tax Increment

Location	Area Tax Base	Anticipated Tax Increments
Favorable	Relatively Stable or Increasing	(1) Sufficient to finance local costs (net), not otherwise subsidized, within economic planning horizon
		(2) Marginal gains in new tax increments, averaged over project life, exceeds normal marginal changes in tax revenue of the area without urban renewal
Marginal	Declining	(1) Sufficient to finance local costs (net), not otherwise subsidized, within economic planning horizon
		(2) Marginal gains in new tax increments, averaged over project life, increase at a rate which at minimum *stabilize* property values (for example, to stabilize a three percent annual decline in tax revenues, at least three percent in tax increments would have to be generated yearly)
Unfavorable	Increasing or Declining	(1) Total tax increments unable to finance local costs within economic planning horizon (or, without resort to federal or state subsidy)

exceed normal tax revenues. (Of course, a "favorable" location might be socially or environmentally disastrous while an "unfavorable" one could have nonmonetary benefits unquestionably warranting some form of subsidy.)

Where a LPA is forced to perform as a for-profit entity—with uncertain or no resource to federal or state subsidies—critical tolerance for public investments become well defined. Under urban renewal, the federal government could be counted on to put up at least two-thirds of net project costs. This meant that the risk and cost of poor LPA decisions about project location were two times greater for the federal than the city government. In fact, the use of noncash credits further shifted the risk and costs by a factor of 4:1, 5:1, or even higher. That is, for every (net project cost) dollar expended in a poor project location, an LPA would bear only 20 to 25 cents of the cost liability. Accordingly, a major difference between federal and nonfederal projects was the difference between who bore the cost of poor locational decisions.

2. **Project Timing.** The primary feature distinguishing a conventional LPA, content to rely upon the federal subsidies, from one performing as a

for-profit public investor is the manner in which the latter schedules redevelopment. The LPA emphasizing tax increment financing,

a) Invests money to make money in tax increment revenues;
b) Minimizes front end costs by the timing and scale of project boundaries and the competitive marketability of the reuse plan;
c) Implements so as to maximize marketability, land turnover and pricing, and assessment generation; minimizes interest costs on tax allocation bonds; and,
d) Avoids where possible the administrative and programmatic delays associated with the federal program.

Although timing of project initiation and execution would be equally important to federal and nonfederal projects, the federal subsidy cushion could tolerate excessive delays. Delays in nonfederal projects show up relatively faster as monetary costs associated with bond interest charges and intergovernmental friction. To oversimplify somewhat, the cost of delay to a LPA as a quasi-development corporation is approximately three to five times greater than for one relying exclusively upon federal subsidy. In California projects relying primarily upon federal subsidy and secondarily upon tax increments, Ratcliff found project timing subordinated to location, boundary, and reuse objectives. Ideally, "the LPA has strong reasons for the prompt sale of the redevelopment project area—to speed the enjoyment of community benefits, to reduce the costs of delay including loss of tax revenues, interest on borrowed funds, imputed interest on the local contribution and administrative expenses, and finally to bolster public relations by showing action."[18]

As tax increment recapture becomes increasingly important, new strategies have been developed which recognize and exploit the use of time. Three of the more illustrative are briefly described below.

(1) *Beating the Assessor.* This strategy involves wrapping areas of actual or probable new construction in a "project" boundary before they are reassessed so that the LPA captures the naturally occurring assessment gain. Under this variant, the agency would exploit the time lag occurring between (a) when new construction is announced or begun, and (b) when it is completed for assessment purposes. Accordingly, the object is to freeze the old assessment base, wrap it up as a project, capture the new tax increments, and then decide how to redevelop the neighborhood.

(2) *Multiple Project Staging.* Another variant would be to pool tax increment revenues in a common fund and to stage development of multiple projects so that the most lucrative is begun first and then subsequently leverages the less favorable projects. Suppose a LPA were considering thee potential project areas—Project A would be highly lucrative for increment revenues, Project B would be marginal, and Project C unfavorable. Standing alone, Projects B and C probably would not be developed due to the LPA's reliance upon tax

increment generation rather than upon a federal subsidy. Standing together, however, all three might prove financially feasible if the LPA wraps project boundaries around the three areas, proceeds with the most lucrative project first, and phases in the more marginal and unfavorable projects as projects revenues and costs permit.

A potential disadvantage would be reverse leverage where, for example, an economic depression or physical catastrophe wiping out the lead project would pull down the linked projects. Careful financial planning should obviate that possibility. Prudent staging of multiple projects could make feasible a more socially balanced redevelopment program with little, if any, sacrifice of financial objectives.

(3) *Project Boundaries.* Definition of project boundaries is a function primarily of tax increment optimization and the geographical distribution of "blight." Similarly, it is clear that increment optimization dynamically interrelates with other project variables including location, timing, and reuse marketability. Tax revenue flows would be to a for-profit LPA what cash flows are to a developer: both are essential and needed as early as possible in the project's life. Boundaries for the project area and redevelopment site need not be coidentical. The broader the project area—but not necessarily the site area—and the earlier its definition in the planning process, the greater the tax increment capture.

How boundaries are drawn could determine, of course, tax capture potential as well as reuse marketability. While social, political, and neighborhood factors could be significant, they would be subordinate to the first order requirement for tax increment optimization. Once that requirement is met, however, these nonfinancial factors could be elevated to meet multiple community objectives or to stage multiple projects.

The size of project boundaries could be important for other reasons. One might be to stabilize declining property values, and household and investor disinvestment due to uncertainty about the future of a particular neighborhood. In some cases lending institutions have been willing to finance commercial and residential improvements in a "blighted" neighborhood once it had been made part of a project. Prior to that loans had been notably scarce. Another related reason for large projects might be to facilitate an owner participant financial involvement to help realize project objectives.

The economics for determining boundaries and reuse marketability are straightforward. Tax increments are optimized for the financial planning horizon by maximizing new assessments while minimizing local project costs. Since tax increment revenues must equal total net project costs, this means that increment revenues must equal the local tax rate multiplied by the increment base (new assessed valuations less frozen assessed valuations) over a specified period of years. To illustrate, suppose a project has:

a total (net) cost to the community of $980,000;

a total local tax rate (municipal, county, school, and so forth) of 14 percent of assessed valuation;

a projected increment base of $7,000,000 within 20 years; and

the marginal gain in tax increments exceeds the normal marginal gain in tax revenues without renewal.

The project would break even because 14 percent of a new increment base ($7,000,000) would meet local net costs.

Another method would be to surround the project with a special district known as a benefit district. A benefit district would capture the *external* benefits generated by the project but spilling over its legal boundaries. A special benefit district could be used where:

a) The neighborhood encompassed by the project is "blighted" but the area surrounding the project cannot support a reasonable legislative finding of "blight;"

b) the project neighborhood is "blighted" *and* so is the area surrounding the project, but political or social factors preclude a LPA from extending the boundaries into the surrounding area.

The theory of tax increment financing in California originally was to promote capture of *internal* benefits assumed to have been generated by the project and the LPA's activity. It was based upon observations that so long as central cities were allowed to decline, the municipality—rather than other taxing agencies—would bear a disproportionate share of the costs as the need for public services increased while the assessment base contracted. Thus, the theory suggested that so long as a municipality would suffer disproportionately from central city decline, it should be allowed to benefit disproportionately from central city redevelopment.

Where tax increments are recovered internally by ad valorem taxation of land and improvements, ideally they should be recovered externally only through taxing increases in land values. The rationale, in its simplest explanation, is that (a) urban renewal should encourage new investment in improvements (houses, stores and buildings), (b) a tax (*ad valorem*) on improvements is counterproductive, whereas (c) a tax on increased land values in no way penalizes improvement investments. The most common illustration is where a new train station is built and neighborhood land values, due to georgraphical proximity with the station, begin to skyrocket. California authorizes use of special benefit districts to finance mass transportation.

California Project Experience

In summary, tax increment financing is a for-profit device enabling a LPA to take out tax flows as a developer takes out cash flows to finance front end, interim, and permanent project costs. In many projects LPAs quite naturally adopt the "in low, out high" investment approach of developers. Of the 42 tax allocation bond issues since 1956, three projects were "predominantly" residential, another three industrial, and 36 were commercial. Although there are sound reasons for not placing labels on these projects, tax increments as a rule are best generated in high rise residential, commercial, and to a lesser extent, industrial projects. Projects that are predominantly comprised of low or medium density residential, neighborhood conservation, rehabilitation, open space, or tax exempt parcels cannot generate sufficient increments to interest bondholders.

Another distinctive query is whether reliance upon increment production distorts broader community and social goals for urban renewal. First, there is still no competent and satisfying method for evaluating a dynamic, multiple objective program such as urban renewal. Accordingly, project labels such as "predominantly commercial" further cloud the issue. Second, Ratcliff observed that the 19 LPAs in 1961—the CBD era of the federal program—were more sensitive to community benefits, public reaction, and political factors than they were to land disposition prices. In selecting prospective redevelopers the LPAs ranked tax revenue generation *fourth* behind low income housing, speed of completion, and local community ties.

On the other hand, 16 allocation bond issues were made between 1956 and 1968, but there were 26 issues after the federal program shifted from a CBD to residential emphasis in 1968. Presumably the post-1968 surge was due to continuing local interest in commercial projects, but it also could indicate LPA acceptance of tax increments especially for small nonfederal projects. In short, the evidence regarding social and community goals is mixed.

A third distinctive feature is that tax allocation bonds have been favorably received by investors and generally rank one grade below general obligation municipal bonds. Forty-two issues totalling $178 million have been issued since 1956 at interest rates one-half to one percent above municipal bonds. There have been no defaults and only one refunding (Sacramento, 1956).

IMPLICATIONS FOR THE NEW TOWN INTOWN PROGRAM

Tax increment financing is a device which supplements more conventional methods of project financing and thereby stimulates intown development. It is a tool: how it is used is determined by the rules of the game. The new towns intown proposed for San Antonio, Pontchartrain, and Roosevelt Island, for example, use actual or imputed tax increment revenues to supplement more conventional revenue flows—cash, capital gains, and tax shelters.

In New Orleans the land price is to be written down from $4,400 to $3,000 per acre as a condition of transfer from a private entity, Centex Corporation, to the public development entity, the New Community Development Corporation. By making the one-third write down, the private entity in effect is using the Pontchartrain site as a seed investment for its surrounding landholdings and is anticipating that write down costs can be recovered as long-term capital gains. Accordingly, within the Pontchartrain project area, land prices assessment valuations, and tax increment generation will increase as: the project area land naturally recovers its former fair market value of $4,400 an acre, and the new town intown and surrounding Centex development proceeds.

Functionally, the Pontchartrain project represents two variations on the California experience with tax increment recapture. One is that the tax increments are not allocated to a special fund of the public entity. Instead the increments flow directly into the municipal general fund where, with city council approval, they can be allocated to the development corporation. Since the public entity lacks exclusive control over the increments, it apparently cannot pledge them against tax allocation bonds for permanent project financing. If the public entity were authorized to leverage the increments, rather than surrendering them to the general fund, the scope and intensity of its operations might be substantially enlarged. For example, the development corporation hypothetically could leverage increments to finance additional low and moderate income housing, public facilities, or active inner city redevelopment.

Roosevelt Island exemplifies another variation employing recapture of *imputed* increments. The land is written down to zero cost under a long-term lease between the Urban Development Corporation and the City of New York. The development corporation, rather than individual families, pays property taxes to the city at an imputed rate according to type of apartment—subsidized, middle, or high income. Although these tax payments are labelled "tax equivalent," that term is a misnomer. The units are to be undertaxed relative to comparable apartments elsewhere in the New York region. While financial and property holding arrangements supporting Roosevelt Island are fairly intricate, one result is that the "in lieu" payments permit the public developer to recapture imputed tax increments generated by the intown project.

In San Antonio, the private entity, SANT Ltd., would hold the project area land under a long-term lease from the Title I LPA, the San Antonio Development Agency. The terms of their agreement enable the private entity to make an in lieu payment of project area taxes. Since property assessments within the project are frozen, there is no tax revenue loss while new town development proceeds, but gains in land appreciation can be recaptured by SANT as imputed tax revenues. It may be observed that while the San Antonio LPA can write down land prices, apparently there is no write-down for assessed valuations.

Some policy implications of tax increment recapture in federal and nonfederal projects, particularly NTITs, need to be stated clearly. The rules of the game for central city development are controlling and likely to remain fixed for many years despite general and special revenue sharing.

The NTIT program copies and also extends federal urban renewal by relying exclusively upon a "market test" to determine financial feasibility of community development. The lead development entity, usually a developer seeking competitive investment returns, invests money in urban development in order to take out money as cash flows, capital gains, and tax shelter. Tax increment recapture facilitates the for-profit motivation of California LPAs and of private or public lead entities under the Title VII program. How the takeout occurs is a function of federal and state rules or the game for federal renewal projects, federal new towns intown, and nonfederal projects. Even the nonfederal projects are governed by the federal game rules. Legislation enabling federal and nonfederal redevelopment in the 50 states was modelled after the federal urban renewal statutes and program.

The resulting implication is apparent: new town intown development will continue to proceed in center cities either as (a) quasi-urban renewal using a LPA for eminent domain, land assembly, write downs, and perhaps tax increment recapture; or, (b) a public development corporation with the same legal powers and, hopefully, without the lockstep project mechanics of urban renewal. If the market test for new towns intown is taken as a given, then a primary objective of federal administration of Title VII, as now constituted, would be to enlarge community benefits consistent with for-profit developer interests. Tax increment recapture, especially to leverage multiple linked new town intown projects within the same community or region, would then warrant serious federal consideration.

NOTES TO CHAPTER THIRTEEN

1. The legal and financial insights provided by two recognized experts on tax increment financing are acknowledged gratefully—Eugene F. Jacobs, a Los Angeles attorney and leading exponent, and T. E. Comerford, first vice president of Blyth, Eastman, Dillon and Co., Incorporated, San Francisco.

2. An Opinion of the California Attorney General states that the essence of tax increment financing is,

> . . . the allocation to repayment of redevelopment indebtedness of the amount of all taxes, otherwise payable to the appropriate taxing agency, which result from any gain in assessed valuation of the property in the redevelopment area occurring after adoption of the project. Conversely, the taxing agency is guaranteed the amount of money it would have received on account of the levy of taxes under the assessed valuation existing at the adoption of the project. The taxing agency is entitled to the same revenue, neither more nor less, than it would have gotten if assessed values had not increased. To insure this, it is expressly stated in the constitutional provision that until the assessed valuation of the taxable property exceeds the valuation shown on the last assessment roll preceding adoption of the project, all the taxes levied and collected must be paid to the respective taxing agencies. Once

that value is exceeded, however, the division of taxes goes into effect. That is, the levied taxes are allocated according to the formula specified, and as they are collected they are divided between the taxing agencies and the redevelopment agency in accordance with the allocation. (27 Ops. Cal. Atty. Gen. 352 at 354 [1956]).

3. Cal. Health and Safety Code § 33000 *et seq.*

4. Stats. 1951, c. 710, p. 1922, Section 1 and other subsequent statutory provisions.

5. 36 Ops. Cal. Atty. Gen. 102 (1960).

6. Cal. Health and Safety Code § 33250–33254.

7. Cal. Const. Art. 13, § 19.

8. In Connecticut the state has created a $25 million loan pool for assisting community redevelopment. The loans are repaid from increases in tax revenues resulting from redevelopment projects. Connecticut Development Commission, "Urban Renewal in Connecticut–1964 Report," State Office Building, Hartford, p. 6.

9. Cal. Health and Safety Code §33670(a).

10. 35 Ops. Cal. Atty. Gen. 211 (1960).

11. Cal. Health and Safety Code § 33673.

12. Cal. Const. Art. 11, § 18.

13. Marini, F., *Local Bond Elections in California–The Two-Thirds Majority Requirement,* (Institute of Governmental Affairs, University of California, Berkeley, 1963), p. 1.

14. There are 49 different types of special assessment districts in California. Consider the following legislative committee report.

> At present, Article XI, Section 18 of the Constitution of California regulates the incurring of long-term indebtedness by cities, counties, and school districts. Intended as a bulwark against the extravagant and unwise commitment of tax funds to sometimes questionable public improvements, the constitutional provision has become a sieve through which our tax funds flow for the most part without let or hindrance.

Local governing boards faced with the need for public improvements and fearful of the results of an election requiring approval of two-thirds of those voting, have evaded the constitutional restriction by resort to "lease-purchase," "special fund," and "special district" arrangements which avoid the requirement of voter approval. Sometimes this has been done after voter disapproval of a bond issue. Such financing methods are more expensive to the taxpayer than general obligation bonds. "Most of the witnesses appearing before the committee had no conception of what a fraction-of-a-percent increase in bond interest rates could do in dollar and cents toward skyrocketing the price of bond financing. . . . " Subcommittee of the Revenue and Taxation Committee on Public Indebtedness, "The Cost of Public Financing for Necessary New and Expanded Facilities on the State and Local Level," (California State Assembly, Assembly Interim Committee Reports, 1959, Vol. 4, No. 5, pp. 14, 16.

15. *In Redevelopment Plan*, 61 Cal. 2d 21 (1964).

16. Ratcliff, R., *Private Investment in Urban Redevelopment—A Study of the Disposal Phase in Urban Renewal* (Institute of Business and Economic Research, University of California, Berkeley, 1961), pp. 16—29.

17. Ibid., p. 17

18. Ibid., p. 20

Chapter Fourteen

Towards Design Criteria for Housing in New Town Intown Programs[a]

Introduction

The new town intown program is unique among federal programs in permitting an integrated approach to the housing problem as seen in a broad social context. Virtually every housing program attempted in recent years has seen housing as a problem to be solved in isolation and not as part of a larger system. The original public housing program, as well as the newer section 236 and rent supplement programs, was concerned only with expanding the physical supply of housing and its occupancy by groups not otherwise able to afford it. The urban renewal program went somewhat further; it was able also to deal with certain neighborhood conditions, street patterns, utilities, recreational facilities in some cases, and public services in others. But even its focus was physical, with other activities undertaken secondarily so as to attract occupants to new housing and to meet their needs once in it.

The new towns intown program could open broader vistas. It could tackle housing problems as part of a total urban system. On the physical end, it is ideally suited to: (a) coordinate use of existing housing with new housing, and (b) provide in a rational market oriented fashion some relationship between a person's ability to pay and the quality of the housing he occupies subject to publicly determined minimums. Further, it can, as part of a single program, deal with neighborhood problems, safety, recreation, public facilities, and transportation at the same time it deals with the quality of individual units of the physical housing stock. It can also provide the educational, health, welfare, manpower training, employment, and other programs needed to maximize the opportunities derived from an improved housing stock.

A number of proposals can be suggested, and even worked out in some detail, by which this might be accomplished. At the most conservative

a. by Helmut Schulitz, Peter Marcuse, and Sean O'Laoire.

extreme, an NTIT program could simply marshal public programs in a coordinated improvement effort, one part of which would be raising the housing stock to stated minimum levels. Outside of a new town or large scale urban renewal program, such an effort has never been undertaken with anything approaching success. Such is one possibility for NTITs, but lessons from previous experience with redevelopment seem to point toward another more radical direction.

In the past, redevelopment tended to shift the income scale of housing clients. Even if development costs could be substantially reduced, they would probably still be high enough to push rents above low income means. Old housing for the poor was demolished and replaced with new housing for the middle class. A housing allowance program appears to have problems. Rather than increase, through the market, the supply of adequate housing for the poor, it may simply bid up the cost of the present supply—indeed, it could be an inflationary force on the price of *all* housing. The mortgage assistance program has proven less than successful as witnessed by the recent disclosures of corrupt practices by lending firms.

All these programs had a common failure: they were all examples of the "from the top down" approach in housing administration—an approach whereby programs were developed in Washington and applied across the board without much regard for local institutions and processes.

Another approach is necessary—a "from the bottom up" approach—to complement centralized authority and to achieve any marked improvement in housing. A collection of authorities at the community level would be a powerful addition to implementation of a national policy and also would provide a local perspective at the planning and implementation stages.

But such an approach demands community organizations of sufficient scope—and power—to mobilize and channel community resources with effectiveness. For a particular community, this means two things. First, there must be a close involvement of the local mayor and city council (or similar officials). They can provide, through the city's administrative and legislative process, valuable assistance. For example, in Los Angeles Mayor Thomas H. Bradley has proposed a community resources bank to help finance development and redevelopment projects.

Second, a broad based, community "cutting-edge" development entity is needed that can view housing with a sense of community and regional needs. Such a community development agency of corporation should have sufficient scope to be able to try innovative approaches to improve the quality of housing. For example, if the NTIT program set up a community development corporation authorized (a) to marshall all housing allowances allocable to that community, and (b) to provide all those eligible for such allowance with decent, safe, and sanitary housing (meeting whatever standards the federal program might establish), a fully coordinated, integrated program could then be established to handle the whole gamut of "housing" problems.

While there are many such potential approaches and they each would have to be examined in more detail, the point is that a community based strategy allows for a diversity of responses tailored to *local* needs and attributes. Within broad policy, guidance, and support provided by the federal level, local development corporations, based upon their own assessment of housing and related needs, would be free to strike out in the most promising directions.

But what of the broad policy, guidance, and support from the federal level? If federal money is to be spent, what kind of questions should HUD ask of the agencies making proposals based upon local needs? This is a highly complex area that requires some subtle but important shifts in perspective. Previous HUD efforts at establishing guidelines have concentrated upon a too narrow range of concerns—for example, the shelter component of housing. A house is, after all, not simply a physical structure, but a complex system through which certain services are provided to residents. Its outputs are shelter from the elements, to be sure, but ideally it is also a place from which a job is easily accessible; in which a family can be raised, friends entertained, and an education achieved; in whose improvement money and labor can be invested; and a place that is part of a community in which a person can live in dignity, exercising self-government, feeling secure and independent.

Because an NTIT program could see and deal with housing as part of an intricate web of physical, social, economic, and psychological factors, all of which it can in some fashion directly influence, NTITs could also deal directly with what we call the "outputs" of housing. Outputs are those items by which a housing policy truly should be judged—not the gross number of units built, the percentage of substandard housing, or the progress in achieving some fixed numerical national goal, but rather the satisfaction of people with the housing in which they live, and the contribution it makes to their health, economic prosperity, development of their children, and strength of their community.

These appear to be broad generalities, as useless as they are true. The effort to make them operational may not heretofore have seemed worthwhile because no programs heretofore had the capacity to direct themselves at these outputs systematically. The breadth and depth of the analysis should match the breadth and depth of the tools available to implement its results. With the expanded tools potentially made available by NTIT, an expanded and more thoroughgoing analysis of housing problems is needed. This chapter begins to fill that need—first, with an overview of housing as a system, and second, with an example of how such an approach can yield *specific criteria* for future housing programs under the direction of local development corporations and other developmental agencies. The main focus is to suggest the kind of guidelines that HUD could establish for cities or agencies seeking federal assistance for new towns intown. Specifically, this outlines the kind of information about housing development that should be supplied by any entity undertaking a new town intown.

The Housing System as Part
of a Larger System

We do not intend here to present a thorough and academically rigorous formulation of the systems view of housing. Such a formulation requires much more time than has been available in the present study. But, beyond that, a complete formulation is not necessary for present purposes. What is important is to highlight the fact that the NTIT program almost uniquely makes relevant such a systems approach, and indeed demands it, for the NTIT program *can* deal directly with the full range of outputs of housing policy.

Where housing subsidy policies were forced to deal separately with construction of housing or its rehabilitation as part of the physical inputs into housing, or where landlord-tenant relations reform and management policy can deal with some of the social and organizational inputs into housing, or where housing allowances or welfare programs can deal with some of the income and economic inputs into housing, or where crime prevention programs (often not even considered relevant to housing policy at all) are generally only seen separately as inputs to housing, NTIT could marshall and coordinate all of these efforts in a single program. In doing so, it both can and must be conscious of the desired outputs of the total package of policies subject to its influence. Some of these outputs are here discussed in their intermediate form: quality of maintenance, safety, employment, neighborhood stability, and others. They can ultimately be discussed in terms of shelter, security, health, income, self-government, communality, control over the environment, and parallel categories.[1]

The failure to adopt this kind of orientation has resulted in many failures of housing policy in the past. Physically sound housing was designed (although such implications are not thought through by its sponsors) to optimize the output of shelter, but totally neglected the outputs of communality and safety (Pruitt–Igoe being an extreme example). Ownership of housing was encouraged to optimize the output of control but at the expense of income (Section 235). Communality could be emphasized at the expense of shelter (tenant control in public housing, nonprofit sponsorship under Section 236). And possibly income may now be optimized as an output, but at the expense of shelter and communality (certain forms of housing allowances).

For the sake of brevity, the systems view described here will simply be illustrated by a diagram. Using this diagram, the balance of this chapter will be devoted to one key application of it—the selection of the criteria for housing programs in the community oriented approach outlined above. The diagrams that follow are, indeed, illustrative only, and should only serve as a useful framework to approach the problem.

Diagram 14–1 suggests the full scope which a systems approach to housing encompasses. The Primary Inputs can be categorized in a number of ways: the division among resources, social organization, and individual develop-

Diagram 14—1. Elements of a Systems View of Housing

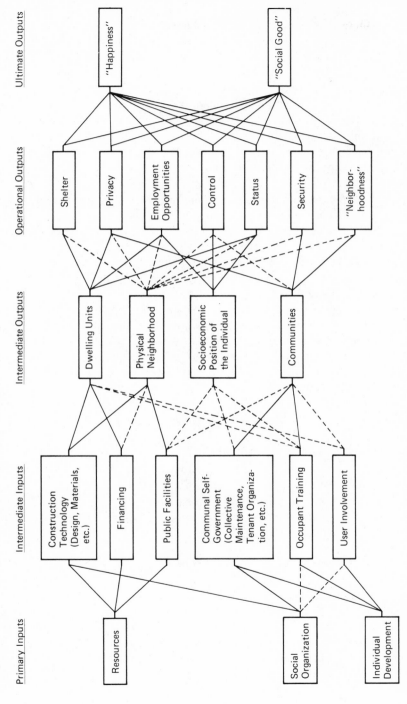

ment is an arbitrary but useful one. It highlights the alternatives among public policies by separating out their costs in resources (that is, generally, their budget cost), the social organizational changes required for them (generally by legislative changes or public action), and the opportunities for individual contribution.

Intermediate Inputs categorize the types of programmatic actions through which the Primary Inputs can be brought to bear on housing problems. They are, in effect, the distinct components of the packages of inputs of which each proposed or existing housing program is made. Again, separating the existing program packages (that is, urban renewal, public housing, housing allowances) into their ingredients, including the Intermediate Inputs of which they are composed, helps to clarify the results they produce and the possibilities of changes and rearrangements that may exist.

Intermediate Outputs is a category that serves an evaluative rather than an operational purpose. This category highlights the major areas in which the impact of housing policies (Inputs) can be seen, and thus can be evaluated. Their use in measuring the success of various policies is key, and they may serve as indicators (at an operational level) of the success of housing policy. For other purposes, however, they may be unnecessary, and the impact of Intermediate Inputs can be traced directly to Operational Outputs.

Operational Outputs are differentiated from Ultimate Outputs only in their level of refinement. Obviously the process of analysis can be pushed even further, to a formulation of some ultimate output of "human happiness" or "the social good," but such formulations are of little assistance in policy making. The level at which Ultimate Outputs are here suggested is no doubt beyond the capability of immediate measurement, but yet serves as a reminder that Operational Outputs can be seen as only steps towards broader goals, and their interrelationship and ultimate consequences cannot be ignored. The Operational Outputs, on the other hand, can indeed be measured and the extent of their achievement evaluated. It is one of the intellectual weaknesses of existing federal housing policy that only one of these outputs, shelter, is generally even considered in the evaluation of policy. One of the lessons to be learned from the existing failures of that policy is that other outputs are at least equally important, and that their reciprocal relationship can be ignored only at the peril of jeopardizing even that single objective.

Criteria for NTIT Housing Efforts

So far we have argued for two important shifts in housing administration. One shift is toward a greater appreciation of the systems nature of housing and the variety of trade-offs to be made among the variety of outputs. It is by comprehending *all* the outputs of housing that a housing policy should be judged. Secondly, we have argued for a community based input into housing administration. Many housing programs suffered from over-centralized planning and implementation that tended to disregard local peculiarities and needs. A central point in our argument is the need for local development corporations which put housing in perspective with other local needs and devise local programs within a broad national policy. But such an approach raises questions of what criteria a federal housing administration should use in judging local agency proposals.

Clearly, such criteria should be based upon a systemwide perspective and should not revolve strictly around physical design features—that is, number of rooms, square footage, utilities, and so forth. In spite of much rhetoric about providing everyone with a "decent home," the decent home has never received further definition than the one outlined by minimum property standards and by housing and building codes. Much of the current dilemma in attempts to provide housing for lower income groups is due to a too technical focus on standards and a too narrow appreciation of the trade-offs to be made. Any program to provide low income housing should have broader goals than so many houses of so many rooms for so many people.

The remainder of this chapter will indicate the complexity and kinds of interrelationships involved by focusing attention on one of many intermediate outputs: the dwelling. This is intended mainly to exemplify the types of trade-offs generally involved in making decisions about dwellings under the constraints of current design concepts.

The current approach toward minimum standard housing—to make all trade-off decisions in favor of basic shelter needs and to disregard most psychological needs—seems at first glance to be in line with the notion of a hierarchy of needs as put forth by psychologists.[2] This hierarchy suggests that before trying to fulfill a higher level of needs, basic physical needs have to be met. The hierarchy is postulated to have five levels—a physical requirement (food, shelter, and so forth), a security requirement (stability, freedom from fear, and so forth), a social requirement (group interaction, friendships), a self-esteem requirement (respect, love), and a self-actualization level.

The difficulty of applying such a concept to the design of housing lies in determining the threshold where basic physiological needs are met. The threshold varies for different people. Yet we are used to accepting public housing, FHA, and VA minimum standards as an absolute indicator of habitability, and we assume that these physical standards take priority over all other nonphysical needs such as need for security, need for social interaction, need for self-respect, and so forth—that is, other outputs of a housing system.

For a slum dweller, a house may mean more than just shelter. He might be willing to trade off better sanitary facilities against the image of his dwelling, or his personal attachment to a house he himself took part in designing, or the social fabric of his neighborhood. This is not to argue for the continuation of slums, but rather to reinforce the idea that housing, important to the way people find fulfillment and self-actualization, is a complex system with many subtle trade-offs.

For an arbitrary cross-section of users, the house has a varying relationship to people's psychological, social, and physical needs—a relationship that is by no means permanent or static. Current efforts at physical and social planning have been insensitive to the "relativity" of the role housing plays in the social scheme of things by overstating the importance of shelter.

Rather than prescribing arbitrary physical standards, general criteria for housing should be based upon a broader assessment of the complex ways in which changes in the quality of the environment affect the quality of life.

One way to begin to assess these complex interrelationships is with the aid of a *Cross-Impact Matrix*. Such a device allows for investigating, one at a time, the variety of interactions possible in such a complex system. By listing housing characteristics as columns of the matrix and problem areas as rows, each cell of the matrix can be filled to indicate the magnitude and direction of the interaction. Often in this type of analysis, one has little more than intuition as a guide because so little is known, but the order and the structure of the exercise help to eliminate inconsistent assumptions.

In Diagram 14–2, 21 major housing characteristics have been investigated for their positive or negative impact on problem areas often associated with inner city housing. These problem areas are simply another way of looking at the outputs of a housing system; it is a lack of one or more of the outputs shown in Diagram 14–1 that defines a problem. This cross-impact exercise gives a clue to the relative importance that each housing characteristic would have in an attempt to increase the level of all outputs.

When this analysis was begun, it soon became clear that there were gaps in the knowledge needed to assess all the impacts. Very little is known, in fact, in a rigorous scientific sense about some of the interactions. Basic research is needed to put things on a firmer footing. (The analysis serves to identify some of those research needs.) Some of the results shown are little more than educated guesses, but rather than wait for future research, it seemed important to establish the applicability and usefulness of the approach. However, it should be clear that the conclusions shown are tentative and might be changed in light of new research.

The results are summarized in a number of general criteria. The list is by no means complete and should be seen as only a preliminary framework for evaluating NTIT projects proposed by local development corporations and other developmental agencies.

Criteria
The following criteria represent a synthesis of the observations derived from the cross impact matrix: housing characteristics and their impact on inner city housing problems. (As indicated earlier, these are set down in a highly simplified manner.)

Diagram 14-2. Housing Characteristics and Their Impact on Inner City Housing Problems

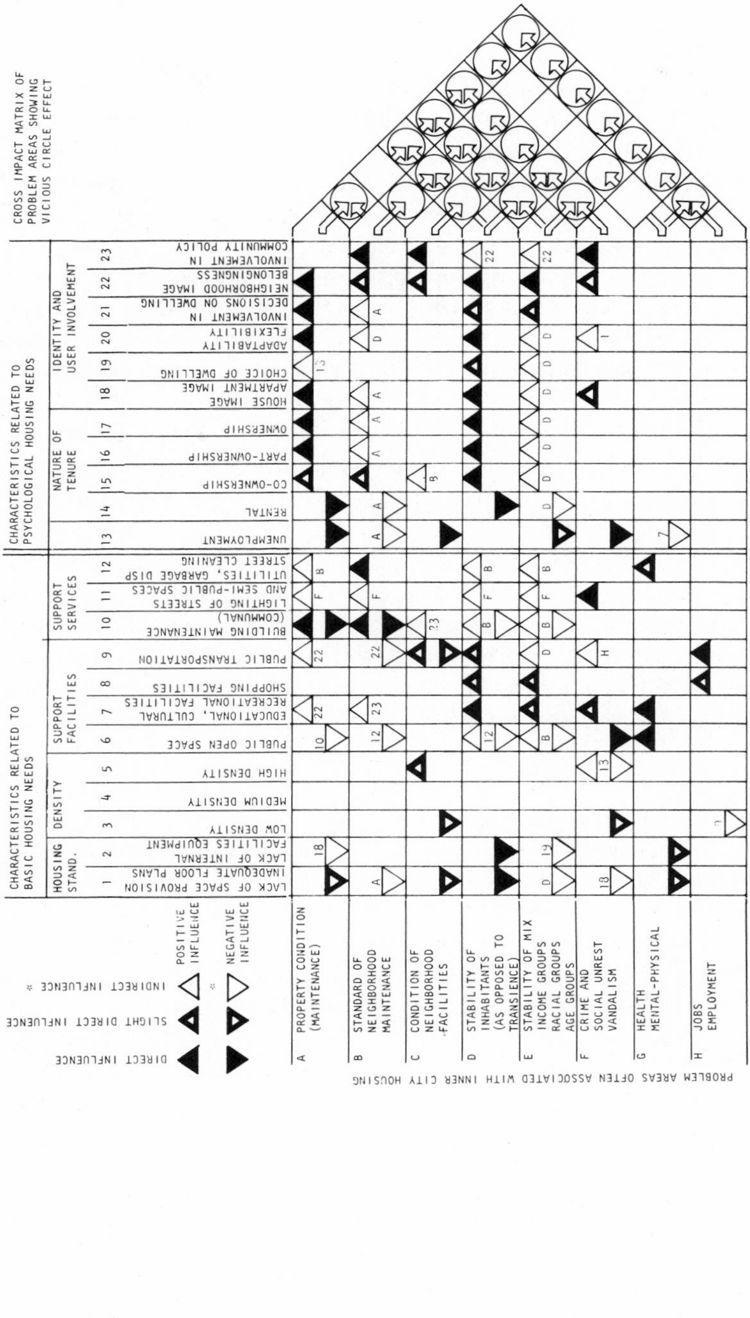

Note: For detailed description see synopsis of cross impact matrix
*Letters and numbers indicate primary source of indirect influence

1. **Variability of Floor Plans in Response to Individual Dweller Needs.** Current design methods and building technology allow the future user of a dwelling to take an active role in shaping the dwelling according to his specific needs. Involving the user in the design process is important for insuring a high degree of user satisfaction and commitment.

2. **Adaptability of Floor Plans.** Present technology can also allow for considering second and third user's layout preferences if adaptability is considered a design priority at the outset of a project in addition to the initial variability of the dwellings. Adaptability will also contribute to the user's needs to adapt to family growth, nonconforming life style, and so forth. This allows for maintaining the usefulness of dwelling over time and consequent neighborhood stability. Adaptability of floor plans may imply not only the ability to adapt floor plans to user needs within a fixed physical framework, but also the ability to expand and contract space as requirements demand. Adaptability and growth potential have implications for initial capital investment in housing, but provision of potential for development and user involvement in addition to basic accommodation and utilities seems in most instances preferable to a slightly better but fixed accommodation without hope for development and improvement. Technology and design have already solved the problems implicit in this directive.

3. **Variety of House Images and Building Forms.** This objective can be addressed by the provision of a cross section of dwelling types (single family house, apartment, duplex, and so forth) in combination with technologically and socially practical variations in each of these categories (on the level of individual units as well as aggregates).

4. **The Provision for Various Densities.** The need to provide for various densities reflects the need to provide choice. This objective suggests a need to think in terms of aggregate densities rather than discrete areas of low, medium, and high densities.

5. **High Density Medium Rise as an Alternative to High Rise.** It is a substantiated fact that densities achieved in high rise development can be achieved in medium rise building forms. Intensification of land use[3] the benefits of which will be outlined later, is a by-product of this type of development.

The inevitably increased amount of semipublic access associated with this form of development can be traded off against more useful and controlled public spaces.

6. **Provision for Mix of Functions in Buildings.** The mechanics of financing housing often preclude the possibility of including support and integral

housing facilities in housing structures—that is, shops, schools, day care centers, and commerce. Especially in areas of poor public transportation or low car ownership, the benefits of proximity of functions to housing should be obvious. The financial and social planning benefits are many.

In new town intown housing there would seem to be a potential for innovative ways of financing housing by giving tax and planning concessions to developers in return for financing housing as an integral part of their developments, thereby providing them with something of a market base (for example, Foundling Hospital, London; Houston Center, Houston, Texas). The self-policing and security associated with areas of intense and constant activity promises a reduction in crime.

7. Design of Semipublic Spaces. Underused spaces, such as corridors, alleys, lanes, are generally the backdrop against which crime occurs, garbage gathers, and so forth. The problem could be best addressed at the individual design proposal level, but avoiding these types of spaces should be seen as a design priority. Clearly identifiable boundaries between private and public spaces, and provision of more individual private space combined with the intensified use of public space can help reduce the problems associated with non-defined semipublic spaces.

8. Avoidance of Disruptive Discontinuity of Neighborhood Image (Physical-Spatial). The introduction of a building form which disrupts the existing physical fabric of an area and has negative or undesirable connotations turns the eyes of the community on the new building. The building is stigmatized and residents, in turn, are castigated and victimized.

As a design directive, efforts should be made to relate new developments to the scale and fabric of their physical and social context.

9. Avoidance of Disruptive Discontinuity of Neighborhood Image (Construction and Phasing). The appearance of the "federal bulldozer" on a renewal site often meant the effective demise of an area's social fabric. In programming construction for a new town intown housing project, cognizance of social structure should allow planners to consider not only construction staging but also the staging of "people removal" to adjacent accommodations (if they wish to remain in the area) and the gradual integration of newcomers into the area.

10. Payments for Housing (Initial Costs). Traditionally, high initial construction costs often precluded the possibility of adequate support facilities which might have provided communities with an integrated base for growth. A reduction in initial construction capital costs (even if this means a cutback in the provision of space) in favor of financing integrated support facilities should be considered where lack of funds is a problem.

This directive implies a review of financial programming, budgeting, and design, that is, architectural design should allow later expansion as growth demands.

The provision of a tax base "nucleus" as suggested above could be seen as a way for partially financing physical and social growth if complemented by an ongoing development budget.

Alternatively, residents could directly undertake expansion, as their needs demand, if provided with basic utilities, and structures.

11. Intensification of Land Use. The arguments for intensive land use are many, particularly in central city situations where land and land development costs are high. Intensification of land use does not necessarily mean the sacrificing of open space and support facilities; rather a reconceptualizing of the role and form of these facilities in the neighborhood is needed—school yards as community open space; multiuse recreational facilities, shops, commerce, and housing in same structures—all of which have benefits of reducing cost, increasing proximity to users, and insuring intensive and full usage.

12. Building Maintenance Via User Involvement. There are many ways of involving the user in maintenance directly and indirectly. There would seem to be a number of prerequisites to achieving a state of concern that produces good maintenance:

a) Give the user a dwelling that fits his needs and aspirations (by providing choice);

b) Provide as much opportunity as possible for the user to own his own dwelling;

c) Failing that, provide for maintenance costs in the form of rental concessions or grants;

d) Provide good quality public maintenance;

e) Reduce amount of associated semipublic space.

A consequence of a high degree of private maintenance would be a substantial saving in public funds now allocated to (often deficient) maintenance.

13. Neighborhood Maintenance Via User Involvement. The provision of a neighborhood environment that fits users' aspirations would seem to be a prerequisite: the standard of neighborhood maintenance by user involvement can be addressed by,

a) Reducing the amount of public open space in favor of more private open space;

b) Giving the individual the opportunity to co-own open space and facilities;

c) Physically and functionally defined spaces related to community traffic and usage patterns would reduce the crime potential and redundancy inherent in amorphous public open spaces.

14. Job Creation. The potential for involving local unemployed and future users in the construction of their housing is rarely exploited. This possibility is either ignored or precluded by the nature of the particular technology or union regulations. If employment in initial construction activities proves impractical, there may be other possible sources of employment such as security, maintenance, sanitation, and the like.

15. Ownership Whenever Possible. The benefits of ownership are many and varied; making ownership increasingly possible would seem to have many social and financial advantages:

a) Ownership implies a commitment to a place for some duration of time, contributing to social growth and stability of a neighborhood;

b) Ownership implies a commitment to the physical health of buildings, ensuring high standards of maintenance in the private sector which would have benefits for the public sector;

c) Ownership fosters a sense of belongingness and self-esteem among other things.

16. Decrease of Rental in Favor of Ownership or Part Ownership. Rental situations contribute to transiency, lack of commitment, and physical decay through lack of maintenance. Alternative tenure structures such as co ownership and part ownership should be pursued, because the social and financial benefits are substantial in promoting belongingness, self-esteem, community involvement, and better maintenance. Besides the alternatives mentioned above, existing methods such as rental leading to ultimate possession should be pursued. Part ownership, that is, provision of a physical shell or infrastructure by a public agency with the user providing his own dwelling, is a possibility worth pursuing (Experiments by S.A.R. in Holland).[4]

17. Involvement in Decisions Affecting Dwellings. The products of autocratic decision taking and alienation from the decision making process are loss of commitment and concern. In the realm of decision taking on housing and associated issues, the right of the user (whether renter or owner) to be involved in decisions concerning his dwelling should be acknowledged and reciprocated, whether the issue by the demolition of an apartment building or house or choice of paint color for his front door.

Current experiments in user participation in predesign decisions and ongoing involvement in planning, particularly in Europe, bode well for administrative structures that facilitate a high degree of user involvement. The results of these experiments seem to indicate greater social and community stability and health.

18. Potential for Cooperative and Co-Owner Cultural, Commercial and Recreational Facilities. The benefits of co-owner and cooperative ventures are largely manifest in community stability, and social health while also compensating, in some situations, for lack of full ownership of individual dwellings. Some degree of financial involvement in community facilities encourages usage and maintenance. The potential for a cash return or savings to shareholders in ventures such as co-op grocery stores and bars, pubs, and the like is considerable.

19. Community Involvement in Planning and Maintenance. Experience with involving the community in planning and maintenance is sufficient to show that trade off between the difficulties of involvement versus the social benefits accrued make such efforts and costs worthwhile.

Conclusion

The criteria above represent the first step in establishing guidelines for evaluating a set of community housing proposals.

In application of the criteria, a number of current building techniques and phasing concepts can usefully be introduced. Another impact matrix was prepared. The various building and staging concepts are identified as rows and the criteria are identified as columns. The cell of the matrix is filled with some description of a given technique's potential for satisfying a given criterion.

The results shown in Diagram 14–3 suggest that building technology is of surprising significance when it comes to satisfying a broad range of housing criteria, many of which at first glance seem to. be little related to building production processes. (Few criteria turned out to be indifferent to building production processes.)

A further conclusion which can be drawn from Diagram 14–3 is that certain of the industrialization technologies (5–8) which have been pursued in the United States by private industry as well as by federal programs (such as Operation Breakthrough) have less potential for meeting the stated housing criteria than more traditional techniques. The diagram indicates that in order to satisfy the suggested housing criteria with industrialized building techniques more radical approaches have to be used. These might take the form of "open building systems" with exchangeable components (4) based on generally accepted conventions of modular coordination and on methods such as those developed by the Dutch Stichting Architecten Research (S.A.R.)[4] In situations where such industrialization methods are out of reach, one would fare better with traditional techniques which at least potentially could be superior (to closed systems industrialization) in terms of variability, variety of dwelling units, prevention of neighborhood disruption, and the like.

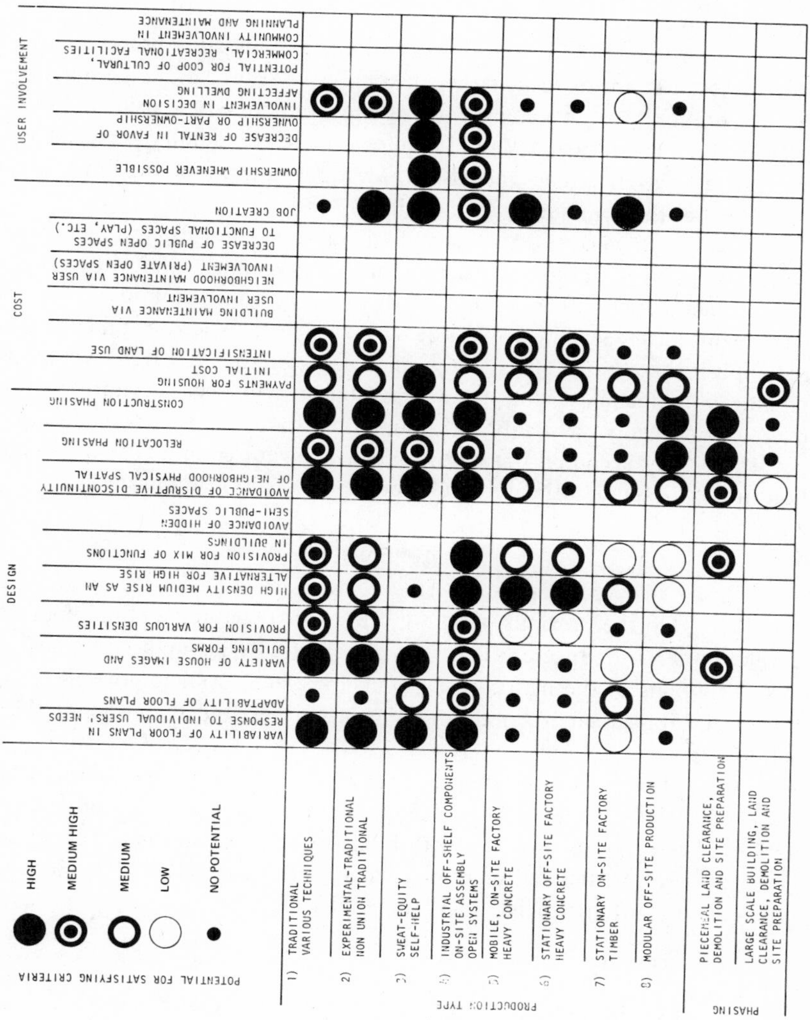

Diagram 14–3. Implications of Housing Criteria on Implementation

POTENTIAL FOR SATISFYING CRITERIA

- ● HIGH
- ◉ MEDIUM HIGH
- ○ MEDIUM
- ○ LOW
- • NO POTENTIAL

USER INVOLVEMENT

- PLANNING AND MAINTENANCE
- COMMUNITY INVOLVEMENT IN
- POTENTIAL FOR COOP OF CULTURAL, COMMERCIAL, RECREATIONAL FACILITIES
- AFFECTING DWELLING
- INVOLVEMENT IN DECISION
- OWNERSHIP OR PART-OWNERSHIP
- DECREASE OF RENTAL IN FAVOR OF
- OWNERSHIP WHENEVER POSSIBLE

COST

- JOB CREATION
- TO FUNCTIONAL SPACES (PLAY, ETC.)
- DECREASE OF PUBLIC OPEN SPACES
- INVOLVEMENT (PRIVATE OPEN SPACES)
- NEIGHBORHOOD MAINTENANCE VIA USER
- USER INVOLVEMENT
- BUILDING MAINTENANCE VIA
- INTENSIFICATION OF LAND USE
- INITIAL COST
- PAYMENTS FOR HOUSING
- CONSTRUCTION PHASING

DESIGN

- RELOCATION PHASING
- OF NEIGHBORHOOD PHYSICAL SPATIAL
- AVOIDANCE OF DISRUPTIVE DISCONTINUITY
- SEMI-PUBLIC SPACES
- AVOIDANCE OF HIDDEN
- IN BUILDINGS
- PROVISION FOR MIX OF FUNCTIONS
- ALTERNATIVE FOR HIGH RISE
- HIGH DENSITY MEDIUM RISE AS AN
- PROVISION FOR VARIOUS DENSITIES
- BUILDING FORMS
- VARIETY OF HOUSE IMAGES AND
- ADAPTABILITY OF FLOOR PLANS
- RESPONSE TO INDIVIDUAL USERS' NEEDS
- VARIABILITY OF FLOOR PLANS IN

PRODUCTION TYPE

1) TRADITIONAL VARIOUS TECHNIQUES
2) EXPERIMENTAL-TRADITIONAL NON UNION TRADITIONAL
3) SWEAT-EQUITY SELF-HELP
4) INDUSTRIAL OFF-SHELF COMPONENTS ON-SITE ASSEMBLY OPEN SYSTEMS
5) MOBILE, ON-SITE FACTORY HEAVY CONCRETE
6) STATIONARY OFF-SITE FACTORY HEAVY CONCRETE
7) STATIONARY ON-SITE FACTORY TIMBER
8) MODULAR OFF-SITE PRODUCTION

PHASING

- PIECEMEAL LAND CLEARANCE, DEMOLITION AND SITE PREPARATION
- LARGE SCALE BUILDING, LAND CLEARANCE, DEMOLITION AND SITE PREPARATION

The most suitable building technique would certainly be combinations of various production types. Diagram 14–3 can be seen as a rough guideline for selecting various techniques in response to the resources and demands of a given situation and in order to satisfy the housing criteria; for instance, open building systems (4), involving sweat equity concepts (3) and certain on-site subsystems production.

While not in final form, the criteria and selection processes presented here project one major idea: rather than have the federal agency evaluating each housing proposal within a community as a separate item (and using only physical criteria), the federal agency should require a broad community perspective showing how any given project increases the various *outputs* of the housing *system* and improves the community's well-being.

Such a requirement would expand the list of topics to be covered in a proposal; and it would also strain administrative and technical capabilities of local agencies. In the early stages of this new approach to housing administration, many local agencies would not have sufficient expertise and experience to accomplish these basics. It is likely, in the short term, that HUD would have to provide both technical and planning assistance. While such a short-term investment could involve a significant amount of resources, such a commitment is needed to fully accomplish a necessary shift toward community involvement in housing policy—and, ultimately, to improve the quality of housing.

APPENDIX

On the previous pages we briefly discussed the methodology used to develop criteria for future NTIT housing efforts. By listing housing characteristics as columns of the matrix in Diagram 14–2 and problem areas as rows, each cell of the impact matrix indicates the magnitude and direction of the interaction.

The following synopsis discusses the interactions in more detail and gives a few indications of how magnitude and direction of the interaction was derived. The synopsis proceeds with a one-by-one description of the selected 23 housing characteristics and their interdependencies with other characteristics and problem areas often associated with inner city housing.

Housing Standard

1. Lack of Space Provision/Inadequate Floor Plans.
A. Impact on Property Condition/Maintenance.

While there is no magic formula to indicate minimum space provision in housing, there is substantial evidence to suggest that overcrowding, through sheer stress of use, affects the physical fabric of housing. Inadequate or inappropriate floor plans are generally an associated factor. The lack of incentive to maintain property is not only a function of overcrowding and inadequate floor plans, but is also related to the user's stake in the dwelling (14–21).[b]

B. Impact on the Standard of Neighborhood Maintenance.

As overcrowding and inadequate floor plans reduce the user's incentive to maintain his dwelling, this inevitably is expressed on a community scale with compounding effects on the physical condition of a neighborhood. The nature of tenure and quality of public maintenance could ameliorate this situation (14–17).

C. Impact on the Condition of Neighborhood Facilities.

Lack of internal space conditions will tend to externalize living/social patterns with an ensuing need for (and stress on) neighborhood facilities such as community centers, cafés, schools, and playgrounds.

> Parents in high density housing evidently do not discourage their children from leaving the house, thereby temporarily relieving the high densities. But this solution to high densities tends to reduce the parents' knowledge of and control over their children.[5]

Also, inadequate or inappropriate internal planning can often be compensated for by complementary public facilities (that is, clubs, day care centers, and so forth) (7C).

D. Impact on Stability of Inhabitants.

Lack of space provision and inadequate floor plans are not attractive to individuals or families making a permanent commitment to a dwelling; consequently the quick turnover of residents contributes to physical and social decay and instability (17) (19).

E. Impact on the Stability of Social and Racial Mix.

Factors outlined in (1D) above lead to situations where only the financially and socially impotent inhabit dwellings of inadequate space and floor plans—with consequent homogeneity of income groups. This thereby reduces the possibility of interaction between income and racial groups. Technology allowing change and extension of building according to needs could help stabilize communities.

F. Impact on Crime and Social Unrest.

(1E) illustrated the relationship between inadequate space provision, internal planning, and social instability. (1A) (1B) (1C) indicated the inevitable externalizing of dissatisfaction. This dissatisfaction can find expression in violence, rioting, defacing of homes and facilities, and crime. The accumulation of factors (1A–1G) produces a stigma and feeling of social ostracism which will be addressed in (18A–18D).

G. Impact on Health.

The issue of health and space/planning relationships is difficult to tie down as the variables are complex. As stated in (1A) there is no universal for-

---

b. Numbers in parenthesis refer to sections following that relate to the item(s) in question. Thus, (14–21) refers to section 14 through 21.

mula for a minimum per capita space requirement. Neither is there a definitive societal yardstick to indicate spatial separation within dwellings (sleeping quarters, sexual separation). We can state that inadequate space for those with contagious disease might foster epidemics. The broad issues of the relationship of space provision to mental health and educational development is quite uncertain.

To quote from a HEW Conference on "Health Research in Housing and Its Environment"

> In considering man's life space there is an unfortunate tendency to restrict attention to lack of space, based primarily on the concern that "crowding" results both in transmission of disease and "stimulus overload." This is a restrictive view in that it is difficult to correlate infectious problems to specific densities while "stimulus deprivation" can result from too much space.[6]
>
> Perhaps the most interesting finding was the apparent cultural and social class differences in the perception of space, the value placed upon it and the consequent differences in space utilization. A summarizing typology was constructed which suggested that the major differences on the continuum from lower to upper social class lies in a shift from a polychronic orientation to space to one of monochronism. That is, territoriality is exchanged for notions of compartmentalized space and space use. Furthermore, as more space is acquired, there is a shift in space utilization from providing for fundamental needs to space used as a symbol of cultural status.[7]
>
> We said that according to present evidence, space and privacy have only dubious and and perhaps undiscovered causal relationships to health or illness. Some concern was expressed that our measuring techniques may be too crude to find the relationship between space, privacy, and health which many of us believe exists. But I think what we were saying to ourselves is that we know what we are finding is not true but we don't know how to prove that it isn't.[8]

H.   Impact on Jobs, Employment.

Very little relationship can be detected between spatial needs and employment, but the quality of housing may conceivably influence productivity.[9]

2.   Lack of Internal Facilities and Equipment.

A.[c]   Impact on Property Condition.

While pursuit of minimum space standards is a fruitless task, the provision of basic sanitary hardware, electricity, cooking facilities, plumbing, and bathroom has been accepted as a societal requisite. To what extent lack of

c. Letters refer to items in Diagram 14–2 and are shown in entirety in previous section.

the above may lead to lack of long-range commitment to dwelling and therefore to a lack of incentive to maintain the property is difficult to assess.

D. Impact on Stability of Inhabitants.

The lack of commitment to a dwelling with primitive internal facilities leads to a quick turnover of inhabitants. The stigma associated wih a dwelling with little or no internal facilities contributes to alienation and rejection of dwellings and neighborhoods. The application of modern technology, plug-in bathrooms, prefab utility cores, and similar innovations could upgrade existing situations (18) (19) (20).

E. Impact on Stability of Social and Racial Mix.

Issues discussed in (2D) affect the stability of mix of an area. The upwardly mobile may drift to the suburbs while those remaining may well make ghettos of their neighborhoods (2D) (18) (19) (20).

G. Impact on Health.

Lack of internal facilities and equipment has a more direct and measurable relationship with health than space deficiencies. But the impact of lack of basic bathroom equipment on the creation of situations conducive to epidemics and other diseases appears to be generally overweighed.

> . . . Application of minimum standards today may make little contribution to improved physical health because the problems they attempt to tackle are more effectively resolved via other means.[10]

> Contrary to expectations, rates of utilization of medical services appeared relatively insensitive to changes in the quality of the residential environment.[11]

> The strongest conclusion was that the removal of rat infestation produced the most marked reductions in utilization rates. Contrary to expectations, far less important were the more customary inputs of space consumption per person and plumbing facilities; and, as noted, overall change in housing quality had a dubious impact.[12]

> The two structural elements of the dwelling most significantly affecting the change in visits were changes in the adequacy of plumbing and waste disposal facilities.[13]

Density

3. Low Density.

A. Impact on Maintenance.

There is no direct relationship between low density and property maintenance; a more meaningful relationship might be that of "nature of tenure" (14–17) and property maintenance. Other determinants of property maintenance might be the quality of neighborhood maintenance (10B–12B).

C. Impact on the Condition of Neighborhood Facilities.

The nature of low density single family housing is such that public facilities are expensive to provide within walking distances because of lack of support population (7–9). Public utilities are more expensive in initial cost as well as maintenance (10–12).

D. Impact on the Stability of Inhabitants.

Low density housing is not any more *innately* stable than other forms of housing. The variables are:

1. Nature of tenure (ownership, rental co-ownership);
2. Items discussed under column (1);
3. House image/community image/belongingness (18);
4. Ability of individual to choose dwelling (19);
5. Individual's involvement in community (23);
6. Quality of support facilities (6–9).

Individuals will make their commitment to "place" relative to their status, income, race, age, and related factors.

F. Impact on Crime, Social Unrest, Vandalism.

There have been claims that lack of pedestrian traffic or sidewalks may contribute to crimes like mugging, rape, and other assaults.

> . . . the problem of insecurity cannot be solved by spreading people out more thinly, trading the characteristics of cities for the characteristics of suburbs. If this could solve danger on the city streets, then Los Angeles should be a safe city because superficially Los Angeles is almost all suburban. Los Angeles' crime figures are flabbergasting. . . . And this is markedly true of crimes that make people fear the streets. . . . The reasons for Los Angeles' high crime rates are undoubtedly complex, and at least in part obscure. But of this we can be sure: thinning out a city does not insure safety from crime and fear of crime.[14]

The view that low density reduces crime is as oversimplified as the argument that high density creates crime (see 5F). The variables are complex; building design, access, street pattern and overall how people view and use their city. For pedestrians, that is, for those who cannot afford to drive a car, a low density environment might be unsafe at night but the Angelinos do not behave as if their city were a pedestrian environment. Public security is less efficient over larger, less dense areas.

G. Impact on Health.

A positive aspect of low density housing relating to health is the potential availability of open space and light depending on layout and location. It is, however, difficult to measure any direct health benefits derived from lower density, unless it is compared to abnormal densities combined with crowded apartments. The missing sense of safety due to not being allowed to walk the streets at night (see 3F) might affect those who are unable to drive.

H. Impact on Jobs and Employment.

Access to jobs for those who do not have a car decreases, as does the chance to find a job.

4. Medium Density.

A. Impact on Property Condition.

Comments as (3).

B. Impact on Neighborhood Maintenance.

There is a greater probability of higher quality public maintenance standards as density (and support population) increases.

C. Impact on Condition of Neighborhood Facilities.

The larger support population makes better public facilities at closer distances possible.

F. Crime and Social Unrest.

Higher density does not, in itself, give rise to crime, but rather the combination of factors already referred to and many more such as involvement, tenure, image, and belongingness can help create a positive as well as negative impact on crime. Police and security are sometimes more efficient and effective in medium density situations.

5. High Density.

(Note: For the purposes of these comments, high density is not synonymous with 'high rise.')

A. Impact on Property Condition.

Features (1–2) in combination with, say, (18) (image), (21) (decisionmaking), and (23) (involvement in policy) may produce in a high density situations an incentive or lack of incentive to maintain property, but high densities by itself normally cannot be expected to have such an impact.

C. Impact on Condition of Neighborhood Facilities.

High density situations generally require a substantial amount of public facilities; theoretically these facilities can be supported by a high density situation, but are often inadequate, overused, and overstressed. Factors outlined in (1) plus whether or not the population has any stake in the facilities, are other determinants of condition.

E. Impact on Stability of Mix.

It is only societal mores that would seem to suggest a negative relationship between stability and high density. High density housing, like any other housing, must provide basic facilities, room for family expansion, open space, good support facilities, and security—those factors which contribute to an individual or family putting down roots.

Again, if a high density situation offers the potential of "place" and "something you call your own," why should not a mix of income groups, races, and age groups be stable? If it is unstable, it will be more likely to be for "stigmatic" reasons (18); for example, middle income groups not wishing to associate with lower income groups, or because the building type is associated with public housing.

F. Impact on Crime, Social Unrest, Vandalism.

There would seem to be little societal connection between crime, unrest, and so forth, and high density.

> ... That high density development by itself is not synonymous with "congested instant slums" is clear to any stroller along New York's Park Avenue between 59th and 96th Streets, where low density is hardly the term to describe the canyon wall of tall apartment buildings standing shoulder to shoulder on each side of this famous millionaires' row. That plenty of distance often has little relationship to healthful housing is equally apparent to any visitor to the shacks of Appalachia or the hovels of a score of Indian reservations.[15]

The "bogey man" is not high density, but rather the social context and the fact that housing design and form in a high density context tend not to foster belongingness, bad image associations, inadequate facilities for individual expression, and a lack of neighborhood facilities and support facilities. If these factors and others are combined in *any* density situation, the result will be crime and social unrest. The most extreme example is the often talked of Pruit–Igoe development.

Theoretically, a positive aspect of high density living in an integrated and well-serviced neighborhood is the fact that constant traffic and usage become a policing factor in the street and in public places.

G. Impact on Health.

Only when prerequisites for health are not met (that is, if high density is achieved by lack of personal space (1) and overcrowding) could high density actually affect physical and mental health.

Support Facilities

6. Public Open Space.
A. Property Condition.

A frequent assumption is that if there is little or no private space associated with the dwelling other than public open space (whether in the form of a roof top, common balcony, park, or playground), these spaces will assume the function of private open space. In terms of maintenance such public spaces are often the most neglected spaces in the building or neighborhood because the responsibility is shared among many. The lack of maintenance, in turn, has an adverse affect upon the maintenance of the individual properties.

B. Impact on the Standard of Neighborhood Maintenance.

Standards of maintenance of public open spaces are not only a function of pressures of usage, but also of a commitment of the individual to his community which is very difficult to influence. The maintenance costs tend to rise with growing trouble in the community. Large public open spaces often have to be maintained by inadequate rental income. This is clearly demonstrated in the failure of maintenance of Pruit–Igoe.[16]

D. Impact on the Stability of the Inhabitants.

A run-down public open space influences the character of the whole community. A run-down community will foster transience, that is, people who can afford it move, while those who can't stay. Public open space can often compensate for deficient private space and facilities. Yet is is argued here that excessive public open space can foster community problems rather than cure them.

E. Impact on Stability of Social and Racial Mix.

In a socially mixed situation, public open space will inevitably have a different meaning for different ages and income groups (old to sit, young to play). Sidewalks may be a better potential catalyst for mix of all sorts, community interaction and communication, than spacious parks. On the same line, playgrounds and community centers might better serve the young than endless lawns and carefully designed flower strips.

F. Impact on Crime and Social Unrest.

In certain conditions, well-designed, well-located and well-maintained public open space can alleviate the social problems of overcrowded apartments. Conversely, public open space associated with a community of despair (D) can become the scene of all sorts of crime. Public open spaces should be identifiable, well controlled through continuous activities, and responsive to diverse community needs (E).

> More Open Space for what? For Muggings? For bleak vacuums between buildings? Or for ordinary people to use and enjoy? But people do not use city open space just because it is there and because city planners or designers wish they would. . . . Parks are not automatically anything, and least of all are these volatile elements stabilizers of values or of their neighborhoods and districts. . . . Unpopular parks are troubling not only because of the waste and missed opportunities they imply, but also because of their frequent negative effects. They have the same problems as streets without eyes, and their dangers spill over into the areas surrounding, so that streets along such parks become known as danger places too and are avoided. Moreover, underused parks and their equipment suffer from vandalism, which is quite a different matter from wear.[17]

G. Impact on Health.

Public open space, when adequately and appropriately designed and provided, probably helps the mental and physical health of a community (through sports, play, and spontaneous interaction).

7. Educational, Cultural, Recreational and Medical Facilities.

A. Impact on Property Condition.

The quality of public facilities is an intrinsic part of the community's image and in turn influences the relation of people to the community and to the maintenance of property.

B. Impact on Standard of Neighborhood Maintenance.

Educational programs in schools can teach community sense and public-mindedness which directly affects neighborhood maintenance.

D. Impact on Stability of Inhabitants.

The quality and sensitivity of education and the provision of cultural and recreational facilities have a potential role in stabilizing what otherwise might be a transient, quick turn-over type of community by providing an extension and a compensation for inadequate homes, and by inducing pride and community sense. Schools are one of the most important determinants in the decision to move.

E. Impact on Stability of Racial and Social Mix.

The rich will not send their children to school in a neighborhood they believe to have bad schools and therefore will move out, whereas the poor and deprived have no choice and stay on. Thus, the provision of *good* quality educational facilities is a major determinant of the stability of mix. It is necessary to consider the possible role of schools and of school yards as extended community facilities (with extensive multiuse spaces) and to ensure that educational, recreational, and cultural facilities are integrated with, rather than stand apart from, the community.

F. Impact on Crime.

Although a direct cause-effect relationship between crime and social unrest and the provision of adequate and appropriate schools, medical facilities, youth clubs, dance halls, vocational and trade education is difficult to detect, one can safely conclude that absence of such facilities may be an alienating factor.

G. Impact on Health.

Medical facilities and free clinics can be expected to have a direct impact on the health of any community, but it is also necessary to consider the fact that,

> with respect to features in housing which are claimed to reduce the ravages of certain illnesses a much wider range of substitutes are available. Preventive medicine, development of drugs to expedite

recuperation during illnesses, access to superb health facilities, or improved nutrition are all examples of alternatives.[18]

8. Shopping Facilities.

D. Impact on Stability of Inhabitants.

Besides providing an immediate source for food, clothing, shopping facilities also have a social and cultural role. The need for accessible shopping by foot in communities with low car ownership or poor transportation is also a prerequisite. The presence of a "corner shop" provides many communities with a social hub.

E. Impact on Stability of Social and Racial Mix.

The provision of a variety of shopping facilities, from luxury to basic, is necessary to preserve the stability of mix of a community—(this fact would presume a support population (5)). These facilities should be accessible, if not by foot, by public transportation or car.

F. Impact on Crime.

In areas of deprivation, the rate of pilfering and burglarizing shops is very high. Concentrated shopping areas induce street life and community life, and provide in some part at least their own security (5). The location of shops vis-à-vis the community is crucial in this respect. With increasing burglarization of stores, the risks to store owners—and subsequently prices—tend to rise. This again affects (C) (D) and (E).

H. Impact on Jobs and Employment.

Local shopping facilities can provide limited employment.

9. Public Transportation.

A. Impact on Maintenance of Property.

Lack of good public transportation, particularly when coupled with unemployment, can contribute to the "locked-in" noncaring ghetto mentality which contributes to poor maintenance (22).

B. Impact on Neighborhood Maintenance.

Expression of (9A) at community scale (22).

C. Impact on Neighborhood Facilities.

Availability of public transport may relieve the necessity of neighborhood facilities to a certain extent. Competition with nonlocal shopping facilities may lower prices in local stores or lead to deterioration and closing of local stores.

D. Impact on Stability of Inhabitants.

Public transportation (or the lack of) is a factor in determining the stability of a community, particularly as it relates to ease of access to work, schools, and shopping. To the non-car-owning family, the choice is often between living on welfare in the ghetto or trying to move nearer to work, shopping, or schools. This contributes to transience.

F. Impact on Crime.

Public transportation means access to work, recreation, and education—all factors which reduce crime (H).

H. Impact on Jobs and Employment.

Particularly in blue collar areas, access to work by public transportation is crucial to the economic and social survival of a community. Four-fifths of the new jobs gained in the nation's large metropolitan areas during the 1950s and 1960s were gained in the suburbs. Hence the growing trend in "reverse commuting," especially by Blacks, Puerto Ricans, and Mexican—Americans, who head from city homes to suburban plants in the morning and back in the evening.

> The need for distant commuting presents a sizable difficulty for city dwelling blue collar people. Commuter rail and bus fares, usually far higher than city transit fares, take a heavy bite out of working class paychecks. And because public transit frequently is spotty in automobile oriented suburbia, commuting is time consuming as well as expensive for any reverse commuter who is too poor to own his own automobile or unable to join a car pool, and whose factory is not within walking distance of a commuter railroad or bus station. These difficulties must certainly be considered factors in the high rate of unemployment among big city Blacks.[19]

Support Services

10. Building Maintenance (Communal).

A. Impact on Property Condition.

Good quality building maintenance can affect to some degree the incentive an individual has for maintaining his own dwelling. This maintenance may be administered directly or by grants, equipment complemented with educational programs, and the like. Maintenance without participation of the individual may lead to a lack of responsibility by the individual, that is, to the assumption that the community will take care of all maintenance problems and thus add to staggering maintenance costs and, eventually, result in poor maintenance services.

B. Impact on Standard of Neighborhood Maintenance.

The quality of communal maintenance, whether publicly administered or privately instigated, will dictate to a large extent the quality of neighborhood maintenance. This is a case for questioning the way public funds are administered for maintenance in certain situations. Perhaps monies should be available at the individual or block level for house improvement so as to create a context for more private and community involvement in maintenance. Density and size of support population are also determinants of the quality of neighborhood maintenance.

C. Impact on Condition of Neighborhood Facilities.

The appropriateness and social usefulness of facilities will be a determinant. Co-ownership of public facilities may influence the condition of neighborhood facilities, as for example in Co-Op City (New York).

> . . . Each household holds shares in the nonprofit corporation that controls and manages Co-Op City. Residents vote upon policy issues concerning the maintenance and operation of the community and can collectively hire their own management. This quality alone is largely responsible for Co-Op City's residents perceiving themselves as a unique autonomous community[20] (22).

D. See B.

11. Lighting of Streets, Semipublic Spaces, and Parks.

B. Impact on Condition of Neighborhood Maintenance.

Relationship only visible if deficient lighting is part of overall deficiencies. The crime association of badly lit streets and spaces may affect standard of individual neighborhood maintenance.

D. Impact on Stability of Inhabitants.

The association of crime with badly lit streets would certainly not help the mental and physical stability of inhabitants. It contributes to defensiveness, minimal social interaction, and quick turnover of inhabitants because of lack of commitment; conversely, good lighting can contribute to stability.

E. Impact on Stability of Mix of Income Groups, Races, and Age Groups.

See D.

F. Impact on Crime and Social Unrest.

Research has shown that high quality lighting of streets and semiprivate spaces has considerably reduced the incidence of street crime, that is, rape, muggings, robbery, burglary, attacks, and molesting—particularly in ghetto areas and areas of low traffic density. As a design directive, good lighting and avoidance of dead-end and redundant spaces would seem to be priorities.

G. Impact on Health.

The relationship would appear to be only marginal, but more important in the area of mental and social health; that is, where the association with crime would distort social and sociomental attitudes and development.

12. Utilities, Garbage Disposal, and Street Cleaning.

A. Impact on Property Condition.

Inadequate utilities (or none) and lack of garbage disposal contribute to the general degradation of individual dwellings and reduce the incentive to care. Careful planning of garbage disposal systems becomes important. Innovation, for example, internal trash smashers, recyclable waste collection, and so forth, are worth consideration in new projects to alleviate solid waste problems.

   B.   Impact on Standard of Neighborhood Maintenance.

   Inadequacies of garbage disposal, street cleaning, and the like, have manifestations on the community maintenance scale with compounded consequences.

   D.   Impact on Stability of Inhabitants.

   Who wants to live in an environment of trash cans, litter, germs, and so forth? The mobile will leave while the impotent poor will stay and compound their own degradation.

   E.   Impact on Stability of Mix.

   Broadly the same as 12C. The rich and upwardly mobile will move to areas with better services.

   G.   Impact on Health.

   There probably is a slightly direct relationship between lack of hygiene facilities, poor garbage disposal, street cleaning, and health.

13. Unemployment.

   A.   Impact on Property Maintenance.

   Not only will the unemployed poor be forced to gravitate towards people of similar status, but, also, the total environment will reflect despondence, lack of care, and generally will not be conducive to maintenance. This is not to say that unemployed people are generally unwilling to take care of their homes, but lack of funds or credit in combination with a generally deteriorating and deprived environment will foster lack of care.

   B.   Impact on Standard of Neighborhood Maintenance.

   The despondence and lack of self respect, *culturally* associated with being unemployed will reflect itself at the individual dwelling and neighborhood level in terms of maintenance and care. A large contributory factor must be the fact that lack of ability to pay rent and taxes affects the quality of public maintenance.

   C.   Impact on Condition of Neighborhood Facilities.

   In areas of high unemployment, which invariably show ghetto symptoms, there is also a general association of poor and poorly maintained neighborhood facilities which contribute first to ghetto conditions and then cannot be improved for a variety of economic and social reasons. (Lack of buying power to support shopping facilities, lower revenue of store owners, higher risks, lack of tax base for public provision and maintenance.) Deterioration of neighborhood facilities coincides with lack of certain facilities and overabundance of others (for example, liquor stores and churches).

   D.   Impact on Stability of Inhabitants.

   Areas of high unemployment tend to be monolithic in structure for the very worst reasons—social stigma and inability to move. The social repercussions are well known.

E. Impact on Stability of Mix.

The common denominator of employment can facilitate a mix of incomes, races, and ages. (13D) shows that lack of employment has the reverse effect.

F. Impact on Crime, Unrest.

Unemployment as a component of other social ills, contributes to unrest, crime, and so forth (13C).

G. Impact on Health.

The relationship between unemployment and health has physical health implications with lack of food and access to health facilities, and mental health implications such as retarded, distorted outlook and social development.

Nature of Tenure

14. Rental.

A. Impact on Property Condition.

The nature of being a renter, and the implicit lack of commitment to time or place or inability to conceive of owning a "home of your own," have repercussions on physical conditions and maintenance. Rental concessions for maintenance and property improvement should be reviewed as a method of attacking this problem.

B. Impact on Standard of Neighborhood Maintenance.

Implicit generally in predominantly "rental communities" is a lack of commitment to neighborhood. Perhaps shareholding or some other financial interest scheme might be considered.

C. Impact on Stability of Inhabitants.

Almost by definition, rental is synonymous with quick turnover, lack of commitment to time/place, and consequent lack of social stability.

15. Co-Ownership.

A. Impact on Property Condition.

The concept of co-ownership has many expressions, but most of all it implies a personal and communal commitment to a place. This increases the likelihood of better private dwelling maintenance.

B. Impact on Neighborhood Maintenance.

Fallout from (15A) Co-Op City, New York:

I feel that it is mine: it is a place where I belong. Social, political, and environmental problems can be confronted with mutual efforts toward solution. Co-Op City residents have a real sense of participation in welfare of their immediate environment.[21] (See also 10C.)

C. Impact on Condition of Neighborhood Facilities.

Fallout from (15A and 15B).

D.   Impact on Stability of Inhabitants.

The commitment to co-ownership enhances stability.

E.   Impact on Stability of Mix.

The likelihood is that co-owners will be of similar background, age or income, and thereby will exclude other groups. Perhaps their concern for where and with whom they live can be lessened by their commitment to co-ownership. Co-Op City, New York:

> Co-Op City is much more of a diverse community in the true spirit of Jane Jacobs than any of the more publicized Restons or Columbias. Although Co-Op City was built primarily for people of moderate income, there is a wide mix of race, ethnicity, and age. Such a characteristic certainly distinguished Co-Op City from the majority of developments in suburban America.[22]

16. Part-Ownership.

A.   Impact on Property Maintenance.

If this implies owning an apartment within a block or a mobile home without the land, it is an option that will probably improve commitment and maintenance.

B.   Impact on Neighborhood Maintenance.

If this implies (16A) plus a share in common facilities, pool, recreation, or pub, then the probability of better maintenance or revenue for public maintenance at a neighborhood scale becomes greater.

D.   Impact on Stability.

When there is an even limited stake in a place, the greater the probability is of a time/community commitment, thereby stabilizing the social situation.

E.   Impact on Stability of Mix.

Same as above.

17, Ownership.

A.   Impact on Property Condition.

"If you own a house, and are happy with it, then the chances are you will look after it."

B.   Impact on Neighborhood Maintenance.

Ownership, expressed on a neighborhood scale, will be an individual concern multiplied by the number of individual owners, with a consequently high level maintenance.

D.   Impact on Stability of Inhabitants.

Financial commitment implies commitment to place and in turn contributes to stability.

E.   Impact on Stability of Mix.

If ownership is restricted to high income groups, then other groups are excluded, reducing the variety of mix.

A more adequate knowledge base is needed in order to determine the feasibility of socioeconomic residential mixing. More information is needed about why people live where they do and, specifically, about (1) housing preferences and attitudes; (2) "real costs" for different socioeconomic groups; (3) public sector costs and benefits, both perceived and actual; (4) alternative approaches to correcting public sector costs and changing individual "real costs;" and (5) the "human costs" of socioeconomic stratification.[23]

Identity and User Involvement

18. Home Image/Apartment Image.

A. Impact on Property Condition.

If there is not a "fit" between a resident's image of his home or apartment and his needs for self-esteem and aspirations, and if he is trapped in that situation for any reason, this will in all probability lower his degree of involvement and thus degree of maintenance.

> Government sponsored housing developments in America, for a variety of reasons seldom articulated, are designed so that they stand out and are recognized as distinctively different residential complexes. It is our contention that this differentiation serves in a negative way to single out the project and its inhabitants as "easy hits." The idiosyncratic image of publicly assisted housing, coupled with other design features and the social characteristics of the resident population, makes such housing a peculiarly vulnerable target of criminal activity.[24]

D. Impact on Stability of Inhabitants.

(17E).

E. Impact on Stability of Mix.

As suggested in (18A) only those who have the economic power to reject a house/apartment image in pursuit of another image will be able to do so, compounding the presumably undesirable image of those left behind. Images as a constituent of why people live in or reject a place or dwelling is a factor in protectivism and exclusivism of a particular area (for example, Beverly Hills). Can the poor produce a desirable image?

> One of the reasons for intentionally maintaining the visual stigma of public housing was suggested by Adam Walinsky in his article, "Keeping the Poor in Their Place." He reasons that in this country, unlike our Western European counterparts, the middle- and working-class population do not look favorably on those members of our society who require government assistance to pay their rent. While we have come a long way from our laissez-faire attitudes of the 1920s in developing a more enlightened approach toward less able

members of our society, we are still apparently incapable of providing housing for them which looks better than the worst we provide for ourselves.[25]

F.   Impact on Crime and Unrest.

Image and connotation contribute to rejection or acceptance of a neighborhood. In the case of bad image and connotation, aggressiveness, crime, social unrest, or rioting may be among the social products.

19.   Choice of Dwelling.

A.   Impact on Property Condition.

This can be addressed largely as was (18A). If you have *chosen* to live in a house (as much as any one can make that choice), then the chances are you will care for it.

B.   Impact on Stability of Inhabitants.

Having been offered and exercised choice in dwelling type and location implies commitment and ensuing stability

D.   Impact on Stability of Mix.

Initially, the availability of a choice of dwellings may accommodate a mix of incomes, races, and ages, but cannot determine stability of mix over time (15) (16) (17). The newly built physical environment tends initially to be relatively free of stigma. The stigma is created through the social context over a number of years, but the stigma is a driving force, because those who can afford to move do so.

> There is no evidence from field studies that socioeconomic mixing is feasible. The trend in the movements of urban population is toward increasing separation of socioeconomic categories. The tendency is manifested among Blacks as well as among whites.[26]

E.   (18D).

F.   Impact on Jobs and Employment.

The importance of housing as the locational base for access to employment and other services is stressed by various reports. As the Kaiser Committee put it:

> The location of one's place of residence determines the accessibility and quality of many everyday advantages taken for granted by the mainstream of American society. Among these commonplace advantages are public educational facilities for a family's children, adequate police and fire protection, and a decent surrounding environment. In any case, a family should have a choice of living as close as economically possible to the breadwinner's place of employment.[27]

20. **Adaptability/Flexibility**.

A. Impact on Property Condition.

The degree to which a dwelling is adaptable will influence the commitment of its user. Technology can provide internal and external adaptability as a response to changing user needs and thereby help solve some problems such as quick occupant turnover, and consequent community instability. If time commitment is a consequence of an adaptable dwelling, then the probability of good maintenance is also higher (1) (2) (16) (17).

B. Impact on Standard of Neighborhood Maintenance.

Fallout from (20A) (20D).

D. Impact on Stability of Inhabitants.

A flexible dwelling which can be adapted to changing needs; (for example, larger family or nonconventional life style) offers the user the choice of staying in a home and remaining part of a community and contributing to its stability rather than being forced to leave because of the change. (20A).

E. Impact on Stability of Mix.

Fallout from (20D). Adaptability does not contribute to stability of mix *per se*, but the likelihood of more nonhomogeneous life styles being absorbed in the community is theoretically greater.

F. Impact on Crime and Unrest.

To the extent that lack of space or redundant space in a house is a factor in externalizing stress, a more adaptable and flexible home has the greater chance of containing stress (1A) (1F) (2A) (2F).

21. **Involvement in Decisions Affecting Dwelling**.

A. Impact on Property Condition.

The possibility of involving users in residential decisions exists to a lesser or greater degree under every tenure structure from rental to ownership. If user rights as they pertain to the home are not acknowledged, then subsequent alienation will contribute to noncaring and lack of maintenance. The converse is also true.

B. Impact on Standard of Neighborhood Maintenance.

(21A).

D. Impact on Stability of Inhabitants.

Potentially a factor contributing to time, place, and community commitment.

E. Impact on Stability of Mix.

Fallout from (21A) (21D).

22. **Neighborhood Image**.

A. Impact on Property Condition.

(18A).

B.   Impact on Standard of Neighborhood Maintenance.

In the event of a lack of fit between aspirations, status, and neighborhood image, a lack of concern of standards of maintenance will be a feature of the transient mentality. Lack of motivation will be a quality of those who have no power to change their locale or environment (18A) (18B).

C.   Impact on Condition of Neighborhood Facilities.

The condition of neighborhood facilities will be a function of the fit mentioned in (22B) in terms of their appropriateness and relevance. It will also be a function of the quality of public maintenance and the stake of the individual in the facilities. (15, 16, 17)

Co-Op City, New York:

> Co-Op City is a real community. Few new developments of the New Town genre are as urbane or an intensely active. Literally hundreds of voluntary organizations flourish. Ethnic associations, political clubs, and religious groups play a major part in the lives of Co-Op City residents. Of the three commercial areas that are in the process of completion, one already teems with activity. A variety of community facilities, social services, and a preschool that also are located within the center provide opportunities for different age groups to come into contact throughout the course of the day.[28]

D.   Impact on Stability on Inhabitants.

All the factors which combine to give an individual a sense of belongingness, image included, will be determinants of the commitment to a neighborhood and the level of neighborhood stability.

E.   Impact on Stability of Mix.

The rich "exclusivise" their image and thereby exclude other groups, while also creating images for the upwardly mobile (19E).

F.   Impact on Crime and Unrest.

A too-facile association of crime and social unrest with certain neighborhoods can distort and compound the level of crime and unrest in that community, while destroying any sense of belonging:

> Society may have contributed to the victimization of project residents by setting off their dwellings, stigmatizing them with ugliness, saying with every status symbol available in the architectural language of our culture that living here is falling short of the human state. However, architecture is not just a matter of style, image, and comfort. Architecture can create encounter and prevent it. Certain kinds of space and spatial layout favor the clandestine activities of criminals. An architect, armed with some understanding of the structure of criminal encounter, can simply avoid providing the space which supports it.[29]

23. **Involvement in Community Policy.**

B. Impact on Standard of Neighborhood Maintenance.

Involvement in community policy can be voluntary or induced, but either way has beneficial results for maintenance. The amount of direct maintenance by user then should increase.

C. Impact on Condition of Neighborhood Facilities.

Community involvement in planning and maintenance could ensure a better fit between needs and community, and also ensure use, care, and pride.

D. Impact on Stability of Inhabitants.

If a person is encouraged or chooses to become involved in the community, by implication he is making a commitment to the community and contributing to its stability.

E. Impact on Stability of Mix.

Involvement in policy does not necessarily imply stability of mix; for example, the rich might organize to exclude the poor or Blacks. Blacks might organize to exclude whites.

F. Impact on Crime and Social Unrest.

Involvement in community policy can directly affect the motivation of potential criminals; it also contributes to a sense of belongingness and security.

> Pruitt—Igoe remains a shattered community in the midst of a blighted area, but there are now some who see reasons for hope, if only the new beginnings are nourished by more sensible planning and government support. . . . One is increased involvement of tenants in project management. Another is the organization of tenant security guards, some of whom were once among the project's most troublesome citizens.
>
> Unarmed and without direct police power, the guards are nonetheless credited with helping reduce crime. They shepherd children to school, escort women to buses, and patrol the dangerous hallways.[30]

NOTES TO CHAPTER FOURTEEN

1. "Homeownership for Low Income Families: Legal Implications," and "Homeownership for Low Income Families: Financial Implications," (Washington, D. C.: Urban Institute Working Papers, April 1972).

2. Maslow, Abraham H., *Motivation and Personality,* (New York: Harper and Row 1954).

3. Martin, Leslie, Lionel March, *Urban Space and Structures* (Cambridge, Massachusetts: Cambridge University Press, 1972).

4. Work of the SAR, Stichting Architecten Research Group, Eindhover, see: Habraken, N. J., *The Pursuit of an Idea, Plan 3* (The Netherlands, 1970).

5. Mitchell, Robert E., "Personal, Family and Social Consequences Arising from High-Density Housing in Hong Kong and other Major Cities in Southeast Asia," *Proceedings of the First Invitational Conference on Health Research in Housing and Its Environment* (U. S. Department of Health, Education and Welfare, U. S. Government Printing Office, 1970, p. 94.

6. de Groot, Ido, Robert S. Carrol, Ray M. Whitman, "Health and the Spatial Environment," *Proceedings*, op. cit., pp. 87, 88.

7. Wilner, Daniel, William Baer, "Sociocultural Factors in Residential Space," *Proceedings,* op. cit., p. 106.

8. Johnson, Ralph, in *Proceedings of the First Invitational Conference*, op. cit., p. 10.

9. Victorisz, Thomas and Barnett Harrison, *Economic Development of Harlem* (New York: Praeger, 1970), p. 59.

10. Mittelbach, Frank G. and Leland S. Burns, "Housing Codes—Selected Economic Implications," *Proceedings,* op. cit., p. 95.

11. Burns, Leland S. and Frank G. Mittelbach, "What Economists Think of Housing and Health," *Proceedings,* op. cit., p. 86.

12. Ibid., p. 87.

13. Burns, Leland S. and Frank G. Mittelbach, *A House is a House is a House,* International Housing Productivity Study (UCLA 1972), p. 12.

14. Jacobs, Jane, *The Death and Life of Great American Cities,* (New York: Random House 1961), pp. 32, 33.

15. Fried, Joseph P. *Housing Crisis in U. S. A.* (New York: Praeger Publishers, 1971, Penguin Books, 1972), p. 44.

16. *L. A. Times,* August 30, 1971.

17. Jacobs, Jane, op. cit., pp. 90—95.

18. Mittelbach, Frank G. and Leland S. Burns, *Proceedings,* op. cit., pp. 49, 50.

19. Fried, Joseph P., op. cit., pp. 49, 50.

20. Hinshaw, Mark L., "Whatever Happened to Radiant City?" *Architectural Design,* (November 1972).

21. Ibid.

22. Ibid.

23. "Socioeconomic Mixing in Metropolitan Areas," *Freedom of Choice in Housing,* National Academy of Sciences, National Academy of Engineering, p. 41.

24. Newman, Oscar, *Defensible Space,* (New York: MacMillan 1972) p. 102.

25. Ibid., p. 105.

26. "Socioeconomic Mixing." p. 36.

27. Kaiser, E. F., *A Decent Home.* Report of the President's Committee on Urban Housing (U. S. Government Printing Office, Washington D. C. 1969), p. 35.

28. Hinshaw, "Radiant City?" (November 1972).

29. Newman, *Defensible Space,* p. 12.

30. *L. A. Times,* August 30, 1971.

Part V

Summary and Recommendations

Chapter Fifteen

Summary and Recommendations:

Introduction

We undertook to study the federal new town intown program, starting two years after it had been launched under Title VII of the Housing and Urban Development Act of 1970, in the hope of providing guidelines for its administration, assisting in the design of new town intown programs by major cities across the country, and making suggestion for its ultimate improvement.

We approached the study by (1) examining the few new towns intown already under way or planned, (2) reviewing the national experience with previous central city development programs, particularly urban renewal and model cities, (3) polling the views of experts in the field as to what had been learned from our previous experience and how best the new town intown program might proceed, and (4) examining what it would take to carry out a substantial development program in a major city within the framework of new town intown concepts.

As a result of the search, we made what we consider to be some key discoveries about central city development. These have to do with the clarity of objectives, scale and scope of development (program versus project), programming and implementation strategies, and the need for federal leadership and financial assistance. These are briefly summarized in the sections that follow.

OBJECTIVES

What Should be the Objectives of New Towns Intown?

Federal housing and urban development programs from the New Deal forward have had two core objectives: (a) to help modernize and revitalize the central city, and (b) to assist less advantaged families acquire needed housing and basic services. While the individual programs—public housing, housing subsidies, urban renewal, and model cities—tended to interpret these objectives narrowly and to deal more with manifest problems than underlying causes, there was an inherent logic in the objectives themselves. Our study has strongly underlined this logic. It is important to appreciate that it was not the *objectives* of urban development that were at fault in the failures and limited successes of the past, but rather the failure to define them properly and then to make them operationally viable.

Title VII treats new town objectives in very general terms. Thus, national policy is declared to: "refine the role of the federal government in revitalizing existing communities and encouraging planned, large-scale urban and new community development, . . . treat comprehensively the problems of poverty and employment (including the erosion of tax bases, and the need for better community services and job opportunities) which are associated with disorderly urbanization . . . , and . . . develop means to encourage good housing for all Americans without regard to race or creed."

Current HUD Guidelines, rather than further defining these basic objectives, merely hint at their underlying purpose. Thus, they require that each new community ". . . must contribute to the social and economic welfare of the entire area which it will importantly affect" (HUD Office of New Communities Development Guidelines 720.6 (a) (3)).

New guidelines—and new national legislation on central city development—should indicate that contributing "to the social and economic welfare of the entire area" is to be interpreted as covering twin, closely interrelated goals:

(1) to assist in the modernization and revitalization of the central city in terms of strengthening its basic socioeconomic and physical foundations (rather than necessarily aiming at quantitative growth); and

(2) to assist in improving the range of opportunities available to the less advantaged in the central city.

The interrelationship of these overriding objectives should be made clear. The first should be seen as essential to developing more job, income, and cultural opportunities for those most needing such assistance, as well as safeguarding the future welfare of all central city residents and businesses. Alternatively, the second objective should be seen as key to modernizing and revitalizing the central city as a whole, making it a good place to live, work, and play, and strengthening its inherent, long-standing function of giving the less advantaged a boost up the urbanization ladder.

The key elements of modernization should be seen as including considerations of efficiency, equity, and quality of life.

Efficiency considerations involve essentially the objective of adjusting the urban fabric to those functions logical for the modern (and future) central city, and at a scale and density appropriate to present and anticipated needs. These considerations particularly involve modernization of infrastructure; locational relations among work, residence, and other activities; adequacy of the transportation system; and competence of governmental and social institutions to guide and manage these functions.

Equity considerations involve those adjustments for a fairer balance of gains and losses among social groups than has occurred in the provision of governmental services and facilities. This applies particularly to those which touch upon the major human activities in the city (work, residence, neighboring, play, and so forth.)

Quality of life considerations are particularly hard to pin down, but no less important for that reason. They involve those factors which touch on the city as a healthy and satisfactory place in which to live and work. Beyond efficiency and equity, there are qualitative aspects that determine whether people will want to live in the city or will live there only when they have no other choices.

Clearly, these three elements need to be spelled out in operational standards for judging the relative worth of proposed NTIT and other central city development efforts. While tools and techniques for central city development would vary from city to city, the probability of achieving these goals should be the common standard for evaluating the relative worth, locally and nationally, of a given NTIT proposal or program.

DESIGN OF NTIT PROGRAMS

What Functions and Activities Should a New Town Intown Encompass?

A key purpose of incorporating new town intown assistance into Title VII was to enlarge the scope and content of central city development and thereby overcome recognized inadequacies in urban renewal, housing, and model cities programs. To those involved in drafting the NTIT legislation, it was clear that integral features of both urban renewal and model cities should be incorporated into a more comprehensive new town intown program. The record shows, for example, that Congress intended the renewal program to supplement Title VII new towns intown through redevelopment subsidies, land assembly powers, and necessary capital improvements.

Once it is recognized that what is involved is town scale development of total communities, it should be clear that all significant elements of community development and life must be incorporated into new town intown planning and development as they are in suburban new communities. Thus, new towns intown should not emphasize merely physical and housing development but the social and economic organization of a community as well. This, in turn, implies that all forms of federal urban assistance be coordinated and made available for new town intown development.

What Are The Models for New Town
Intown Development?

Although all new town intown projects have the same ultimate objectives (increase employment, provide additional housing, create viable "community scale" living environments, and so forth), each adopts different strategies to achieve these ends. To properly address the policy issues involved in central city development, attention must be directed first to these alternative strategies, because the different approaches present different constraints, requirements, and levels of potential for overall impact. Based on our analysis of central city development experience, with special regard to the varying levels of innovation and potential represented by recent new town intown projects and proposals, two models for new town intown development can be identified:

> MODEL IA: Most new town intown projects to date have involved development of large parcels of vacant land within the central city but beyond the central business district (Fort Lincoln, Washington D. C.; Roosevelt Island, New York City; and Pontchartrain, New Orleans).
>
> IB: Several proposed projects involve the development of under-utilized or vacant land in a contiguous section of the inner city and closely related to the central business district, (for example, San Antonio).
>
> MODEL II: Several new town intown proposals now in the discussion stage (Hartford, Cleveland, and Chicago) advocate a different approach involving development of a set of linked project areas throughout the central city, both within and without the central business district, in staged sequences. This third approach is essentially a development program while the first two are project oriented.

Model IA has the narrowest applicability due to the relative scarcity of suitable sites in most central cities. Also project potential is most constrained as well, because developers must accept the given location and physical size. The popularity of this approach, it should be noted, derives from (a) the need to minimize costs of land acquisition and resident relocation, and (b) the $50 million per project ceiling for Title VII mortgage guarantees.

Model IB could be more pervasive than Model IA because abandoned and underutilized land is common in older sections of many cities. This alternative model is similar to the most advanced urban renewal projects. It is more flexible than Model IA or urban renewal since project boundaries can be better shaped to maximize returns on available physical and human resources in the central city.

Model II attempts to exploit the advantages of Model IA and Model IB while overcoming some of their defects. In some cases a Model IA or

Model IB new town intown can be generally beneficial, but the possibility of displacement—merely shifting the socioeconomic problems of one section of the city to another—is also apparent. Moreover, most experience with central city redevelopment indicates that a project by project approach is, in general, relatively ineffective because it operates at too small a scale to have major impacts on the central city. Where individual projects have been comparatively effective (for example, Boston), they were conceived and implemented as part of a strong program of redevelopment that envisioned specific sequences and overall city-wide impacts.

Our own analysis suggests that comprehensive central city modernization will require programmatic linkages between locations with high development potential (resource and opportunity areas) and areas of high socio-economic need (or primary impact areas). These linkages must be made explicit, feasible, and defensible in order to realize the overriding objectives of central city modernization and assistance to the less advantaged. Moreover, with a comprehensive development program involving a series of functionally linked projects, shortcomings of one project can be traded off and remedied by other project locations. For example, some projects could provide housing for relocatees from other sites; others could concentrate on industrial and job development; finance problems of marginal projects could be balanced out with tax revenues generated in projects with higher economic potential.

Our emphasis on a programmatic approach to central city modernization does not imply that NTIT Models IA and IB are not valuable and significant in their own right. Certainly both models are noteworthy improvements over most previous redevelopment and related projects. Model II does, however, argue for a higher degree of sophistication in development in which Model IA and Model IB projects can be combined for greater impact in the more ambitious programmatic approach suggested by Model II.

What is Appropriate Scale for a New Town Intown?

HUD Guidelines set 100 acres and 12,000 population as minima for new town intown federal assistance, derived essentially from the first approved NTIT project (Cedar–Riverside). While arbitrary, these minima can be defended as being not inappropriate for Model IA development of single projects on vacant land—if adequate employment opportunities and public services are provided by off-site surrounding areas. A more "balanced" community in terms of employment and public services, however, would dictate much larger scale—probably no less than Fort Lincoln NTIT scale (335 acres) and quite possibly approximating San Antonio NTIT scale (500 acres and 10,000 jobs projected on-site).

In the past, renewal project boundaries generally were determined by physical blight while model cities areas were the function of "worst" slum and poverty conditions. Neither of these, our study has found, were adequate bases for determining project size as seen in the light of the central city modernization and broadening-of-opportunities objectives. Availability of vacant or abandoned land in the central city, similarly, can be inappropriate for determining the scale of new town intown projects.

NTIT scale should be determined by development potential of an area rather than physical blight, "bad" social conditions, or available vacant land. The aim is to create a viable community. The new town intown, it follows, normally should encompass more territory than a typical urban renewal project or model cities neighborhood. Size should depend on the requirements of central city modernization and should consider: (a) type and location of public service systems and facilities, (b) present and future economic potential for development, (c) type and configuration of transportation networks, and (d) community awareness, relative strength of community institutions, and citizen participation.

Actually, developmental scale should be viewed from two perspectives. One is in terms of single project scale, that is, how large should be the boundaries of a particular project. The viability of scale in this instance would be a function of the objectives of that particular project and would vary enormously from case to case. Much more important in terms of our analysis is the relationship of scale to overall impact, that is, how many projects and other efforts are needed to significantly impact the city as a whole (and thus to achieve the overall objectives of central city modernization). In the past, such impacts were given little thought because federal programs focused on individual projects. By arguing for a programmatic approach involving designation of an area of significantly larger scale, we suggest that impacts beyond project boundaries must be taken into account consciously so that individual projects are located, designed, and implemented with the express intent of influencing a larger area.

NTIT Model IA clearly has limitations from both views of scale. In terms of project size, its flexibility is limited to available vacant land (although in some instances a Model IA project could be well suited for developing particular parcels of vacant land). In terms of wider impacts the picture is more bleak, because it is most unlikely that a single Model IA project could have significant citywide impacts in most sizable central cities in the United States.

Model IB and even more so Model II are considerably more flexible and likely to be effective in terms of scale. A Model IB project, by encompassing part or all of a central business district and its environs, could in many cases begin to approach scale sufficient for citywide impacts. A Model II program approach, which could incorporate a series of Model IA and IB projects, would naturally offer the greatest potential for significance in terms of scale.

Thus, in our opinion, the much larger scale appropriate to Model II programs, makes the most sense as the main base for a federal new town intown program. In terms of Model II, this does not mean that the entire area encompassed (which might be half of a city, as in Hartford) would actually be redeveloped, but it does suggest that analysis and evaluation would focus upon this larger program "zone" and not alone upon individual projects within such a zone.

Given the need for a programmatic approach, the question of maximum (rather than minimum) scale also becomes an issue, but it is one that can be determined only by (a) the inherent logic of the proposed development program for the central city, and (b) the availability of funds for development.

How Should a NTIT be Programmed
to Modernize a Central City?

In more recent years, a few urban renewal agencies became expert at programming renewal projects so as to integrate well with each other and into the urban system. This gave a renewal agency flexibility in designing strategies for upgrading very large areas because it could link together areas of high development potential. For instance, a set of linked projects could include an underutilized railroad yard potentially developable as an office complex, a residential neighborhood needing rehabilitation, and a shopping center requiring modernization. Because each project was mutually reinforcing, the total impact was much greater than if planned in isolation.

With establishment of workable program provisions by the Housing Act of 1954, all renewal agencies were nominally required to take a programmatic approach. The Housing Act of 1959 went further with its Community Renewal Plan requirements. However, the state of the art for such planning in the 1950s tended to leave much to be desired. And the renewal program's narrow emphasis upon removing blight foreclosed serious consideration of social and economic development concurrent with physical redevelopment. Nonetheless, a handful of renewal agencies (such as Boston) eventually became adept at programming projects to maximize program impact. The neighborhood development program was another step toward more programmatic development.

The Model Cities program, by contrast, in actual practice emphasized concentrating resources in one target area within a city, the model neighborhood. Despite its laudatory objectives, this represented a step away from a programmatic approach. Although many model neighborhoods encompassed large areas, boundaries were drawn with little regard for social or economic feasibility; indeed, quite the reverse was the case. Instead of combining areas of strength with problem areas to achieve a balanced program of linked projects, in actual practice the model city program focused almost exclusively on the least viable areas of a city. Not surprisingly, this led to relatively small marginal returns for public investment, because the limited funds were never really sufficient nor concentrated to create the critical mass necessary to make the program successful or even plausibly cost-effective. While quantitatively significant in terms of number of acres designated, the program was not significant in terms of the types of acres included. Accordingly, size of program area was not enough; much more important should have been the potential of project sites within the program area and their ability to contribute to citywide goals.

Thus, the NTIT program could combine the best features of model cities and urban renewal by utilizing renewal's potential for programmatic approaches to attain comprehensive socioeconomic development objectives generally similar to those implied by model cities. For maximum development impact, such a strategy would link strong areas of a central city with "need areas" within broadly defined development sectors. (These concepts are discussed throughout this volume, but particularly in Part III.)

Problems of low income, unemployment, and slum living probably cannot and should not be solved solely within a poverty ghetto. Opportunities for upward mobility for the less advantaged would need to be developed, but not necessarily within a ghetto's boundaries. For example, job opportunities might be better created in economically viable locations easily accessible to the ghetto rather than in the ghetto itself.

However, investments in physical and human capital should occur inside the ghetto to enable residents to take advantage of extraghetto opportunities as they become available. Job integration and upgrading of ghetto workers into the economic mainstream undoubtedly depend, to an unknown but surely significant degree, on the total quality of life that each individual experiences. As Vietorisz and Harrison put it, a worker cannot be "exiled every night to a rat-infested, overcrowded, personally hazardous, and miserably serviced environment while being expected to deliver a high degree of productivity on the job."

Similarly, opportunities for better residential environments need not be developed solely in the worst parts of the city. They could be developed through projects in areas offering greater socioeconomic potential such as converting vacant or underutilized land to house socially integrated communities, or through improvements of areas with some initial advantages such as unusually well-organized minority groups. Thus, all NTIT components need not be developed on one contiguous parcel of vacant or underutilized land.

We believe this linked area approach is best achieved along the lines suggested by a Model II new town intown program. Obviously, if financing or commitment are not sufficient, individual Model IA and Model IB projects scattered across the city could also have positive impacts. Indeed, all else being equal, five projects approached from the viewpoint suggested by the new community legislation will accomplish considerably more in terms of jobs, housing, and other objectives than five traditional urban renewal projects. Thus, we are stressing that much more could be accomplished by integrating these projects as common elements of a development program.

How Should NTIT Components Be
Chosen and "Balanced"?

There is no formula answer because local needs should primarily determine the type and relative balance of the developmental components of a new town intown. Specific program and project emphases accordingly should vary with the nature of the central city and its design. Ideally a Model II NTIT should be viewed in part as constituting the process by which these specifics are identified and ranked by the local jurisdictions themselves.

National experience does indicate, according to our study, that the traditional, unquestioning emphasis on developing public and assisted housing units is probably misplaced. It is interesting to note that in a Delphi, carried out in connection with this study, the more experienced urban experts believed that housing should be de-emphasized. Moreover, housing development should not be treated merely as production of physical shelter but incorporated systematically into larger service and neighborhood environments.

Similarly, more attention should be directed to economic and employment development. Each NTIT should be designed and implemented with an awareness of its relationship to the economic processes of the surrounding central city and urban region. Regardless of its specific components, a NTIT program should generally concentrate on moving with, rather than against, the powerful forces in the regional economy unless unlimited development subsidies can be assumed realistically.

Experience with inner city development also leaves little doubt that central city programs should give greater consideration to human oriented services. Too often redevelopment and Model I NTIT projects have concentrated on physical development, leaving social needs to the care and funding of other agencies. "People" improvement should have equal emphasis with "place" improvement in new towns intown. In fact, as some experts have suggested, NTITs should be able, if necessary, to encompass all life support systems of the central city. In addition, they should include those services needed to modernize the central city.

More specifically, NTITs should be cognizant of the underlying factors which would influence the relative emphases of major program components. Key considerations for each component are discussed below:

1. Economic/Employment Development. As Goldstein (1972) and others have observed, with some notable exceptions, efforts at job development in and out of urban renewal and model cities were relatively unsuccessful. However, important lessons were learned in these efforts as well as those of the Office of Economic Opportunity and Departments of Commerce and Labor.

a) Central city development programs are more successful if they move with, rather than against, the powerful socioeconomic forces shaping the spatial configuration of the region. Bringing manufacturing and wholesaling activity back from land intensive sites in the suburbs would require massive subsidies. However, due to agglomeration economies, central cities are attractive places for many office based service and financial firms and some kinds of manufacturing. Assistance in land assembly, provision of infrastructure, and coordination of public and private investment decisions would help the central city economy move "in the direction it wants to go."

Following this approach, the development entity could generally avoid monetary outlays to induce firms to locate in uneconomic locations. However, such inducements might be justified where a firm is providing jobs uniquely suited for the resident work force.

b) The NTIT program could stimulate the central city to generate jobs, income, and overall economic viability in much the same way as the renewal program. It could accomplish this by:

1. Eliminating or compensating for negative neighborhood effects;
2. Assisting in land assembly for firms needing more space to expand their operations;
3. Preserving and strengthening important urban institutions which are key to the urban economy;
4. Investing in public facilities that complement the central city's expanding role in office based activities;
5. Improving transportation where this serves to increase employment opportunities.

c) Some economic/job development must take place within the ghetto in order to develop the thrust necessary for ghetto dispersal. It is unlikely, however, that unemployment and low income problems can be solved within the ghetto. As previously mentioned, this underlines the logic for a set of projects in "opportunity" areas linked with projects within "need" areas.

d) HUD should require from cities seeking NTIT assistance a detailed analysis of economic problems and potential of the central city and anticipated impacts on designated development areas as well as on the central city as a whole.

2. Service Development. Past experience points to several lessons concerning services.

a) The importance of services within central city development areas cannot be overemphasized, and if the NTIT program is to be successful, more emphasis must be placed upon developing better education, vocational training, health, day care, personal security, and the like. Better services, particularly manpower and other educational programs, render a work force more productive and boost the competitive advantage of the area. Better services also add to the amenity of an area which is an increasingly important factor in the location decisions of firms. In addition, jobs are created through the provision of services.

b) Development of a new town intown will not be successful if a reasonable amount of personal security cannot be assured. Methods generally listed for improving security include better physical design ("defensible space") and lighting, provision for adequate and more personalized policing, and encouragement of more street activity and around-the-clock use of facilities. However, it is extremely doubtful whether a NTIT could be maintained as a secure, but isolated, island in a sea of unrest. Thus, security programs to be effective must cover not only the NTIT area but surrounding areas as well. Moreover, security programs can be effective only when established as an integral part of a broader scale *social development effort.* Since our knowledge in this realm is extremely limited, this will involve social innovation and experimentation. The new town intown program should encourage carefully designed programs of this type through special incentives.

c) Increased production in the central cities is due primarily to increasing concentrations of labor intensive, office based service and financial firms. From the public finance standpoint, however, this may create problems for those cities which in actual practice tax only property and therefore do not tax the increased value added. Thus, they finance improved services for industry and disadvantaged populations by a property tax system more sensitive to the central city's declining residential base (with out-migration of middleclass residents) than to its increasing importance as a service and financial center.

3. Housing Development. Many costly lessons about housing have been learned from the housing and renewal programs.

a) Even with land write-down private redevelopment of cleared sites, following market dictates alone, will generally result in upper middle to high income housing and with lower income families included in token fashion only. Strong federal pressure and incentives are essential to achieve new towns intown that are "balanced" economically and racially. In Model II NTIT development, questions of economic/racial balance can be treated more flexibly than in Model I projects. In the former, it is expected that the low income and minority communities would be involved in working out trade-offs between progress in housing integration and tax increment generation (and therefore more funds for public services and housing).

b) Great care must be taken not to reduce the total supply of existing low and moderate income housing to achieve other objectives. HUD should require a "housing budget" as part of every NTIT proposal that would show losses and gains in low and moderate income housing for every stage of development. Trade-offs anticipating any *net* losses in existing stock would have to demonstrate substantial gains in general community welfare to be justified.

c) Housing subsidies will undoubtedly be required if low and moderate income families are to afford decent housing (except, perhaps, in some areas of the Southeast United States where construction costs are still relatively low). In general, without public subsidies NTIT developers cannot construct much, if any, low and moderate income housing. Our analysis shows that without substantial land writedown or other "deep" subsidies, housing programs of the type available in the early 1970s (for example, Section 235, 236, and public housing) normally could not generate large amounts of low and moderate income housing.

d) Adequate compensation for relocation costs is expensive. Since enactment of the Uniform Relocation Act of 1970, estimated relocation costs have risen to $8,000 for each homeowner displaced, $2,500 for each tenant, and $5,000 for each business. High relocation costs obviously make vacant or underutilized land and rehabilitation more attractive than renewal (and obviously much more cost effective as well). However, a NTIT program could conceivably manage essential development without being overcome by relocation costs. For example, it could entice residents into equity participation in the development process so that they would personally gain from property value increases and therefore have a stake in community improvement. Residents would be expected, under such arrangements, to be interested themselves in minimizing relocation costs in order to maximize equity returns. Experiments of this type will be needed to break through the present relocation impasse.

4. Neighborhood Development.

a) Neighborhoods of poorer and less advantaged families are important parts of the central city fabric. They have many social assets (as well as problems); they are not merely places "to be cleaned up." Not only do such neighborhoods provide better homes for these families than can be afforded elsewhere, but also they provide preferred locations for public transportation, public and private services, shopping, and family and friends. They are also places where minority groups can mobilize political power and bring leverage to bear on public and private institutions. It is not necessary to glorify such areas to appreciate their assets as well as liabilities. Central city programs must come to grips with this fact; otherwise, unthinkingly, they can tear and disrupt the community fabric.

b) A central city development program is not likely to achieve significant net gains unless it can simultaneously improve the physical environment and social and political assets of these neighborhoods. Benefits must be readily apparent to residents if they are to support the program and maintain neighborhood improvements over time.

c) Great care must be taken to help assimilate newcomers and accelerate upward mobility. For example, some NTIT neighborhoods could serve as places where newcomers are assimilated. Once the newcomer has consolidated his position, he could leave the NTIT area altogether or relocate to take advantage of opportunities in other linked areas. The central city should, in general, be approached in terms of its own built-in dynamism rather than in terms of the values of stability and neatness associated with middle class suburban living.

IMPLEMENTATION

What Finance Strategies Have Developers Used in the Central City?

In the past the most direct solution to financing central city development was federal subsidies for land write down, housing, site clearance and improvements, interest, planning, and so forth. While undoubtedly "costly," the effectiveness of such direct monetary transfers from federal to local governments cannot be denied.

Also, federal loans were used to reduce interest costs and to finance development not possible with conventional financing. Mortgage guarantees, the financial device for Title VII new towns, has been somewhat successful but only for a small handful of Model IA projects. And finally, new issues were raised with the passage of the Housing and Community Development Act of 1974 as to the feasibility of using general and/or special revenue sharing funds and attendant eligibility requirements.

Although each finance strategy had its own unique feature, they were means to the same end: utilizing federal funds to compensate private parties for investment in an uneconomic (or "not fully economic") situation. Naturally, the more uneconomic the situation, the greater the public subsidy required to induce private involvement. Regrettably, too often in the past sizable amounts of federal funds were expended to bring about modest levels of private activity in problem burdened locales when more cost effective results could have been attained had the same funding been (a) concentrated and (b) carefully targeted to areas of greater potential.

In any event, assuming governmental encouragement of combined public-private development to be the best method of stimulating central city modernization, the amount of the central city development activity generated ultimately will probably be a function of the level of governmental funding.

In addition to federal transfer of funds, other techniques have reduced capital and operating costs of central city development to competitive levels. In some cities, areas can be developed with relatively little federal financial assistance when vacant land is involved. Much of the NTIT activity to date or planned, in fact, is on vacant land with no relocation, land clearance, or related costs. In some rare cases, such land may be in public ownership, as in Fort Lincoln. Unfortunately, the availability of vacant public or private land in appropriate sections of the central city is quite limited.

Creation of new land may reduce costs of development where it is cheaper to fill or dike than to build upon built-up land. An example is Battery Park, New York City, where it cost approximately $40 per square foot to create land worth $400 per square foot on the open market. Environmental problems and limited applicability are major drawbacks, however. Air rights over existing facilities is another method of creating development space in the central city, but costs are often prohibitive.

Also, development of underutilized land in the central city may sometimes be feasible with minimal subsidies. Certain large publicly owned parcels (for example, military bases) are especially attractive, if political and administrative hurdles can be leaped. In some cases leasing of public land for private development may be an especially workable strategy since it eliminates the problem of setting a fair market price for what may be valuable real estate. Large privately held parcels (railroad yards, port facilities) that have outlasted their usefulness may be developable without major public investment, especially if already under single ownership.

Some experts advocate redevelopment of abandoned residential areas, arguing much of the property could be acquired relatively cheaply by the city for unpaid back taxes. While attractive on the surface, in most cases such an approach is probably not an efficient means of lowering redevelopment costs to competitive levels, since the basic social maladies that induced abandonment in the first place must be overcome before rebuilding will occur. As has been noted in reference to model cities, such "worst first" approaches require massive expenditures for limited results. Thus, even with free land, redevelopment of such areas in most instances is not economically feasible.

In some cases innovative manipulation of tax laws may also serve to induce private development in the central city. In the NTIT Delphi, developers as a group assigned high priority to property tax incentives as an inducement to private investment. Boston has had considerable success in encouraging private development by granting property tax abatements.

Both Cedar–Riverside and the Hartford Process have devised means of channeling tax benefits to individuals and corporations so as to encourage investment in central city development. Tax benefits include tax shelters for wealthy investors, sharing of capital losses, exploitation of tax loopholes, and the like. Utilization of tax laws to encourage central city modernization is still a fairly *ad hoc* private procedure, suggesting that greater public attention needs to be directed at the potential of this area of program "financing."

What Strategies Have Been Used for Improving the Welfare of the Less Advantaged in Intown Development Efforts?

It is generally conceded that central city development and redevelopment efforts that concern themselves only with physical and/or economic considerations are likely to be ineffective. Social problems must be addressed as well, both to effectively impact the central city and to gain the most benefit from public investment.

The following strategies have been found useful in improving the welfare of the less advantaged through intown development efforts:

Housing subsidies are one of the most common means of aiding the less advantaged in development and redevelopment programs. Significantly, all NTIT developers have applied for federal housing subsidies, implying developers will normally not be able to build new communities with significant levels of income integration without public support. In the past, this public support has taken the form of "235" and "236" programs, housing allowances, subsidy of interest costs, various state and local programs (for example, Mitchell–Lama in New York), support of efforts to lower building costs (Operation Breakthrough), or innovative new forms.

Subsidies for social services is also a direct method of aiding the less advantaged, although this approach has been insufficiently exploited, perhaps due to difficulties of interagency coordination. Experience to date indicates rich benefits can be reaped by involvement of social development programs with ongoing central city development efforts. Fortunately, this lesson is taking effect, judging by the increased emphasis placed on social services in later urban renewal projects planned and under way. Financial support for human oriented services might be obtained by involvement of appropriate federal or state agencies, local contributions, use of internal subsidies, and/or application of general or special revenue sharing funds.

In addition to prividing for subsidized housing, educational, health, and other opportunities they otherwise could not afford, the less advantaged can be assisted by enhanced incomes so they can afford more of these services. Intown development efforts can assist in this direction by increasing directly the quantity and quality of employment opportunity and indirectly by including job training programs in development programs. A more controversial and untested strategy would be to give interested less advantaged groups, or even individuals, a "piece of the action" so they might participate in the returns from NTIT development.

If the intown development involves a Model II programmatic approach, the less advantaged also might be aided by improving accessibility to housing, services, and employment through improvement of the region's transportation system.

Of course, merely creating new housing or services is insufficient if less advantaged groups cannot gain access to the new opportunities. To prevent such exclusion, HUD guidelines require Title VII applicants to create and enforce an affirmative action program assuring that housing rentals and sales will be "open," that minority groups will be represented in construction employment, that minority subcontractors will be involved in the development, and that some employment opportunities be allocated to minority businessmen. The effectiveness of these affirmative action programs depend on how rigorously they are enforced.

What Political and Institutional Arrangements Facilitate NTIT Development?

It is evident that the success of even a limited new town intown project of the Model I variety, no less than a major citywide program of the Model II type, requires substantial political support at every level, from the local community up to the federal government, which cuts across all of the various major public functions and services of importance to an intown community. Of critical importance is the strong support of the central city decision making groups and, in a more general way, of the community at large. This is essential because the creation of a new town intown inevitably requires many changes in laws, regulations, and procedures, and often the granting of high priority standing in terms of both funds and timing of activities. The importance of this element has been highlighted in the studies which we have carried out on NTIT projects under way and planned. The types of assistance that have been provided to new towns intown by supportive local governments is indeed impressive— covering such items as the extremely attractive leasehold arrangement of city owned land granted by New York City to Roosevelt Island and the uniquely designed institutional and financial arrangements worked out by the City of New Orleans for Pontchartrain—but equally significant is the fact that this type of support is essential for the success of a new town intown effort.

Building on even the limited experience with new towns intown to date, it would be possible for HUD guidelines to establish the elements of community, local governmental, and state support required of a NTIT effort before a proposal would be considered for federal government financial assistance. Not only would such a requirement help protect the federal investment, but also it would provide a useful checklist for those undertaking a NTIT effort and generate, as well, a useful type of pressure from above. A NTIT developer should not be permitted to apply for federal assistance unless the necessary local support (as well as state backing when new state legislation is required) has been obtained.

In terms of institutional arrangements, experience to date suggests that there are many potentially valuable forms, no one of which has yet proved itself obviously superior. The main organizational problem is somehow to combine the advantages of the private entrepreneur (with the relatively great flexibility, ability to mobilize resources and organizational talent, and freedom from the more obvious kinds of political pressures) with the advantages and powers of a public entity. In several of the NTIT projects, a partnership between a private developer and the local renewal authority has proved itself a workable arrangement, with the private developer providing the entrepreneural skills and the local agency the powers of eminent domain and land write-down, as well as access to the local, state, and federal bureaucracies.

A public development corporation as the entrepreneur, be it locally or state based, also seems to offer great potential, although the relative advantages and disadvantages of this institutional form at Roosevelt Island (state, plus local subsidiary) and Pontchartrain (local) are as yet undetermined. The extensive and complex institutional requirements for planning and carrying out a broad based Model II "linked area" kind of NTIT development suggests there well may be need for a "lead agency" that can serve as an umbrella (or parent) organization which, in turn, can spin off a variety of subsidiary corporations or work out arrangements with private corporations for the management of the individual NTIT projects within the new town intown program.

An examination of the various tasks to be accomplished in a Model II kind of development—as highlighted in specific terms by our study of what it would take to launch a new town intown program in a city like Los Angeles—suggests that such a public development corporation would need to have substantial powers. These powers would include:

a) Preparation of physical, economic, social, and financial plans for the "development sectors," in relation to broader planning for the city and region (with prior approval of the mayor and city council); primary responsibility for zoning, land use, and building controls within these sectors; and coordination and phasing of public improvements in the designated sectors;

b) Operation as a developer with powers to buy, sell, and lease land; acquire, construct, and rehabilitate buildings and other property; and condemn, assemble, bank, and write down land and other property;

c) Operation of public facilities and quasi-public enterprises (such as minibuses);

d) Issuance of tax exempt bonds and other obligations;

e) (Possibly) certain specified overriding of local zoning, building, and housing codes;

f) Establishment of public, joint public-private, and private subsidiaries, and undertaking joint activities with existing entities.

A "joint venture" approach between a public and a private entity, as is common in outlying new towns, has not yet been tried or even proposed for any NTIT effort, but it is a possibility that should be considered.

From the standpoint of the federal administration of the new town intown program there is not reason to specify, or to favor, any particular institutional form for NTITs. Clearly, experimentation with institutional forms is a necessity at the present time and should be encouraged. On the other side, HUD might well expect a full explanation for the particular form chosen for a given

NTIT effort and an indication of how the essential entrepreneurial and operational tasks are to be accomplished under the proposed form.

PROPOSALS FOR NTIT FINANCING

Introduction

Title VII and other provisions of existing HUD programs have been instrumental in the launching of a number of suburban new communities, but have not had a similar impact within central city areas. Although several projects exist under the NTIT designation, most have received a major part of their financing through urban renewal or other programs.

Additional sources of financing to supplement Title VII are required to provide the same encouragement for projects in central city areas as compared to those in outlying areas. There are several major differences between suburban and intown developments. Primary among them is the level of public facilities and services required by the higher density configurations encountered intown. It is a widely accepted principle that higher densities result in increased demands for public facilities and services. Further, the employment objectives of intown development—so integral to the success of an intown project—create even further demands for public facilities. Title VII on the other hand was designed merely to help finance land development costs regardless of whether the land is located in a central city or suburban area, and essential public expenditures were not adequately provided for.

A second flaw in Title VII for intown purposes is the too small amount of the mortgage guarantee. We have documented elsewhere the high cost of land acquisition, relocation, clearance, and infrastructure which are typical intown costs. The Title VII maximum of $50 million is not enough for comprehensive town-scale development of the type envisioned for a new town intown program in a large city.

Assistance for financing of low-moderate income housing has also been shown to be an absolute necessity. The Nixon administration's suspension of housing programs may have been another factor in the failure of Title VII to induce much intown development.

A number of additional financing sources must be made available for central city development if NTIT goals are to be met. The financing of successful central city development programs will necessarily be a joint effort involving the private sector and local and federal governments. There is no way to predict how much of the development capital needed can be provided by the private sector, nor which levels of government are best able to bear the public costs. At one extreme, it is possible to envision projects where the only public assistance would be that of land assembly (through eminent domain) and provision of some minimal level of infrastructure. A more likely case would require a very high level of participation by the private sector, local government, and federal government. The other extreme is the case where heavy reliance on federal assistance—especially HUD—is necessary.

Magnitude of Total Financing Needed

A brief overview of a major urban development project will give some idea of financial magnitudes which will be required. Table 15–1 shows the range of costs for various intown projects for which data are available. The costs are on a "per project" basis, rather than a cost per unit area or other basis, for reasons to be described later; note also that a Model II NTIT may include several projects. The amounts shown, based on existing proposals, may not be appropriate for Model II NTITs (for which no data are available). They are nevertheless suggestive.

1. **Land Development.** Land development costs for intown projects for which data are available range from $83 to $265 million, as shown in Table 15–1. Many factors (other than project size alone) affect the magnitude of land development costs, including:

a) The costs of land which are typically higher in larger cities and in locations near the central city;
b) The degree to which existing infrastructure can be re-used. Projects proposed on essentially vacant or underutilized land receive no benefit from existing infrastructure;
c) The amount of relocation and demolition required;
d) The amount of fill, grading, diking, or other site preparation required;
e) The density of the proposed development. Higher densities require more expensive site preparation and infrastructure.

2. **Low-Moderate Income Housing.** Table 15–1 also contains an estimate of the costs of low-moderate income housing. The point was made elsewhere that financially assisting construction of low-moderate income hous-

Table 15–1. Loan Amounts for NTITs by Function [1]

Function	Range of Actual NTIT Projects [2] ($ Millions)
Land Development	$ 83–265
Low-Moderate Income Housing	66–124
Public Facilities	9–85
Total	$158–474

[1] Costs are on a per project basis. Note that Model II NTIT may encompass several such projects
[2] Based on NTIT projects for which data are available

ing, as part of the project financing package, can determine the ability of a developer to deliver such housing.

3. Public Facilities. The final item in Table 15–1 is the cost of public facilities. This includes public facilities to be provided by the developer as well as local government agencies. A partial list of public facilities for a high density intown development could include:

> Streets and highways;
> Mass transit;
> Sidewalks and lighting;
> Parks, open space, recreational, and cultural facilities;
> Sewer and water distribution;
> Wastewater treatment;
> Libraries;
> Schools and other educational facilities;
> Neighborhood facilities.

The importance of providing for the capital requirements of these facilities cannot be overemphasized. Intown developments cannot be successful without high levels of public facilities and supportive services.

Moreover, an intown developer must deal with a well-established city government, typically with limited capacity and/or funds for providing public services and facilities in new development areas, even though the eventual returns may be great. The suburban developer, by contrast, often creates new political jurisdictions to provide public services without having to convince a local government to bear the capital costs. As a result, an intown development must be prepared to bear the capital costs of public facilities.

The dollar amounts required for public facilities are affected by many of the same factors affecting land development costs. Most important factors are density (demand for public facilities rises sharply with density) and the reuse capacity of existing facilities. The range of public facilities' costs for intown projects for which we have data is $9 million to $85 million. The low figure is probably unusual; it is for a fairly low density project with many existing facilities in place. The New York Urban Development Corporation, in its 1970 report, estimated public facilities' costs as nearly 1.5 times land development costs for all projects then under way.[a]

---

a. New York State Urban Development Corporation and the New York State Office of Planning Coordination, *New Communities for New York,* (December 31, 1970), p. 60

SOURCES OF FINANCING FOR CENTRAL CITY DEVELOPMENT

Private Sector Participation

Recent urban renewal experience in many cities has shown that the private sector *can* provide substantial amounts of equity and loan funds for central city projects when those projects are economically sound, well coordinated, and fully supported by local government. Private sector participation will ultimately determine the success or failure of central city development; federal and local government participation can provide the legal powers needed for development and some of the infrastructure funding but the private sector will eventually have to provide the greater part of the capital.

Local governments can do a great deal to so encourage private sector participation. The willingness of local government to exercise its powers in a concentrated, coordinated way within development areas is essential to success. The private sector needs to be convinced that local government will give full support to development before committing itself to the greater part of the financing requirements.

Tax Increment Financing

Tax increment financing is likely to become an integral part of financing for urban development, because it enables local government to assist in the financing of capital outlays without direct financial participation.

Tax increment financing establishes a way to borrow against anticipated increases in property tax revenues, which result from development activities, in order to provide the capital needed for investment in development. The usual method consists of an agreement between the developing entity (LPA, CDC, and so forth) and local agencies (city, county, school districts) which receive property tax revenues. The property tax base taxable by those agencies is frozen at the existing levels; subsequent increases in the tax base during the specified period of time (usually 20 to 30 years) are assumed to be the result of development activities and are assigned to the developing entity. The developing entity then issues tax increment bonds whose interest and principal are to be repaid from property tax revenues derived from the anticipated increase in the tax base. The bonds are secured only by this anticipated increase in tax revenues; there is no liability on local government, and no voter approval is required.

The amount of capital which can be raised by tax increment financing is a function of the anticipated increase in the property tax base. The increased tax base will consist of land value appreciation, the value of new structures, and increases in the value of rehabilitated structures. The success obtained by development entities in raising capital through tax increment bonds depends on the evaluation by the financial community of the chances that the project will achieve the projected level of development. The degree of commitment to the project by the local government is an essential element in making tax increment financing possible.

Increases in the tax base can result from growth unrelated to activities of the developing entity. Public investment in such projects as transportation systems, hospitals, and educational facilities may accrue to the developing entity as an "unearned increment." Such investments by local government may help the developing entity obtain the capital needed for its development activities.

Local agencies who give up their rights to the increase in the tax base during the financing period benefit in the long run. After the tax increment bonds are retired, the full tax base including the increment resulting from development is returned to the local agencies. The agreements between the developing entity and a local agency may establish a way to fund any increase in demand for services provided by the agency which may occur during the financing period, so that the agency is never any worse off as a result of the tax increment agreement.

Tax increment financing can be viewed as a process by which part of the benefits from development are returned to the developing entity and are used to offset capital costs. The method can provide substantial amounts of capital for projects which generate large amounts of new construction and increases in land value. While tax increment financing alone simply cannot return enough capital for major development programs, it may be very effective in conjunction with Title VII and other methods of financing.

Urban Development Loans

The cornerstone of a central city development program is the capacity of developers to borrow substantial amounts of long-term capital at reasonable interest rates. Provision must be made for future commitments so that renegotiation contingencies and associated uncertainties would not jeopardize the project schedule. In addition, flexible repayment is necessary since most expenditures occur early in a project, long before offsetting revenues are generated. Finally, some kind of guarantee is needed, because private lending institutions are not willing to assume the risks of major urban development projects with very long payback periods.

A federal bank for making loans to urban development entities would have several advantages over the Title VII guarantees. To begin with, capital could be raised at lower interest rates by a single centralized bank than is now the case with a multitude of local agencies. Reasons for this include better flow of information to the financial community and the existence of a secondary market for federal agency securities. The fact that existing Title VII issues bear interest yields near those of AAA industrial bonds, despite the federal guarantee, supports the argument that multiple bond issues by local development entities is not the most economical way to raise development capital.

An additional advantage of a federal bank would be that the staging requirements of various projects could be used to reduce the peak debt. As early projects begin repayment, these funds could be loaned out to subsequent projects without the bank having to raise new capital.

A Federal Financing Bank which was set up in 1974 can conceivably be used in conjunction with the Title VII apparatus to satisfy certain of the needs for federal banking assistance. The Federal Financing Bank can supposedly provide lower interest rates (because of its larger and more frequent security issues, better flow of information to the investment public, and the existence of a secondary market).

A full-fledged federal urban development bank would be even more desirable as it could make direct loans to promising development projects earlier in the project's life and before the requirements for Title VII have been satisfied.

Community Development Revenue Sharing

Community development revenue sharing (CDRS) could conceivably become an important part of a NTIT financial program. CDRS is seen as a replacement for five previous programs (urban renewal, model cities, open space, rehabilitation loans, and neighborhood facilities) as well as providing additional funds required in "community development."

CDRS can provide localities with funding needed to satisfy several critical urban development needs. Perhaps most importantly, special revenue sharing can provide seed money for initial planning and feasibility studies, as well as administrative and operating costs incurred early in the program's inception. These early costs may total at least $2 million, and there is no assurance a feasible program and/or projects will result. Most cities would be unwilling to risk that amount from general revenue sources for determining program/ projects feasibility.

A second use of special revenue sharing funds could be to finance public facilities in NTIT projects. Studies of local allocations of general revenue sharing funds show conspicuous amounts being spent on capital improvements. There is reason to believe that cities would be willing to devote sizable amounts of CDRS funds to the capital investment uses most needed by NTITs.

Finally, CDRS could finance some of the software programs not firmly provided now under Title VII provisions or administration. The other special revenue sharing components (manpower, law enforcement, transportation, and education) now under discussion should also be viewed as potential funding sources of NTIT development.

One of the earlier conclusions of this volume was that urban renewal, model cities, and other development programs had been thwarted by the fragmented, dispersed application of funds over both location and time. Conversely, our recommendations for the NTIT program are based on highly selective and concentrated funding of central city development.

Public Facilities Financing

A review of the costs associated with the initial NTIT projects makes it evident that the community development revenue sharing amounts currently projected (mid–1974) would not enable cities to provide the investments in public facilities required for major NTIT physical development, much less finance software programs. Such a review also serves to underline the importance of incentives for cities to concentrate development in a few areas with high program potential.

A program of federal public facilities grants and loans in direct association with the NTIT program could significantly help cities provide the public facilities needed for central city development as well as create incentives for cities to concentrate development activities. A public facilities grants/loan program should be very selective, funding only those development programs concentrated enough to make substantial central city modernization possible.

A likely combination would be some minimum amount of "first phase" combined grants and loans for public facilities—enough to fund the most critical public facilities outlays very early in a NTIT development program—coupled with more substantial public facilities loans. The loans, made directly through a federal bank (such as an urban development bank or federal financing bank) should be at lowest possible interest rates (such as those charged to federal agencies), and should have deferred principal repayment provisions.

These grants and loans should be made available to the developer (or local government agency) at a time well before the major project funding (such as Title VII) is actually drawn upon, so that public facilities essential to project success can be in place when marketing of the earliest phases of development begins.

Summary

Title VII alone has not been enough to stimulate major urban developments in central cities. A variety of additional financing sources must be made available if central city development is to succeed.

The private sector can probably provide a major part of the development capital where central city governments commit themselves fully to supporting concentrated development programs with all available governmental powers. The same commitment by local government can make tax increment financing a very powerful method for raising development capital.

Federal programs which are needed include an urban development bank to reduce borrowing costs and provide direct loan funds for expenditures early in the project; special revenue sharing for community development which also can provide outlays early in the project as well as to fund public facilities; increased loan ceilings (either under Title VII or through direct loans from a federal bank); and public facilities grants and loans in direct association with

NTITs to help provide the high quality of public facilities necessary for high density central city locations. The modernization of central cities will necessarily be an expensive undertaking. Various approaches and sources of funding will have to be employed to make the task economically, financially, and politically feasible.

ATTACHMENT A

WHAT RESEARCH IS NEEDED TO GUIDE SECOND GENERATION CENTRAL CITY DEVELOPMENT?

While the present study hopefully has provided new insight into the problems and potential of comprehensive central city modernization, it has also brought to the fore one very evident fact: there are many key issues in central city development about which (1) we still know relatively little, but (2) urgently need to know more.

Our study, by tracking what is known about central city development and by attempting to think through the design and implementation of a new town intown program in a given city, has identified many issues central to formulating a second generation national program. They are the issues discussed in this summary; namely, (1) objectives, (2) design of Model I and II NTIT programs, and (3) implementation. However, the study also highlighted certain subissues which deserve early and special attention:

1. Objectives. Even assuming broad agreement that the appropriate purposes of a second generation national program of central city development are modernization and assistance to the less advantaged, these objectives should be defined more sharply than we have been able to. Thus, the following types of questions should be addressed:

a) How should present and anticipated central city functions be described as operational program requirements?
b) More specifically, how can the economy of the central city be strengthened in the face of evolving trends and what are the locational implications?
c) What can central city development contribute to modernizing local government?
d) What kinds of social innovations should the national ᴎTIT program sponsor in order to speed the modernization of social patterns; and, conversely, how would the existing "out-of-dateness" of social patterns influence design and implementation of local NTIT programs?

2. Design of NTIT Programs. Here, each of the issues we have discussed needs more analysis and drawing of specific implications for programs, policy, and operations:

a) What kinds of specific functions and activities should local new town intown programs encompass?

b) What alternate forms might NTIT projects take in addition to the two models we have described?

c) What is the appropriate scale of a NTIT in different sizes and kinds of cities: We are clear that the HUD established minimum (100 acres/12,000 people) is indeed a minimum, but more needs to be known about the appropriate scale of Model II development.

d) How should a NTIT be programmed to revitalize the central city: Here, more in-depth analysis of urban renewal, model cities, NTIT projects and programs is called for. A specific issue is: how can a NTIT be programmed so that improvements in jobs, services, and housing within a NTIT project do not produce offsetting losses elsewhere in the central city. The question of displacement effects (the shifting of socioeconomic problems from one part of the city to another through development activities) deserves special attention.

e) What factors and criteria should determine the relative emphasis placed on each development component of a NTIT? Also: how best to determine the quantity and quality of public facilities to be included in a NTIT; how to determine the viability of different income and racial mixes in residential areas; and what packages of residential services (educational, cultural, recreational, security) are most effective and marketable?

f) What is the impact of alternative densities on the social and economic viability of intown development?

3. Implementation.

a) How can private developers be attracted to NTIT projects? What strategies can intown developers use for achieving competitive capital and operating costs in the central city? While we have devoted substantial attention to this question, much remains unknown and needs early attention. For example: what is the relative importance of three major sources of private profit from NTIT development: cash flow, tax shelter, and capital gains? How does the attractiveness (and cost to the government in terms of taxes lost) of each vary for investors in different tax positions? How do different types of government assistance (loan guarantees, tax increment, tax abatement, capital grants, and so forth) affect profitability? What variables determine what kind and how much public subsidy or incentive is needed to attract investors to a given site? The various ways of reducing private development costs in central city projects equally deserve research attention. Also, how feasible is the use of the concept of transfer of development rights to complement and partially finance more concentrated development in central cities?

b) What strategies should be used to improve the welfare of the less advantaged in intown development efforts? This has been a major theme in our study, but it is only too evident that our present knowledge in this realm is extremely limited.

c) What kinds of political conditions and institutional arrangements are most conducive to NTIT development? Our study has outlined many questions and possibilities for developmental institutions, but these require further study to provide more definitive answers. Also, how can the capacity of these institutions to generate wide political and financial support be increased? How can the capacity of these institutions for mobilizing risk capital, owner participation, and corporate shareholding be increased? What are the appropriate roles in central city development of state and regional governments? How can citizens effectively be involved in decision making in these organizations? What are the possible relationships of such institutions with federal, state, regional, and local governments? We would also stress the importance of evaluating NTIT program management at local and federal levels.

d) What forms of financing could be utilized for local NTIT programs and projects? This is closely related to the fourth major issue—federal government leadership and assistance. The key question here is what kinds of federal financial assistance are needed to encourage central city development in the coming decade(s)?

HUD Research and Evaluation

Based on our own observations and proposals by other research groups in the field of housing and urban development (for example, those sponsored by the National Academy of Science and RANN of the National Science Foundation), we can recommend that HUD needs greater internal capability for direct operational research while it also supports external research aimed at some important knowledge gaps.

As far as research approach is concerned, it should be evident that most of the operational questions can be answered only through experimentation, careful observation, and evaluation. These, of course, are closely interrelated. The new town intown program clearly needs to be carried out in an experimental mode and to draw upon continuous evaluation and feedback. Accordingly, we would strongly suggest establishment of a monitoring system within the NTIT program or HUD to ensure continuous high level evaluation and feedback as a matter of course.

Index

Your Memory

Your image was a contour on my atlas,
Holding your throbbing reminiscence in the cracks of my mind,
And with vigor I rubbed till there was only a smudge,
With the stubborn resolve to forget.
But your smudge remains more stubborn,
As prominent as valleys and peaks on the scale,
Blocking road symbols with its silent illustration,
Which the waves of the Pacific won't wash.
And the motive not to reflect,
Twists and squirms in your reflection,
And though your eyes shall flicker no more,
I see them open against my verdict.
In speech or in dialect our senses mirrored,
Akin to the sea and sky where blue divides,
I knew the lines of your skin and the shades in your conviction,
But a logical path I cannot find.
However, if I sit solidly here with the ticking of time a blur
And let emotion take me back to our sacred tie
I shall become a callow stream with obstructions at every turn,
And I shall fade.
No other shall venture into my contemplation,
With the equal empathy as your expression verified,
Now my sentiment shall emulate in tears alone as death looks on.

Melissa Smith